Time Present, Time Past

Bill Bradley

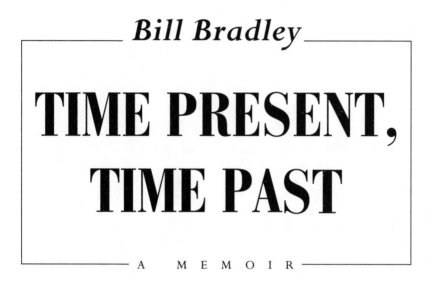

TIME PRESENT, TIME PAST

A MEMOIR

Alfred A. Knopf   NEW YORK   1996

THIS IS A BORZOI BOOK
PUBLISHED BY ALFRED A. KNOPF, INC.

Grateful acknowledgment is made to Michael Lewis for permission to reprint from "Where He Is; Senator Bill Bradley's Speech at the Democratic Convention" (*The New Republic*, August 3, 1992).

ISBN 0-679-44488-2

Manufactured in the United States of America

First Edition

For
Ernestine and Theresa Anne, and
for Mom and Dad, too

Time present and time past
Are both perhaps present in time future,
And time future contained in time past.

"Burnt Norton"
T. S. ELIOT

Contents

Preface   XI

1   Crystal City   3

2   The Garden   17

3   The Walking Town Meeting   29

4   The World's Greatest Deliberative Body   59

5   The Big Picture   91

6   Outside the Frame   117

7   The Media Burn   145

8   Money Is Power   162

9   Night Thoughts   194

10 The Closed Frontier   214

11 Getting to Billings   236

12 Trouble with Unions   250

13 The Scotch-Irish Nation   267

14   The Original Americans   290

15   The Creedal Society   317

16   Across the Great Divide   354

17   Promises to Keep   394

18   A River That Still Runs   416

      Afterword   425

      Acknowledgments   427

      Index   429

Preface

I HAVE always preferred moving to sitting still. For ten years after finishing college, I made my living by running around in short pants in drafty arenas across America, as a professional basketball player. The rhythm of the road—a drive, a flight, a performance, a hotel, a sleep, and a drive, a flight, a return—provided a frame through which I saw America and myself. The perspective had its limitations, but it ordered my movements. In 1976, I published *Life on the Run,* a book about my decade as a player on the road.

For the past seventeen years, I have crisscrossed America as a politician, a United States senator from New Jersey, following the familiar rhythm—a drive, a flight, a performance, a hotel, a sleep, and a drive, a flight, a return. I have spoken in convention centers, union halls, churches, hotel ballrooms, college campuses, and the living rooms of wealthy contributors. I have autographed T-shirts and auctioned basketballs. I have shaken hands at factory gates, commuter stops, farm picnics, and state fairs. I have dedicated new buildings and eaten endless varieties of ethnic food, including white-bread sandwiches with the crust cut off. I have spit out ten-second TV interviews and taken part in two-hour panel discussions. I have appeared in support of senators, governors, congresspeople, and mayors. By 1994, I had campaigned in forty-six states.

I threw myself into these political trips around America. Give me eight hours in a hotel room for sleep, phone calls, and reading, and I could stay on the road for weeks at a time. I enjoyed listening to the people I met. They told me their stories, got me to laugh, made me wince, angered me. These encounters were the meat and potatoes of my travels—and the spice. As I moved from place to place, I inevitably brushed up against history—the story of what had happened to people living in that part of America. Slowly, as the number of places I visited increased, I saw past events not only in their particularity but also in their sweep. The expansion of the United States westward became more than the founding of St. Louis, or Custer's last stand, or wagon ruts in the Wyoming rock beds of the Oregon Trail. The ruins of dwellings at Chaco Canyon in New Mexico triggered my imagination about the Anasazis, who lived there long before the first European arrived in America. An exhibit in western North Carolina on the Scotch-Irish immigration confronted me with my own roots and spurred me to look into the lives of my ancestors. Civil War battlefields like Gettysburg and Antietam conjured up images of Americans fighting each other in defense of liberty as each side defined it. The tensions and contrasts in America between freedom and order, the individual and the community, material well-being and spiritual transcendence, a common culture and ethnic diversity, pop out at anyone who travels with open eyes and a curious mind.

Sometimes during these campaign journeys I encountered the fruits of my legislative efforts in the U.S. Senate, for which I was either damned or praised, picketed or presented awards. I also came face-to-face with the unmet needs of Americans who were living in poverty, many of them paralyzed by self-doubt and terrorized by violence: I saw mothers in urban America afraid to send their children to school through neighborhoods controlled by gangs; families in Appalachia living in bone-chilling poverty with their Scotch-Irish independence beaten down; the colossal failure of our Native American reservations. I saw fear of the future in the faces of middle-aged men who had lost their jobs; what they thought would never change had disappeared, and they had nowhere to go. In these pockets of America, I was reminded that I am in politics to take action, to stop the suffering, and to promote opportunity. Without a new approach and more resources, the cycle of despair in the inner cities, in Appalachia, in the Dakota badlands, would never be broken. Without more good-paying jobs, the hopes of middle-class families would never be realized.

Yet much of the devastation in our country has originated in the realm of lost values. Do people really care anymore? I wondered. We need firm standards, yet daily there are reminders that our standards have slipped, or never were. What happened to the commonsense notion that two parents are better than one? What happened to making the effort and taking pride in a job well done? What happened to the widespread belief that volunteering for the PTA, the Red Cross, or the Boy Scouts is one way not only of helping others, but of finding one's own self-fulfillment? What happened to employer loyalty and employee conscientiousness? Telephone operators cut you off; clerks act as if they're doing you a favor to take your money for a purchase; packages you send through the mail never reach their destination; somebody else's mail is delivered to your address (who is getting yours?); police sleep on duty; government workers want civil-service security and private-sector pay; executives cash in stock options after firing employees to improve the bottom line; corporate limousines clog the streets even as companies cut workers' pension benefits; parents make excuses for their children's lack of discipline; the well-off elderly complain, unsatisfied with generous benefits; young professionals live increasingly selfish and tangential lives, shying away from commitment.

Self-indulgence has infiltrated America, even as more people struggle to make ends meet and frantically search for meaning beyond their individual lives. We want certain things, but we don't want to pay for them. The national budget deficit is mirrored by excessive personal debt. Between 1980 and 1987 in this country, personal debt increased by 80 percent. The cost of health coverage rises in part because of unhealthy habits; people smoke, drink, neglect to exercise. From the fat bodies that come from consuming too much of the wrong kind of food to the slow economic growth that comes from our inability to reduce the deficit, there seems to be less discipline. Few are willing to give up anything, no matter how small, for the sake of a better tomorrow. In such a society, surfeited by images of immediate gratification and hedonistic sexuality, telling kids to avoid AIDS by practicing abstinence is either folly or hypocrisy: the abstinence message—however correct—is often overwhelmed.

Though there are still extraordinary individuals in communities across America, too many of us are losing a conception of the whole, and of our connectedness to one another. To believe that a leader can solve our problems is wrong. Leadership is not something that is done to people, like fixing their teeth. Rather, it is what unlocks people's potential, challenges them to become better, calls them to task for the lies they have told themselves. It also sees the goodness in even the most intractable knave. The answer to our problems, individually and as a nation, rests within each of us. A worker who doesn't give an honest day's work for a day's wage forfeits the moral claim he has on the company's management to treat him with respect. A manager who fires workers at the first hint of recession can't expect loyalty from those who remain. A television-network executive who exercises no judgment about the violence or hedonism of the network's programs can't escape the charge that he or she is contributing to national self-destruction. The newspaper publisher whose only concern is to print whatever sells loses the right to criticize politicians who pander to voters. Too many Americans abdicate their individual responsibility.

Government is only as good as the public servants who work in it and the people who delegate to it great powers. Today citizens are confused about what they can expect from government and what it can expect from them. Fifteen years ago, they would ask my Senate office to help them with a lost Social Security check or a problem with the Immigration Service and be grateful if we succeeded and understanding if we failed. Today they begin by threatening to withdraw their political support unless they get immediate results. They want government to guarantee their happiness as well as their minimum wage, and they demand it as if it were an American's birthright. Congressman Barney Frank once joked at a political roast that the voters think of politicians as corrupt, lazy, and ineffective, but what the congressman wanted them to know was that from his perspective the public wasn't so hot either.

On my campaign trips over the years, I found myself assessing what kind of political action was needed to reconstitute not just people's faith in government but their commitment to each other. Modern campaigns, with their sound bites and attack ads, deaden democracy, undermine the moral authority of government, and contribute to resentment and anger among the voters. A few times—particularly during Bill Clinton and Al Gore's postconvention bus tour—I observed a reassuring expectation in the eyes of people who had come out to see their candidates. Increasingly, I came to feel that American democracy is an ongoing experiment with an indeterminate outcome. The only constant is the potential to change national direction.

In 1992, I traveled to twenty-seven states for Clinton. With each trip, my journey became more personal. As I campaigned for him, I did so aware that for the past seven years people had been urging me to run for president. I had rejected their suggestion; the time was not right for me. I was at peace with my decision and reconciled to living with its consequences. But from time to time, I found myself wondering what it took to be a good president, and what it cost a person to become president. Nineteen ninety-two was also a year in which personal tragedy made its appearance in the Bradley family and among some dear friends. My wife developed breast cancer, underwent a mastectomy, and had six months of chemotherapy. My father went blind, received radiation for skin cancer, and showed less and less energy and ability to engage anyone in a consistent way. My mother began to struggle against advancing emphysema, with its diabolical trade-offs between breathing on the one hand and debilitated muscles and tissue-paper-thin skin on the other. My secretary of fourteen years took a leave of absence to fight ovarian cancer. Two acquaintances died in plane crashes, and one friend committed suicide. Each of these events reminded me of mortality and the ever-present chance for catastrophe to overtake the best-laid plans. Certainly millions of others have experienced pain greater than mine. Still, these new circumstances in my life had an effect. The thought that maybe there wouldn't be a tomorrow had never seriously occurred to me. Now it went with me everywhere.

In my travels across America over the years, I had taken along small notebooks and jotted down what I heard, saw, sensed, and felt. I filled the pages of notebook after notebook. In 1992, I realized I was writing with more intensity than usual. Perhaps because it was a year of great pressures and decisions, I was more reflective than I had been in other years of campaigning, seeing things on more levels. I felt an urge to declare myself—to get beyond the politician's pragmatic ambiguity to the clarity of the facts as I saw them. I wanted to sum up my position at midpassage of my life. Having gone from growing up in a small town to working in a global arena, from a controlled intellectual commitment to the public interest to a belief that expressions of the heart count more, I wanted to write about that passage. I decided to order the thoughts in the 1992 notebooks, amplifying where appropriate from the notes of past years and the feelings of the moment. The story that emerges is not a portrait of George Bush or Bill Clinton or Ross Perot. It is certainly not a chronicle of the 1992 campaign, or of my career in the U.S. Senate. More than anything, it is my attempt to come to terms with our country, its history, its people, its problems, its potential, its current circumstance, even as I struggle with where I am in my own life and in my career as a public servant. The candidates and the campaign in 1992 gave a context to some of my travels. But my observations and comments about the events and their effects on me come from thoughts that have been germinating for many years and are the result of countless other journeys across America and into myself.

Time Present,
Time Past

1

Crystal City

I COME from Crystal City, Missouri, a small town on the banks of the Mississippi River, thirty-six miles south of St. Louis. My parents, Warren and Susie Bradley, married late in life. He was forty-three and she was thirty-five when I was born, and my arrival surprised them. I am their only child. My father had moved to Crystal City in 1912 with his mother and two sisters, after the family home in Ironton burned down and his father, who had run a general store there, died of cancer. To help support the family, he quit high school at age sixteen and went to work for the St. Louis–San Francisco Railroad. He sold tickets, loaded baggage, and kept track of the train schedules. At night, at a big oak table, he would sit with a sharp pencil and a crane-necked lamp, taking messages from the telegraph line. Morse code became the only language other than English that he would ever learn. He said, "Once you know how to take down the code, you have learned how to concentrate." At age twenty, he went to work at the local bank, in a job that entailed, as he would later say, "shining pennies." Slowly he advanced to assistant cashier, cashier, and then president, acquiring stock along the way, until by 1942 he had controlling ownership of the Crystal City State Bank (now owned by the Boatman's National Bank of St. Louis).

Ever since I was a young child, my father's health was the family's number-one priority. He lived every day with a painful, calcified arthritis of the lower spine. I never saw him drive a car, throw a ball, or tie his shoes. I never knew him to sleep longer than six consecutive hours. He could walk, but only on hard, even surfaces, and never for a distance much farther than the two long blocks from our house to the bank. My mother and I would dress him, tie his shoes, attach his suspenders, and pick up his newspapers from the floor. The world below his thighs and above his head was totally inaccessible to him.

Books about non-Western medicine and positive thinking dotted his library shelf. He had high blood pressure, so we radically changed the family diet. He had a gall-bladder operation, from which no one thought he would recover. He had intestinal problems, which he treated by eating Black Strap molasses. The stress of daily existence he handled with bourbon and water—two per day—and a wintertime vacation in Palm Beach, which he had first visited in 1928, when it was little more than a glorified sand dune. These visits lengthened from two weeks to two months as his career prospered. "If I get a phone call from the bank, I've failed," he would say. "Vacations are for relaxation, not business." He sat on the beach in his white wooden folding chair every day from 10 a.m. to 2 p.m., protected from the wind by a blue canvas cabana. After a shower, he took a nap, had a drink, and read the newspapers until dinner. He perfected the art of immobile relaxation, practicing it with the single-mindedness of a professional golfer facing a ten-foot putt.

My father lived for the bank and for his family. He walked to work every morning at 8:15 and back every evening at 5:15. Often he came home for lunch. He served as treasurer of the school board for thirty years, but he never went to a meeting. He rarely attended any events in town, other than my Little League baseball games in summer, my school basketball games in winter, and (although he was suspicious of religion) Sunday-morning services at Grace Presbyterian Church.

Small-town banking was a trust-based profession. When there were panic runs in the early thirties, my father stacked up cash in the bank's window, so depositors could see that the bank was solvent. People came to my father with their money problems as they would go to a doctor for their health problems. His proudest achievement was that throughout the Great Depression he never foreclosed on a single homeowner. He felt he could work with people, help them manage, carry them for a while. He had a clear sense of ethics and lived by a rigid code of conduct. If you missed a loan repayment without a good reason, you became a different kind of person to him. Modest and reserved personally, and deeply affected by the Depression professionally, he believed that risk in anything should be avoided at all costs.

My mother, a former schoolteacher and the daughter of a devout Methodist, was energetic, churchgoing, and civic-club attending. She was born in Poplar Bluff, Missouri, not far from the Arkansas border. Her father, Samuel Howard Crowe, was a salesman for Old Judge coffee, along a route from St. Louis to Little Rock, and he did very well at it. He wore a big black Stetson hat, told hundreds of jokes to his customers, and played seven musical instruments. When my mother was nine years old, he moved his wife and their six children to Riverside, a four-story, twenty-two-room Victorian mansion of brick and cut stone which sat on thirteen acres of barns and orchards overlooking the Mississippi River near Crystal City, just north of Herculaneum. I never knew him. He burned to death in a car crash on his way home from visiting my parents when I was eighteen months old. (He told my parents that he would pay for my college if they named me Samuel Howard, after him, instead of William Warren. But my father could never be bribed, not even by his father-in-law.)

My mother graduated from Central Methodist College, where for four years she dated the star football player. She became a fourth-grade teacher in Brentwood, a suburb of St. Louis. Thirty years after she quit teaching, full-grown strangers would appear at our door to express their appreciation and respect for Miss Crowe. At my father's funeral in 1994, one of her former students, who was dying of cancer, showed up to convey his sympathy and take inspiration from her one last time. As the daughter of a disciplinarian, she insisted on protocol and performance in her only child. On many an afternoon, I was called into the living room to say hello to her bridge club and otherwise demonstrate my manners. "Sir" or "ma'am" was how I invariably addressed an adult. Her conversation with my teachers after a PTA meeting focused more on my deportment than on my academic performance.

To my mother, pain was something to rise above. "Look at what happened to your father," she would say. "He just gave in to pain." She believed that endless energy and the human will could conquer any situation, and she also believed that activity was an acceptable substitute for thought: I therefore took lessons in piano, trumpet, French, swimming, basketball, boxing, and the French horn. My father said no to dancing lessons ("Babe Ruth didn't have dancing lessons"). My mother to this day says that I would have had better coordination as a basketball player if only I had taken ballet.

My mother always wanted me to be a success. My father always wanted me to be a gentleman. Neither wanted me to be a politician.

When I was growing up in Crystal City, it was a town of 3,492 people. Today it has topped 4,000. Back then, most of the men in town worked in the Pittsburgh Plate Glass factory. At its peak, PPG employed more than four thousand people in its Crystal City plant; they came from all over Jefferson County. The company owned many of the houses in town until the late 1940s, when it asked my father to sell its holdings to the townspeople.

The first sign of trouble at the factory came in the late 1950s, when there was a lengthy strike. I remember crossing the arched concrete bridge over the railroad tracks on my way to school and seeing hundreds of angry men listening to speeches by union leaders. The men wanted higher wages and better working conditions. They got them, but a few years later the union accepted the new "float" process of making plate glass—a process that had just been imported from England and would reduce the size of the workforce. In the 1970s and 1980s, the plant continued to downsize. Crystal City's fresh white silica sand, which inspired the word "crystal" in the city's name, and its proximity to rail and river transportation no longer counted for much; new industrial processes had been introduced in plants elsewhere. Pittsburgh Plate Glass finally closed the factory in 1992, after more than one hundred years of operation, and today with the giant industrial buildings torn down and weeds covering the vacant land, it is as if someone has removed the photos of my childhood from the family album.

While I was growing up, I had several brushes with politics. My first political memory is of listening to my father denounce Ed Eversole, the local Democratic kingpin. Eversole had at various times been county prosecutor and circuit judge. He manipulated county politics from his law office above the Miller Theater, on Main Street in Festus, the other half of what was self-importantly known as the Twin Cities. At night, the glass-speckled sidewalk in front of the Miller glittered in the light from the marquee. During the day, in front of the door that led to the second floor, the sidewalk was flat and plain, like the entrance to a trap should be.

Ed Eversole had a capacious face with a large nose, reddened cheeks, and eyes that were often bloodshot. He gave the profession of politics an air of intrigue and corruption. Around the Bradley house, he was thought to have been in cahoots with a bank competitor of my father's who later went to jail.

Ed and his wife, Nancy, did not have children, and they often professed a relative's interest in me. Nancy sang solos in the Grace Presbyterian Church choir. My father liked her voice. My mother thought she was a pleasant person. But Nancy's personality and talent couldn't overcome her husband's calling in the eyes of my father. My father was a Republican. But he was more apolitical than partisan, taking a dim view of politics. Politics for him was personified by local Democrats such as Ed Eversole, who he felt cheated people out of what was due them. Throughout the Depression, a picture of Herbert Hoover hung on my father's office wall, even though in later years he admitted that he had been wrong about Franklin Roosevelt, and that at a moment of great international crisis FDR, far from promoting socialism, had saved capitalism. Ultimately, Richard Nixon and Watergate drove my father to become an independent. He saw his grand old party acting just like he thought the local Democrats did—corrupted by power that rightly belonged to the people.

One November evening in 1948, when I was five years old, I sensed that something special was happening, because my parents were preparing to give a sizable party, which they had never done before. It was election night: Truman against Dewey for the presidency of the United States. My father wanted a Dewey victory; in fact, he had agreed to be an elector for Dewey. The celebration was in anticipation of his actually taking his instructions from the voters and casting his elector's vote for a president. But as the night wore on and I sat listening to the returns with my back against the big floor radio, the mood turned somber. Slowly our guests left. The iced champagne bottles remained corked. Truman had held on to the presidency, duplicating his 1940 run for re-election to the Senate: once again, he had come charging from behind by emphasizing his record and his plans to help working people.

In 1952 and 1956, I was my grade school's leading supporter of Dwight Eisenhower for president against Adlai Stevenson, the Democrat. Although my father had preferred Senator Robert Taft of Ohio, he stayed with the Republican nominee. On Election Day, I wore to school a shirt full of Republican political buttons. The one I liked most changed as you moved past it, from the "I Like Ike" slogan to a picture of the smiling candidate. My best friend, whose father was an active trade unionist at PPG, supported Stevenson with a passion equal to mine for Ike. Apart from the fact that we were walking in the political footprints of our fathers, what most struck me about the race was that both candidates were bald. I wondered whether anyone with hair would ever run for president.

My Aunt Elizabeth—or "Bub," as I called her—ran for Jefferson County assessor in 1960 on the Republican ticket. When she became a candidate, she was serving on the Herculaneum school board and made her living by operating a hamburger shop across from the high school. She ran for assessor because she personally disliked the Democratic incumbent. Being assessor was not as important to her as beating him, or, better yet, tarring him. She had virtually no campaign funds—just a mouth full of caustic comments. The county was 60 percent Democratic. Still, she ran. Our spirits soared one Saturday morning in October as we draped three cars with bright-colored crepe paper, armed ourselves with signs, and set off on a countywide caravan of horn blowing and sign waving. My aunt thought the caravan might make the difference. The caravan was fun, but she got 40 percent of the vote.

The only time Crystal City High School ever allowed a television set into the school-library study hall was for the inauguration of John Kennedy. I was a high-school senior then, and still my father's son politically. Nixon had been my candidate. I had watched the Nixon-Kennedy debates, but I understood very little of what was said about the issues. My life was playing basketball, choosing a college, and doing well enough in school to have a choice. As I watched the inauguration, the thing that hit me was not the prospect of a new president, or the soaring delivery of "Ask not what your country can do for you, but what you can do for your country." Instead, it was the vulnerability of the old men in the ceremony: the poet Robert Frost, who struggled against the glare of sun and snow to read a poem dedicated to his fellow New Englander, and Cardinal Richard Cushing of Boston, who fought the wind that blew his script as he offered the inaugural prayer, and whose red hat and flowing cloak reminded people that America now had a Catholic president. Frost and Cushing seemed to be passing the torch to this young man, and in their vulnerability to snow and wind and age reminded us that even this forty-three-year-old president would someday grow old.

When I was a senior at Princeton and asked my father whom I should talk to about entering politics, he advised me to consult Ed Eversole. I made the appointment, and went to see the kingpin late one winter afternoon in his office above the theater. It was a sparsely appointed, rather shabby office, with little evidence that any work actually went on there. He sat behind his desk in a three-piece suit, just as he sat on Sunday mornings across the aisle from my father in the last pew of the Presbyterian church. He told me what many others would tell me in the years ahead. If I wanted to get into politics, I had to start at the bottom. Run for city council, he said, and then try for county office. He implied that he could be helpful, but he didn't say that he would be. After all, I was the son of the town's most prominent Republican. Notwithstanding my declared intention of becoming a Democrat, he behaved toward me as I imagined the head of one organized crime family might behave toward the son of his rival. There would be other political bosses as I made my way through politics—the Pendergasts, Tweeds, and DeSapios of history books, the Lerners, Kennys, and Errichettis of New Jersey. Each of them wielded more power than Ed Eversole, but to me none of them would be as intimidating as he had been, sitting behind his desk in his lair above the Miller Theater.

Crystal City was a multiethnic, multiracial company town. When Little League started there in 1952, it was racially integrated; after *Brown* v. *Board of Education,* the schools followed. There were no problems, chiefly because PPG's college-educated, enlightened engineers dominated the school board. The school district had high standards, and the families in the town encouraged the academic success of their children. When it came to racial issues, the rest of Missouri wasn't always that way. For many years after *Brown* v. *Board of Education,* the color of your skin continued to impose limits on your possibilities if you were black. I remember staying in a run-down hotel in Joplin during a Little League playoff, because the better hotels wouldn't take our black players. I remember traveling as a teenage player in the American Legion baseball league to New Madrid, in the bootheel—the part of Missouri that protrudes into Arkansas—and being refused service at a restaurant there because our catcher and a left fielder were black. And I remember Alex Maul, the bank's black janitor, who did so much for us as my father's spinal arthritis worsened. With my mother's help, Alex set up my first basketball goal ("Your father used to play baseball before he got arthritis, not basketball—why basketball?"). When my mother insisted that Alex teach me how to box, just as he did for the kids who fought in the Golden Gloves competition, he showed me how to punch the speedbag ("Make it sing"). I took over his duties as bank janitor each summer during his vacation, and he taught me the mysteries of wet mopping ("Keep the strands spread wide").

Crystal City's families—the Vacarros, Auddifreds, La Prestas, Pouliezoses, LaRoses, Ryans, Picarellas, Goldmans, Shapiros, Potsterioffs, Salvos, and Magres—had come to America from all over the place. There was always the odd racist joke or ethnic slur, but somehow the fault lines of the town weren't laid out that way. The violent stories of my youth had more to do with high-school rivalries (Herky-Crystal, Festus-Crystal) and class conflict ("Let's get the banker's son") than with race or ethnicity. As my father always said, "The color of your skin doesn't predict whether you'll save money or pay your bills."

IN MARCH 1992, I agreed to speak at a campaign ice-cream social in Crystal City for Dick Gephardt, who was then the majority leader of the House of Representatives. As I drove into town, I noticed that old Highway 61-67 was now Truman Boulevard, but it still had only the one stoplight of my youth. Sam Temperato's first Dairy Queen, which my father had financed (Sam now has seventy-one of them), was still there, and so was Gordon's Stoplight Drive-In. The First Baptist Church still stood on the corner, with the Sacred Heart Catholic Church up on the hill behind it. A mall had replaced the American Legion baseball field. Interstate 55 now flanked the southwest side of town, and another giant mall separated it from the old highway. The ice-cream social was to take place in the VFW hall, out by the town's landing strip; you couldn't call it an airport, really—there were no runway lights and no control tower. One night in the early seventies, I had come close to dying at that airstrip. I had chosen to fly back from a political meeting in the bootheel through a thunderstorm, in a single-engine plane. The lightning flashed around us, the thunder cracked, and torrents of rain streamed past the windows. The plane was thrown up and down like a ball bouncing on the floor. As we headed in for a landing, the pilot couldn't see the runway and had to rely on his memory to locate it. I still thank God that he remembered right.

Gephardt's staff expected a hundred people at the social, and three hundred showed up. I was pleased and surprised by how many old friends were there: Alex Maul and his wife, Margaret; Boston Richards, my Little League coach; Jerry Ryan, my sixth-grade teacher and grade-school basketball coach; Arvel Popp, my high-school basketball coach; Mae Hunt, the secretary of the glassworkers' union for thirty years; Donny Howard, a bully who had beaten me up in second grade.

Shaking hands and signing autographs, I felt a certain loss. My parents were old and their health was failing. For the last twenty years, they had lived in Palm Beach and returned to Missouri only for the summer months, to escape the Florida heat. This year they wouldn't even be doing that. They were too frail; my mother's emphysema and my father's growing weakness made the trip unthinkable. It was as if our family's Missouri life had ended. The old friends seemed older. Coach Popp had emphysema, too. Alex Maul was fragile and slow-moving, and so were my mother's friends from the bridge club, the golf course, and the Grace Presbyterian Church.

I was a politician, speaking on behalf of another politician, as I had hundreds of times in my fourteen years in national politics. But this event was different. These were the people I had spoken in front of as a teenager, in church or at a high-school assembly or a civic club. Now I felt as if I were seeing some of them for the last time. Jerry Ryan handed me a note critiquing my speech: "You need better posture; your points don't follow logically." Others came up to shake hands. One man said, "I bet you don't remember me."

I said no, I didn't.

He identified himself. I said I was pleased he had come to support Dick and to hear me speak.

"I didn't come for that," he said. "I don't have enough money to eat these days. I came for the free ice cream."

THE BIG CITY makes you feel "behind" if you come from a small town. When I played high-school basketball, the challenge was to show the world that we could compete against the big-city schools. I never liked being called a hick. I never liked being looked down on by players I had just beaten, only because I came from a small town. My father wasn't rich compared with big-city bankers. My house wasn't big by suburban standards; my family wasn't educated by intellectual standards; my relatives weren't worldly by cosmopolitan standards. I didn't exactly have a chip on my shoulder, but I felt I had something to prove: that I could win, that I was as good as other people. These feelings ran deep for many years—before I came east, before I won my share, before I saw the individuals beneath the expensive suits and the academic tweeds.

I ache on occasion for the certainty and familiarity of small towns. I view urban America with provincial alarm as well as with a certain provincial awe and exhilaration. Main Street shapes my reaction to K Street and Wall Street, in subtle and powerful ways. That's just who I am. Even after ten years of playing professional basketball for the New York Knicks and living most of those years in New York City and more than twenty years in New Jersey and Washington, I still have impulses that are rooted in my adolescence, when I was part of a high-school class of ninety-six in a town with one stoplight.

I have flown over Crystal City many times on my way to other places. Usually, I can see the bluffs of Crystal Heights to the north and Buck Knob to the south, lining the Missouri side of the river like praetorian guards. These are the bluffs I crawled along as a kid, whose caves challenged young boys to find them and enter the dark without running into bats, snakes, spiders, or foxes. Along the base of the bluffs I would find fossils of carboniferous ferns and arrowheads from the Osage and Kaskaskia tribes. Beneath the bluffs are railroad tracks that parallel the river. I would walk along them with my German-born stepgrandfather, who had married my father's mother after my grandfather died. He told me stories about his childhood in Germany, with its corporal punishment from disciplinarian teachers; we drank from a spring that trickled down from the limestone bluff, and he carried a .22-caliber rifle and a box of .22 longs, with which we shot at logs in the river. On the paths from the railroad tracks up to the caves sat the occasional bum, the last representative of the army of hoboes who rode the empty boxcars during the Depression. Years ago, in the early 1970s, I almost bought a house on one of these bluffs, about ten miles south of Crystal City. Life changed, and the house wasn't bought, and my attention moved from the bluffs along the Mississippi to the Jersey Shore.

In the bottomland between the bluffs along the river is Hug Farm. As a kid, I used to do cross-country training there in the fall, before basketball practice began. I ran from my home past the city's water-filtration plant, and onto a gravel road along the cracked mud fields, through the cottonwood trees to the edge of the Mississippi. There, before I ran back,

I would stop for a few minutes and watch the river flow. No one swam in the river. The whirlpools made it too dangerous. On the very rare occasions when it froze over, one of my uncles would sometimes venture out onto the ice.

In the early 1970s, PPG sold Hug Farm to me and a friend. I keep my share of it for sentimental reasons. There is no house on the property, only the foundations of one that burned down many years ago. The levee offers little protection from the floods, which come every four or five years. The brother of one of my Little League teammates farms the land, and he shares the proceeds with my partner and me. Until 1992, my father handled all the details of the farm—it gave him something to do after his retirement from the bank—but then he went blind and I had to step in.

Every time I'm in Crystal City, I drive down the alley behind City Hall, just west of Hug Farm, or to the parking lot of the town library, just north of it. I get out, look the property over, and estimate the acreage in soybeans or corn. When I bought the farm, I knew I was buying a permanent place in Crystal City. From time to time, somebody shows an interest in buying the property, but I doubt I will ever sell it, because of its powerful place in my memory.

To stand alone next to the river is a special kind of solitude. You can feel the incredible power and sense of possibility that no doubt struck the explorers who came upon this river and these bluffs more than four hundred years ago. The wind rushes through the cottonwood trees and the currents lap the shore. The water looks thick and muddy with upstream topsoil. It carries giant logs from the north. It transports the man-made residue of tin cans and plastics scoured from half a continent. In the spring, its rising waters deposit part of its richness on farms such as Hug and then it recedes, resuming its meandering path south to New Orleans. By August, the sloughs dry up and occasionally dead carp lie stinking in the sun. One mile east sits the bottomland of Illinois, separated from Missouri by the treacherous eddies of what Native Americans called the Great Water.

The Mississippi River has always been a powerful metaphor for me, not just a physical divide but a historical one. When you grow up along its banks, its history lives, and you absorb it before you can interpret it. Thirteen miles from Crystal City is De Soto, named for the Spanish explorer Hernando de Soto, who died in 1542 on the western bank, the first European to explore the southern Mississippi. Within a sixty-mile radius of Crystal City are Ste. Genevieve, Kaskaskia, and Cahokia—outposts established by compatriots of Jolliet and Marquette and the great La Salle, who claimed the river's entire length for France but failed to interest the French crown in exploring the opportunities offered in the Valley of the Great Water.

When I was a student at Princeton, the first art paper I ever wrote was on the work of a Missouri artist named George Caleb Bingham, who painted boatmen involved in trade on the Missouri and Mississippi Rivers. These were rogues and adventurers, unlike the families who had pooled their possessions and set out in flatboats of varying quality, braving outlaws and Indians, on their way to a distant destination where land would be cheap and fertile. Though the naïveté and majesty of the settlers' journey inspires admiration, it was the boorishness and audacity of the boatmen that captured my imagination. In his *Mighty Mississippi,* the Pulitzer Prize–winning Missouri journalist Marquis Childs portrays them as American originals—"half horse and half alligator," as the saying went. They floated down the river with relative ease, drinking whiskey, eating slabs of burned meat, playing the fiddle, dancing the jig, and whoring along the way. Coming back upstream was a different order of experience. It was as hard as work gets. Each man poled and pulled, sweating under the scorching sun to propel the boat and its tons of cargo north against the current. They used poles to push off the river bottom. They tied ropes to trees and tugged, or got off along the bank and shouldered the ropes to haul the boat upstream. Caleb Bingham caught these rivermen in countless paintings, such as *The Jolly Flatboatmen, Raftsmen Playing Cards, Watching the Cargo by Night,* and *Boatmen on the Missouri.* It was a time in American history when humankind and nature still seemed in harmony.

Floods are dramatic and biblical, evoking images of power and devastation. They reveal us as impotent in the face of their violence. In the great flood of 1993, one and a half million cubic feet of water flowed past Hug Farm every second. The water poured over the Hug Farm levee, across the Missouri Pacific Railroad tracks, and into the high-school football field, where it crested several yards above the crossbars of the goalposts. It backed up Plattin Creek and flooded under six feet of water the stoplight intersection of my youth, which lay two miles from the river's edge. The Baptist church was sandbagged. The Chevrolet dealer was sandbagged. Gordon's Stoplight Drive-In and the Dairy Queen were abandoned to the rising waters. The bank's new building on Truman Boulevard was sandbagged, but the water kept coming. Eventually, an enormous crane was sent down from St. Louis by bank headquarters, and the safe-deposit boxes were removed to higher ground. The post office didn't fare so well; the flood nearly covered it. The flood of 1993 caused twelve billion dollars' worth of damage to crops, levees, and structures along the length of the river.

But for all their Wagnerian drama, floods come and go in a natural cycle. Far more dangerous is the continual soil erosion in the Mississippi Valley. The virgin forests were nearly gone by the early twentieth century: as much as half the forest area of the North was burned over. The Mississippi and its tributaries have been scooping up precious topsoil ever since. Without the forests, the flood levels are higher. The river receives much more in topsoil washing down the tributaries than it deposits on the bottomlands along the main stream. In 1935, President Roosevelt's Mississippi Valley Committee found that annual damage from soil erosion just on the western half of the Mississippi drainage basin was twenty times the losses in the same area caused by annual floods. Yet we continue to worry about floods more than we do about soil erosion.

In the late nineteenth century, railroads under the control of Eastern banking interests received large federal subsidies, and with the help of these public grants they displaced much of the river traffic. Although a Mississippi River Commission was created in 1879, it wasn't until the early 1930s that sizable federal spending backed it up. As the Depression deepened, the congressmen who represented districts along the rivers of the Midwest successfully pushed for spending huge amounts on flood-control projects and other river improvements along the Mississippi and its tributaries. Out of this commitment came the twenty-six locks and dams on the upper Mississippi and miles and miles of federal levees along the entire length from St. Paul, Minnesota, to New Orleans. In 1934, the Public Works Administration alone got over thirty-three million dollars for river work. But, as Mark Twain wrote, "Ten thousand River Commissions, with the mines of the world at their back, cannot tame that lawless stream, cannot curb it or confine it, cannot say to it, 'Go here,' or 'Go there,' and make it obey; cannot save a shore which it has sentenced; cannot bar its path with an obstruction which it will not tear down, dance over, and laugh at." These attempts to direct or control the

Mississippi are testimony not so much to our technological acumen as to our arrogance. To subsidize river traffic in this way is to obligate taxpayers at great expense to wage a battle against the power of the Mississippi year after year. It is a battle that we will ultimately lose.

The river for Mark Twain symbolized freedom, defiance, and rebellion, in an age in which he thought that the petty and the narrow dominated life. For me, in an age shattered daily by sound bites and news on the hour, with abrupt shifts in the fortunes of whole nations, with continuity more difficult to find, the river and the bluffs above it came to represent permanence. They were always there, as they had been for thousands of years. They guaranteed a kind of stability. You could count on them to anchor your life.

Wherever I go and whatever I do, the experience of growing up in Crystal City travels with me. The memories are too deeply etched to fade. Things that happened in high school or even grade school seem to have happened only yesterday, and there are places in the town that still glow with the expectations of my youth. Even the old family battles resonate: I didn't return from Princeton and run the bank with my father; I "made a mistake" going to Princeton in the first place. Part of my mother wishes to this day that I had stayed in Missouri, gone to Mizzou (the University of Missouri), married my high-school sweetheart, and come back home.

I did not go back home. But in a sense, I also never left. I will always be as much from that small town between two limestone bluffs on the banks of the Mississippi as I am from anywhere.

2

The Garden

I N T H E S U M M E R of 1992, I was back in Madison Square Garden, to give one of the three keynote addresses at the Democratic National Convention. It was my first performance in the Garden without teammates. Indeed, other than jersey-retirement nights, when the management hung a player's oversized jersey from the rafters, it was only my sixth time back since I retired from professional basketball in 1977. The workers in the Garden greeted me warmly. They were older now—ethnic representatives of the old New York, when the Knicks were winning it all and everyone seemed to have a place in the parade. The hallway walls held some of the memories—a picture of me leading a fast break, with teammate Walt Frazier in his muttonchop whiskers and Afro to my left; a picture of me jumping into the arms of our center, Willis Reed, the moment we won the world championship in 1973.

At the convention, the locker room of the New York Rangers hockey team served as a hospitality suite for Democratic Party officials. The Knicks' locker room of my days with the team had been converted into a VIP waiting room, in which, on this opening night, sat another keynote speaker, Barbara Jordan of Texas. I waited out the time before my speech by reclining on the Knick training table, much as I had twenty years earlier before basketball games. When the word came ("Time to go, Senator Bradley"), I walked out of the locker room, through the halls, and up the wooden steps in back of the giant stage. "Good luck, Dollar Bill," someone yelled, "go get 'em!"

I felt good about the text of my speech, but uneasy about my perennial problem: delivery. My ability as a public speaker was comparable to the rhetorical skills of an inmate of Madame Tussaud's wax museum. For many years, I had never thought much about my speaking skills. After all, I had done well in speech class in high school, and had spoken often as the president of the Missouri Association of Student Councils. Sports banquets and churches were my forums of choice in college. During my years in pro basketball, public speaking and media interviews were everyday occurrences. Still, I knew little of technique, timing, tone, pace, and structure. My college-basketball coach would say to me when we left an engagement that the audience had laughed at my jokes because of who I was, not because the jokes were any good.

When it came to political speaking, for some reason I froze. The day I declared my candidacy in 1978 before the four television cameras, six print reporters, and fifty campaign workers assembled at my headquarters in Union, New Jersey, I was so nervous that I could hardly speak. My voice cracked. My breath was short. I kept my eyes glued to the written announcement, and I felt like someone clinging to a raft bouncing down the rapids.

One of my commercials in that campaign required me to look into the camera and say, "We all want to cut the fat out of government, but my opponent wants to cut out the heart." On a blazing September afternoon in Los Angeles, with the temperature over a hundred degrees outside the offices of Michael Kaye, my media adviser, I did twenty-six takes. I said, "My opponent wants to cut out the heart" with my voice lowering on "heart." "Cut out the heart" with my voice rising in pitch on "heart." "Cut . . . out . . . the heart." "Cut out the . . . heart." "Cut out . . . the heart."

"Say it this way," the director said, " 'Cut out the heart,' with empathy. Say it with feeling! Make it emotional!"

"Cut-out-the-heart," I said, hitting four middle Cs in a row.

"No, no, too monotone! Make your voice higher and lower on different words."

"Cut . . . out . . . the HEART!"

For years, any speech I made on the Senate floor I read—including one that was forty-seven pages long, a real snoozer. Although little premium was placed on rhetoric in New Jersey politics, I recognized early my deficiency as a speaker and as a television performer. Various people offered their suggestions on how I might improve, but finally I decided it was time to seek advice from the pros.

"When Demosthenes practiced oratory, he put pebbles in his mouth," Lilyan Wilder, my newly engaged speech coach, asserted. "Now, you don't have to do that—although marbles would serve the same function—but speaking is like any other discipline: it's a series of habits. Practice good habits and you will improve." She said that speech was all a matter of breathing and that you have to breathe from your diaphragm. That my voice was so full of breath, and I often lost my voice because I spoke from my throat, not my diaphragm. After a while, I would strain my vocal cords, because they were doing all the work, and a few simple practice routines would make all the difference. "Focus on a spot far away. Try to get your voice to reach that spot, and say, 'Charge, Chester, Charge,' using your diaphragm. When you say 'Charge,' you should pull in your abdominal muscles and push out the air. Open your mouth wide, keep your pitch low, and let the words come out. Go ahead, do it!"

After ten minutes of having me bark, "Charge, Chester, Charge," she shifted emphasis to what my mother would call elocution. "Say after me. PPP-PPP-PPP-Pah, PPP-PPP-PPP-Pay, BBB-BBB-BBB-Bee, BBB-BBB-BBB-Bow."

"What?"

"PPP-PPP-PPP-Pah. Each 'P' pronounced clearly. BBB-BBB-BBB-Bee. Each 'B' begun and completed on its own. Let your lips shape the sound. The more you get comfortable breathing, the easier it will be to speak without strain. Also, listen to Frank Sinatra, and sing along, noticing how he breathes and phrases his lyrics."

Back at our house, I put on a record by Ol' Blue Eyes. "I've got you . . . under my skin. I've got you . . . deep in the . . ." Somehow it never came together for me.

"The way I look at it," said Don Penny, a communication coach in Washington, D.C., "you're Gary Cooper. He didn't say much, but every word counted. You gotta know who you're trying to be. You're a natural Gary Cooper. Or for humor just look at Jack Benny. His humor was in his pauses. He waited and the laughs came. You can do that. Deliver deadpan and wait. Like this . . ."

For ten years, advisers suggested changes in techniques, which overshadowed any focus on conviction:

"Don't hold your hands like that."

"Raise your cheeks, so that the camera sees you smiling."

"Sit up straight, but not stiff."

"Don't use your hands so much in gestures."

"Smile when the red light goes on."

"Look into the camera."

"Don't look into the camera!"

"Look at the interviewer."

"Don't raise your eyebrows."

"Keep your chin up."

"Don't speak so close to the microphone."

"Look at your audience and invite them to listen."

"Tell the audience what you're going to say, say it, and then tell them what you've said."

"Above all, be natural."

I PAUSED on the steps that led up to the convention platform, waiting to be introduced to the crowd in the Garden. Twenty thousand people created a familiar rumble. A security official approached and said, "Jerry Brown's people have just disrupted [Democratic National Committee Chairman] Ron Brown's speech. Jerry Brown is about to enter the arena. Expect that there will be a demonstration, and there might be a charge of the podium at some point in your speech. Good luck."

The last time I had spoken to an audience in Madison Square Garden was the night in 1984 when my jersey was retired. That night, Knick fans made up the crowd. For over a decade, the crowd in the Garden had booed me and cheered me. It had derided me and given me standing ovations and tingled my spine with chills. It was the crowd that set high standards for play and, above all, valued victory. In the Garden, the spoken word—unlike the action of the game—invariably invited ridicule. I had seen it happen many times; the crowd had no patience for words, or for politicians. The crowd had booed Mayors John Lindsay and Abe Beame when they tossed up the basketball at opening tip-off. The crowd that night in 1984 made me nervous; still, I had wanted to say goodbye to a game I loved, in the arena where I had played. To my surprise, they actually listened to my three-minute speech. There was a bond between those who played and those who cheered. And nowhere was that bond stronger than in Madison Square Garden on those nights more than two decades ago when the crowd roared, the building shook, and we gave our best.

In the summer of 1992, I would be speaking about America and our common future, not about my years as a Knick. I would be speaking about a beginning, not an ending. But the basketball years followed me. Three of my former teammates, Dave DeBusschere, Earl Monroe, and Phil Jackson, and my old coach, Red Holzman, were in the audience. Pictures of my retired jersey hanging from the rafters were blown up on the convention's big video screens, and some of the queasiness I had felt about using words to reach the Knick fans in 1984 came back, too.

A three-minute videotaped Bradley biography was running on a big screen over the podium; my friend Bruce Hornsby's song "The Way It Is," which I had chosen for its theme of race relations, started to play; and then a voice over the loudspeaker said, "Ladies and gentlemen, Senator Bill Bradley."

I went out to a cheering audience, looked up at the familiar spoked ceiling of the Garden for reassurance, settled myself behind the podium, and began: "Bill Clinton will be the next president of the United States."

Throughout the speech, the Brown people chanted, "Let Jerry speak. Let Jerry speak." Jerry Brown had been Clinton's most tenacious primary opponent and still had not released his delegates. I tried to ignore them, but it was like trying to ignore a pebble in your shoe—it couldn't be done. A convention speech is two speeches—one to the hall and one to the TV viewers. Since the hall was unruly, and would have been even without the noise coming from Brown supporters, I spoke to the television audience. This time, I knew the networks would cover the speech. In 1988, I had delivered a speech to the Democratic National Convention in Atlanta while gazing into a camera that was recording nothing. My speech was considered so minor that only C-Span, which covered the convention from beginning to end, carried it.

This time, I had also decided that I would say what was on my mind, as opposed to issuing partisan one-liners or a political-science lecture. I couldn't do any worse than I had done in 1988, when, one week before the convention, I had been asked to talk about "the role of the presidency in American life." I took the assignment seriously, and put the crowd to sleep. In 1992, I wanted to keep people awake, but I also wanted to tell the truth as I saw it about our national circumstance.

I had completed the basic text ten days before the convention and sent it to a number of friends for comment. Some liked it; others felt it was not a very good political speech because it wasn't partisan enough. One friend urged me to try to get the audience involved with a funny refrain, reminiscent of FDR's "Martin, Barton, and Fish" during the 1936 convention. I decided to go for an alliteration about President Bush—to say he "waffled and wiggled and wavered." I settled on my three words by laying out all the verbs in the dictionary beginning with "w." I discarded "whistled" as irrelevant, and "weaseled" as too crude, and "wimbled" or "warbled" as too esoteric. I placed the refrain at the beginning of the speech, where I had decided to add a partisan section. I was not fully comfortable with this attempt to stir the Democratic pot, but I knew that to ignore party sentiments and say only what I wanted to convey to the American people would also be out of place. After all, it was a Democratic convention.

The rather frivolous partisan refrain was particularly risky, because I had also decided to use a refrain with serious intent, borrowed from Langston Hughes: "Let America be America again. Let it be the dream it used to be." It struck me that the sentiment of that refrain was just right. It said that the American dream remained unfulfilled yet still offered unlimited promise if we would simply live it out.

I knew it would be difficult to pull off my two refrains—one political, one substantive—in the same speech. I would be playing fast and loose with structure. I also knew that I had to acknowledge, in some way, that I was not a stranger to Madison Square Garden. A remark such as "This is the first time I've performed in Madison Square Garden in long pants" seemed too flippant. Besides, I had said it in Atlanta four years earlier, referring to the Omni. I decided to use the venue to make a larger point:

> For ten years I played basketball for the New York Knicks in this building. The guys on the team came from many places—a variety of backgrounds. We respected each other. We gave up our own personal agendas so that the team could win. The idea of giving up something

small for yourself to gain something big for all of us is not new, but putting that ancient idea into practice is the central necessity of our new age. Giving up the desire for more of everything now is the key to having more of something better in our future.

My unselfishness as a player had not come naturally. When I was a small boy, my mother would oversee our backyard games. Often when I beat a cousin at baseball or Ping-Pong or basketball or badminton, my mother would unilaterally declare him the winner. "You have to learn to share," she'd say.

I had also been impressed at an early age by Aesop's fable about the ant who, unlike the grasshopper, confronted the winter prepared, because it had spent its summer working instead of playing. I liked the discipline of staying in good physical condition, and I liked the structure of a personal budget. The message of Michael Jordan's virtuosity cannot be found in Nike ads. Rather, it is as old as the game: Hard work counts. Even though the convention was a political event, I tried to raise a moral question:

What is life worth if we don't strive to build something that is bigger than we are and lasts longer than we do? For too long, we have not worried about future generations or met our obligations to each other. Instead, we have lived for ourselves and for today. Such a world is simply not sustainable.

It was not the kind of speech that electrifies an audience, but I wanted to preach a little. I wanted to say that there were many things more important than material success. I wanted to try to get beneath the ridiculous hats and the continuous hoopla and reach for people's brains and hearts. What did we want our children to have: an understanding of what it meant to be human and how to care for others, or an understanding of what it took to step on someone else for success and how to tell more effective lies—individualism degenerated into greed, without agreement on its limits?

The microchip may be faster than the human brain, but it's not connected to a heart. A new drug might defeat a disease, but it won't eradicate hatred. Technology can't tell us what's right and what's wrong. Achieving personal excellence and extending a helping hand are indispensable elements of an American future that works, and they are both parts of something larger—assuming responsibility for ourselves and our country.

And then I hit it: "Let America be America again. Let it be the dream it used to be."

The issues of race and ethnicity had always been two of my central preoccupations. If I was truly saying what I felt in the speech, I had to raise those issues candidly. The racism of our history toward people of different skin color or different eye shape had to be overcome. We could no longer afford that kind of stupidity. I reminded the convention that, just as slavery was our original sin, so race remained our unresolved dilemma. But it was no longer a matter of white Americans' allowing nonwhite Americans entrance into "their" society by desegregating restaurants and schools. The reality is that African, Asian, Latino, and Native Americans are at the heart of what America has been and is. I said that if a new woman or a new man could be formed out of the ashes of the twentieth century, with all its wars and hatreds, it would be done here in America.

I pointed out that at another time in our history, Martin Luther King, Jr., had written from his jail cell in Birmingham, "We will have to repent in this generation not merely for the vitriolic words and actions of bad people, but for the silence of good people." And I asked:

> Isn't that our challenge as a party and a nation—to reach out to our fel-
> low Americans and mobilize the good people of all races for action—
> action that will stop the random violence in our cities, rebuild
> economic opportunity and jobs for all, and provide the moral leader-
> ship worthy of our ideals? Let America be America again. Let it be the
> dream it used to be.

The day after the speech, the press focused more on the fact that I was "back in the Garden" than on the speech itself. *The New York Times* did draw attention to my call for sacrifice and teamwork. Pete Hamill, in the *Daily News,* reviewed my performance by recounting my answer the next morning on the *Today* show to Bryant Gumbel's question: "So, Senator, was it your biggest night in the Garden?"

Senator: "No."

Dave Gergen said I was not Cicero but Cato. Dan Rather said it would read better than it sounded. Tom Brokaw said I still had a long way to go as a speaker. Once again I had failed the pundit test.

I was disappointed by the responses, yet they were understandable. I've always preferred the written to the spoken word. I was no Bryan— or Cuomo. Making music out of a speech is a special skill. It comes from going out on the road as if you were a musician, playing the small clubs until you get it down. Until I did that, I would have to absorb the criticism. It was just not possible to deliver a stem-winder once every four years.

Michael Lewis, a writer for *The New Republic,* took a different tack in his review of my convention speech. He had come to my rehearsal the day before I was scheduled to speak. In his piece, he recalled that between the ages of ten and twelve he had practiced basketball by pretending that he was me. He quoted from *A Sense of Where You Are,* John McPhee's basketball biography of me at twenty-one, including McPhee's description of my practice routines and the account of how I complained once, correctly, that the basket was an inch and a half low. "That was written when I was four," Lewis wrote. "I am now thirty-one."

But the grip of childhood fantasy leaves a mark on the adult mind. And as I sat in the front row of Madison Square Garden watching Bradley work hard at something that did not come naturally to him, I realized that the effects of our auto-brainwashing had not entirely worn off either of us. (I could now read his lips. "Let America be America again," he was saying. "Let America be the dream it used to be." He paused for applause, which I supplied, and he ignored.) Unlike the politicians who failed to turn up for practice, Bill Bradley thought he could will himself to move people with his words. And the idea itself I found moving.

Watching him, I felt a rogue surge of patriotism, perhaps because I have just returned from eight years in England, where people cringe at the thought of being seen to try. I had not thought it possible to love my country this week; I had thought all such sentiments of mine, such as they were, had gone underground to avoid the cynical attempts to exploit them, not just by the Democratic Party but also by every enterprising Manhattan merchant. . . . But Bradley, as usual, caught me off guard. His faith that he can will a jump shot or a speech is a small, beautiful corruption of our founding principle, that we are all created equal. I clapped loudly from my front row seat as he finished for the last time; he glanced down and smiled.

The next evening I entered the Garden once again to witness the triumph of Bradley. He was preceded by a short film of his life, which included a hook shot made at Princeton and a jump shot made from the floor beneath my feet. And then something went badly wrong. In his taped interview, he seemed forced and artificial. He came to the podium crouched and anxious and delivered what was, by far, the most wooden speech of the evening. He could hardly be heard over the crowd, which, after the film, grew bored. On television, the effect was worse still: the lines from his TelePrompTer could be read in the background. The expressions of his face were clownishly inappropriate, as if someone else, not he, were controlling them. And in a sense they were. He has learned the painful lesson that cameras will not reward his qualities. Instead they reward a caricature of his qualities, which is more easily provided by one who does not actually possess them. He is cursed, I thought, by his virtue.

I appreciated Lewis's insights. Yet the article was colored by something I had encountered before. When I was in my late teens, younger kids began patterning their basketball styles after mine and expressing a desire to follow in my footsteps. As the sport became dominated increasingly by African Americans, I emerged as a role model for many slow-footed white boys. If I could do it, they could too; all they had to do was to practice. Many of them wrote to me over the years, expressing admiration and gratitude. Some of their letters were truly moving. I felt a bond of sorts between us. The connection was a kind of mutual understanding about striving, a shared love of the game, an acceptance of the standards of academic performance and playing by the rules, which at its core was an expression of agreement with those rules and a belief that under them self-fulfillment was possible.

In politics, more than once, I've met men who stood in awe of me when they were younger. They are now adults. They have developed skills of their own, yet they still remember how they felt about me when I played with Princeton or the Knicks. They recall specific games. They can describe the Christmas Holiday Festival Tournament at Madison Square Garden in 1964, when I scored forty-one points against Michigan, the nation's number-one team, before fouling out with Princeton ahead by twelve points, only to see Michigan win it. They describe the fifth and seventh games of the 1970 NBA finals, in which Willis Reed severely injured his hip in one, and hobbled courageously onto the court in the other; the team pulled itself together and won both games and the championship. They expect the same exhilaration from my political performance as a speechmaker that they experienced in their adolescence watching me on the basketball court. When those magic moments don't materialize, they feel doubly let down. They have difficulty tolerating human shortcomings in someone whom they once invested with such an expectation of excellence.

The reaction of these young men is part of a larger problem. To some people, I will always be a basketball player first, a politician second. Byron White, former justice of the Supreme Court and former All-American football player, once told me that to people who were five years on each side of his college senior class he would always be "Whizzer" White, the football star. There is a group of Americans between thirty and sixty to whom I will always be Dollar Bill. Sometimes I like it. Sometimes I don't. But it's as permanent a part of me as the color of my eyes.

Although the 1992 convention speech was an improvement over the one I gave in 1988, I still had not been able to capture the crowd. I was reminded of that as I sat in a television booth lodged in the green seats high above the Garden floor and observed the speech of the Reverend Jesse Jackson. I heard a roar and saw the delegates surge to their feet, then a hush as they sat back down listening intently to every word, and then again a surge forward, as if they were waves in the sea. Jackson was in control of his listeners in a way that I could only achieve in my dreams. Yet I felt confident that I had said what I wanted to say.

THREE DAYS after I had given my wooden speech, I stood in Madison Square Garden listening to Bill Clinton accept the nomination of the Democratic Party. The failure of his own 1988 convention speech, which had gone on forever, was a distant memory. Clinton had taken the hits during the primaries and survived. He was bright, well intentioned, and appeared to enjoy what he did. The newsreel showing him as a high-school student shaking hands with President John F. Kennedy provided a memorable moment, and by implication said that if you elected Bill Clinton you would finally get the heir to the president who still captivated our imaginations, and that in some way our long-frustrated aspirations and our national potential would be realized.

I joined other Democrats on the podium after his acceptance speech. The applause and the cheers and the clapping and the waving extended interminably. Confetti and balloons fell from the ceiling. Music blared, backs were slapped, hugs were exchanged, flashbulbs popped, and cameras whirred, until the Clintons left the hall.

I remained on the stage, surveying the Garden as it emptied. The people passed through the exits like water flowing down a drain. The roar of an hour earlier was replaced by silence, punctuated by the odd shout. The lights dimmed, and the television crews departed. The Spanish-speaking cleaning ladies would soon arrive. Presidential nominating conventions, like circuses, come and go, but the Garden stays. In a way it's "my place," a home warm with familiarity and the memories of when I was young and could run forever. I leaned back and gazed up at the spoked ceiling, and then at the green seats near the ceiling, which even high-school kids could afford twenty years ago, and from which the players looked about an eighth of an inch high. I checked out the scoreboards at each end of the arena. No ambiguity: only a win or a loss.

I climbed down from the stage and made my way to where my fifteen-year-old daughter was sitting, in a chair on the Garden floor amid the red-white-and-blue campaign posters and confetti. It reminded me of when her mother used to sit among the popcorn boxes and beer cups waiting for me after a Knicks game. The resemblance of the moment was eerie. I glanced around one last time and then we walked out of the Garden and into the night and the 1992 campaign.

3

The Walking Town Meeting

URING MY EARLY YEARS in New York with the Knicks, I made an occasional appearance for a New York politician—a state-assembly candidate in Westchester, a Long Island congressman, a Democratic candidate for the U.S. Senate—but the first political dinner I attended was for the chairman of the House Judiciary Committee, Peter Rodino, at Thom's restaurant in Newark, New Jersey, midway through 1972. I was there in part to plead my case that the committee should not condone a monopoly by granting basketball an exemption to the antitrust laws, an action that would have reduced competitive bidding for players. I had lobbied senators the previous year and testified before the Senate Judiciary Committee on the same issue, and I had seen for the first time that even senators fawned over basketball greats—such as Oscar Robertson and John Havlicek, who were my fellow lobbyists and respectively the president and vice-president of the players' union.

Later that year, with little preparation and no experience, I thought about running for office myself. Our team had won the world championship in 1970 and I wondered whether I shouldn't move on after the completion of my four-year contract. After all, basketball was just a game, as my father constantly reminded me. When I first told him I was going to play professional basketball, he asked, "When are you going to get a real job?" Then I told him what I would make playing pro ball. He replied, in one of the few comments I ever heard him make about money, "Not a bad job!" But apart from the good pay, the real world awaited, and in thinking about what I might do, politics appealed to me, because it was (at its best) work serving others, and it was sufficiently respectable—just.

I was naturally drawn back to Missouri, where a few Democrats urged me to look at the office of state treasurer. I took soundings, only to discover that I had been away too long. I had lived in the East for over a decade, and now I felt more comfortable there than in Missouri, accustomed to the Eastern Seaboard's rhythms, its ethnic diversity, and its urban/suburban setting. Jefferson City, the Missouri state capital, was a long way from New York.

In 1974, I seriously considered running for a congressional seat in New Jersey, where my wife and I had bought a house after our marriage. With the Watergate scandal mushrooming, it looked increasingly as if it would be a good Democratic year, but several factors gave me pause. I was writing a book (*Life on the Run*), in which I felt I had a unique opportunity to depict what it was like to be a professional athlete on the road. We had just gotten married, and I didn't want to jump right into a campaign. Besides, I was still making good money playing a game I loved (after the second world championship, in 1973, knowing that the team and my abilities meshed, I derived a unique enjoyment from the game), so I gave up the idea, fully aware that I might never have as good a chance to win a congressional seat in New Jersey. But I knew that if I had run I would have been running for the House only so I could position myself to run later for the U.S. Senate. That's where I wanted to serve, because that's where I could get the most done.

Time passed. The book came out. I got a step slower. The team changed. In the fall of 1976, I knew I was going to quit after the 1976–77 season, and, looking at my possibilities, I decided to take a shot directly for the Senate. Whatever else one might say about that decision—and in different quarters it was met with varying degrees of resentment, incredulity, curiosity, and enthusiasm—one thing was for sure: I wouldn't be following Ed Eversole's advice. I would be starting at the top.

I ran for the U.S. Senate in 1978 as a citizen-politician. I played up the fact that I had taken a different road to a Senate candidacy from my two main opponents in the Democratic primary, one of whom had held appointed office at the state level while the other had served in the state legislature. Although I had had no experience in government, I had appeared on television in people's living rooms for ten years. They had seen me perform under pressure as a player; they felt that they knew me. In my first poll, I had a higher name recognition than Clifford Case, the Republican incumbent of twenty-four years.

In the general election, I faced Jeffrey Bell, a vigorous opponent who had upset the venerable Case in the Republican primary. Bell, who as a student had been a college-basketball announcer on the Columbia University radio station during the years I played at Princeton, was a campaign planner for Governor Ronald Reagan in 1976, when Reagan challenged President Gerald Ford for the Republican presidential nomination, but he had no more government experience than I had. Although he had spent part of his youth in New Jersey, he had moved back into the state only about eighteen months before the primary-filing deadline. I had gone to college in New Jersey, and I had spoken there frequently at sports banquets, schools, churches, and community groups during my college- and pro-basketball years. I had served in the Air Force Reserve at McGuire AFB in Wrightstown, New Jersey, and my wife had been a professor in the New Jersey college system since 1971. Our decision to move to New Jersey from New York had been based on a convergence of personal history and political dreams, but Jeff Bell was in no position to charge me with being a carpetbagger.

Bell's central issue was a proposal for a 30-percent cut in federal income tax rates. In addition to offering my own tax cut, targeted particularly to the middle class, I contrasted what I called "our respective commitments to New Jersey," and promised that I would be a fighter for the state's interests. I pointed out that for every dollar New Jerseyans sent to Washington we got back only sixty-seven cents in federal funds, making us forty-seventh in the nation in return on tax dollars paid. Not realizing that this ranking was largely due to the state's high per-capita income (second in the country) and a dearth of defense contracts, I pledged to "get more for New Jersey." We debated each other twenty-one times. Each debate gave me greater confidence and a chance to show that I was more than a jock. By the end of the campaign, we knew each other's moves better than dance partners in a tango contest.

I tried to illustrate my identification with the state by my campaign schedule. I worked eighteen-hour days, making countless appearances wherever I thought I could meet a few people, shake a few hands, win a few supporters. On one memorable day, as a graphic demonstration of my concern for all of New Jersey, I campaigned in all of the state's twenty-one counties. Starting at 4:30 a.m. in a local bakery in Denville and ending at 10 p.m. in the Golden Star Diner in Totowa, I crisscrossed the state. I milked cows, spoke at corporate headquarters, walked a boardwalk at the shore, greeted commuters and factory shifts, visited hospitals and senior-citizen housing, in a marathon I hoped would make plain my appreciation of New Jersey's diversity—economic, geographic, and ethnic—and my dedication to serving every part of the state. The debates, the touring, the eighteen-hour days, the excellent TV ads, and the novelty of my candidacy brought me 56 percent of the vote.

HAVING REPRESENTED New Jersey for seventeen years, I am not surprised when major polling firms assert that the state is a microcosm of the country. New Jersey offers unexpected physical beauty, surprising economic opportunity, and vital human diversity. Those who make jokes about its notorious gangsters and its legendary industrial pollution have never bothered to discover its true richness.

Flying north from Washington at three thousand feet in a small plane as the sun is setting, you reach a point where the sunlight on the Delaware River turns it into a shiny metallic-looking band extending all the way from Trenton to the Water Gap. There lying before you is the New Jersey peninsula, bordered on the west by the Delaware and on the east by the Atlantic. Tens of thousands of years ago, the glaciers stopped at about where the New Jersey Turnpike sits. North and west of the turnpike are rolling hills or the ribs of low mountain ranges (the foothills of Appalachia), with glacial lakes nestled in them. South and east of the nation's most traveled toll road lies a flat sandy plain, some of it similar to farmland in Illinois or Indiana, the rest covered by a dense pine forest that forms a unique ecosystem known as the Pine Barrens and is protected from development by a joint state and federal commission. A friend once gave me a box labeled "New Jersey Rocks," in which the state's sixteen varieties of rock were laid out as if they were the choice pieces of a Whitman's Sampler—the perfect gift for a budding geologist or a junior senator.

New Jersey is the most densely populated state in the union, with areas of some counties having as many as forty thousand people per square mile. Given that the Pine Barrens occupies more than 20 percent of the state's landmass, the density is even greater than the statewide numbers imply. A neighbor is never far away. There is little open space outside the Pines. Townships run into each other, connected by venerable highways—Route 10, Route 46, and Route 80; Route 22 and Route 78; Route 70 and Route 55—that cross the state like stripes on a barber pole. And extending the entire length of the state, from the New York border to Cape May at the mouth of Delaware Bay, is one of the most beautiful highways in America, the Garden State Parkway.

The state's economy today is much different from the way it was twenty-five years ago. In the 1970s, old manufacturing industries left New Jersey, and major service industries moved in to take their place. Corporate headquarters for everything from heavy equipment (Ingersoll-Rand) to foodstuffs (Nabisco and CPC International) moved to New Jersey from other places. Bell Labs, RCA Labs, research-based pharmaceutical companies, Rutgers and Princeton universities have all put research and development at the core of the state's economy. At the same time, the environmental movement brought a vast improvement in the quality of New Jersey's ecology. The oil refineries along the turnpike, with their stench of sulfur, shared the fate of the massive landfills of garbage in the Meadowlands and the hundreds of toxic-waste dumps— all harnessed by tough environmental laws. The Delaware was a dead river in the late sixties, poisoned by chemicals and sewage, but now it is swimmable, with shad in its clear waters for a hundred miles. Like a neglected child reclaimed by attention and care, the New Jersey environment has been given a second life.

New Jersey is an upper-middle-class state. Four counties in New Jersey are among the fifteen richest counties in America. Yet the level of poverty and violence in such cities as Newark, Jersey City, Paterson, Elizabeth, and Trenton is shocking. Newark ranks seventeenth in the nation in homicides per capita, and a doctor in a Newark hospital once told me that by 2000 he expected 10 percent of Newark's citizens to die of AIDS. Because the townships are jammed so close together, you can drive in fifteen minutes from the mansion districts to neighborhoods of distressing squalor.

New Jerseyans think of themselves more as residents of townships than as residents of a state. The absence of a true state-based, statewide television station contributes to this lack of identity. (New Jerseyans get more news about the mayors of New York and Philadelphia than they do about their two U.S. senators.) From the volunteer fire departments and rescue squads to the intense high-school athletic rivalries and the tight ethnic enclaves, the quality of life derives from the nature of your township. Probably the strongest statewide identification New Jerseyans feel is with their one hundred and twenty-seven miles of beaches, including several barrier islands honeycombed with houses and connected to the mainland by causeways. "Goin' down the Shore" was always the quintessential New Jersey experience, long before Bruce Springsteen told the world about Jersey girls, Asbury Park fortune-tellers, or the motorcycles on Route 9. Millions of New Jerseyans, as well as tourists from as far away as Montreal, spend more than twelve billion dollars a year for small second homes, rented apartments, motel rooms, restaurants, and fun along the Jersey Shore; and the Garden State Parkway, the Atlantic City Expressway, and Route 195 bring in New Jerseyans and Pennsylvanians on daytrips. Atlantic City, with its gambling casinos and boardwalk, attracts more visitors annually than any other tourist destination in America.

New Jerseyans have emigrated from all over the world, and the Statue of Liberty rises from New Jersey waters. Kids in our high schools speak one hundred and twenty different languages at home. It is virtually impossible for me to go through an active campaign day in the state and fail to hear the accent of a language other than English. (And then there is the special New Jersey accent. I came from Missouri, the land of the flat "or"s, as in "barn again" and "knife and fark." New Jersey is the land of "chawclet" and "cawffee.") Many New Jersey parents came from New York or Philadelphia to New Jersey townships for the schools. Many others left New Jersey cities for the suburbs, so that their children would have a better chance to learn. Education is viewed as the great equalizer. New Jersey aristocracy still live in their estates behind high hedges and manicured lawns and socialize down winding country roads that lead to elite clubs. The fox hunt in Far Hills is a long way from the St. Rocco Festival in Elizabeth. But what I like most is that the New Jerseyans at the ethnic festivals could care less about the steeplechase. People seem satisfied to be who they are. There is an inarticulate roughness about many New Jerseyans. Subtle generosities of spirit exist alongside a striking directness. They tell you what they think, and if you are a politician, you had better be able to explain yourself or be prepared to suffer the consequences.

THE TWENTY-ONE-COUNTY tour of my first campaign was the brainchild of my campaign manager, Susan Thomases, who was one of the first women in the country to manage a Senate campaign. She was a creative political strategist and a superb scheduler, who recognized that part of any campaign should be the fun inherent in the enterprise. After my election, she went on to become a corporate lawyer, but she retained her interest in my career and in that of another politician, Bill Clinton, whom she had met in 1972. Over the years, her friendship with Bill and Hillary Clinton strengthened, and in 1992, after playing a counselor role during the primaries, she became Clinton's chief scheduler in the general-election campaign. She enthusiastically backed the idea of a bus tour after the Democratic convention. It was a stroke of genius that confounded the polling and media gurus of modern politics.

From the Democratic National Convention in New York to Camden, New Jersey, then across Pennsylvania and down the Ohio Valley across Illinois to St. Louis, Bill and Hillary Clinton and Al and Tipper Gore traveled from big-city to small-town America, in the first of what would be several such bus tours during the campaign. Moved by a yearning for answers in hard economic times, by the convention films about Clinton's boyhood in Hope, Arkansas, and about his youthful encounter with JFK, and by the ebullient compatibility of the Gore and Clinton families, great crowds turned up everywhere. In Vandalia, Illinois, people lined the roads for ten miles. In Erie, Pennsylvania, three thousand people waited until 1 A.M. to greet the candidates. In Davenport, Iowa, the bus arrived three hours late, but there were still five thousand on hand to greet it.

The visits were a way of telling people in the country's heartland that they were important, and, given the originality of the idea, the media projected those old-fashioned whistle-stop images to millions of citizens across the country. Plugging into nostalgia was a way to make Clinton seem older. Moreover, millions of Americans who had grown up in small towns and left still carried their experiences and loyalties with them, as surely as I carried Crystal City with me. The message was that Clinton was a regular guy who was skeptical of big government and corporate institutions and who understood and enjoyed the American people as they were and where they were. Deeper than that was the identification of Clinton with the road, which from the days of wagon trains to the days of the motorcycle had lived in the national imagination as a symbol of a path to a better future.

In August, I joined the Clinton/Gore bus tour in Ohio for a day. The six-bus caravan drove from Cleveland south to Parma, then east to Youngstown and on to New Castle, Pennsylvania. The roads Clinton traveled were not the interstates but the back roads of America—two-lane highways whose concrete slabs clicked as the tires rolled over them. It was a trip back in time. Driving past the roadside bars and the Gulf stations and the small farms, I remembered the roads of my youth—blacktop Missouri highways named TT or AA that wound their way through the Ozark foothills, where you had to pay attention at night, because there was no white line in the middle, and the shoulder between you and the drainage ditch was perilously narrow.

As we left the rolling farmland of Ohio and moved into the Alleghenies, people came out of their red-brick houses, their white frame houses, their trailer houses up on blocks, and stood at the road's edge to catch a glimpse of the future president. Sometimes what looked to me like three generations stood next to each other, the entire twentieth century spanned in their faces. Some pointed; some laughed; others stood quietly and watched. A few drank beer sitting astride their motorcycles. Did these people believe once again that a Democrat could win and that with his victory things would get better? That a political leader could give them back some control over their lives?

Many of the factories and coal mines in the small towns of western Pennsylvania had closed. The lives of many people here had been all but destroyed. Trying to cope had become an interminable endeavor for more than a few. Unemployment and welfare rolls continued to grow. I knew that they saw themselves as very different from the heroic common man of many a politician's imagination. I knew that what we see is often what we want to see. Nevertheless, I had also learned during my twenty-five years on the road in America that a passing glance is often enough to form a correct impression.

More than a few people on the bus felt lumps in their throats, me included; the very presence of these people was a genuine and spontaneous expression of support. More than this, it was a reminder to us of how sterile the politics of the last twenty years had been, with its attack ads and its stage-managed crowds. There had been an absence of spontaneity, and no true political dialogue in American politics. An excessive security apparatus had blocked the leader from the people by erecting a protective cordon that was more a capitulation to fear—and in some cases an excuse for political detachment—than a necessary security measure. The outpouring of goodwill, the yearning for hopes to be fulfilled, the impatience with cynicism, the anger with the corruption of the recent past—all this was palpable. Not simply as a politician but also as a human being, I was certain that these people by the side of the road had not given up hope that their lives might improve.

FOR ME, two constantly energizing aspects of politics are the people and the unknown that they represent. For over seventeen years, my most memorable moments have come from the people I have met. Encounters with them are the raw material of politics. It's through the stories of people's lives that I am moved and that I gain a hesitancy about universal solutions. It's from their stories that I see what a small role government plays in most people's lives, and, paradoxically, it's where I most feel the impact of decisions taken in Washington. I can't understand how politicians can connect with people, or begin to represent them, if they do not listen to their stories. How else can they determine whether their judgment about an issue is different from that of their constituents, or what principles they share with their constituents? Stories give substance and emotion to abstractions about democracy. Interactions with people and the sharing of their life circumstances show me the boundaries of the possible. The cumulative impressions form a context for policy. Ultimately, I rely on my own judgment, but that judgment needs to be built upon the voices of real people.

The town meeting offers one such forum. The elected official stands before his or her constituents, accountable for actions, answering questions. For the constituents, an exchange with an elected representative provides not only information but a sense that they are heeded. Sometimes they vent their anger and frustration, and just by listening the politician encourages catharsis. The exchange allows the elected official to educate by pointing out the consequences of a particular action, and to state forthrightly where he or she disagrees with a constituent. It leads to a mutual recognition of concerns and duties. It allows the official to hear stories, to learn, to grow in awareness, to hone answers, to discard what doesn't connect, to expand on what does. Like the press conference but much wider-ranging, the town meeting is essential to maintaining political sharpness.

After my first term in the Senate, I developed a variation on the town meeting. I call it the walking town meeting. Instead of waiting for people to come to an appointed place, such as a high-school auditorium or a town hall, to ask me questions, I go where they are and ask them questions: "What's on your mind?" "Anything you want me to know?" "Anything you want to ask me?" Their reactions to my presence give me a good barometer of what they're thinking about that day. An aide stands behind me, tabulating the number of comments and questions by category—twenty-eight on the budget, sixteen on health care, six on Bosnia. Another aide stands to the side of the flow, ready to swoop in and handle matters of constituent service: "I lost my Social Security"; "The IRS lost my tax refund"; "My father never got his Bronze Star"; "I have a problem with immigration"; "My ex-husband won't pay his court-ordered child support." At the end of the session, my staff follows up, and I write down the memorable stories. (Since 1979 my office has helped more than sixty thousand people handle specific problems with one or another federal bureaucracy.)

People who come to a town meeting may have specific things on their minds, or they may come simply out of curiosity. In either case, they come with some sort of preconceived purpose. But when I go where they are—say, to the New York–New Jersey Port Authority Bus Terminal, where six thousand New Jerseyans pass me in a single hour— my unexpected presence makes for spontaneous responses. I put myself out there and see what happens. I can't avoid criticism or derision or anguished complaints; I often find humor and wisdom. I have to deal with all comers.

"What is your stand on abortion?" a woman asks me.

"I think it should be safe, legal, and rare. I'm for a woman's right to choose," I reply.

"Yeah, that's what I thought. I like you and all you do, but that. I hope you'll reconsider. I have two kids and the time for choice is when you're out on a date, before you have sex. That's when you should choose what to do. Not later. It's just wrong. It's really wrong. Our country is stained by this. I hope you'll think about it."

"I once had a good job," a man says; "then you deregulated trucking, you creep."

"Do something about the crime in this terminal, it's an outrage!"

"What can you do about lowering these bus fares?"

"You're the only Democrat I'll ever vote for."

"Number 24 from the corner, yes." (My Knick jersey number was 24.)

Where I have done walking town meetings the most is along the Jersey Shore. New Jersey's coastline extends from Cape May to Sandy Hook. Every summer, I walk for some distance in forty-eight of these shore townships over a period of four days. I look forward to this walk every year; it's my political bellwether.

I walk the water's edge, preceded by two aides, who carry a six-foot-by-four-foot sign reading "Meet Senator Bill Bradley." I shake hands, and I answer questions from bikini-clad women on beach blankets, from grandfathers with their grandchildren in tow seeking an autograph, from families playing ball or building sand castles. I make sure I say hello to the lifeguards on each stretch of the beach and greet the local mayor or councilmen if they come out to say hello. I keep a tight schedule, which my office publishes in advance, telling people exactly what time I will appear on their beach. When I'm walking and talking, I also check out the beach erosion and the water quality. On occasion I confide to a well-wisher, "If I represented Montana, I couldn't do this."

Before 1990, when I nearly lost my Senate seat, I had assumed that most people in the state liked me, and that the occasional negative comment was the exception. Then, in June 1990, Democratic Governor Jim Florio rammed a $2.8-billion state-tax increase through the legislature, with inadequate efforts to explain it to the public. (Even I had thought it was a cynical move—too much, too soon; as the gubernatorial candidate, Florio had stated that he saw no reason for a tax increase.) By August, I saw the outrage my constituents felt toward Florio. They literally screamed epithets at him for what they claimed was taking money from their pockets and giving it to liberal bureaucrats. But I sensed that none of the fury was aimed at me. Not until October did I realize that the public had linked me to the governor. I knew I was in trouble when I stood outside Giants Stadium before a football game in late October, and then at the Port Authority Bus Terminal a week before the election, and instead of hearing affection, as I had on the eve of the 1984 election, I heard anger and resentment directed toward me—words and looks that refuted the latest poll, which showed me eighteen points ahead of Christine Todd Whitman, my Republican opponent.

"I like you, but I'm voting for your opponent to send Florio a message."

"I'll vote for you for president, but not for the Senate again. We need a change."

"I'm voting against you Tuesday to wake you up and tell you to pay more attention to the people."

"Senator, you're going to lose, and the Teamsters will be happy, because you have done nothing for us."

"I'd like to vote for you, but I'm Republican."

"I'm shaking your hand as a Knick only."

The 1990 election, with its three-point margin, was a terrible blow; it was essentially a rejection of me, for not appreciating how much people wanted candor, responsiveness, and a demonstrated caring about their plight. I had been intimidated by the state's roiling political atmosphere, which was dominated by anger about the state-tax increase and worries about tough economic times. My television commercials had been made for a different atmosphere: two of them emphasized my basketball career, which for over a decade I had de-emphasized. Instead of helping, these commercials hurt.

I had spent my Senate career arguing that the best income-tax rates were the lowest tax rates possible. Florio increased rates. It should have been a clear matter of blasting the tax increase, or at least saying that he went too far. After all, no one ever likes to pay more taxes. But it wasn't that simple. Florio had been one of three elected officials statewide to support me in the 1978 primary. I felt I had an obligation to him not to trash his program; moreover, his tax plan had positive features, among them balancing the budget, which his Republican predecessor, the popular Tom Kean, had left grossly unbalanced because his economic assumptions had proved overly optimistic. At the same time, to support the tax increase would have been not just highly unpopular but contrary to the tax principles (lower rates and fewer loopholes) I had espoused over twelve years. The solution my advisers and I decided upon was to say nothing—that is, to say the literal truth: that as a federal official I had nothing to do with state taxes.

Many New Jerseyans interpreted my refusal to take a position on the tax issue as indifference to their economic predicament. But with the Congress in session trying to enact a federal budget before the government shut down, I was stuck in Washington until October 28. I missed the eighteen-hour campaign days that would have been my early-warning system of impending disaster. By the time I sensed the dimensions of the electoral tide, it was too late. I squeaked by, 50 percent to 47 percent, with a margin of fifty thousand votes. One postelection poll I heard about said that more than half of those who voted for Whitman had done so to protest Florio's policies or to send me a message, thinking I would win anyway.

As they say in sports, "If you win the world championship by one point, you're still the world champion." A win should be a win, but the near defeat hung over me like a bad dream. A friend of thirty years, the editor of a national newspaper, called and said, "I'm personally glad you won, but professionally the other would have been a good story."

"What do you mean, a good story?" I asked.

"Oh, you know," he said, " 'Golden Boy Falls on Face.' "

For many months to come, I looked at each person who approached me as if he or she had voted against me. In a reversal of my previous attitude, I expected negative comments and took the positive comment as the exception. I began to shy away from contact. For someone who had worked very hard for twelve years and had incessantly been told how good he was, the close re-election was an abrupt reality check, a painful revelation of the volatility of support.

My constituents began to resemble "the crowd" from my basketball days, whom I could never trust to be constant. The bond I had imagined between me and my constituents had proved evanescent. In basketball, one was only as good as the last game. In politics, one was only as good as the last campaign. All the years of service seemed to count for nothing.

Or did they? Another way of looking at the 1990 campaign was to see its strategy and execution as such a disaster that only the people I had touched over the years with all the long days and the beach walks and the town meetings and the constituent service had pulled me through. After the election, special-interest groups told me that I had won only because they were behind me, and that as a consequence I owed them. In 1984, when I won with 65 percent of the vote, no one had claimed that I had any obligation to his or her group.

In the long run, the close election was the best thing that ever happened in my political career. It forced me to face up to what I needed to change, both organizationally and personally; it forced me to go deeper into my emotions and to speak from values and convictions in ways I had avoided before. It freed me to share what was in my gut as well as in my mind. From another standpoint, it was worse than defeat, because I couldn't put it behind me and go on to other things. My predicament forced me to try to regain people's trust and support without a way to measure my efforts; not for another six years could a new election ratify my progress in reaching out to New Jerseyans. The beach walks and the other walking town meetings became minireferendums on how I was doing.

The day after the election, I began to make changes. Staff members who had been with me for years moved on, either because of burnout or because of what appeared to be the disappearance of my 1992 presidential prospects. My new staff was a generation younger, but provided a continuity of quality with a commensurate commitment to our shared values. I spent more time communicating with the people of New Jersey about my efforts on their behalf. For example, I developed and introduced a new way to pay for college education (income-contingent direct loans) and then told New Jerseyans about it repeatedly. I also spoke out more often on issues in the news—the economy, race relations, America's role in the world. I no longer pondered each statement endlessly, imagining every possible reaction to it before I made it. As my statements tracked my real feelings more fully, I felt surer in my contact with voters. I began to trust my instincts more. In the summer of 1991, as I walked the Shore again, I found, out of the many thousands I met in four days, only five people who were hostile. Maybe the election had been a temper tantrum, I hypothesized. Maybe the people's anger with me had passed. Maybe now they would give me the benefit of the doubt. After all, one political maxim is that an election only measures how voters feel on a single day. Maybe nine months had given the people of New Jersey a different perspective. Maybe they saw how I had tried to change. Maybe the views they held of me before the election were reasserting themselves, after the catharsis of the vote.

I was reminded along the Shore of how long I'd been a public figure:

"I remember you at Rahway, when you spoke at the Presbyterian church in 1964."

"Hey, Bill, you spoke at my college graduation at St. Peter's in 1973."

"Senator Bradley, do you recognize me? I was an intern in your office in 1980."

I was always pleased but surprised when I encountered the results of something I had done. One couple wanted to take a picture of me with their little boy: "He's named for you, because your bill made it easier for us to adopt a foreign-born baby." This was a reference to a law passed in 1989 that eliminated the five-year waiting period for citizenship in the case of foreign infants adopted by American parents.

One man supposed I was at Island Beach State Park because on Tuesdays admission was free. An elderly lady on the Point Pleasant boardwalk said hello and asked me to take a picture of her with her two female friends. After I took the snapshot and returned the camera, one of the friends, who hadn't recognized me, confessed that she'd been worried that I was one of those boardwalk con artists who take your picture and then run off with your camera.

I began to feel connected again.

"Thanks for cleaning up the water. It's great to return to a clean Shore."

"When will that college-scholarship program be available in New Jersey?"

"Cut spending."

"Thanks for helping my mother with Medicare."

"Can you help our son get leg braces from Medicaid?"

"I like you, but you politicians have to start talking about the issues and not simply attacking each other."

"I see you here every year. I'm glad you come."

As I walked along the water's edge, people rushed up. There were pictures, autographs, questions, complaints, stories. A woman in tears told me about the death of her seventeen-year-old daughter, overdosed by an anesthesiologist prior to a liposuction treatment. Another woman told me the story of her son, who was taunted at school with shouts of "Nazi" simply because his mother was German.

"I know why you're walking the beach, Bill," said an older man with two young women he claimed were his daughters.

"Why?" I asked.

"To look at the girls."

With each passing day, these random contacts knitted my confidence back together. I began to relax. The fever broke. Once again I was feeling close to the people of New Jersey.

SINCE THE slow-motion depression began in 1990, the people I have met on these walks have told of a persistent condition: they are afraid. "What should I do?" asked a woman who came up to me. "My husband and I have five kids. We live in an apartment. I need to find a job to help out, but first I need some training, and there's no money for me to take a community-college program in production design." Another woman, whom I met at the Barnegat lighthouse, said, "Six months ago, my husband lost his job. Two months ago, I lost my job. We have three children, and now we have no health insurance. I went to my pediatrician, and he said that if the kids get sick he'll help out. But, you know, Senator, this is America. You shouldn't have to have a friendly pediatrician to get health care for your kids." A man said, "I lost my health insurance and now I'm afraid to let my two-year-old son go to the playground. If he got hurt, I couldn't pay for a doctor." Another man said, "I don't want to be at the beach on a weekday. But nobody brings cars to my transmission shop anymore, and the three cars that are there now can't be picked up, because the people can't pay the bills." A woman pushing her disabled teenager in a wheelchair along the boardwalk said angrily, "Somebody's got to do something to help me. I'm desperate. I get no assistance from any level of government. If you're not rich or on welfare, you're forgotten."

The 1990 campaign had been the harbinger of a changed political atmosphere. People's suspicion of government was intense, surpassed only by their anger at big business. When Governor Florio raised their taxes, New Jerseyans objected to it partly because they denied reality (the budget had to be balanced under New Jersey state law), but also because they had lost confidence in government. They failed to see how any government spending helped their families. Little did anyone guess that the turmoil of 1990 was about problems even more fundamental than taxes and government spending.

During the early 1990s, five economic crises arose in this country: a deep and slowly responding recession; mushrooming budget deficits and rising national debt; the end of the cold war, with its imperative for downsizing the defense sector; international competition that increased pressure on labor and management; and the spread of personal computers and computer networks into the workplace. Because financing the budget deficit and national debt took 20 percent of all private savings, that money was not available for personal loans. As a result, people paid higher interest rates on borrowing to buy cars, homes, and college educations. Economic growth was slower. Postponement of serious action on the deficit reduced their children's prospects for having a higher standard of living. (Democracies often pass tough decisions on to those not yet living.) What people feared most was not being able to work. People were losing jobs that they had always assumed offered them lifetime employment—in companies such as AT&T, IBM, Sears, GM. They could not see technological progress as a good thing, when it destroyed their jobs. But they were also slow to realize that failure to introduce information technology into the workplace endangered, in the long run, not only their jobs but whole industries. The price and quality advantages of open trade weren't readily apparent on the individual level. But people who lost their jobs because of international competition lost something large and obvious, and they became angry. Finally, Americans might feel safer now that the threat of a full-scale nuclear exchange was gone, but workers in defense plants couldn't find good second careers easily. Economic dislocation was a shock, especially because the laid-off employees sensed that the situation would be permanent: good jobs at good pay weren't coming back in the spring.

One of the Clinton campaign's well-known internal staff slogans was, "The economy, stupid; keep it simple." It conveyed what was on people's minds. Along the Jersey Shore in 1990–91, and especially in 1992, the message rang true, day after day. People were intensely worried about their economic condition, and they were ready to make a change to improve it. They were willing to move, they were willing to go back to school, the Republicans among them were willing to vote for a Democrat—in order to get better jobs. Social issues like abortion, or prayer in public schools; foreign-policy issues, like the war in Bosnia or continued repression in Cuba; political issues, like voter registration or campaign-finance reform—these all took a distant second place for many.

On one of my walking town meetings a man named Tom (he wouldn't give his last name) exploded in frustration and fear. A college graduate who had married his high-school sweetheart, he worked for an insurance company in New York, commuting each day by bus and subway. Four of his five children were in parochial school and his wife worked as a clerk in the Jersey City office of an accounting firm. As he talked, his voice grew louder and his flushed face turned crimson. "How can I make it? I work ten hours a day; my wife works; we teach our kids to work; and who helps us? Nobody. Everywhere I turn, there're more taxes. I pay school taxes and my kids don't even go to public school. Auto insurance went through the roof. Now health premiums have increased. Tuition costs are higher. Pretty soon I won't be able to pay my mortgage. Is that what you politicians want?"

A heavyset woman sitting on a bench at Bradley Beach shrieked, "You gotta do something about property taxes. They're killing us. Six thousand dollars for a little beach house—I can't afford that. You politicians gotta fight for the middle class." A physically fit seventy-two-year-old, his voice quivering with worry, said, "Senator, I took early retirement from my company and I spent a lifetime saving my money, but it's not enough, and these were supposed to be my golden years."

WHEN THE ELECTORATE focuses on a bad economy, there is not much an incumbent can do, except maybe change the subject. I had tried that in 1990 and failed. If you're the incumbent and the economy is good, then all you have to do is remind people that you're at least partly responsible and prevent your opponent from changing the subject. I had tried that in 1984 and succeeded.

In the late 1970s, when I first arrived in Washington, President Jimmy Carter couldn't run away from double-digit inflation rates and interest rates. It didn't matter that the principal cause was the OPEC oil-price increases, over which he had no control. He was the president, and he had to assume responsibility for the immediate condition of the economy. All Ronald Reagan had to do was ask people, "Are you better off now than you were four years ago?" and he won the election. By the end of Reagan's first term, the Federal Reserve had broken the back of inflation. Never mind that to do so it had to keep interest rates so high that the eventual result was a recession, with more people unemployed than at any time since the Great Depression and billions of dollars in economic output lost forever. By 1984, the economy was booming, the dollar was strong, and, as Reagan's nostalgic re-election campaign reminded people, it was "morning in America." In 1988, the effects of the burgeoning budget deficits, weakened financial institutions, and a by-then depreciated dollar were yet to be fully recognized. The Republicans ignored the bitter fruits of their economic policies, and the Democrats failed to call the public's attention to them (and even to the savings-and-loan scandal) in any memorable or creative way. The election, anomalously, was not about the economy at all, but about social issues such as the furlough of criminals and who was a more fervent patriot.

By 1992, President George Bush, like President Carter, was reaping the whirlwind of poor economic performance. His administration had seen the lowest economic growth of any four years since the Depression, and on top of that, jobs were permanently lost to the economy because of corporate America's aggressive adjustment to technological change, fiercer international competition, and a world with fewer defense contracts. Meanwhile, the Federal Reserve kept short-term interest rates abnormally low, which was good for banks (who borrowed low and invested in high-yielding long-term treasury bonds) but starved small and medium-size businesses (who could not get credit to expand capacity or create jobs). The twelve-year debt accumulation, the unavailability of credit, and the severe job dislocation were evident to millions of Americans; Bush could not change the subject. As Reagan had done in 1980, Clinton needed only to keep the focus on what most people sensed anyway—that the economy was in bad shape and that the incumbent ought to be held responsible.

During my career as a senator, both Republicans and Democrats have been thrown out of office because of bad economic times. Neither party seems to have the key to sustained economic growth. Neither seems willing to follow a fiscal policy that wrests control of the economy from the Federal Reserve. Given the extent to which the electoral fortunes of presidents depend on the economy, it's easy to say that what a party stands for is irrelevant and that only the economy counts. Nevertheless, what a party believes and what its members know it stands for becomes, in such circumstances, even more important. A party's self-image is what keeps it together and sustains its members with the conviction that, once they are running the government, the whole country will be better off. Party affiliation in the best of circumstances becomes a kind of faith. It is the faith not of a technocrat who wants to pull different economic levers but of a patriot who believes that the nation's welfare and security are at stake and that all the important issues outside the economy—the social contract that informs our civil relations, the way we manage our natural environment, the very tone of democracy itself—are shaped differently by each of the two parties. Such a faith rooted in ideas is difficult to sustain, given the nonideological nature of American politics.

The abolitionists, the progressives, the civil-rights activists, and even some of the early environmentalists were willing to take a public-policy stand that was rooted in a moral view of the world and based on individual conviction. Politicians of principle don't always win, but they know who they are. The norm is for politicians to focus on process more than principle. Ideas alienate as well as attract. Presidential candidates who win their party's nomination by appealing to the core principles of the right or left will, in the general election, follow their political consultant's advice and head for the murky, moderate middle. Political principle is tart in many mouths, whereas vagueness tastes like honey. It has always been dangerous—especially, but not entirely, in the South—for an elected politician to take a position of principle on the issues of race or class. The commonsense result has been to avoid the clarity of conviction powerfully expressed. Even the mention of ideology, political philosophy, or principle has been discouraged; just get the politicians together, divvy up the economic pie, and keep the process moving forward toward an undefined end. In such a world, party has little content and becomes more an entry fee than a patriotic faith.

This became startlingly clear to me when, in the early 1980s, as a freshman senator, I was appointed by Senator Robert C. Byrd, then the minority leader, to head an economic task force for the Democratic caucus. My charge was to hammer out a Democratic alternative to the Reagan economic program. Russell Long, the powerful Louisiana senator who chaired the Finance Committee, came to the meetings, and so did Ted Kennedy of Massachusetts and Henry Jackson of Washington. I tried to find out what all of us could agree on. The answer was, very little. Kennedy wanted more government programs and fewer tax loopholes, and he remained unconcerned about the budget deficit or inflation. The cagey Long rarely said what he wanted, but he remained adamant about what he didn't want, which was usually anything that Kennedy wanted. Jackson insisted that we look at the big picture, which usually meant the geopolitics of oil, Soviet global strategy, or whatever interest-rate predictions his Wall Street advisers—and in particular Henry Kaufman of Salomon Brothers—saw as pertinent for the economy.

No one had a counterproposal to Reagan's plan to reduce taxes, cut federal regulation, cut social programs for the poor, and increase defense spending. No one had any idea how important a simple, clear message was for effective communication. President Reagan had fused personality politics and political program, and Democrats couldn't cope. Few were willing to confront him on ideological grounds, or oppose him from a position of principle. Having been in the Senate majority for twenty-six years, Democrats had allowed power to replace conviction as the chief tool of Democratic governance. Though most Democrats could agree to modify Reagan's tax cut by giving less to the rich and more to the middle class, some refused to support even that position. In fact, many Democrats joined Reagan's bandwagon, mindful of the admonition "Never vote against a tax cut." I concluded that the distance between Ted Kennedy and Russell Long was too great to develop a clear, contrasting Democratic alternative to the Reagan agenda. The failure to develop an alternative was symptomatic of a larger problem: what did Democrats believe?

In 1982, I became the liaison between the Democrats in Congress and the business council of the Democratic National Committee. I met with the businesspeople who were its members and listened carefully to their suggestions, which sounded similar to what Reagan was advocating. "Doesn't anyone have something fresh to say?" I asked myself. I was still feeling discouraged by the failure of Senate Democrats to oppose Reaganomics or to develop a real alternative. I decided to canvass the political landscape. I read widely. I queried academics. I talked with political consultants and pollsters. I held long discussions with veterans of past Democratic administrations. Slowly, I realized that our party had no ideas we were willing to fight for. I saw Republicans appropriating the bedrock American values—liberty, courage, optimism, strength, frugality, family. The intellectual momentum and confidence was all on their side. It was their academics who were churning out books attacking the very idea of national government and attributing the failure of the Carter administration to a timidity about international power politics.

The dynamics of a particular politics changes when politicians who think they know their profession are surprised. The 1980 election, which elevated Ronald Reagan and defeated George McGovern and eight other well-known Democratic senators, created that kind of fear. Democrats lost not just their confidence but some of their convictions. Indeed, the beliefs about government of the previous twenty-six years were increas-

ingly seen as the cause of the defeats. Ronald Reagan had tapped the anxiety taxpayers felt about the nature of the federal bureaucracy when he
portrayed it as too big, too intrusive, and too wasteful. A kind of panic
ensued. Democrats in the 1980s began to believe that the voters' basic
impulses went against them. Rather than pointing out the Republican
contradictions inherent in advocating a passive government at the economic level and an active government on the moral plane or in attempting simultaneously to cut taxes, increase defense, and balance the
budget, Democrats simply echoed the notion of less government.

What Democrats needed was a coherent set of criteria for the func-
tions and operations of the federal government. Some government programs had attracted stifling layers of bureaucracy and lines of subsidy
seekers. The real special interests were not the welfare mothers (although some of them were indeed undeserving) but the well-to-do farmers and the wealthy real-estate investors and the corporate miners and
countless others who championed the free market until they were asked
to do without their subsidies, tax loopholes, or special regulations. What
was needed was a purging of the sweetheart deals that larded law and regulations. What existed was the certainty that once a special provision had
been lodged in the bowels of bureaucratic regulations, no politician
would take the time or exert the energy to find it, much less eliminate it.
Government had become an end in itself—a prize to be fought over not
because of what it could accomplish for all but for what it could deliver
to the few. What was needed was a conviction that government, for
those who worked in it, was as much a commitment to serve as it was a
stable job with good benefits; what existed was a surprising number of
no-show or make-work jobs. Without accountability, idealism became
softheaded talk. Without idealism, government itself seemed just another special interest.

Rather than redefine our national circumstance, or admit the valid-
ity of some of the Republican criticism about the debilitating effects that
impersonal bureaucracy had on the people it was supposed to help and
then fight hard against the greed and self-centeredness of Reaganomics,
Democrats hid. In the single most important vote of the Reagan era,
only ten of forty-seven Democratic senators voted against the 1981 tax
bill, which had the effect of guaranteeing huge budget deficits and shifting the tax burden down onto the middle class. (Only three Democratic senators voted for the Reagan spending cuts as well.) Instead of

challenging the violence without context and the sex without attachment that television purveyed, Democrats joined Republicans in seeking to ingratiate themselves with the entertainment industry by
showering it with tax breaks and trade concessions and giving it unprecedented opportunity to concentrate power through mergers and
acquisitions. Instead of focusing on the concrete circumstances of the
poor—the hunger, the homelessness, family breakdowns, absence of
adequate health care, the joblessness, and the violence—and seeking innovative, practical answers, Democrats got backed into a debate about
the theory of government. Instead of abolishing federal programs that
had failed to solve the problems they were created to solve, Democrats
allowed themselves to be seen as the party that wanted to raise taxes so
that an imperial bureaucracy could waste money on what many Americans saw (however wrong the perception) as programs only for ungrateful and undeserving minorities.

Because Democrats refused to modify segments of government, the
citizens became furious with all the government. Democrats frequently
denied what most Americans knew—that government often handed out
benefits to the loudest group or the petitioner with the best-connected,
best-paid lobbyist. Democrats regularly seemed to be dividing up the
economic-and-social pie (into smaller and smaller slices) among different
economic, regional, ethnic, or special-objective groups whose real goal
was to "get theirs" and forget everybody else. More people came to believe that for Democrats compromise that gave everyone something was
preferred to principled appeals that told someone no. Finally, Democrats
were late admitting that some problems, such as the hollowness endemic
in a materialistic society, could not be solved by government. Learning
to speak to the general interest on a consistent basis and developing a
clear set of Democratic principles became the party's most pressing
need, but by the late eighties the party had become the captive of its
parts, and the whole suffered.

The 1994 midterm elections revealed the rot at the core of the old
Democratic coalition. The South was lost. Labor couldn't produce votes.
Blacks didn't turn out. Latinos weren't registered. Women fled the
ranks. Suburban white ethnics voted against the party. The West resented Washington's control of the public lands. Small business felt over-
taxed, and the middle class felt unappreciated by the party.

For the first time since 1954, the House of Representatives went Republican. In the aftermath of the defeat, there was the normal finger-pointing and the predictable but contradictory advice about changing the image of the party, communicating better, moving to the center, reinvigorating the Democratic base. Since only 38 percent of eligible voters went to the polls in 1994, compared with 55 percent in 1992, it was argued that in 1996 the people who vote only in presidential years would return, and Democrats, corralling the majority of those voters, would be victorious. It was hoped as well that Republicans would do too much dismantling of government and go too far to the right in social policy, thereby making Democrats appear moderate. But without a new conceptual framework, the Democratic Party could not stand united. The passage of time had rigidified the elements of the coalition. "My way or no way" was the working hypothesis. Even as interest groups became more strident, Democratic politicians offered varying versions of how to reduce regulation, cut taxes, reduce spending, and protect the moral fiber of America. If Democrats couldn't keep the focus on broadly recognized public needs, on the increasing disparities of power between the individual and the corporation, and on the national importance of unselfish public service, we would end up defending only the materialistic side of government—the side that determined who got what resources. By stigmatizing the process of allocating power and resources through government, Republicans then would be able to deny the modern Democratic Party its legitimacy. Few seemed to understand the depth of the party's problem. "In politics," the political scientist David Green has written, "real intellectual victory is achieved not by transmitting one's language to supporters but by transmitting it to critics." When you adopt your opponents' definition of the situation, including their premises and even some of their substantive analysis, effective opposition becomes difficult. The Democratic identity crisis, accelerating since 1980 and smoothed over in 1992, burst into the open with a vengeance in the aftermath of the 1994 election.

AMERICA'S PROSPERITY and its progress depend on a wise government. Thomas Jefferson, the champion of self-reliant farmers, believed in as little government as possible, because he suspected that it would be dominated by the forces of commerce, which he considered inherently corrupt. Jefferson's fear was Alexander Hamilton's hope, and eventually it was realized. Commerce wrested control from the individual rooted in the land. In the Civil War, the North's economic organization paved the way for a new age, and in the aftermath vast industrial enterprises prospered, dehumanizing as they profited. The progressives tamed industry by breaking up concentrations of power incompatible with democracy, regulating industry's most dangerous activities, and asserting some control over previously unfettered corporate decision making. The Teddy Roosevelt progressives were Hamiltonian, in that they saw that big private concentrations of power needed an active big government to balance them. The Woodrow Wilson progressives were Jeffersonian, in that they wanted to break up the big concentrations of private power and regulate them so that smaller business entities would be less intimidated and more able to compete. Although they differed in method, both sorts of progressives believed that three purposes of government were to prevent exploitation of people by powerful private interests, to help the poor, and to get the economy functioning in a way that provided more chances for better jobs and more resources to more people.

During the Great Depression, private charities and corporatism were not enough to deal with the human suffering. Franklin Roosevelt established new rules for a new time. He signed into law the Works Progress Administration, to put people to work building and refurbishing public structures; Social Security, to remove the elderly from poverty; the Wagner Act, to give labor the tools to fight for its members' economic interests; the Securities and Exchange Commission, to inform investors about the dangers of market speculation. He embarked on a series of sometimes contradictory governmental experiments, whose ultimate benefit may have been not to generate jobs but to keep people believing that things would get better. The Second World War created the jobs, but it did so by dint of even greater government involvement in the economy. The regulated welfare state had been born, and it matured with every passing decade.

Lyndon Johnson followed up the New Deal with the Great Society, which specifically targeted poverty. It recognized the special needs and circumstances of Chicanos working in the fields of California, and Native Americans wasting away on reservations. Much good was accomplished. Much idealism was channeled into government efforts. Many young volunteers gained valuable experience by fighting the War on Poverty.

Many African Americans and Latinos saw new horizons open to them. But by 1994, after sixty years of well-meaning action, the delivery mechanism of government was covered with barnacles. Yet to argue, as Republicans did, that the best government was local government ignored the facts. Civil society was eroding locally, as well as globally. Corruption was infinitely more likely at the local level, and in an increasingly interdependent world, national government was more, not less, important. But if no one made the case for national government, we Democrats had only ourselves to blame for our predicament.

Since the late 1970s, economic challenges have arisen that are not susceptible to traditional solutions: oil-supply disruptions, destabilizing worldwide capital flows, hidden trade subsidies, the virtually unchecked movement of economic refugees, the economic and health costs associated with a polluted environment, and finally the skill disparities between advanced, knowledge-based economies and the economies of the old industrialism. The times call for radical reform—in our economy, our politics, and our social interactions—and only government has the power to effect those reforms. To deny that fact is to be blind. Yet how to effectively use government eludes us.

On national security, in order to shake the "dove" label acquired during the Vietnam War, Democrats gave Reagan and Bush a blank check. With the exception of a minor issue—the supply of arms to the Nicaraguan contras, a policy that took on monumental proportions inside the beltway and among those liberals who saw another quagmire in every exercise of military power—Democrats said little about foreign policy. We might have addressed the international economy, whose monetary system had been broken since the early 1970s, when inflation and Eurodollars forced the abandonment of fixed exchange rates backed by the gold standard, and whose chaotic functioning made business planning increasingly problematic. We might have addressed the cluster of so-called North-South issues, such as overpopulation, economic migration, or the value of the pluralistic ideal in a world of rising chauvinism. We might have drawn attention to the environment, whose protection is essential if our children are to breathe clear air, drink clean water, and have a safe and healthy existence. We might have asked whether including 1.2 billion Chinese and 850 million Indians in the international economy changed any assumptions about how that economy should work. Instead, Democrats argued about whether the use of military power was legal or wise in this case or that. Democrats accepted a battleground the size of a postage stamp. By accepting Republican premises—particularly that the most important or only international issue of our times was the West's conflict with communism—we allowed the Republicans to define us.

Even with these failures, the Democratic Party persevered. Its members might have been disenchanted, but they weren't yet prepared to exit. A political party is more than a political strategy or a set of positions on issues. It is a combination of feelings, a series of shared experiences. It evokes a mood. It has a history. The very mention of its name conjures up a set of images that give it meaning and tell its members who their friends and enemies are. A colleague of my wife's at Montclair State University tells the following story:

> One day I was walking to school in the first grade with my best friend, who turned to me and said, "You're a Democrat. And if I had known that three years ago, I would never have started playing with you."
> "What's a Democrat?" I asked.
> "Oh, it's something terrible. It's what poor people are."
> "What are you?" I asked.
> "I'm Republican. That's what rich people are."
> Throughout the day, I agonized over my best friend's comment. I worried I would never again play circus with him, and I liked playing circus. When I got home that night, I asked my mother, "Am I a Democrat?"
> She said, "Yes."
> "What's a Democrat?" I asked.
> "That's what good people are," she said.
> "Well, what's a Republican?"
> "That's what greedy people are," she said.

For many Americans, that still seems to be the difference between Republicans and Democrats: one fights for the little man and is good, and the other protects the rich and is bad. It's as simple as that, in their view.

Yet true Democrats want the path to wealth open to all, even as they oppose great concentrations of power. True Democrats believe that most parents want their children to have a higher living standard than they do—to have a chance, if not for wealth, at least for comfort. True Democrats not only care about the weak, the poor, and the less well educated but they constantly work to give all Americans an equal chance for material advancement. True Democrats are unwilling to accept the misery of some Americans as the price for the achievement of other Americans. True Democrats don't disparage success.

In 1988, I visited Sam and Kate Kilpatrick, of Hot Springs, North Carolina, up in the mountains in the western part of the state. It was a place where guys driving pickup trucks with empty gun-racks would stop in Hardees to pick up breakfast at 7 a.m. It was a place where the memory lived of rich Northerners who came and plundered the area's coal and timber and then educated the people in the ways of real-estate speculation. These mountains had been the refuge of British Loyalists during the Revolution, of Indians during the forcible removal of the Cherokees to what is now Oklahoma in the 1830s, and of Unionist North Carolinians during the Civil War.

Sam and Kate, both Democrats, were modest and self-reliant. In winter, they lived in a small white frame house. In summer, they lived a few miles away, in a house with outside plumbing and a kitchen that was an open space covered with an aluminum roof. Sam had one good eye. The other one was covered with a black lens. He also had the worst teeth I'd seen in a long time. "Been chewing tobacco since I was fifteen," he explained. Kate, who married Sam when he was twenty-two and she was sixteen, had just had open-heart surgery. They survived on Sam's veteran's disability payments and a small pension. When I arrived, they were sitting in aluminum lawn chairs in front of their open-air house. Oilcloth covered the kitchen table. For breakfast, they offered me fried eggs, unhomogenized butter, bacon, fried potatoes, biscuits, gravy, jelly, and coffee. Kate said that because of the operation she might someday consider changing her diet.

The summer place sat next to a small pond fed by a spring. Sam had built a wooden waterwheel, which turned as the water flowed from the pond into a creekbed and powered a miniature decorative windmill. He had also put together a wire fish trap that looked like a Maine fisherman's lobster trap. He baited it with worms; the fish would swim in to get the worms and find themselves without an escape route. Sam and his friend Charles Dillingham of Bakersville took me on a walk through the forest to an old shed where Sam stored, among other things, a Conestoga wagon. There were stacks of car batteries extending from the floor to the ceiling of the shed. There were machinery parts of every shape and size and of indiscernible provenance. Off to one side lay a large pile of thick wire rope, which looked like a giant ball of yarn. "Maybe someday I'll use this wire to build a bridge over the creek," Sam said. Charlie gazed at the clutter. "Sam would be dangerous if he had a Harvard degree," he said.

We resumed our walk, passing a giant white-oak tree twenty-two feet in circumference, which Sam claimed was the biggest oak in North Carolina. They told me how to make "cow-shit tea": you fill a container one-third with cow excrement and two-thirds with water. You let it settle, and then you put a spout in the bottom and use the liquid that seeps out to water garden vegetables. "It gives you great strawberries," Sam said.

Back at the house, they asked me about basketball and about the Senate. They felt that Jesse Jackson was a rabble-rouser and that Jesse Helms was a disgrace to North Carolina. I asked Sam and Kate what made them proudest as Americans. "We seem to be treating the elderly and disabled better," they replied.

I asked them who their favorite president was.

"Harry Truman, no question about it," Charlie shot back.

"Why?" I asked.

"Because he was one of the people, and when he spoke we could understand him. Just because someone is president doesn't make him better than me."

There it was. To be a Democrat, you had to have a fierce egalitarian spirit. You judged someone without regard to material possessions or social position. You didn't "put on airs." Elitists were out. Each individual soul had an inherent and independent worth, regardless of knowledge or wealth. Times have changed; these feelings remain. There are no unaccountable elites who require deference. Only individual Americans are important, and one is no more important than another.

The Democratic Party of the 1990s has no Depression to overcome, no Vietnam War to oppose, and no civil-rights revolution to champion. But Democrats can invest other troubled areas—such as the rising sense of powerlessness and economic insecurity in the middle class and the fear of social breakdown embodied in things as disparate as the deterioration of families and the escalation of violence—with the same 1930s sense of urgency to find answers and the same 1960s moral conviction that America's future depends on our success.

Given the size of the deficit and the burden it places on future generations, even public finance has a clear moral dimension these days. At the same time, Democrats must speak the truth about race, and about the endangerment of our civil society. Abraham Lincoln once said, "The dogmas of the quiet past are inadequate to the stormy present. . . . As our case is new, so we must think anew and act anew . . . and then we shall save our country." If Democrats can help shape the coming information age so that it adds jobs, builds community, and enhances democracy even as it improves economic productivity, we can offer tremendous hope. Above all, Democrats must give a ringing endorsement to the conviction that America's best days lie ahead of it. When we do all of that, we can start not just to win again, but to lead again.

4

The World's Greatest Deliberative Body

I N T H E S U M M E R of 1964, between my junior and senior years at Princeton, I came to Washington as a summer intern, working first in the congressional office of Richard Schweiker (R.-Pa.) and then in the presidential campaign of William Scranton, the former Republican governor of Pennsylvania. When I wasn't interning, I was researching my senior thesis on Harry Truman's re-election to the Senate in 1940 and training for the Tokyo Olympics, which would take place in October. That summer, Congress adopted a budget that approached a hundred billion dollars; supported the Gulf of Tonkin Resolution, which paved the way for the massive U.S. military escalation in Vietnam; and passed the most important civil-rights legislation since Reconstruction. I was in a corner of the Senate chamber on a hot June evening when the vote was taken on the Civil Rights Act, which among other things desegregated restaurants, hotels, and other public facilities. I heard senators say aye, and I saw them signal nay.

One of the naysayers was Barry Goldwater, soon to be the Republican nominee for president. Goldwater's vote—and Attorney General Robert Kennedy's speech that summer to the college interns, in which he urged us to give our lives to public service—precipitated a decision I had been moving toward for a few years. At Princeton, H. H. Wilson's course on American politics acquainted me with the politics of power—particularly the clout of big oil and the size of the military-industrial complex. President Eisenhower's farewell address in early 1961, which warned the country about the growing power of that complex, had already made a strong impression on me. Martin Duberman's course on the history of the Civil War raised issues about race that seemed as unresolved in 1964 as they were in 1863. A course in twentieth-century history with Arthur Link showed Woodrow Wilson and Franklin Roosevelt standing with the less powerful against the forces of entrenched privilege, whose power was at its core the power of capital. Democrats throughout history (with some notable exceptions) seemed more in tune with values I had come to hold dear. As I walked out of the Capitol that night, I saw senators heading down the steps on the way to their cars accepting expressions of gratitude from black and white supporters of civil rights. It was obvious to me that something of enormous importance had happened. The passage of the Civil Rights Act would make America a better place for everybody. The historical perspective I was acquiring at Princeton joined with the leadership on civil rights by a Democratic president to pull me away from the Republican Party affiliation of my parents and into the Democratic Party.

Fourteen years later, I was elected to the Senate myself, and when I was sworn in at thirty-five, I was the youngest sitting U.S. senator. I knew I had much to learn. I had never served in a legislature. On the one hand, that meant I didn't have to break procedural habits and states of mind acquired in a different house. The U.S. Senate would make its imprint on me as the only legislative body I knew. On the other hand, everything was unfamiliar. My learning curve had to be vertical.

I chose to become a workhorse, a senator who worked hard every day in his assigned committees and sought the respect of his colleagues, rather than a show horse, a senator who defined success by the number of times his name appeared in print. The Washington Post Style section wanted to do a profile of a freshman senator and selected me. I said no. I turned down countless invitations to private dinners and small receptions, accepting only those whose rejection would have become an issue. I talked about basketball only when one of my colleagues asked me a direct question on the subject. For nearly two years I refused virtually all non–New Jersey media interviews, because they obviously arose from my earlier celebrity. I wanted to be a U.S. senator, not a star.

I was assigned to the Finance Committee and the Energy and Natural Resources Committee, and rarely missed a committee hearing. I asked questions infrequently in these meetings, leaving that to more senior members. I did my homework, spending hours studying the arcane details of energy, tax, and trade issues. When a freshman colleague who had served in the House of Representatives proposed an assault on the seniority system, I demurred. I wanted to make it in the Senate on the Senate's terms.

By tradition, a senator's first speech on the Senate floor is supposed to hold significance. In the past, a freshman did not speak on the floor for one year. By 1979, it was a different era—still, I did not speak until May. Consistent with my campaign promise to bring a fairer share of federal dollars to New Jersey, my first speech was in support of an effort by senators from New Jersey, Pennsylvania, and Delaware to have the aircraft carrier *Saratoga* refurbished at the Philadelphia Naval Shipyard instead of at Newport News, Virginia. A victory would mean more jobs for New Jersey. When we won, someone remarked that it was the first time military hardware had headed north since Lee invaded Pennsylvania.

In that first skirmish on the Senate floor, I learned the most important lesson a legislator can learn—count your votes before the vote. The assistant whips are senators from six regions of the country who tally six or eight senators each and give the leadership a sense of where the votes lie on a particular issue. But when it's a regional battle or a nonpartisan ideological matter (such as abortion or flag burning) rather than a partisan fight, the interested senators have to act as their own whips. I talked with sixty senators before the shipyard vote, marking on a long Senate tally sheet whether they were with us, against us, or undecided. In the process, I learned that many senators will say yes if you personally ask them for their vote. By asking face-to-face, you raise the stakes of a no. If the question isn't asked in person, the no is delivered by a staff member to a staff member, and the senators whose votes you wanted haven't risked the consequences of turning down in person someone they may be petitioning themselves in the near future.

Locking up a vote early is important. If people give you a commitment, it is unlikely that they will renege on it; that's part of the honor of the Senate. Your word is one of the few currencies that can be spent. But listen very carefully, so that you don't hear only what you want to hear. An experienced senator will rarely say a flat-out yes or no. "Let me think about it, and I'll get back to you," is the most likely response. That means your colleague hopes you'll forget to bring the matter up again. Other response gradations include: (1) "I agree with your position" (the senator has not promised to vote for it); (2) "You make a powerful argument" (again, no commitment); (3) "I'm with you" (this is the next level, implying sympathy but not necessarily a vote); (4) "Count me a yes," or "Yes, I'll support you," or "Yes, I'll vote for your position." Only these last are certain votes.

If knowing your commitments on substantive votes is advisable, knowing them on votes related to the internal workings of the Senate is imperative. Robert C. Byrd of West Virginia, the majority leader of the Senate when I arrived in 1979, was a master at getting a commitment and looking ahead. When he ran for majority leader, in 1976, he asked Senator Joe Biden of Delaware for his vote. Biden said that he had committed himself to Hubert Humphrey. "What about the second ballot?" Byrd persisted; the rule in the Democratic caucus was that the leader must have a majority vote, so, if no one had a majority, the low man among the candidates would drop out and another vote would be held. Biden said that he had given his commitment on the second ballot to someone else. "Well, what about the third ballot?" Byrd asked. Again, Biden said no. Byrd won by acclamation after Humphrey saw he didn't have the votes and withdrew. Byrd had anticipated the result—but he wanted Biden to say no three times, so that on the next issue Biden would feel a correspondingly greater obligation to go along with Byrd. If you never ask, you never get a no or a yes, with its subtle accompanying obligations; all you get or don't get is a vote.

I learned the most in those early years by observing Russell Long of Louisiana and Henry Jackson of Washington, the chairmen of the two committees on which I served. The Finance Committee, which Long chaired from 1965 to 1980, is the most powerful Senate committee. From sources as diverse as the income tax and tariffs on imports, it raises 98 percent of the money that the government spends, and it determines the rules for how over half of it—Social Security, Medicare, Medicaid, welfare, and trade subsidies—will be spent. Pat Moynihan of New York, who was chairman from 1993 to 1995, has said that the most important achievement of his first term in the Senate was getting a position on the

Finance Committee. For many years, its chairmen have generally been strong-willed Southerners. Before Russell Long, the chairman was Harry F. Byrd, Sr., of Virginia. For ten years—from 1941 to 1947 and from 1949 to 1953—it was Walter George of Georgia. As a leader of the Republican–conservative-Democrat coalition during the first six years of the New Deal, George became a thorn in FDR's side, and in 1938 the president opposed his re-election, going so far as to endorse his own candidate, Lawrence Camp, in the Georgia Democratic primary. At the dedication of a Rural Electrification project in Barnesville, Georgia, and with Senator George only a few feet away, FDR said that George did not have "a constant active fighting attitude in favor of the broad objectives of the party and of the government as they are constituted today" and did not "in his heart, deep down in his heart, believe in these objectives." Senator George told the president that day, "Mr. President, I want you to know that I accept the challenge." Roosevelt's candidate lost. When Senator George returned to the Senate, FDR knew he had a problem, so he sent a young aide to apologize. The young man began by saying what a blunder the president's decision to oppose George had been, but that George should probably let bygones be bygones. "You know the President," the young aide is reported to have said, "he's his own worst enemy." There was a long pause. Then George said, "No he isn't."

Russell Long built his conservative majority on the Finance Committee with Republican as well as Democratic votes. He used all manner of weapons—humor, intimidation, reason, and tactical surprise. He controlled many of the Democratic committee members by convening with them an hour before the full session. At these preliminary meetings, he would listen and assess where the votes were on a particular issue, and if it was clear that someone didn't have the votes for a proposal, he would ask him why he was bothering to bring it up. In full committee, if a liberal Democrat pushed for a vote before Long had his own opposing votes lined up (knowing that he could always get a few Republican votes), Long would launch into a favorite anecdote, usually about his Uncle Earl, the former governor of Louisiana. He went off into these improvisatory diversions like a great jazz musician going into a riff—unsure of its destination but proceeding with full confidence. "What do you mean, I promised a vote on this matter? I didn't say today, did I? Reminds me of a story about Uncle Earl. I was his secretary, and he was governor. A guy from Jefferson Parish walked into the office one day and said, 'My name is Herman Belliveau, and during the campaign your Uncle Earl promised me a job.' I checked the list. No Herman Belliveau. He said he wouldn't leave until he got a job. I went in to Uncle Earl and told him, 'There's this guy, Herman Belliveau, from Jefferson Parish, who says you promised him a job during the campaign, and now he won't leave until he gets the job.' Uncle Earl said, 'That's easy, Russell. You just go back out there, look him in the eye, and tell him I lied.' "

Russell Long was a backer of big oil and his father's son, the former a consequence of being the latter. Huey Long, Russell's father, was first governor of and then senator from Louisiana. Even after he went to Washington, he controlled the Louisiana legislature with an iron hand, once personally overseeing the passage of forty-four bills in a matter of hours during a special session of the state senate. As governor he had paid for free textbooks for schoolchildren and paved roads for their parents by taxing the state's oil-and-gas industry. He might have been president if he had had more discipline. Instead, he was a flamboyant populist who reveled in excess. T. Harry Williams recounts this anecdote in his biography, *Huey Long:* "A phone rang in the busy Roosevelt headquarters that Jim Farley [chairman of the Democratic National Committee] had set up in New York City soon after the [1932] Democratic convention. The secretary who answered it asked who was calling. Huey Long, said the voice on the other end, and Huey Long wanted an appointment to see Farley. Certainly, the secretary said, and where could Senator Long be reached? 'I'm at the Waldorf Astoria,' the Kingfish answered, 'in rooms 1220, 1222, 1224, 1226, 1228 and 1230.' "

Huey Long in the Senate was a study in demagoguery, buffoonery, populism, and special pleading. Above all, he was a performer. Senator Arthur Vandenberg (R.-Mich.), who thought of himself as something of a speech stylist, would come to the Senate floor to listen to Huey, because, even though his idiom was uniquely Louisiana, his sentences and paragraphs always fell together in perfect coherence. He exasperated and intimidated other senators. Alben Barkley (D.-Ky.) said, "Huey, in debate, was like a horsefly: he would light on one part of you, sting you, and then, when you slapped at him, fly away to land elsewhere and sting again." Once, Huey demanded of Vice-President Garner, who was presiding over some measure in the Senate at the time, "How should a senator who is half in favor of this bill and half against it cast his vote?" Prickly Cactus Jack, speaking for most of the Senate, replied, "Get a saw and saw yourself in two; that's what you ought to do anyhow."

Another time, Huey was inciting an enraged Senator Kenneth McKeller of Tennessee with humorous jabs, as the gallery roared with laughter. The presiding officer banged the gavel and said that if the gallery didn't quiet down he would clear the Senate of all spectators. Alben Barkley rose to his feet and asked the presiding officer to reconsider this threat, explaining, "When people go to a circus, they ought to be allowed to laugh at the monkey." Huey jumped up and said, "Mr. President, I resent that unwarranted remark on the part of the Senator from Kentucky directed toward my good friend, the Senator from Tennessee."

Huey Long's slogan, "Every Man a King," had strong appeal in the depth of the Depression, when unemployment was as high as 25 percent. His Share Our Wealth Clubs swept the country. In 1933, he introduced the Long plan to "redistribute wealth." It consisted of a progressive tax on fortunes of over a million dollars, with a requirement that all wealth over a hundred million dollars had to be given to the government; an increase in the income-tax rates to stop anyone from taking in more than a million dollars a year; and an inheritance tax that limited the amount an individual could inherit to five million dollars. Biographer Forest Davis called Huey "Karl Marx for the hillbillies." Huey believed that he could defeat FDR, and he certainly knew he would outpromise him. "His mother's watching him," Huey said. "She won't let him go too far, but I ain't got no mother left. . . . He's livin' on inherited income. I got nothin', so I don't have to bother about that." Millions of Americans listened on March 17, 1933, when he bought time on the NBC radio network and explained his redistribution plan to the country—thereby telegraphing his ambitions and allowing FDR time to thwart his efforts by co-opting Long's constituency with presidential rhetoric and programs. With a poll commissioned by James Farley showing that up to six million people from all regions of the country might well vote for Long for president, FDR had reason to take pre-emptive action. FDR's proposed tax bill of 1935—which increased income taxes on wealthy Americans, established a graduated corporate income tax, and raised inheritance taxes—was clearly a response to Huey's populist calls for wealth redistribution. FDR even said that taxes should "prevent an unjust concentration of wealth and economic power." By the time the bill became law, only the inheritance tax was dropped. LBJ believed that Huey Long was the person who had assured FDR's support for Social Security.

Whether Long would have challenged FDR in 1936, and whether he would have run as a third-party candidate if he failed, we'll never know. Huey was assassinated by Dr. Carl Weiss in the Louisiana state capitol on September 8, 1935, when his son Russell was seventeen years old. I always believed that Russell Long was never able to get over the horror of that event. Once, in the middle of a Finance Committee hearing, an aide brought a note to the chair. Russell read it and then took his glasses off. Tears welled in his eyes, and he looked off into the distance, as the witness continued to testify. The note was passed along the dais; it read, "The Pope has been shot by an assassin and is in critical condition—not sure he'll survive." Russell Long was not a particularly religious sort; the news must have awakened memories of that long-ago trauma.

I am convinced that Russell's support for big oil (and for countless other special interests) stemmed not just from oil's importance in Louisiana but from his desire to show that, unlike his father, he appreciated the importance of wealth and respected economic power. Russell wanted no part of attacking the rich. From time to time I sensed that he felt it was dangerous. Yet he honored his father's populist legacy by establishing the earned-income credit, which gave poor people a tax cut in the form of a cash payment, and by championing employee stock-ownership plans, which sought through tax incentives to compensate workers with stock in addition to wages. Such plans fostered tax equity, industrial harmony, and broad-based ownership; they also constituted Russell Long's own version of "Share Our Wealth."

As a legislator, Russell Long was a genius. He knew the substance of the legislation he dealt with, and he understood how each position could be played in a campaign. He reminded young senators that a carefully delivered tax benefit would never be forgotten by the well-to-do, well-educated recipient, but a structural tax cut for the poor would never be remembered. "Just look at Albert Gore, Sr.," he would say. "Back in 1969, he thought increasing the personal exemption would guarantee his re-election. Hell, nobody who got it ever knew it, and he lost!" When asked on one occasion why he hadn't voted for a measure that the majority leader supported, Long, always disarmingly honest about his political calculations, replied, "Because it's not popular." Sometimes when the Finance Committee was considering a big bill, Long would allow a liberal senator to attach amendments to increase spending for welfare or Medicaid or countercyclical revenue sharing. Then, the next day, Long would discover that there just wasn't enough money to pay for the actions of the day earlier; they would have to be cut back. When the senator protested, Long would shrug his shoulders and say, "You got a nice press release out of it anyway, didn't you?"

When President Jimmy Carter appointed Paul Volcker as the Federal Reserve chairman in the summer of 1979, Long said that he wouldn't have made that appointment—Volcker was too independent. "Any president ought to have a talk with the fella he appoints as Fed chairman and tell him, 'You run monetary policy for three years, I run it in election years.' I'm afraid Carter didn't have that conversation, and all of us Democrats will suffer for it." As it turned out, Volcker's double-digit interest rates brought the economy to a screeching halt, thereby helping to defeat Carter, turn the U.S. Senate over to Republicans, and transfer chairmanship of the Finance Committee from Russell Long to Bob Dole.

What I admired about Long was his unabashed love of legislative combat. Whereas Huey Long had been the "great outsider," using the Senate as a platform to play to the nation, his son was an insider, a legislator who never allowed his performance skills to overshadow his attention to the fine print. In conferences between the House and the Senate, Russell would wear down all but his most intense adversaries. He would sit until 3 or 4 a.m. talking and negotiating until his opponent grew tired or distracted, and then he would move his amendment, like someone darting into a subway just before the doors closed. When Russell took the floor for a speech, you knew it was time to listen, because he would educate you as well as entertain you, both in aid of his larger strategic purpose. Those who opposed his machinations could rarely muster the knowledge or audacity to defeat him. The best many could hope for was a draw.

Another senator worth watching was Henry "Scoop" Jackson, who represented the state of Washington with a personal openness as wide as the wheatfields of eastern Washington and with a personal strength as solid as the Cascades. Scoop, the chairman of the Energy and Natural Resources Committee from 1977 through 1980, played the legislative game the way good generals fight wars: everything was planned; nothing was left to chance. Votes were lined up in advance with meticulous personal lobbying. Outside groups were enlisted to lobby. Certain decided senators were asked to contact other senators who were still uncertain about the issue at hand. For floor debates Jackson prepared a battle book— that's what his staff called it—in which every possible question was anticipated, mastered, and answered. He left as little as possible to improvisation, and he then went out onto the floor and crushed his opponents.

Two examples illustrate his style. The first took place in March 1982. The Reagan administration was intent on building a hundred B-1 bombers to bolster our aging fleet of B-52s, which for a generation had been our main means of delivering a nuclear bomb to the soil of the Soviet Union. The issue was highly charged politically, because President Jimmy Carter, a rival of Jackson's in the 1976 Democratic presidential primary, had canceled the B-1 in favor of the more sophisticated B-2, which wouldn't be ready for a decade. Carter felt that, in the interim, the thirty-year-old B-52s could be retrofitted to carry cruise missiles. Scoop Jackson, always a backer of strong nuclear deterrence, supported Reagan's B-1 proposal, as well as rapid development of the B-2. Along with the new chairman of Armed Services, John Tower, he offered the administration's proposal to establish a B-1 production rate of four planes per month, thereby closing the gap in time between the waning effectiveness of the B-52 and the delivery of the B-2 stealth bomber. The chief opponent was Sam Nunn of Georgia, who argued that the B-1's electronic capability wasn't good enough to jam Soviet air defenses and that therefore it would never reach its target. The wiser course, he argued, would be to wait for the Stealth, which, because of its shape and the composition of its surface, was expected to be able to penetrate hostile air space undetected even by the most sophisticated radar.

Scoop had the full support of the Reagan Defense Department, whose nuclear strategy was shaped by one of his former aides, Richard Perle. Jackson also persuaded the Air Force and Rockwell, the B-1's contractor, to launch an all-out lobbying effort. Rockwell developed a brochure showing each congressman and senator by state and district how many jobs would be created (there were few in Washington State) by building one hundred B-1s. Nunn had the more substantive argument, and was himself a steady and respected legislator, but he could not orchestrate as much political power. Jackson's thorough petitioning, personal relationships, and subtle intimidation, plus support from the uniformed military and the continued existence of the cold war, won the day for the B-1 bomber.

The other fight, a year later, was over honoraria—senatorial speaking fees—which Jackson wanted to limit immediately to 30 percent of a senator's annual salary (at the time, senators earned sixty thousand dol lars a year). He felt that unlimited honoraria compromised the Senate. "There is a general perception," he said, "that we have opened the door to undue influence and serious conflicts of interest. This is a scandal waiting to happen. . . . This is a problem that will not go away, and we must do something about it." Jackson had been giving his honoraria to charity for years. His adversary this time was Senator John Chafee, a Rhode Island Republican, who said full disclosure, not limitation, was the answer. Senator Bob Dole, who the year before had earned a hundred and thirty-four thousand dollars (he gave fifty-one thousand of it to charity) in fees from entities as diverse as Pizza Hut, Citicorp, Warner Communications, the Rotary Club of San Rafael, California, and the Institute of Makers of Explosives, sided with Chafee in opposing an immediate limit. Jackson believed that sometimes a senator has to make his colleagues uncomfortable to protect the institution. He was direct and unrelenting, in his best Presbyterian way, but on this one he lost. Yet, in pushing for an immediate limit, he created room for a compromise. The ultimate bill, which even Dole and Chafee supported, limited honoraria to 30 percent of salary but made the effective date January 1, 1984. When it came to the workings of the Senate, the web of personal relations and mutual obligation served as an impenetrable front-line defense to all but the most determined senator. Scoop knew that silence was often a co-conspirator on questions of ethics. By simply raising the issue, he embarrassed the Senate into action.

By the early 1990s, there were not enough votes to pass a pay raise for senators, and at the same time the public was objecting strongly even to limited honoraria. The solution wasn't complicated: give up the honoraria, which the press looked at as a pay raise through the back door, and bring the salary issue out into the open; the press (many of whose members made more than senators did) would probably approve of a reasonable raise. Eight years after Scoop's initiative had called attention to the practice, honoraria were gone.

Scoop's style illustrated another aspect of the modern Senate—the importance of staff. He surrounded himself with talented professionals and gave them his trust. They, in turn, were fiercely loyal to Scoop. They represented him in countless meetings with other Senate staffers, pushing his agenda in all of them. They always made sure he had the information he needed to be prepared. They amplified his voice and extended his reach. By watching how he gave credit to those who helped him, I saw his generosity of spirit demonstrated every day. Over the years, members of a senator's staff come and go. Yet, like old grads, they continue to think of themselves as Jackson staff or Dole staff or Kennedy staff. For twelve years I was served competently and loyally by Marcia Aronoff, one of the first women to hold the position of senator's chief of staff. In addition, many talented professionals gave me years of their time, and together we accomplished much while building an office in which the person who opened the mail felt as essential as the legislative aide for foreign policy. Some senators are known as impossible to work for, because of their tempers, their work habits, or their egos. Scoop showed me how to motivate people to give 100 percent and keep them headed in a direction that supports the goals I've established.

Although Jackson was chairman of the Energy and Natural Resources Committee, his real love was defense—especially nuclear-weapons strategy. He was a member of the Armed Services Committee for thirty-one years. Committee chairmanships are determined essentially by luck: senators advance when other senators of the same party who are more senior die, resign, retire, or lose. The person in front of Jackson in seniority on the Armed Services Committee happened to be the durable John Stennis of Mississippi, who came to the Senate in 1947 and had served as chairman since 1969. In 1983, Jackson returned from a trip to China (where he was regarded as a great friend, because of his anti-Soviet geopolitical vision and his promotion of better U.S.-Chinese relations) complaining of a cold and chest pains. A few days later he was dead, never having made it to the chairmanship of Armed Services.

Stennis remained chairman or ranking member of the committee until his retirement in 1989. One evening in 1984, after the Senate had adjourned for the day and the chamber was in semidarkness, Senator David Pryor of Arkansas was sitting in the cloakroom reading a newspaper. Suddenly he heard a booming voice coming from the Senate floor. He asked the clerks what it was. They said they thought it might be Senator Stennis, who had recently had one leg amputated because of a malignant tumor. Pryor was puzzled, because he was hearing not just the booming voice but a series of creaking sounds. He pushed open the swinging door and looked out at John Stennis, defender of the Old South and the defense budget. Stennis was a stickler for form (he once told me that the Turks were a remarkable people because they always dressed neatly). Above all, he was a conscientious senator, who deeply respected the traditions of the Senate.

Aware that the rules required a senator to stand when speaking on the floor, Stennis was practicing. At the age of eighty-three, he was lifting himself up from his wheelchair to his full height, grasping two metal handles that had been installed on his desk—lifting himself up again and again—and perfecting his balance by holding on to a handle with one hand so that he could gesture with the other. With each gesture, he was booming out in his rich Southern baritone, assuring himself that when the debate came he would be able to perform as he ought to.

Most U.S. senators remember the first time they were in the Senate chamber. For me, it was during that summer when I was a college intern, on the night the 1964 Civil Rights Act passed. For David Pryor, it came much earlier, because his interest in politics began while he was still a young boy. His mother had been one of the first women to seek elective office in the United States, running for clerk of Ouachita County, Arkansas, in 1922. As a ten-year-old, Pryor used to listen to politicians speak from the steps of the courthouse in Camden, the county seat (population 11,000). He recalls young Congressman William Fulbright stashing his suitcoat in the car so he could mount the steps to address the citizenry in his shirtsleeves during his first Senate campaign in the summer of 1944. When he was seventeen, Pryor wrote a letter to his congressman, Oren Harris, requesting that Harris make him a page in the House of Representatives. Time passed. Nothing happened, and David thought the letter had been lost. Then, after seven weeks, the response came (he still has the letter): he had the job, but only if he could arrive in Washington in four days. Pryor and his mother got into the family's new 1951 Chevrolet coupe and drove the two-lane roads to Washington, where, on his first morning in the city, his mother literally deposited him on the steps of the Capitol. It was pouring rain, and inside he was told to report to the doorkeeper of the House, "Fishbait" Miller. David introduced himself to Miller as the new page from Arkansas. He had hardly gotten past the "hello" when Fishbait barked, "Get over to the Senate! They need pages—they're in the middle of a big filibuster."

"Where is the Senate?" Pryor stammered.

"Down the hall, take your second right, and just keep walking and you'll walk right into it," the doorkeeper said.

Pryor walked across the blue-and-yellow-tiled floor and through the National Statuary Hall, once the chamber of the House, where in 1825 John Quincy Adams had been selected as president of the United States over Andrew Jackson. It was now the repository of state-donated sculpture depicting famous citizens, such as Nebraska's William Jennings Bryan, Hawaii's King Kamehameha, and Utah's Brigham Young. Pryor was nervous and more than a little scared as he crossed the rotunda, whose big domed ceiling loomed a hundred and eighty feet overhead, its walls covered with murals depicting the landing of Columbus, the baptism of Pocahontas, the embarkation of the Pilgrims, the discovery of the Mississippi by de Soto, the signing of the Declaration of Independence, the surrender of Cornwallis at Yorktown, Washington's resignation as commander-in-chief. He then entered the Senate side of the capitol, where the mauve-and-white marble floor had been worn down by the footsteps of millions of Americans who had come to these halls for one hundred and fifty years to petition their elected representatives. He passed the intimate old Senate chamber, where John C. Calhoun and Daniel Webster had disagreed on nullification of the tariffs of 1828 and 1832; where Henry Clay had effected compromise to save the union; and where Sam Houston had sat in serape and bright-red vest, whittling hearts from chunks of pine and tossing them to the ladies who sat in the Senate gallery listening to the debates. He walked down a hallway whose windows opened onto the expanse of the Mall, to the swinging oak-bronze-and-glass doors that had served as an entrance to the Senate chamber since 1859. He pushed open the doors and walked onto the floor of the Senate. The first person he saw was a balding, heavyset man seated at one of the desks a few yards away, who looked directly at Pryor, snapped his fingers, and beckoned him forward.

"Who, me?" Pryor signaled, touching his finger to his chest. The senator nodded. Unshaven and tired, he gave Pryor a ten-dollar bill and a set of keys and instructed him to take a taxi to his apartment in Southeast Washington and fetch his bedroom slippers. This was Joseph R. McCarthy (R.-Wis.), who was in need of podiatric comfort since he was about to resume his filibuster against a State Department authorization bill and he expected to be on his feet for many hours. Pryor made the journey and returned with the slippers, and that night told his mother that he had had quite a day: "It was the first time I'd ever been in Washington, the first time in the Capitol, the first time in the U.S. Senate, and the first time I ever rode in a taxi."

T H E   S E N A T E has its whimsical moments, such as the time Senator Chic Hecht (R.-Nev.) announced his opposition to the nuclear waste repository targeted for his state by saying he was against "any nuclear suppository." It has its solemn moments, such as the time I declared my position in favor of a resolution to expel my New Jersey colleague, Senator Harrison Williams, during the Abscam scandal. There are even frightening moments, such as on an evening in November 1983 when a bomb exploded outside the main Senate conference room, shattering the mahogany doors leading to Minority Leader Robert Byrd's office and spraying bits of glass into the Republican cloakroom. No one was injured only because Majority Leader Howard Baker by chance had adjourned the Senate much earlier than the publicly stated time.

I'll never forget a bizarre moment in 1986 when I got a letter from Countess Sonja Von Drueben, a widowed, elderly lady living in California, with no children and substantial wealth, who informed me that because she admired my work in the Senate she wanted to make me the sole beneficiary of her estate. On its face, it seemed preposterous, and having just joined the Intelligence Committee, I wondered if it might be a setup by a foreign intelligence service to compromise me. I also considered the possibility that the FBI was running a sting operation to tempt unwitting legislators in a kind of test of professional integrity. Common sense told me that only John Beresford Tipton, of the old television show *The Millionaire,* gave millions of dollars to people he didn't know. I contacted the FBI, who after a brief inquiry said that I should just put the whole thing on the shelf and that if the woman was for real she would write again. She never did, and to this day I don't know if I was the victim of a prank, the target of a sting, or the subject of a counterespionage effort.

The Senate also has its moving moments. In the spring of 1994, Senator Howell Heflin (D.-Ala.) spoke in a debate about Senator Carol Moseley-Braun's (D.-Ill.) attempt to deny the United Daughters of the Confederacy a renewal of the patent for their organization's official insignia design. Heflin, who through his actions as a lawyer and judge had long championed racial justice, rose and said, "I have many connections through my family to the Daughters of the Confederacy organization and the Children of the Confederacy, but the Senator from Illinois . . . is a descendant of those that suffered the ills of slavery. I have a legislative director whose great-great-grandfather was a slave. I said to my legislative director, 'Well, if I vote with Senator Moseley-Braun, my mother, grandmother, and other ancestors will turn over in their graves.' He said, 'Well, likewise, my ancestors will turn over in their graves [if you vote against it].' "

Heflin supported Senator Moseley-Braun.

BY THE END of my first Congress, in 1980, it had become clear to me that success in the Senate was a function of the interaction of substance, procedure, and personality. The senators who had an impact and got other senators to listen to them had to know what they were talking about. When Sam Nunn or John Tower stood up to talk about defense issues, not everyone agreed with them, but no one questioned their knowledge of the subject. When Ed Muskie of Maine—or, later, Pete Domenici of New Mexico—explained the workings of the budget, we paid attention. When Bennett Johnston of Louisiana spoke about energy issues, or Jack Danforth of Missouri clarified moments of moral or con-stitutional confusion, or Pat Moynihan of New York described our wel-fare system (or practically anything else), they were listened to. These were all senators who commanded respect because of the knowledge they possessed. They were influential because they had full control of substance. Many senators will simply read a speech prepared by their staff, and are unable to answer questions or debate the issue compe-tently. The senators with substantive grasp of their issues can say some-thing new by the hour. But substance alone does not make someone effective.

The smartest senator in the world is ineffective unless he or she knows the rudiments of Senate procedure, an arcane language that often intimidates a newcomer. Knowledge of procedure and congressional workings allows for tactical agility and informs strategic legislating. In my first year in the Senate, I presided over the Senate more than any other senator, thereby winning the biannual Golden Gavel Award. On the most important close votes, the vice-president presides, and when he is not in the chair the responsibility falls to the majority leader, who del-egates it, often to younger senators in the majority. The assignment is usually considered a chore. As presiding officer, you sit in the chair on the dais and do little more than repeat the rulings that the parliamentar-ian whispers to you—or, worse, you just sit and watch, while those sen-ators in love with their own voices drone on, endlessly. After talking many hours with Floyd Riddick, for years the Senate parliamentarian and now the nation's leading authority on Senate rules, I used my time in the chair to become comfortable with Senate procedure. When Robert Byrd as majority leader in 1979 would duel with Senator Jim McClure of Idaho at three o'clock in the morning over some obscure procedural precedent, the chamber heated up. Both McClure and Byrd were self-made, prideful, and combative. Whichever way the parliamentarian ruled in one of their procedural disputes, he would be creating a precedent that would govern future Senates. Usually, Byrd's position prevailed. It was an unwritten rule; on close calls the majority leader got the benefit of the doubt.

During his tenure, Robert Byrd used procedure as a tool to control the Senate. He intimidated those who might otherwise have challenged him by subtly threatening them with a procedural onslaught—a point of order, a second-degree amendment, an amendment in the nature of a substitute, an amendment to the underlying text; a motion to proceed, to reconsider, to adjourn, to recess; a call for the regular order, a call for a resolution under the rule. He would do whatever was necessary to make them look foolish. By contrast, Russell Long, who didn't have Byrd's leadership responsibility to keep the Senate on schedule, used procedure to bend the legislative body to his will.

In making his procedural moves, Long always had a larger strategic design. For example, in 1979 we took up the windfall-profits tax on oil. Oil prices had doubled in a year, and American oil companies, as well as the oil sheiks of OPEC, were doing very, very well. The Carter administration wanted a windfall-profits tax. Long, from the oil-producing state of Louisiana, opposed it, even though he knew that the president had more cards to play than he did and would more than likely win in the end. Still, Long did not like to lose, and he believed that what a senator told you was never as good as a "look-see vote." So he designed a patently outrageous measure to slash the proposed windfall-profits tax rate dramatically. He calculated that those who voted with him on this chimera were his core supporters. If forty-two senators were with him on the amendment, he could concentrate on the other fifty-eight and identify those whom he could persuade to support something less ambitious. His objective all along was the second amendment; the first just set it up. On this occasion, when he saw that his core support consisted of only thirty-two senators, he knew that the windfall-profits tax was going to pass. He went through the motions and gave some energetic speeches, but after that first test he knew that Carter and his Senate allies had the votes.

Some senators downplay the importance of procedure. When Mike Mansfield of Montana was the majority leader, from 1961 through 1976, he ran a collegial institution, managing to structure debates and reducing the procedural kamikaze attacks. The Byrd leadership, by contrast, was heavy with procedure, both because Byrd liked it and because, ever since the lengthy filibuster on natural gas deregulation in 1977 showed what was possible, other senators used it more frequently than in Mansfield's day. For Byrd, legislative debate was like war, and the element of procedural surprise was a weapon. When George Mitchell of Maine was majority leader (and this was true of Howard Baker when Republicans had the majority) he usually worked out agreements in which a certain amount of time was allotted to floor discussions of an amendment and there was a finite list of amendments permitted under the agreement. Procedural surprise was replaced by comity, constant consultation, and a recognition that, without agreed-upon schedules, the Senate and senators' lives would hover somewhere between uncertain and chaotic (a circumstance Byrd never worried about) as issues constantly encountered procedural obstacles. In a civil Senate, one can be a good senator and leave the procedure to others. But if you wanted to follow an independent course, or reserve your right to protect your state's interest against all comers, you had to know procedure and be prepared to use it skillfully and ruthlessly. Russell Long would rarely accept a time agreement on an issue he cared about. He preferred to begin debate without agreement and see where the Senate was headed. Once, he debated a tax bill on the floor for three weeks.

In order to get a time agreement, all senators have to agree. Any senator can veto it. Therein lay the power of a Russell Long or a Jesse Helms; they wouldn't agree to a proposal limiting the time to be spent on an amendment unless a particular offensive section was removed; or sometimes they wouldn't agree at all, thereby preserving their right to filibuster any added provision they didn't like. When the provision was removed or altered, they would give their approval.

The longest filibuster in Senate history was conducted by Strom Thurmond in 1957, when he held the floor alone for twenty-four hours and eighteen minutes against a civil-rights bill. Robert M. La Follette, Sr., filibustered for more than eighteen hours in 1918, but he had allies in other senators, who helped him by requesting quorum calls. (A quorum call is a slow call of the roll to determine if a majority of senators is present.) In 1935, Huey Long stood alone against a bill to extend Franklin Roosevelt's NRA (the National Recovery Act), an attempt at national economic planning which he had always opposed. He spoke for fifteen and a half hours, with only two ten-minute breaks that, under the rules, he could obtain by calling for a quorum twice. By the evening of June 12, word had spread throughout Washington that Huey Long was filibustering. It was entertainment of the first order, and people in formal dress filled the Senate chamber to see the show. Huey read sections of the Constitution and explained their origins, as well as what they meant to him, prompting Will Rogers to say that many senators "thought he was reviewing a new book." A little after ten o'clock, having spoken for some ten hours, Huey declared, "I seem to hear a voice that says, 'Speak ten more hours.' " T. Harry Williams writes that reporters in the press gallery sent notes to Huey requesting certain speech topics. He discussed Frederick the Great. He described how to fry oysters and make "potlikker." He rolled pieces of sandwiches into small balls and ate them with milk while he spoke. After midnight his voice began to fade, and finally, at 4 a.m., having gone on for six hours without a break and with a bladder about to burst, he yielded the floor. When he returned from the rest room, the opposition had the floor and called for a vote. The NRA was extended 41 to 13, with 41 abstentions, which was a moral victory for Huey.

The modern filibuster has metamorphosed from an endurance contest to a series of feints and threats. Given the hectic nature of senators' schedules, a bill rarely comes to the floor with any part of it likely to provoke a filibuster. A senator can always force the clerk to read a fifteen-hundred-page bill, which could take several days, thereby saving a senator's voice. A senator can kill days with an endless sequence of quorum calls and other parliamentary motions. Sometimes a clear statement of intention will deter a bill's coming up. For example, Senator Bob Dole stopped consideration of national health-care legislation in 1994 simply by conveying that if a bill was brought up ten Republicans would filibuster, giving each plenty of time for rest, and enough Republicans would vote against cloture (60 votes are needed to end debate), so that proceeding was an impossibility. Dispensing with the reading of the jour-

nal and limiting the time for morning business are two preliminary steps
to get around cloture, but such a strategy requires deception and ruth-
lessness over a period of days. When Mitchell took over as majority
leader, he promised Dole that there would be no surprises; that made
Mitchell, in the health-care debate of 1994, a prisoner of Dole's threat.
Robert Byrd thought Mitchell had given up too much.

However strongly I may have disagreed with Helms or Long or Dole
on issues, I supported their right to use procedure to their advantage.
There have been times when I have used it myself. For example, back in
1983, several Southern senators tried at the last minute to change the for-
mula for allocating federal education dollars in a way that would take
money from New Jersey and redistribute it in the South. I used procedure to dispense with their amendment before it came up for debate.
What I did was call for "the regular order," which under the rules automatically returned the Senate to the matter being considered before the
Southerners' amendment was offered. The action blocked their route to
a vote. There is a procedural response to the call for the regular order.
They didn't know it, however, and I didn't tell them.

The reason—beyond aversion to personal conflict—that procedure
is not used more often for substantive ends is that only a few senators
know the rules well. In addition, if you're going to filibuster, obviously
you have to be on the floor at all times and willing to speak at length.
Otherwise an opponent gets recognition by the chair, and because you
no longer control the floor, you cannot speak. A senator is allowed only
two speeches on the same legislative day on any matter before the Senate. He may yield the floor, but only for a question. On the other hand,
any senator can object to a time agreement requested by the majority
leader. But in taking this approach, a senator has to be willing to anger
his fellow senators. An objection will inevitably produce a brouhaha that
requires negotiations among all interested senators and their staffs,
which keeps the Senate in session longer and requires senators to cancel
all their day's and sometimes their week's appointments. Only a senator
tough enough to absorb the bashing by colleagues, or wise enough to
know that such opprobrium never lasts, will persevere and veto a time
agreement that fails to meet his or her terms. A majority leader might be
confronted with ten or fifteen separate objections to a particular agreement, and might be juggling several agreements at any one time, looking
more like an air-traffic controller than a national leader.

When Robert Byrd left his position as majority leader in 1988, I continued to call him Mr. Leader for two years. Byrd had overcome a poverty-stricken childhood; his foster parents raised him in a coal-company house, and he walked three miles to catch a bus for school every day. As a senator, he had delivered untold billions of dollars to the residents of his dirt-poor state of West Virginia. In some counties, 30 percent of the total incomes come from the federal government. He had held every senatorial position possible: majority leader, minority leader, whip, secretary of the conference, and president pro tempore. Byrd's worth was constantly underestimated, because people made judgments of him based on standards outside the Senate. From that standpoint he seemed, like LBJ, parochial and narrow. But inside the Senate he was a genius with a long memory—courteous, unflinching, and proud.

Byrd never took anything for granted. He would personally poll senators to be sure of their votes. He always asked. In 1971, Byrd was contesting Ted Kennedy for the position of whip. The day before the vote in the Democratic caucus, he had Senator Herman Talmadge of Georgia telephone Bethesda Naval Hospital to make sure that his fellow Georgian, Senator Richard Russell (a man Byrd spoke of only as Senator Russell), was still alive, so that Byrd could be assured of Russell's proxy vote in the election. He won by seven votes.

An absolute dedication to his West Virginia constituents gave Byrd the currency he could always count on—the opportunity for continued tenure in the Senate. Night after night, he would sit in his office telephoning West Virginians just to seek their advice, ask their views on several issues, wish them well in college, express his sadness at a death, offer his congratulations for a wedding or a birth. All the work paid off. In one statewide general election, he won all fifty-five counties of West Virginia. He became one of only three U.S. senators in American history to be elected to seven six-year terms. He served under nine presidents, and once said, "Presidents come and go. We have had great ones and we have had some that were not so great. And the same can be said of senators. But senators stay if they give their best. . . . There have been only 1,826 senators . . . since 1789." In July 1995, when the Senate honored him for casting his fourteen thousandth vote, the most in Senate history, Byrd said that he believed, in the words of Robert E. Lee, "Duty is the sublimest word in the English language."

During his early years in the House, Byrd went to law school at night, and when he got to the Senate, he sat for months mastering the Senate rules. When he was whip, there was no favor too great for a colleague to ask. Mike Mansfield delegated authority, and Byrd assumed it, building up long lists of chits. When Mansfield retired at the end of 1976, Byrd had the votes to become majority leader.

But in 1989, he was no longer majority leader. Newly elected senators wanted a new leader. George Mitchell, whom I had urged to make the race, beat Bennett Johnston of Louisiana and Daniel Inouye of Hawaii, and Byrd retired to the barony of the chairmanship of Appropriations and the position of president pro tempore, which usually goes to the longest-sitting senator in the majority party. He insisted on more office space than any president pro tempore or chairman of Appropriations had ever had, and Mitchell agreed to it out of respect and a desire to keep Byrd on his side. Whether that would assure Byrd's loyalty was impossible to tell; Byrd was a man of many parts, but predictability was not one of them. Six years later, when Republicans took charge, they moved Byrd into a space one-sixth as large.

On the afternoon of November 20, 1989, I walked into the Senate chamber to assume my obligation to preside—something I did infrequently after my early Golden Gavel days. It was 1:27, and my time in the chair began at 1:30, but since I was there I thought I would relieve Byrd, the current occupant. He sat erect in the chair, wearing a black suit, black vest, and dark tie, with his white hair swept back. He was reading the Bible; the book lay open at Psalms.

"I'm here to relieve you," I said, thinking I was doing him a favor.

"Could you wait three minutes?" he said.

"Sure, but why?"

"I need three minutes to have one hundred and fifty hours of presiding this year. You just sit there for a few minutes," he said, gesturing at a nearby chair. Then he leaned over, a smile on his face, and said, "I get paid ten thousand dollars more than other senators, because I'm the president pro tempore. If I do a hundred hours of presiding, that works out to a hundred dollars an hour, but at one hundred and fifty hours, I get paid only sixty-six dollars an hour."

He must believe this means something to someone other than himself, I thought. But I didn't know to whom. Maybe he thought his extra ten thousand dollars would be an issue in his next campaign. Maybe fear was a way of life for him. Maybe it was his sense of rectitude—I stayed mystified.

"Is that clock right?" he asked, as the clock above the entrance door turned to 1:31.

"No," I said. "It's one minute fast."

He waited thirty seconds, shut the Bible, picked up his glasses, got up, smiled, shook my hand, and said, "It's all yours."

Byrd's idiosyncrasies are unfathomable. He once issued a record that featured him playing the fiddle. One of the more remarkable political events I ever attended was a Democratic dinner in Newark where Byrd was the guest speaker. After a few words, he took his fiddle (he is no Stuff Smith) and for thirty minutes regaled the bemused New Jersey pols with various Scotch-Irish melodies from the mountains of West Virginia. For the two hundredth anniversary of the Senate, he prepared a history of the Senate from 1789 to 1989, which he read into the *Congressional Record* over months and years, and then, pursuant to a special appropriation, he bound the pages and presented each senator with an autographed Government Printing Office copy. Byrd loves history—the more ancient, the better. In 1995, he gave each senator a copy of his latest book, again published by the Government Printing Office, entitled *Constitutionalism in the Roman Senate*. Another time, he gave several of us a print of an old watermill—a picture he had painted himself during the Second World War, when he worked as a welder in a shipyard in Baltimore. He seems to share easily his nonlegislative passions with his colleagues.

Byrd fights for his convictions. "The Senate is not supposed to be efficient," he said, during his one-man filibuster in 1995 against the balanced budget amendment to the Constitution. "The press can call it 'Byrd-dogging' if they want, but I'm going to exercise my rights as a senator consistent with my conscience. I took an oath to defend and support the Constitution of the United States. When I leave here—and I plan to run again—but whenever that is, I want to look in the mirror and say that I did what my conscience told me; that I was not swayed by the passions of the moment, that I have been similar to Prothonius, of whom John of Salisbury said, 'It was glory enough that he was a man of whom his grandson need not be ashamed.' Republicans are like Lenin, who said, 'We shall destroy everything and on this ruin we will build our temple.' We have a duty to insist that they tell us how they will balance the budget. I

bought a secondhand car once and I insisted on looking under the hood.
We should do the same here."

The final word on Robert Byrd was best expressed, predictably, by
Robert Byrd himself, at one of those senators-only events that imply in-
timacy but often are no more than perfunctory gatherings. This luncheon was different. It was honoring Robert Byrd on the occasion of his
retirement as majority leader. His old adversaries Bob Dole and Ted
Kennedy spoke, as did his close friend Senator Ted Stevens of Alaska.
His West Virginia colleague, Jay Rockefeller (whose Uncle Nelson had
been pilloried by Byrd in the 1970s), reminded us that Byrd had been
valedictorian at Mark Twain High School in 1934, and that he had
worked in gas stations, butcher shops, and shipyards before he began his
extraordinary legislative career. Byrd then spoke about himself to his assembled colleagues:

> I thank you for your understanding and forgiveness over the years. I've
> never made it my purpose to be liked, but I've always liked you. . . . I
> hope you can understand this enigma, [which] doesn't understand
> itself. I've been to one movie in forty years and I walked out of that
> one. . . . I've attended three baseball games, and two of those were a
> doubleheader on one afternoon. And one football game; I went at half-
> time to crown the West Virginia Queen when we played Maryland. So
> you can understand why people scratch their heads when they look at
> Robert Byrd. . . . I don't watch many games on television because I fig-
> ure when you've seen one game you've seen them all. . . . For twenty-
> two years I've been doing what I've been doing on the floor. Perfectly
> wooden, no charm, purple hair. We've heard about all the years of
> hard times he has had. What does he do for fun except stand on the
> floor and make motions? . . . I read all of Shakespeare's thirty-seven
> plays; I've read Plutarch's lives, *The Iliad, The Odyssey*. I've read the
> Bible all the way through; read Webster's abridged dictionary from
> beginning to end; read the history of the world, seven hundred pages;
> read the history of England a number of times—reviewed it, con-
> densed it, put it down on paper in my own words . . . memorized po-
> etry during those eight-hour rides to and from West Virginia on those
> two-lane roads. I've read the thirteen-hundred-page book on Senate
> procedure over and over again. Often I say to myself, How well can
> [our kids] spell? There are different views as to what values ought to
> be. I have my own and I respect others. The Senate leaves its mark on
> us. . . . Editorialists and cartoonists have always lampooned the Sen-
> ate, but the Senate is still what our forefathers intended it to be.

There are only a hundred people in the nation's upper house; most of them have a rather strong sense of themselves. None of them wants to be embarrassed, and all of them want to win—every time. That's an impossibility. Even when substance and procedure go well, sometimes personality differences can derail things. The race for authorship of amendments and laws becomes very competitive. A chairman can take hold of all the power or else hand out assignments, responsibility, and credit to committee members. Scoop Jackson always gave credit and responsibility to the members of the Energy and Natural Resources Committee. He even allowed me to run a series of classified hearings on the geopolitics of oil when I was a freshman senator. Russell Long enjoyed his power but gave each member of Finance some room to do his or her thing. It was almost as if he welcomed a surprise, because he could go into an Uncle Earl riff, tell a few stories, adjourn, and then return the next day with the votes. Legislating with Long was fun.

Lloyd Bentsen, on the other hand, while being courteous, even-tempered, and a man of his word, was a controlling Finance chairman. Bentsen came from the Rio Grande Valley of Texas, where his first-generation Danish parents had created a very profitable ranching and farming operation. He grew up with Mexican kids, spoke Spanish fluently, and became a bomber pilot in the Second World War. He recalls that in his first campaign for Congress, in 1948, an old rancher came up to him and said, "You're running a good campaign, but watch out, they'll steal it from you. . . . I'll help you. Do you need any killin' done?"

Chairman Bentsen detested surprises, and he kept credit for himself. He had a chairman's proposal on practically everything—health care, tax policy, trade. He couldn't tolerate dissent among his fellow Democrats. He bought people off by including a provision favored by a particular senator in exchange for that senator's down-the-line backing. Although Russell Long was the one to coin the motto "I'm against any combine I'm not a part of," Long never made the battle personal, even when you opposed him. He remained jovial even as he shafted you. Bentsen, dignified and reserved, was more like a stern father than a seasoned performer. He administered retribution: sometimes leaking a negative comment to the press, or declining your request to hold a hearing, or withholding credit for hard work that had arrived at conclusions different from those he wanted.

A chairman's power derives from his ability to control his committee, which is where the bulk of legislation is really written. When a bill

proceeds to the floor, getting fifty-one senators to agree to an amendment is more difficult than getting a majority of eleven in committee. On
the floor, the legislative maneuvering becomes a free-for-all. Staffs of
senators often wage feuds over who will write the amendment to be offered to a pending bill, or whose name will go on it first, or whether the
title of the program to be created will be the one chosen by their senator. They battle about who will issue the press release, who will go on
the TV show, who will get the headline. Each event has minimal value,
but in total they are what make a reputation. Within the institution,
someone may be regarded as a greedy, press-seeking egotist; outside it,
he's seen as a leader.

Nonpolitical bonds—friendships among spouses; traveling abroad
together on fact-finding trips; working out in the Senate gym—often
generate the civility that allows gigantic egos to interact and an institution built for conflict to function smoothly. Still, there are clashes, particularly when the issue relates to a senator's power within the
institution. A chairman wants to have control of his committee, which
means being able to get a majority to do the things he wants; therefore,
the composition of committees is important. Both parties have their own
committee on committees, charged with making committee assignments. The positions on the Democratic Committee on Committees are
allocated on the basis of region and by the appointment of the Democratic leader. There are fierce battles within it. The battles are generally drawn along classic lines—liberal/conservative, environmental/
industry, rural/urban, East/West. Under Russell Long, the Finance
Committee was well supplied with a majority of senators who were conservative on social and economic matters and yet willing to give taxpayer
money to the oil industry. On the Energy and Natural Resources Committee, which has jurisdiction over water in seventeen Western states, as
well as over the Park Service, the Bureau of Reclamation, the Bureau of
Mines, the U.S. Forest Service, and the Bureau of Land Management, I
am one of only three members from east of the Mississippi. Western senators dominate the committee. Predictably, the Western resource-based
states, with industries such as timber, mining, cattle, and irrigated agriculture, continue to receive water and access to public lands at little cost,
subsidized by all the nation's taxpayers.

The levels of conflict within the Senate extend even to such mundane
areas as office space, postage, and paperclips. From 1981 to 1986, when
the Republicans controlled the Senate, I was able to use an extra room in

the Hart Senate Office Building for my interns to sit in to help answer the fifteen hundred letters I got every week. When the Democrats took over again, I was booted out by the Democratic senator from Kentucky, Wendell Ford, the chairman of the Rules Committee and my prime opponent on tobacco issues, who wanted to give the space to Lloyd Bentsen for the joint tax committee's additional staff. (To be fair, four years later, when the Intelligence Committee needed my capitol hideaway office, Ford replaced it with one of the best in the Capitol.) Too often, instead of focusing on issues, you have to battle for office space, office supplies, staff slots on committee payrolls, and committee assignments. One of the powers of leadership positions is to grant or reject these requests, which raises the question of how many votes have been sold for extra paper, more space, or an additional payline for a staff member. The answer: more than the public knows.

Because of the jockeying built into the functioning of the Senate, ambitions clash, staffs clash, and personalities clash. Over time, certain senators develop a dislike for other senators. I've seen measures objected to simply because of personal pique. A smart senator approaches such a problem with the balm of accommodation, apology, or pleading. Otherwise, the objection stays. One would be surprised at how few senators are smart in this regard. I've seen tempers flare and senators nearly come to blows. One night in 1980, at 2:30 in the morning, I was awakened from the catnap I was taking off the Senate floor by the bellowing of Senator John Culver of Iowa, a man known for his explosive anger, who had once ordered his driver back in Iowa to drive across a golf course to escape a traffic jam. He was holding forth on the floor, in a blistering tyrannical rage at Senator John Tower over some weapons system. On another occasion, Senator Lowell Weicker of Connecticut, angered by the suggestion that a position he took on an issue had been influenced by a company that formed the foundation of his family's inherited wealth, said to his accuser, Senator John Heinz of Pennsylvania (a senator of even greater inherited wealth), in the well of the Senate, "If you don't take back what you said about me, I'm going to punch you in the mouth." Heinz apologized.

Senator Ted Stevens of Alaska, who knows that he is renowned for his temper, uses it effectively. When the Senate is moving toward completion of a measure, Stevens has more than once launched into a tirade, threatened to filibuster, and usually succeeded in getting the offending provision either modified or thrown out. Stevens once became so enraged at Senator Howard Metzenbaum of Ohio for stopping Alaska from purchasing a federally owned railroad within its borders that he didn't speak to him on the floor for two years. He also waged a personal vendetta in 1980 against his fellow Alaskan, Mike Gravel, because he felt that Gravel was grossly inconsiderate at the time of Stevens's first wife's death; as a consequence, he settled on the charge that Gravel wasn't doing enough to protect Alaska in the fight over the Alaskan Lands bill. In my first Congress, I saw Jim McClure frustrate his fellow Idahoan Frank Church every time Church tried to pass a bill out of the Energy Committee. These were the only times I witnessed conscious delay in committee, and it was the most intimate battle I've ever seen. McClure would sit three feet from Church and demand roll call after roll call, talking endlessly between each of Church's amendments and then offering more of his own. It was purely a partisan antagonism, as far as I could tell. McClure, a conservative ideologue, simply wanted to rid Idaho of its senior senator for the past twenty-three years. He succeeded.

During William Proxmire's thirty-two years as a senator from Wisconsin, he railed about government waste, popularizing the Golden Fleece Award, which he bestowed on the most outrageous government expenditure of the month. In the early 1980s, the Senate opened a new office building, in which the plans called for a gym on the top floor. Proxmire, who ran six miles to work each day, forced a vote on money for the gym, and of course it was eliminated. Majority Leader Howard Baker was so angry that he closed the shower room in which Proxmire changed each morning after he arrived at the Senate.

If Jesse Helms offers anything, most Democrats will oppose it practically without looking at the substance. When Howard Metzenbaum offered anything, most Republicans would oppose it practically without looking at the substance. Democrats dislike Phil Gramm because Gramm is seen as disloyal (he switched from Democrat to Republican in 1982) and dismissive of the normal rules of courtesy (his language is often strident). Richard Shelby of Alabama was seen as an opportunist by fellow Democrats even before he switched parties after the 1994 midterm elections. His record, however, was not much different from that of his Alabama colleague, Howell Heflin. Heflin talked about his feelings and beliefs; Shelby just voted and rarely explained.

In the midst of all the swirling personality interactions, friendship doesn't follow a partisan path. John Chafee, Nancy Kassebaum, Bill Cohen, and Dick Lugar are Republican senators whose decency, balance, sensitivity, and courage I have come to count on. Jack Danforth, an ordained Episcopal minister, was someone I often sought out for counsel on many personal and political issues, and Al Simpson over the years became a steadfast friend. Trust was the bridge we crossed together even as partisan waters swirled below. Simpson's conservatism and Danforth's opposition to many of my initiatives just didn't seem important when compared with their humanity. The capacity to listen, to empathize, and to shoot straight wasn't the province of one political party. Once, during the Anita Hill–Clarence Thomas hearings in 1991, Simpson and I participated in a lengthened *Nightline* show that became very heated. We exchanged sharp words before six million people. When Ted Koppel closed the program, my adrenaline was still pumping. Then, as I sat in my chair and turned my mind to other things, I remembered that on my way home I needed to get a quart of milk for my daughter's breakfast. I checked my wallet. It was empty. What to do? Whom did I feel comfortable enough to ask for some money? No doubt. I walked across the set to Simpson, who was himself recovering from the angry exchanges. "Al, can you loan me ten dollars?" I asked. While continuing his conversation with a reporter, and without hesitating, he gave me a ten-dollar bill. Driving home, I thought about the levels of our lives as senators, about how much the public never knows, and then at the all-night grocery, after buying the milk, I bought a box of Wheaties with some of the change and thought of Al.

One of the things that many Russian politicians said about Mikhail Gorbachev was that on his way up, particularly when he was Secretary of the Central Committee, he always had time to listen to a colleague's worries, angers, or problems, and usually he tried to help. Like Gorbachev, a skillful senator understands when a colleague needs the friendship of someone who knows the pressures of public life and the difficulties of coping in public with private tragedy.

Joe Biden was twenty-nine when he was elected to the Senate in 1972. By the time he was sworn in, he had reached the legal age of thirty and he had lost his wife and daughter in a tragic automobile accident. Biden was so thrown by the loss that he couldn't bring himself to assume his Senate position. Finally, by March of his first year, he started taking the train every day from Wilmington to Washington, and on one of his first days on the job he went into the senators' private dining room for lunch. When he got up to get a salad, the venerable and dour John McClellan of Arkansas summoned him: "Biden?"

"Yes, sir?"

"Lost your wife, huh?"

Biden bristled. The remark had the tone of "Lost the election, huh?"

"I think I know how you feel," said McClellan.

Biden didn't believe that the older senator had a clue about how he felt, but he held his tongue.

"Sit down, son," said McClellan, who then proceeded to share a part of his life with the young senator. "When I was thirty-six, my wife and I were driving back to Arkansas," McClellan said. "We got down in the Ozarks of Missouri, and suddenly she took sick. Within a few hours, she died. I had to raise three boys. It was difficult, but I did it. Twenty years later, I got a call from Aramco, in Saudi Arabia, where one of my sons was working. I was told he had been crushed to death on an oil rig and his body was on its way home. I went back to Little Rock and called another of my boys to ask him to join me and meet the plane that carried his brother's body. On the way to the airport, his motorcycle crashed, and he died. So there I was, with two dead boys arriving on the same day. So, son, I think I do understand. Now, let me give you this advice: work, work, work, work. That will pull you through."

EVERY DAY, an effective senator calculates the interaction of substance, procedure, and personality in his dealings with his fellow senators. To have command of only one of these and not the other two dooms one to failure. The skillful senators know what they're talking about and have mastered the substance of at least two or three subject areas, such as tax, defense, criminal justice, transportation, or trade. The skillful senators use procedure to further their goals. They don't let Senate leadership arrange their procedural lives. The skillful senators are at home with their colleagues. They maintain more than a modicum of interest in their fellow senators as human beings. Speaking ability has little to do with being a great senator. I once asked the chairman of the Liberal-Democratic Party in Japan, "Who is the best speaker in the Japanese Diet?"

"The worst politician," he replied. He could have been talking about the U.S. Senate.

Until the institution confers authority on a senator by virtue of seniority, playing the supporting role is the key to Senate success—sometimes even a majority leader will shun the limelight. Mike Mansfield delegated much power to his committee chairmen, who wrote the laws on Medicare, Medicaid, federal aid to education, federal loans for college education, the Clean Air Act, the Clean Water Act, and countless other pieces of legislation that transformed America. His skill was getting agreements among giant egos and then giving them the credit. Even his television interviews, with their nos and yeses instead of personal posturing, were meant to be self-effacing. (No wonder he did so well as our ambassador to Japan in the 1980s.) Mansfield was the antithesis of his predecessor, Lyndon Johnson, who dominated the institution personally and dictated its agenda. In my entire tenure in the Senate, I've never heard anyone say a negative word about Mansfield. The key to leadership in the Senate is found in an ancient Chinese proverb holding that there are four kinds of leaders: those who are laughed at, those who are feared, those who are loved, and those who lead without anyone's knowing they have led. There are only a few who know how to be the last kind of leader, and I think they are the very best.

Finally, the behavior of every senator, be that senator collegial or not, is affected by the quest for re-election. Senators running for re-election often do not act normally. They justify an egregious legislative position or their sudden support of the other party's amendment or their participation in outrageous pandering to special interests as being absolutely necessary for re-election. In the months leading up to the election, they rush to offer amendments that will illustrate how hard they fight for "the little guy" or how deeply they are cutting spending, even though the rest of their record leads to the opposite conclusions. The last year of a Senate term is full of ultimatums ("I won't vote for the budget unless I get . . ."), paranoia ("My opponent will run a negative ad if I take that position"), and quirks ("I can't get back from my state for a vote on any Monday before 3 p.m.") that have become part of the institution. Requests (or, more often, demands) to select specific dates for recesses or to delay votes so that Fridays or Mondays are free for fund-raising work make the majority leader's life a constant round of negotiations.

During the national health-care debate in the 1993–94 Congress, Senator George Mitchell summoned a bipartisan group of senators known as the mainstream group to his office overlooking the Mall, in an effort to agree on a bill that could overcome a threatened filibuster. Senators for much of the twentieth century had sat in this office to hash out tough decisions behind closed doors. On one wall was a painting of FDR delivering a fireside chat. Across the room hung a portrait of Harry Truman. Out the window that afternoon, the sun was setting rather spectacularly behind the Washington Monument. "I get five or six ultimatums every day," Mitchell said. "Drawing a line in the sand is the new senatorial tactic. A senator tells the press in his state what his position is before he talks with me, and then, when he talks with me and I try to persuade him otherwise, he says he can't change his position because he's already talked about it to the press and it would hurt his re-election chances if he reverses it."

Harry Truman, uncomfortable during his early days in the Senate, was once counseled by Senator Ham Lewis, the Democratic whip: "Harry, the first six months you're here you'll wonder how the hell you got here, and after that you'll wonder how the hell the rest of us got here."

After seventeen years in the Senate, I've concluded that being a U.S. senator is the best elective job in the world. It affords complete independence. A senator is accountable only to his conscience and the voters of his state, and then only once every six years. A senator sets his own schedule and determines his own style. A senator can call virtually any American for advice and get it. In that sense, serving can be a constant learning experience. In the Senate, you know that you're in the middle of the action and that what you do has an impact. Sometimes you feel it with one vote on a critical issue or one speech watched on C-Span by millions; other times you sense it through an accumulation of committee decisions, floor votes, press conferences, and public reactions. Occasionally you see bridges built, water cleaned, or children fed because of your action. You know that serving in the Senate makes you a part of an institution that stands for minority rights over the roughshod sweep of popular passions. Paradoxically, the Senate's promise as an institution that will bring rapid change remains unfulfilled even as its purpose to moderate passions is realized. I ran in 1978 as a citizen politician, and I always rejected the idea of senator for life. I've always said I would stay as long as I felt effective for New Jersey, challenged by the work, and able to see that what I cared about most for America is being advanced. There are other places for public service, equally as rewarding, both in and out of government. But for me, during these seventeen years, the place of service has been the Senate—that rectangular room with the swinging oak-bronze-and-glass doors, where bombastic voices and soft-spoken words of wisdom have an equal right to the floor.

5

The Big Picture

REFORM has no friends," Machiavelli is supposed to have said. About the time I entered college, my mother began commenting in a mildly disapproving way on my defense of "the underdog." Although she admitted that concern for the poor and disadvantaged could be found in Christian doctrine, it made her uncomfortable. She wanted a religious faith that was a personal support; she had no interest in its applications to the rest of the world. She most certainly did not want a morality-based concern to shake up the status quo. My father, on the other hand, always wanted to know where the money flowed, how the world really worked, and, if things were to be changed at all, how they could be made more equitable without destroying what we had. From early March 1933, when FDR temporarily closed all the banks to prevent further runs on them, to the day my father retired in 1973, he was preparing for another depression. He made only one investment in his life—in stock of his own bank. He preferred knowing one thing well to knowing a hundred things superficially. Somehow, out of these two influences—my mother's religious sensibility and my father's prudence—and perhaps in opposition to aspects of them, came my impulse to make the world a better place.

In the Senate, I found that big reform is as easy as small reform. A complete overhaul takes the same amount of time, the same number of meetings, the same energy level as a more modest objective. In legislating, work really does expand to fill the available time. Given that fact, I always preferred trying for big reform to sticking a small provision in one place and another one somewhere else. If you succeed with small reform, all you get is a slightly different set of complaints and another, related task next year. If you succeed with big reform, you can change the country.

During my 1978 campaign, in which the principal issue was the 30-percent tax cut proposal of my opponent, I decided I wanted to be on the Finance Committee. Before I had even won the election, I lunched with Russell Long to get his support in the Democratic Committee on Committees, and I lined up liberals, such as Ted Kennedy, who saw me as an ally. In 1977, Kennedy had offered me a job on his staff. I replied that I was thinking more along the lines of a job like his own, but from that encounter, as well as from all the Robert Kennedy Tennis Tournaments that I had participated in while a Knick, Ted, assuming a greater agreement on tax issues than actually existed, supported me for a place on the Finance Committee.

When I first started playing professional basketball, my tax attorney told me that I had to make a decision about how much I wanted to pay in taxes. At age twenty-three, I found that hard to believe. How could I decide how much to pay in taxes? He said that I could take my pay as salary, or defer all or part of it, or take it as property, or take it as a long-term consulting contract, or take it as employer-paid life-insurance and pension plans, or take it as payment to my own corporation, or take it . . .

"I just want to play basketball and be paid well," I said.

"It's not so simple," he said.

"Taxes," observed Supreme Court Justice Oliver Wendell Holmes, Jr., "are what we pay for civilized society." Yet, ever since I read articles by the economist Milton Friedman and Harvard law professor Stanley Surrey in the mid-1970s, I believed that the income-tax system was inequitable and in need of fundamental restructuring. After I was in the Senate less than a year, I realized that most Americans paid at higher tax rates than necessary so that a much smaller group of Americans could take advantage of loopholes. These loopholes (credits, exclusions, and deductions) for the few distorted the market's role of allocating resources, and this meant that taxpayers with the same income paid varying amounts of taxes, depending on their personal probity or the acumen of their accountants.

In the early 1980s, a poll by Daniel Yankelovitch asked, "If you abide by the rules, will you get ahead in America?" An astonishing 81 percent of Americans said no. While many breaches of the social contract no doubt contributed to that answer, certainly one of them stemmed from the set of rules that affects a hundred million taxpayers annually—the tax system. As long as the code was so complicated that only experts could understand it, as long as almost as much money was excluded from tax collection as was collected (and for reasons that were never examined), and as long as the system produced widely disparate effects on similarly situated taxpayers, many Americans would remain convinced that you were a sucker if you played by the rules.

After a few years on the Finance Committee, I floated my version of basic tax reform—lowering tax rates and eliminating loopholes. Russell Long, the king of the tax loophole, told me I was "barking up the wrong tree." He would fight me at every step of the way. Journalists laughed at me. Other senators ignored me. I wrote a book called *The Fair Tax* about my ideas, and I tried to sell tax reform to Walter Mondale when he was running for president in 1984. Though he rejected my proposals initially, the Republicans thought he might take them up, so they called for a study of tax reform themselves. The study was adopted by the Reagan administration as a position partly out of fear that, by advocating the fair tax, Democrats would reassert control over the issue of cutting tax rates for the first time since the administration of John Kennedy.

In his second term, Ronald Reagan proposed a version of the fair tax. It was known as the Tax Reform bill of 1986. I had opposed simply cutting tax rates in 1981 as an act that would increase the deficit, but I supported cutting rates if the cuts were paid for by eliminating loopholes. That way the deficit would not increase. I became the president's strongest ally in Congress, selling the idea to Dan Rostenkowski, the chairman of the House Ways and Means Committee, and to Republican Senator Bob Packwood, who was by then the chairman of Finance. Both Rostenkowski and Packwood were used to the loophole habit, but when they went on the wagon they became tenacious advocates of lower rates and fewer loopholes.

Before the bill passed out of the Finance Committee, Russell Long made sure that it had his fingerprints on it. On a tally in the committee's backroom, he prevailed by one vote in his effort to save one of the oil industry's loopholes. He did not think the issue would be addressed again, on the assumption that what was done in private would not change in public. Yet I felt one of his votes might be soft. When I insisted on a public vote in full committee, he was livid. Long won again by one vote, and afterward he got me up against a wall and said, "Well, you made your point, and if you want a bill on the floor, don't try to repeal this one again." I thought that if the king of loopholes had only that one request, we had truly changed the terms of debate on the tax system. On the floor, I said that though I opposed the oil provision, it wasn't worth a filibuster from Long, so I voted against the attempt to knock it out and convinced Packwood to oppose all other amendments, too. In the end, even Russell Long voted for tax reform.

The day the 1986 Tax Reform Act passed was a moment of great pride for me. It was a major reform, clearly the biggest of the Reagan years. The top tax rate for individuals dropped from 50 percent to 28 percent, and what amounted to nearly two hundred billion dollars annually in loopholes were eliminated. What separated the 1986 bill from other tax-reform bills was that it was based on the principles of equity (equal incomes should pay equal taxes), simplicity (eliminating loopholes reduced complexity), and efficiency (the market was a better allocator of resources than a member of the Finance Committee with a pocket full of subsidies). It appealed to Republicans because it lowered rates and to Democrats because it decreased loopholes. (I once told President Reagan that he and I were interested in tax reform for two different reasons. He was interested because as a highly paid actor he had had to pay a marginal tax rate—the rate by which the highest dollar of income is taxed—of 90 percent of his salary. I was interested because as a professional basketball player, given the tax law's treatment of player contracts, I had been a depreciable asset.) Tax reform, in defiance of the odds, upheld the public interest against the special interest, and in so doing it gave me hope that victory could be achieved on other thorny issues, such as reducing the budget deficit. I felt that this bill was an example of how tenacity, clarity of purpose, and the promise to overturn what the public saw as a fundamentally unfair system could overcome the destructive undertow of the status quo.

In addition, tax reform helped the state of New Jersey. Because New Jersey had the second-highest per-capita income of all fifty states (Connecticut being the first), high tax rates took large amounts of money out of the state. If those rates were cut, New Jersey would therefore gain disproportionately. In addition, for some inexplicable reason New Jersey taxpayers used fewer loopholes, so if these were reduced New Jersey would be hurt less than other states. The result was that New Jersey got one of the biggest individual-income-tax cuts (amounting to a total reduction of about a billion dollars a year in personal income taxes) because of the reduction in the top rate. But (as I would find out in 1990), given the increase in state and local taxes, few New Jerseyans remembered that they had gotten a federal tax cut.

I told Gina DesPres, my legislative assistant for taxes, that even before the ink was dry the lobbyists would be making plans for reinstituting their favorite loopholes. To avoid such an onslaught, I urged the Treasury to include an explanation of the bill in each 1987 income-tax form. After Social Security had passed in 1935, FDR had insisted that each working American be given a Social Security card with an individual Social Security number, which would suggest that there was a special account for each person. When an actuary told FDR that the social-insurance program didn't work that way, the president laughed and said that the card did not have an economic purpose. It had a political purpose—to build support for Social Security so that "those SOBs on Capitol Hill won't repeal it." I urged the Reagan administration to follow FDR's example. They demurred and within a few years tax reform began to unravel.

NEXT, I turned to an even more complex issue—Third World debt. It was an issue that affected international bankers, New Jersey exporters, and *campesinos* throughout Latin America. Unlike tax reform, Third World debt was not neatly confined to one committee and one body of regulations. Instead, it involved many countries, many economic structures, many political systems, and many congressional committees. A reform law was unlikely. My task here was to influence the opinion leaders by using the bully pulpit afforded by the Senate.

The substantive problem was clear. During the oil boom of the 1970s, many oil-producing Third World countries had more money than they knew what to do with. They put their excess dollars into the world's private banking system, which in turn lent it largely to Third World countries that had big oil bills or good long-term prospects because of their natural-resource base. That debt often was not prudent, but bankers lined the waiting rooms of finance ministers in Mexico, Brazil, and Argentina, literally pushing money on these countries. In 1982, the bubble burst. Oil prices plummeted, and in the meantime interest rates had skyrocketed. Nearly a third of all the export earnings of the debtor countries were being used to pay interest to foreign banks. Obviously, since the money was going to banks, it wasn't being invested in the debtor country itself, which meant slower economic growth and fewer jobs for developing nations that desperately needed high job creation and a high economic-growth rate. It also meant fewer U.S. exports. The imbalance between repayment terms and the long-range capital needs of these Third World countries could be corrected only by help from the lending banks themselves and from public-interest, multilateral financial institutions.

In 1985, when the International Monetary Fund (IMF) stepped in, its cure was worse than the disease. The IMF wanted the debtor countries to run their economies through a wringer by reducing their budget deficits, privatizing state industries, depreciating their currencies, and cutting wages—all in order to keep current on their interest payments. When countries took such painful steps, people were hurt, and the only benefit was to receive short-term financing that put them further in debt. If a country failed to follow the rigid repayment terms, it could never receive IMF funds. I believed that this way of dealing with the problem was a recipe for disaster. The rigid application of IMF strategy would make poor countries much poorer and risk destabilizing their governments.

I had begun to worry about the interaction of recession and Third World debt in the summer of 1982. That July, the head of a major American bank came to see me. He denied categorically that there was any problem with Mexican debt. One month later, Mexico almost defaulted, because it was unable to get the cash to make its bank payments. Bank after bank across the United States faced potential catastrophe from profligate Third World lending. Bank examiners were allowing banks to carry loans on their books at a hundred cents on the dollar, while in the market the debt was selling at fifteen cents on the dollar. I was certain that if the public ever woke up to this exposure, there could be a run on bank stock, and perhaps on banks themselves, as consumers realized that these institutions were primed to go under. Bank failures could ripple through an economy already stung by farm-loan defaults and a growing S&L crisis. For the first time, my father's fifty-year fear of another depression could be justified.

For all these reasons, I laid out my objections to the IMF approach in speeches on the Senate floor as early as 1983. I urged that banks face reality rather than hide from it. I pointed out repeatedly that a Third World in depression hurt our export industries, and that high interest rates caused by financial instability could lead to higher interest rates for American homebuyers. I predicted that without economic growth fledgling Third World democracies would be endangered. I made speeches in places where I knew officials of private banks, the Treasury, and the Federal Reserve would be in attendance. I wrote articles championing debt relief for debtor countries as a reward for sound economic policies. I had private talks with bank officials, asking them to declare a moratorium on interest payments from debtor countries. I threatened them with legislation that would impose an immediate writedown of their Third World debt to market value.

The response of the banks, as well as the Treasury and the Federal Reserve, was to say that if countries were given debt relief they would never again be eligible for loans in the private market. No matter how destructive the transition, these countries simply had to repay the loans, with virtually no flexibility on terms. Treasury Secretary Jim Baker, who had taken over from Don Regan in 1985, expressed the official reaction when he said, "Debt forgiveness is a mirage." Major U.S. real-estate firms could always find a sympathetic ear at Treasury for some kind of tax or regulatory relief, while Third World debtors never even got a consideration. The vehemence of the rejection surprised me.

To complicate matters, when Chemical Bank announced in December 1986 that it was taking over Texas Commerce Bank, in which Baker's family owned large amounts of stock, the treasury secretary had a financial stake in a major Third World creditor. By opposing any action on Third World debt that would endanger the earnings of Chemical or impose stricter accounting on worthless loans, Baker, of course, risked the appearance of conflict of interest. When his holdings finally became public—in 1989, after the crisis had ebbed and after the confirmation hearings on his appointment as secretary of state—he pledged to sell the stock, taking offense at the suggestion that his debt decisions had been based on personal considerations. I believe they were based on the national interest as he saw it. Yet his background of old Texas money, his career as a corporate lawyer, his years as a private investor, and his tenure as White House chief of staff all argued for his listening more sympathetically to board chairmen concerned about quarterly earnings than to the pleas of liberationist theology priests concerned about grinding poverty.

When George Bush won the presidency, Nicholas Brady, a mutual friend and former senator from New Jersey, took over at Treasury. I visited him and lobbied hard several times to get him to provide debt relief. I played on his desire for favorable comparison with Jim Baker, suggesting that debt relief could be his legacy and that of President Bush. These efforts—plus news of riots in debt-burdened Venezuela; a rivalry between Baker and David Mulford, the assistant secretary of Treasury for international affairs; a call for voluntary debt relief by a commission of thoughtful bankers under the auspices of the U.N. Association; and (most important) the passage of time, which had allowed banks to strengthen their balance sheets—led to adoption of the Brady Plan in March 1989. The plan called for an end to the banks' practice of loaning debtor countries just enough money to pay interest back to themselves. Instead, Brady's action sent the signal to banks that it was time to recognize some losses and provide some debt relief. Brady rejected the assumption of the Baker years that debt reduction would prevent debtor countries from returning to the private capital markets as credit-worthy players. Participation was voluntary, and involved an IMF/World Bank guarantee on the interest of the remaining debt after a bank reduced a portion of the Third World country's existing debt. In addition, the World Bank, the IMF, and Japan established a thirty-billion-dollar fund for debt relief. Finally, no U.S. government funds would go to the banks. The goal was to reduce the cash drain of interest payments by lengthening the term of debt and lowering the interest rate. I remember walking out of the State Department with Paul Volcker, after Secretary Brady had announced the new direction in a speech to a group meeting in the plush diplomatic reception room on the eighth floor. Volcker was skeptical, intimating that it might well be years before a Third World country could go back to the private capital markets for bond financing. But as it turned out, he was wrong.

Mexico was the first country to seize upon the Brady Plan's offer to lessen its debt burden. As it happened, instead of discouraging the loan of capital, the plan made Mexico more attractive to lenders, because it stabilized the debt situation there and made it predictable. Billions of dollars that Mexicans had kept abroad out of fear of inflation, a declining peso, and statist government began to come home. Not long after that, foreign investors saw opportunity, and the result was an infusion of billions of dollars in investment. Debt relief had achieved its immediate objective. Costa Rica and Ecuador followed Mexico's example, and Argentina enacted market reforms to prepare it for Brady. Debt relief was only a limited success in the long run, however. As the peso crisis of 1994–95 would demonstrate, a good economy one day is no guarantee for the next day. Keeping the confidence of international investors requires managing the economy for the long term and assuring political stability. Erratic behavior in either area spells trouble.

One day in 1986, William Casey, the director of the CIA, invited me to breakfast at the sprawling CIA headquarters in Langley, Virginia. I had been on the Intelligence Committee for almost two years, but prior to that invitation I had known Casey only through his books on tax shelters and his appearances before the committee, where his answers to members' questions were often incoherent or inaudible. The committee exchanges with Casey were peppered with such admonitions as "Mr. Casey, could you speak up? I can't understand you." He would then speak louder, but because he slurred most of his words, we often still couldn't understand him. Among committee members, he quickly became known as "Mumbles."

What could this summons be about? I wondered, as I made my way through the various security checkpoints to the director's office. The breakfast was straight government issue: scrambled eggs and bacon served on plain government plates and accompanied by watered-down coffee, toast, and jam. After discussion of various everyday intelligence matters in the presence of his staff and mine, Casey said that he wanted to see me alone. He's going to tell me something I don't want to hear, I thought apprehensively, and then he'll leak it and deny he told me. We sat down. He twitched a few times and mumbled something about the CIA. Then, out of the blue, he said, as if he were whispering a code into my ear on a street corner in Vienna, "Keep your eye on the big picture. I liked what you did in tax reform, and now what you're doing for Third World debt. You're right. The banks are wrong. The real action in politics is the big picture. Keep it up."

Reform might have no friends, I thought, but it had strange allies. Casey was right. I find the big picture the most interesting to look at. I always liked macroeconomics more than the economics of the firm. I liked Fernand Braudel, Arnold Toynbee, Henry Adams, James Billington, Daniel Boorstin, James MacGregor Burns, James McPherson, and other historians of sweep better than historians of cotton planting in Alabama during the 1850s or other in-depth looks at a specific place at a particular time. When I hear from individual Americans, I ask myself what is the big-picture issue behind their stories. Working on the big-picture issues gives me a chance to have the greatest impact on the greatest number of people. Moreover, questions of structure interest me more than issues of marginal gain or questions of blame. If we got the structure right, we would need less congressional oversight and micromanagement—even less government. If people of equal incomes paid equal taxes, there would be more faith in the tax system, and consequently more mutual respect between the people and their government. If the economies of Third World countries grew, poor people could have a better chance to feed their families, American exports would rise, American jobs would increase, and the U.S. banking system would be stronger.

The big bold reform, founded on principle, had the potential to truly change things for the better. It rarely was achieved overnight, but I gained great satisfaction when I committed myself to a multiyear effort. I liked getting the press to believe that what had never happened before was now possible. I liked knowing a subject so well that opponents feared embarrassment if they challenged me. The very complexity of the big issues fascinated me. The management of diverse personalities and political interests, as well as the mastery of technical detail necessary to push big reform forward, made each day's effort exciting.

The pressures of electoral politics often crowd out work for structural reform. Politicians consumed by re-election rarely take the time to master a subject, and their legislative activity often mirrors what their polls say their constituents want. A small amendment on a crime bill serves a senator's campaign more than it serves the criminal-justice system. It's easier to understand a single change than a reform of the entire system. Securing passage of a larger IRA deduction to increase personal savings marginally is easier than reducing the budget deficit to increase national savings significantly. Providing a tax cut for those who drill oil is easier than finding a way to cut tax rates for everyone. Finally, the larger the reform, the more outspoken will be those who stand to lose from it. Often it's 55–45 for reform in the polls, which means that if you use reform as a campaign issue, you start out with 45 percent of the people potentially against you.

BY THE TIME I completed my second term, I had concluded that success in the Senate could be defined as getting a major reform bill passed every four years. It takes that long to develop an idea, prepare the public, marshal the support, and enact the law. In 1988, within the jurisdiction of my committees, there was one issue on the environmental front that was as important as Third World debt on the international front and tax reform on the economic front. It was an issue essential to life and central to our economy—water.

From 1987 until 1995, I was chairman of the Subcommittee on Water and Power of the Energy and Natural Resources Committee. The subcommittee has jurisdiction over the Bureau of Reclamation, which built and runs America's largest dams. Growing up in Missouri, with its forty inches of annual precipitation, next to America's greatest river, I had never thought much about aridity. Though the Mississippi was usually narrower in August than in May, it never dwindled to a trickle. Yet I knew that man's attempt to control nature in the West meant damming, storing, and distributing the waters of the great river basins: the Colorado, the Columbia, the Missouri. I also knew that people had been fighting over water in the West for a long time. The movie *Chinatown* only dramatized the corruption and greed surrounding attempts to bring farmers' water to Los Angeles. Water played a central role in the politics, economy, and life of seventeen Western states, and by understanding water issues, I could learn much about the uniqueness of this American region. Of all the water projects, I was told, the Central Valley Project (CVP) of California had the most intractable and important set of problems and opportunities—and "Oh, by the way," these same experts said, "forget it, you'll never reform it." That piqued my interest and got my competitive-reformer juices flowing, but first I had to learn all I could about California water. In particular, I had to learn about the Central Valley, an area three times the size of New Jersey that extends over four hundred miles from the foothills of Mt. Shasta in the north to the Tehachapi range in the south, in an almost perfectly flat swath some fifty miles wide.

The first hearing on California water held by my subcommittee took place in August 1989, in Sacramento, where I sat through seven hours of testimony. Subsequently, I read widely and held hearings in Los Angeles, San Francisco, back in Sacramento, and several times in Washington. I visited farms in the Central Valley and farms in San Diego County. I talked with water experts, water-policy makers, and water lawyers. I talked to commercial salmon fishermen, whose livelihoods had been endangered by drought and the excessive allocation of water to agriculture, which lowered stream flows and endangered habitats. I talked to businesses that needed water desperately for their industrial processes. I talked to farmers who were fearful that water reform would push them off the land. I talked to the owners of vast agricultural tracts concealed through interlocking trusts and sale-repurchase agreements. I talked with farm workers who were worried about their future. I talked with professional environmentalists, friends of the environment, and people who wanted to preserve wetlands so that they could hunt migratory ducks and geese. I talked to politicians—local, state, and federal politicians. In the subcommittee's hearings, I heard testimony from seventy-five people, and literally hundreds more passed through my office from 1988 on, talking about California water. To some people, water policy becomes boring very quickly, but if you're going to achieve big-picture reform as a legislator, you have to investigate the subjects in mind-numbing detail, for only out of understanding the facts can the shape of reform emerge.

The important thing to remember is that California is largely a desert. The winter winds blow off the Pacific full of moisture, which condenses when it hits the Sierra Nevada, on the eastern edge of the Central Valley, depositing tons of snow and rain. Some experts have estimated that by spring there is enough snow in the Sierra Nevada to cover the ten million acres of arable land in the Central Valley with four feet of water. The problem is that meltwater never comes in a steady flow. Instead, with the spring thaw it gushes from the mountains in a mad race to the sea. From April to November, there is virtually no rain at all, and by August the torrents from the meltwater have fallen to a trickle. The annual runoff from the Cascades and the Sierra Nevada finds outlet through two great rivers: the Sacramento, which flows some three hundred and twenty miles south from the region around Mt. Shasta to Suisun Bay, the eastern arm of San Francisco Bay, and the San Joaquin, which flows west from the Sierras and then north to the same bay. The two rivers have a common delta, a rare phenomenon. In the years before the CVP, these rivers flooded along the way, leaving a trail of devastation in their wake even as they deposited topsoil on the valley floor.

For centuries after the conquest of the Indians, the land of the Central Valley was owned by only a few people. The vast concentrated ownership of the Spanish and Mexican land grants gave way to the Kings of Wheat in the late nineteenth century, with their twenty-thousand-acre farms in the Sacramento Valley. At first, those who had property next to the rivers—the Sacramento, the Feather, the American, the Mokelumne, the Stanislaus, the Tuolumne, the Merced, the Chowchilla, the Fresno, the Kern, the San Joaquin—claimed the right to use river water indiscriminately. One cattleman, Henry Miller, who owned nearly three million acres in California, controlled both sides of the San Joaquin for a hundred and twenty miles. He also changed the course of the Kern River by building a canal a hundred feet wide and fifty miles long to take the river water to his own land. Such abuses of concentrated power were not uncommon, but by the late 1920s California courts had rejected the right of property owners to use the waters of neighboring rivers indiscriminately, declaring that any water use, even by an owner of riverbank land, had to be "reasonable and beneficial." Then, in 1983 the California Supreme Court said that water users, in the exercise of their water rights, could not disregard "public trust values" related to the environment and recreation. In other words, the public interest was more important than the property interest.

Before the CVP harnessed the rivers, farmers used groundwater in such quantities that by 1929 more than one-quarter of irrigated lands were irrigated by water pumped from beneath the earth's surface. Since the aquifer was finite, the farmers had to pump ever deeper. By 1936, land was being abandoned, because the groundwater, now dangerously low, had turned salty as the aquifer level approached bedrock.

The Central Valley Project, initiated in the 1930s, called for construction of the Shasta Dam in the north, at the headwaters of the Sacramento, and the smaller Friant Dam near the headwaters of the San Joaquin, in the Sierras. In the north, where two-thirds of the surface water flowed, the objective was to shift a part of that Sacramento Basin

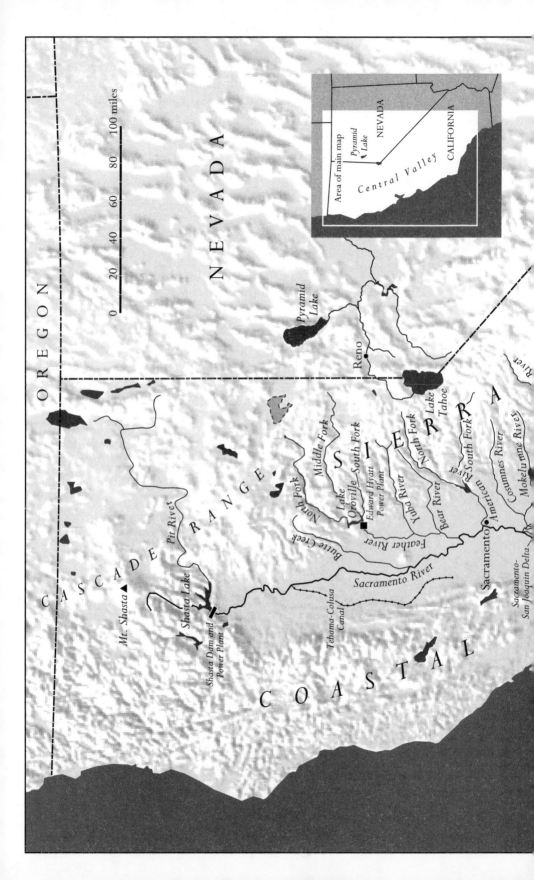

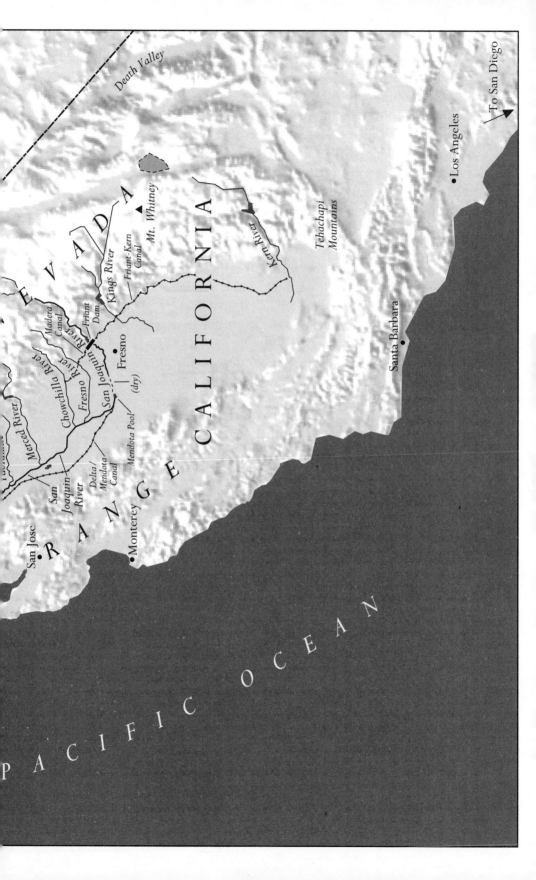

water to the San Joaquin Basin, which had two-thirds of the state's need for agricultural water. In the south, the plan was to divert the westward flowing San Joaquin into a canal running thirty-seven miles north from the riverbed and a hundred and sixty miles south to formerly arid farmland. Instead of flowing west and north to Suisun Bay, the bulk of the San Joaquin water would thus head south (this was called making the San Joaquin run backward). Under this design, the original riverbed of the San Joaquin would go dry for miles, from near the point where the canal—its northern section to be known as the Madera Canal and its southern as the Friant-Kern Canal—intersected it to the point where the Fresno, the first of a series of rivers flowing down from the Sierras, emptied into it and headed toward the Suisun Bay delta. Many of the farms in the southwestern San Joaquin Valley would therefore be left without water. The planners' answer to that problem was another canal—the Delta/Mendota Canal.

The great stream of water from the Sacramento River pouring into the delta at Suisun Bay now flows through a series of dredged channels, to the delta's south side. There the water is sucked two hundred feet aloft in seven giant pumps at Tracy and deposited in the Delta/Mendota Canal, which slopes gently to the south. Gravity carries the water southward for a hundred and seventeen miles, until it debouches into the original bed of the San Joaquin at Mendota Pool, whence it flows north again—joined at intervals by the Fresno, Chowchilla, Merced, Tuolumne, and Stanislaus—back to its old delta.

In its scope, the Central Valley Project is the most ambitious water project in history, with three hundred and fifty miles of canals and two hundred miles of high-voltage power lines. Neither the Shasta Dam nor the Friant Dam is as high as Boulder or as massive as Grand Coulee. They are not as big as the Kuibyshev Dam on the Volga, or the Itaipu Dam on the Paraná River, between Brazil and Paraguay. But for sheer imaginative breadth the project is unmatched. As Secretary of Interior Harold Ickes said in 1939, upon the beginning of work on the Friant Dam, "This is a line of creation built to unlock the fertility of the rich soil, to resist drought, to overcome floods, to provide outdoor recreation, and to generate cheap power that will lighten the labors and improve the living of millions of our citizens."

I remember flying over this vast public-works project one spring day a few years ago. The giant pumps on the south side of the delta, and the dams themselves, looked like tourniquets applied to the human circulatory system. The vast stretches of green fields next to the desert gave a graphic picture of the Central Valley before and after its Project. But the most memorable sight was a ten-mile stretch of the old San Joaquin riverbed. I saw water to the east, water to the north, and in the middle, desert where once a river had run. That dry, brown gap beneath the plane looked as if it were a mistake made by an ancient highway engineer who was drunk when he laid out a serpentine roadway. It was upon seeing this dry span that the audacity of the project dawned on me. In Russia during the 1980s, there was an intense environmental debate about whether or not to turn the direction of the Ob River so that it would flow south to irrigate the deserts of Central Asia, making them bloom with cotton. Here in California, the CVP had already achieved such a feat, albeit on a smaller scale. What nature took centuries to evolve, the Bureau of Reclamation had destroyed and rebuilt in thirty years.

The CVP, the crown jewel of the bureau's system of two hundred and fifty-four diversion dams, was completed in the late 1960s. It supplies 20 percent of California's water, and water from the project goes to nearly as many acres of farmland as from all the rest of the dams in the seventeen-state national reclamation system combined. An agricultural economy has developed, based on cheap, plentiful, and certain water provided by the federal government.

The generosity of the federal government is hard to understand absent politics. Large growers have always been active in political fundraising. They have friends, good friends, in the statehouse in Sacramento and among the state's congressional delegation in Washington. My first trip to the valley was in 1982, when Congressman Tony Coelho of Merced hosted several fund-raisers for my 1984 Senate campaign. I had not put two and two together. I was naïve enough to think that the contributors must like basketball. But those in attendance were the water boys, gaining what they hoped was a little insurance on the vote of a new, Eastern member of the Energy and Natural Resources Committee.

As a consequence of their connections, large landowners of as much as twenty thousand acres benefited from subsidized water that was supposed to go only to farms of less than one hundred and sixty acres (raised to nine hundred and sixty acres in 1982). The big farms were skillfully using the image of the struggling farmers to retain their subsidies. Near Fresno, in the Westlands area, the state's largest and most powerful agricultural water district, vast tracts of land got water at a price of $7.50 per acre foot (325,000 gallons), a subsidy equal to $2,200 per acre. By contrast, a farmer in San Diego County (outside the CVP service area) paid as much as $400 for an acre-foot. A resident of Santa Barbara, if forced to turn to desalinization as an answer to drought, would have to pay as much as $1,900. What Wallace Stegner labeled as "the iron triangle of growers, politicians, and bureaucratic experts" perpetuated these outrageous subsidies. If you argued that water prices should reflect demand more clearly, you would soon be presented with a family out of a Walker Evans photo of the Depression portrayed as those who'd get hurt by your rather mild policy change.

Federal policies that kept water prices artificially low threatened the financial viability of the project. The first reclamation projects in the West were supposed to pay off their interest-free loans in ten years by charging the local irrigation districts fees for the water and the local hydropower users fees for power from the dams. Over the years, the ten-year payback period for projects stretched to twenty, then to forty years. By 1989, the CVP had not begun to meet its repayment projection, or even to cover its annual expenses. By the year 2030, nearly seventy years after its completion, only about $230 million of the $3.7-billion debt would be repaid by the users, which amounts to a 95-percent subsidy paid by the nation's taxpayers. The outlandish federal subsidy was one of the reasons New Jersey agriculture had declined. Campbell's Soup, a company that grew tomatoes in my state for nearly a hundred years, moved its crop operations to the Central Valley years ago, unable to resist the lure not just of good weather but of massive subsidies as well.

The CVP has also had a considerable negative impact on the environment. The delta pumps at Tracy suck up eighty million young striped bass each year. The Pacific salmon is headed for the endangered-species list, with only two hundred Chinook moving up the Sacramento in the winter run of 1991 (in 1968 there were one hundred and eighteen thousand). Wetlands have been shrinking because of agricultural encroachment. As water evaporated from the irrigated fields each year, salts came to the surface, poisoning the soil and eventually turning farmland into alkali flats. But worse still, in 1990 toxic pesticides were found in runoff from the San Joaquin Valley orchards and row crops.

Because of the CVP and other smaller but similarly biased water projects, roughly 85 percent of California's water was being used by agriculture, even though agriculture represented only 4 percent of the state's economy and 3 percent of its jobs. In San Diego County, I remember seeing grapefruit trees being watered through tiny plastic pipes that were under strict control and flooded the roots with small amounts of water twice a day, while in the Central Valley unpaved irrigation canals were drained by giant sprinkler systems that sprayed water over vast fields as if it were rain in New Jersey. The drip versus the spray was a vivid picture of how agricultural water usage depended on cost.

By 1990, I realized that the first step in water reform required bringing the price of CVP water more in line with what the market would dictate in a world where entrenched political power did not guarantee outrageous subsidies. With higher prices, conservation had to improve, as farmers, like the San Diego grapefruit growers, made greater efforts not to waste such a precious commodity. If agriculture simply conserved 10 percent, it would double the water available for the residential and commercial sectors. A more efficient use of water, monitored by price, in turn would mean less pollution from agriculture. Water purity would be enhanced in the long run for millions of Californians, and water would flow more easily to the industries that generate the jobs of California's future.

The environmental abuse and overconsumption in the CVP were not just California issues. They affected the entire West. To begin with, there were fewer wetlands for migratory birds on the Pacific flyway from Mexico to Canada. In addition, fishermen in the Pacific Northwest had been hit nearly as hard as California fishermen by the decimation of the Pacific salmon and the steelhead-trout population. I will never forget a fisherman at a hearing in Los Angeles telling the roomful of farmers that too much water for their crops meant too little water for fish, and that meant he couldn't support his family. More important, proper management was vital to the protection of the water resources of neighboring states. To the extent that federal law prevented California from transferring water out of the Central Valley to meet its growing urban needs—eight hundred thousand people were arriving in California each year—the state would be obliged to try to find water somewhere else. To senators from Arizona, Nevada, Colorado, Wyoming, Utah, and New Mexico, this meant that California would seek to modify the Colorado Basin Compact, so that more of that water would go to California.

This prospect contributed to the acceptance of CVP reform by senators from neighboring states, even though they realized that the precedents set by the reform would affect their own states in time.

My fundamental objective in sponsoring CVP reform legislation was to give farmers the right to sell their water to the highest bidder; to improve water usage and efficiency so that less water went farther, thereby freeing up water for cities; and to require the CVP to pay its environmental costs as well as its fiscal debt. When these objectives were achieved, the costs to the taxpayer would be reduced and the need for new, environmentally damaging dams would diminish. Above all, the residential consumer would pay a lower price for water and face less interruption in water flows. In the wake of mandatory residential-conservation measures imposed on urban California during the 1987–92 drought, there were five-year-olds in Los Angeles who had never seen a green lawn.

The bill allowed water transfers out of the Central Valley to other places in California but retained for CVP users the right to buy the water first. In no circumstance could more than 20 percent of the water be removed from a single water district without that district's approval. The bill established water metering, water-conservation standards, and tiered pricing, whereby the last bit of water purchased would be a little more expensive than the first—a discipline encouraging conservation. The four hundred and eighty-two CVP water districts themselves would have to see to it that farmers in their district no longer washed pesticides into the river, as if it were the other guy's problem downstream. The bill allocated nearly a million of the seven million acre-feet of CVP surface-water yield for fish and wildlife (both for in-stream flow and refuges) and established a fifty-million-dollar environmental-restoration fund for devices at dams to facilitate the arrival of spawning salmon and the departure of their young. The Friant system would contribute no water for fish or wildlife. None. But the users of the Friant water system would pay a small surcharge to help mitigate some of the environmental damage caused by the CVP as a whole.

These measures radically altered the way California did its water business. Water could now move from agriculture to urban use; government would be getting out of the way and reducing its subsidy; fish and wildlife would finally be protected. It created a convulsion in the traditional water community. For years this community had expected low-cost water as a right, and environmental concerns were nonexistent. The governance of many water districts was based on votes related to land ownership. A twenty-thousand-acre farm had more votes than a thousand-acre spread. A few large landowners in such an undemocratic arrangement could control massive amounts of land and water. Conservative businessmen had become accustomed to federal subsidies. They were as dependent as some welfare mothers, and they were afraid of the market. With so much at stake, they played politics for keeps. The legislative battle to gain passage of CVP reform was a cliffhanger right to the end.

In March 1992, we tried to hammer out a compromise in the Energy and Natural Resources Committee. We were headed for an agreement until Senator John Seymour of California balked. Seymour had in January 1991 been appointed by Governor Pete Wilson, who had loyally served the agribusinessmen of the Central Valley when he was in the Senate. Soon it became clear that Seymour was taking his orders from the governor who had appointed him. Wilson did not want a compromise. Bennett Johnston, then the chairman of Energy and Natural Resources, after consultation with me, gave Seymour two choices. Seymour could continue to work with me to arrive at a compromise, and if compromise was reached the Senate would stick with it in negotiations with the House in conference committee. Seymour's other option was for the Energy Committee to pass his version of CVP reform with none of my suggestions included, and with a recommendation that the Senate pass his bill unchanged, by voice vote. But there would be no commitment by Johnston or me to fight in conference for the provisions of Seymour's bill. The first option required intense negotiations and compromises now; the latter was an invitation for those who disagreed with him to roll him in conference. He opted for the latter—the one-day-headline approach. He boasted that he had "dribbled between my legs." The Energy Committee duly reported out his bill, and the Senate passed it on a voice vote.

The chairman of the House Interior Committee was George Miller, who represented California's seventh congressional district, which included municipal and industrial users of CVP water. He was steadfast, knowledgeable, principled, and detested by that part of the water community averse to change. Miller's father, a California state senator, had never been able to beat the water interests, and Miller had grown up in a house full of lore about "those SOBs." We worked out a compromise version of the bill and announced it two weeks before the end of the session. Seymour didn't like our version and complained that he hadn't been consulted. Nonetheless, the House-Senate conference adopted the Miller-Bradley compromise, which would become the final law when both houses adopted it. To enhance the chances for passage, Miller and I merged the CVP reform into an Omnibus Water bill that included twenty-seven other water projects in the West.

The water boys still had hopes of killing the bill; during the previous Congress, then Senator Pete Wilson, by letting the clock run out, had defeated a bill that would have ended the loopholes in the 1982 law limiting subsidized water to farms under nine hundred and sixty acres. During the last week of a congressional session, two years of work telescopes into a few days. If bills are not enacted before adjournment, they die, which means that they must be reintroduced in the next Congress. New hearings must be held, and many of the same scraps must be fought again at each step in the legislative process. Because there is so much at stake with so little time left, pressure is high. Everything has to operate by unanimous consent. That's when deals are made fast and furiously. Senators opposed to bills relent as they find their own bills blocked in retaliation. During the session, a threat of filibuster can be broken by forcing a senator to hold the floor until he or she gives up. The end of a session normally doesn't afford enough time to wait someone out. With a firm adjournment deadline announced, one person can filibuster a bill to death. That was Senator Seymour's strategy.

A senator usually keeps several legislative efforts going simultaneously, and that activity intensifies at the end of a session. At the end of the 1992 session, I was also trying to get agreement on passage of bills that prohibited sports betting, established a study to make a portion of the Delaware River "wild and scenic," and one that created a high-school exchange program to bring as many as five thousand high-school students here from Russia, Ukraine, and other former Soviet republics for up to a one-year stay with American families. Each of these bills was important to me, and, together with a bill passed earlier establishing a new way for students to finance their college education, they would form a successful legislative session. If the bills floundered, I couldn't point to my effectiveness or deliver on promises I had made to myself and to New Jersey in 1990. Much was at stake.

Legislative pressures merged with the particular political demands of an election year. In the last days of the 1992 session, senators wanted to get home to campaign for re-election. Others wanted to campaign for the presidential ticket of their party. Still others simply wanted a rest after the hectic session. All wanted the session to end. In such an atmosphere the clock can also work against the filibuster. If the leadership calls the bluff and extends the date for adjournment, then the filibusterer, if he is alone and if he persists, angers the rest of the Senate and loses support for his cause.

In the last week of the session, Senator Seymour joined Senator Alfonse D'Amato of New York in a filibuster, because D'Amato's filibuster, on a bill unrelated to CVP, had the effect of delaying even further the consideration of the water bill. I persuaded Majority Leader Mitchell to tell Minority Leader Dole that the Senate would stay in session until we finished the water bill. Once Dole was convinced that Mitchell meant business, he told Seymour the bad news: Seymour could delay passage of the agreed-upon water bill for a few days, but that was all, because Mitchell would extend the adjournment date to break any filibuster. Seymour was fighting alone. Many Republicans whose states' water projects were in the Omnibus bill were opposed to the filibuster, among them Senator Jake Garn of Utah, who had worked to pass the Central Utah Project for twenty years and who was retiring from the Senate in a few months.

Seymour finally accepted an agreement that allowed him to pass his version of the CVP bill in the Senate again on a voice vote, thereby giving him the fig leaf of being able to claim that the Senate had supported his bill. Then the Seymour bill would be sent to the House, where it would die by prearranged agreement with Miller and the House leadership. Final arguments were made. The Senate vote on the Miller-Bradley bill took place, and the bill passed, 83–8.

ON THE LAST MORNING of the session and the final day that the water bill was being debated, Governor Bill Clinton's campaign headquarters in Little Rock called and asked if I would defend Clinton against President Bush's attack on Clinton's youthful trip to Russia during his time as a Rhodes Scholar. As a Democrat and as a Rhodes Scholar who had traveled to Russia during my own Oxford tenure, I was the natural person to wage the defense, and I said I would do it. So, after the water bill passed, there was no time for celebration. The demands of a presidential campaign swallowed up the sense of legislative accomplishment. I took the few pages my staff had prepared and added some personal references. Then I rose to the Senate floor to chastise Bush:

> I went to Russia when I was a Rhodes Scholar. It was a great trip. I saw totalitarianism up close and was revolted by it. I met hundreds of Russians and Ukrainians. I found them to be warm, open people who, I hoped, would triumph as they have in throwing off communist rule.
>
> What does the president imply? That we were unpatriotic to go? That anybody who, as a student, traveled to Russia is unpatriotic? What hogwash! I thought education was learning about the world firsthand as well as from books. This is a smear.
>
> Should President Bush be held accountable for every trip he's made abroad as a private citizen? Has he been to the former Soviet Union as a private citizen? How many times did he go? What did he do? Whom did he see? Also, what about any trips as a private citizen to Iraq, China, Libya, Iran, or Panama? How many? When? What did he do? Whom did he see?
>
> This would be ridiculous, if it weren't so sad.

As I left the Senate floor, a few Republicans gave me dirty looks and Senator Ted Stevens of Alaska stood up and said that Clinton's trip was a legitimate issue.

My job on the water bill now required luck plus a strategy. Before nearly four years of work could come to fruition, President Bush had to sign the bill. I knew I had the difficult job of getting a president whom I had just attacked to do something I wanted. I knew I would have to persuade Western Republican senators and California Republican businessmen, Chief of Staff Jim Baker, and anyone else who counted in the White House to urge the president to sign the bill. It meant holding out the possibility that Western Republicans would lose Senate seats if he vetoed it. It meant evoking the specter of a Clinton administration even tougher on Western agricultural interests than this bill would be. It meant persuading Western newspapers to publish editorials in its favor. The president had a little over three weeks before his failure to sign the bill would automatically veto it. With the Senate out of session, this pocket veto was a dangerous prospect.

Two weeks later, President Bush had not yet signed the Omnibus Water bill. I urged Republican businessmen in California who supported

CVP reform to call the White House. The CEOs of Pacific Telesis, Hewlett-Packard, Bank of America, and Security Pacific Bank did so, after I argued that if they didn't call, the president might listen only to Governor Wilson and to some of his major fund-raisers, who were wealthy farmers benefiting from vast water subsidies at the expense of the rest of the California economy. I called Jake Garn and reminded him that time was running out for the Central Utah Project. I called Senator Malcolm Wallop of Wyoming and reminded him that Clinton was ahead by ten points in the polls and that in a Clinton administration a different water bill could set even more stringent regulations for Western water interests. I called Senator John McCain of Arizona and reminded him that the fate of our efforts to save the Grand Canyon by altering the operation of Glen Canyon Dam was tied to the fate of the CVP. I contacted Bob Grady, who handled water issues for the Office of Management and Budget. He was from New Jersey, and had been my opponent's speechwriter in 1984, but he was committed to water reform in California and had supported my efforts throughout. He said he would do everything he could to help get President Bush's signature, but he worried that California's politics, and Governor Wilson, might interfere and persuade the president not to sign.

Four days before the pocket-veto deadline, President Bush still had not signed. I was told that Governor Wilson had flown to Kentucky, where Bush was campaigning, to plead his case with Bush personally. A leaked threat of Sunday editorials was my last means of bringing pressure on the White House. While I was driving from event to event in New Jersey on the Friday before the election, I called editorial writers of the Salt Lake City, Denver, and Los Angeles newspapers. I urged them to publish negative Sunday editorials on Bush if he hadn't signed the bill by Saturday night, which was the deadline; twenty-eight water projects for the West were at stake, I reminded them. I argued that he would be doing no better for the West than Jimmy Carter did when he attacked Western water projects in 1977. Most of the editorial writers seemed receptive.

On Saturday I learned that Bush had signed the Omnibus Water bill the night before, twenty-four hours before the pocket-veto deadline and over Governor Wilson's vehement protests. Nearly four years of work had come to an end. I called George Miller, who was ecstatic. One of his father's goals as a state senator, and one of George's since he came to Congress eighteen years before, had been fulfilled. We shared a tremendous feeling. You knew that the big-money water interests would challenge the law in the courts, hoping to wear down the government. You knew that next year the Permanent Government of Lobbyists would try to undo the law's intent by influencing the way the executive branch wrote the regulations. You knew that the water boys would go to work on new Senators Dianne Feinstein and Barbara Boxer, trying to convince them that if they just repealed a few provisions of the CVP reform, such as those guaranteeing water for the environment, they would lock up the votes of the Central Valley and guarantee themselves re-election. You knew there would be sneak attacks to gut the reform with amendments attached to appropriations bills. You knew that attempts would be made in the Energy and Natural Resources Committee to riddle the law with destructive amendments, perhaps even to repeal it.

But all doubts about being able to achieve another major reform were gone. You knew that lives in the Central Valley would change. You knew that the water wars in California between urban, agriculture, and environmental interests would ease up just a little. You knew that you had laid the foundation for the state's future economic growth. You knew that substance, procedure, and personality had come together again. You knew that you had counted your votes. You knew that you had won.

6

Outside the Frame

G ROWING UP in a small town engendered a curiosity about the wider world. I had no conscious desire to leave Crystal City. I liked it, but I also sensed that the world offered greater variety than the confines of a factory town of thirty-five hundred people. International affairs were never discussed at our kitchen table, and I knew no returning war veterans with stories of the South Pacific, D-Day, or Korea. There were no linguists in my family, no globetrotters or international businessmen or students of the world. The radio shows we listened to were Jack Benny's program on Sunday night, *The Shadow,* and *Henry Aldrich.* With the arrival of a seventeen-inch Motorola television set, the Red Skelton and Ed Sullivan shows, *Dragnet,* and *Martin Kane, Private Eye* topped the family's viewing list. (Actually, they were my father's favorites. My mother rarely watched television.) Occasionally, my father and I watched *Victory at Sea,* a documentary on the Second World War, but my primary windows on the world were the magazines and phonograph records my parents accumulated.

I practically memorized Edward R. Murrow's recorded series called "I Can Hear It Now," chilled by the eerie cadences of Adolf Hitler's speeches at Nuremberg rallies. I can still summon up Churchill: "We shall fight on the beaches, we shall fight on the landing grounds, we shall fight in the fields and in the streets. . . . If the British Empire and its Commonwealth lasts for a thousand years, men will still say, 'This was their finest hour.' " The first awareness I had of New Jersey was a record that contained the radio broadcast of the *Hindenburg* dirigible disaster at Lakehurst.

In our basement were stacks of old *Life* and *Look* magazines from as far back as 1938. They smelled of mildew and age, but I sat looking through them for hours at a stretch. By the time I was thirteen, I had read and reread them all. The Second World War came to life in the war pictures in the magazines. The Berlin airlift, the Geneva Conference of 1954, the rise of Khrushchev became part of my awareness because I read the magazines. Pictures in *National Geographic* of Asian cities and African veldt, of the ruins of ancient civilizations, of natural wonders like the Amazon, Victoria Falls, Mt. Everest, the Nile, all lived in my imagination. Every time I put the magazines away and climbed back upstairs, I had the same thought: When will I ever visit those places in person? When will I see what lies outside the frame?

In May of my senior year in high school, I decided to accept a basketball scholarship to attend Duke University, in Durham, North Carolina. Although my mother preferred Mizzou, she thought Duke offered the right combination of academics, sports, and, as she said, "the spiritual." My father was less enthusiastic. Over the last three years of high school, when I received offers of basketball scholarships from seventy-five colleges, he had come to prefer Princeton. Ironically, Princeton, like other Ivy League schools, offered no athletic scholarships. My father would have to pay my tuition and expenses.

Whether by design or in all innocence, he put me on the *Queen Elizabeth* and sent me on an Olson College Tour to Europe shortly after I accepted the scholarship to Duke. Little did either of us know that the tour, which consisted of thirteen girls and me, would affect my life in fundamental ways. To me, it was simply the chance of a lifetime—a chance to spread my wings and to see Big Ben and the Tower of London, to steam down the Rhine, to stand in the Roman Colosseum, and to indulge my imagination as the landscape changed before my eyes. My thirteen female tourmates, on the other hand, were unable to understand why I'd chosen Duke over Yale or Princeton.

A visit to Oxford planted the seed of desire to return there someday. The warm yellow sun of a June morning and the smell of the freshly cut lawns seemed to invite you to sit under a tree and read, and I saw many students doing just that. Parts of some of the colleges dated back to the fourteenth century. Portraits of peers and prime ministers hung in the eating halls of Balliol and Christ Church. Oxford seemed steeped in a casual excellence I was determined to know. And finally, on my return, I broke my foot, and for the entire month before I was due at Duke I sat facing the possibility of a world without basketball. While recuperating, I read books about Oxford and the Rhodes Scholarship, and I discovered that Princeton had produced more Rhodes Scholars than any other university. Four days before the Duke freshman class convened, I switched from Duke to Princeton, and arrived on the campus at 9 p.m. the night before the first meeting of the Class of 1965.

In retrospect, that decision was the turning point of my life. Princeton ignited my intellectual curiosity and introduced me to a new social world. It brought me to New Jersey, and it challenged me on the most fundamental levels imaginable. It was where I became a man.

The day after I arrived I ran into the basketball coach crossing campus. He was flabbergasted, having written me off as a Duke Bluedevil months before. Gradually, I found my way around. By mid-October, with my foot healed, I was appearing daily in Dillon Gym. One afternoon during a preseason pickup game, a mustached man wearing cut-off khaki shorts and carrying a squash racquet walked onto the court. "Odd-looking guy," I thought as I glanced at him. He asked to join the workout, in an accent that I mistook as Scottish.

The tall stranger got an elbow and returned one; then he took a pass, swept across the lane, and hit a fifteen-foot hook shot, took another pass, hit another hook. "Couldn't be Scottish," I thought. He said, "Belz the name, basketball the game, and South Jersey is my home." Later Carl Belz, one of Princeton's greatest basketball players ever, trumped my expectations again, when he asked if I liked Manet's *The Fifer*. And why didn't I take Art 101?

"Art," I said. "You mean drawing?"

"No, art history," he said. "Learning to see with a new set of eyes, just like you see the whole court." So it happened: at first an introduction, then a coexistence, and finally the unlikely union of art and basketball in my own mind—a union that was decisive in the years ahead as I learned to trust that artistic part of me that was determined to perform professionally, wearing short pants and playing the game I loved.

One of the benefits of playing basketball at Princeton was international travel. In October of my senior year, I played in the 1964 Tokyo Olympics. The university allowed me to miss the first half of the semester because I had worked on my senior thesis during the previous summer in Washington, and I took my course books (including a tome on Russian history) along to the Olympic training camp and on to Tokyo. It was my first time in Asia. I hit my head constantly on doorframes and subway entrances. I got used to ducking. I didn't get used to the Japanese laughing and pointing at the giants walking down the street.

During the Tokyo Olympics, I met Jack Horton, whom a friend in Princeton had asked to look me up. At the time, Horton was flying Naval intelligence missions out of Japan to unknown destinations. He was the Republican son of a prominent Wyoming family. He loved his family's fifteen-hundred-acre dude ranch, which backed up against the Bighorn Mountains, in Saddlestring, Wyoming; there he would roam the range on horseback with the deer, the antelope, and the cattle. He also loved cloak-and-dagger intelligence missions, interesting women, and exotic destinations. After a year at Oxford as a Rhodes Scholar, restless as ever, he had left and enlisted in the Navy. He thought he might go back to Oxford someday. He lived in a small house set in the mountains outside Tokyo, with a housekeeper and a dog. An air of mystery surrounded him, and he courted it. I found him fascinating. I have always been somewhat guarded myself, but his guardedness was even more intense than mine: his tales of exotic places and people did not include his own reaction to them. He appealed to the side of me that wanted to go everywhere, see everything, know all the subtle customs of the locals, and reach a level of understanding deeper than was possible from reading magazines in a small town or traveling with a sports team. He would tell me about a hotel in Bangkok that had a particularly interesting "kitchen" and a corner room with a remarkable view, which you could book if you asked for the right clerk at the desk and mentioned that the right person had sent you. He could name the provincial capitals of Italy and what dishes were their specialty. He knew obscure mountain passes in Tibet and Nepal. He speculated about the linguistic differences between Cantonese Chinese and Szechuan Chinese, and about the interaction of Buddhist, Shinto, and Confucian traditions in Japan. I found his stories magnetic. They drew me to imagine a life on the road in new and exciting ways.

After the Olympics, I toured Asia under the sponsorship of a program called Princeton in Asia, which sent recent Princeton graduates to teach in a few non-Mainland Chinese colleges. I was a gold medalist and a forthright Christian, and people apparently wanted to hear about both experiences. I went to Taiwan, where I spoke at Tunghai College and heard whispered comments from students about governmental efforts to inhibit open debate. At the U.S. embassy in Taipei, I cast my first ballot for president, voting for Lyndon B. Johnson. In Hong Kong, I spoke at Chung Chi College, walked the narrow alleys of Kowloon City, bought a tailor-made tweed sports jacket, and ate my first Peking duck at the favorite restaurant of Chung Chi's President Andrew T. Roy. Dr. Roy, whose parents had been missionaries in China and whose son would later become U.S. ambassador to China, told me that few in Washington understood either the dangers or the opportunities that China represented for the United States, and that no one fully appreciated China's potential economic dynamism. When he spoke of his early years in China—about the people he knew and the communist terror that followed—tears welled up in his eyes. Later I would read about Mao's genocide immediately after assuming power, and about the excesses of the Cultural Revolution, and I would remember Dr. Roy's face in that Hong Kong restaurant in 1964.

After my senior year, I headed back to Europe, this time to Finland, Prague, and the World University Games in Budapest. Hungary was still occupied by the Soviets. The basketball competition took place in an outdoor arena that seated about twenty thousand people. We defeated the Soviet team to win the gold medal, and each American player received a medal and a bouquet of flowers. After accepting them on an elevated stand in the middle of the stadium, we walked around the infield track, waving to the crowd, who clapped and cheered wildly. After that, the Soviet team got their silver medals and took their walk. I looked back from the exit ramp, and I'll never forget what I saw. The Russians walked and waved as we had, but the Hungarian crowd was hushed. Instead of clapping, they moved their hands as if to clap, except that one hand passed above the other in a silent, scissorlike motion. It was a chilling act of defiance, and in its collective expression richly affirming of Hungarian national identity. For me that moment, more than a hundred accounts of the uprising of 1956, conveyed the unmitigated hatred that Hungarians had for their Soviet occupiers. Years later, when I stood in Hungarian

American halls in Carteret or New Brunswick listening to Hungarian Americans castigate the Soviets, I knew they were not simply a disaffected and bitter interest group. Like the people in the arena that night in 1965, they were representative of millions of their countrymen.

In December of my senior year at Princeton, I had been selected as a Rhodes Scholar. The series of qualifying interviews was extensive and idiosyncratic. I remember a discussion about nineteenth-century British history, with special emphasis on Gladstone and Disraeli. Then, as I was walking out of the room, one interviewer tried the trick question: "Oh, Mr. Bradley, one thing more. Who plays tight end for the Chicago Bears?" There was a saying among Rhodes Scholars that it was great to be a Rhodes Scholar except that you had to live two years in Oxford. I felt the opposite. If I had not gotten that scholarship, I would have applied for others until I made it to England. The goal was Oxford, not the Rhodes.

Press attention during my last year in college had mushroomed, including magazine cover stories and hyperbolic accounts of my academic and basketball talents. I received forty letters a day from strangers applauding my performance, seeking advice, and inviting me to speak. The amount of attention surprised me. I began to see that another advantage offered by Oxford was refuge, a place to leave the public eye and get back some sort of perspective.

My desire for anonymity was put to the test on the trip over—again on the *Queen Elizabeth*—with the two dozen other American Rhodes Scholars of 1965. As it happened, my roommate was Jack Horton, full of stories as usual, who was returning to finish his tenure at Oxford after five years in the Navy. On the last day of the voyage, I received a telex saying that the international wire services wanted to get a photo of the "great American basketball player Bill Bradley" disembarking at Southampton. The spotlight was the last thing I wanted, so Jack and I decided that he would identify himself as Bill Bradley and walk down the gangplank wearing a cowboy hat and carrying a lacrosse stick, which he would identify as a basketball stick. The English, we knew, were notoriously ignorant about American sports (the reverse is just as true, it should be noted), and they seemed particularly uninterested when it came to basketball.

After we arrived, I got off the boat and told the three photographers on the dock that Bradley was coming. Horton walked to the bottom of the gangplank, placed the stick against his shoulder as if it were a musket, and posed first with his cowboy hat on and then brandishing it as if he were waving to a Fourth of July crowd in Cody, Wyoming. Neither picture ran, but I have always wanted to see the face of the *New York Post*'s sports-picture editor when he got the photo of the great American basketball player on the docks of Southampton.

During the two years at Oxford, I lived in a foreign world. I thrived, even though, every day, my experience told me I was an outsider. I learned the truth of the observation that some of the English are self-made and worship their creator. I also formed friendships that have lasted a lifetime, and found loves that still linger in memory. I traveled widely, indulging my yearning for new places: Italy, Spain, Czechoslovakia, Hungary, the Soviet Union, France, Syria, Israel, Lebanon, Jordan, Switzerland, Poland, Yugoslavia, East Germany, West Germany. I commuted to Milan once a month, where I played basketball on the team of the Simmanthal meat-packing firm and lived with four of my Italian teammates in a house owned by the club. I drove and camped through Byelorussia, Russia, and Ukraine, encountering the quixotic and incompetent state police for the first time.

Heading south from Moscow, three friends from Oxford and I, driving in an Austin station wagon, were followed by two Russians in a Skoda. When we stopped, they stopped. When we moved, they moved, always maintaining a comfortable distance, but always sloppy enough to show us they were there. They mysteriously disappeared when we entered Ukraine. Two weeks later, after taking a boat from Yalta, we arrived at a campground in Odessa, and were told that an unspecified epidemic had forced its closure, but that for the same one-dollar coupon we could stay at the best hotel in Odessa. After checking in, we went out for dinner and returned to find that our room had been ransacked by security agents. Later, when we tried to cross into Hungary, border guards detained us, searching every inch of our station wagon and looking at every scrap of paper in our wallets. One of the guards found a map on a small piece of paper in my wallet. He claimed it was the map of a military installation. I knew it was a drawing of directions to a good restaurant in Warsaw. During a three-hour standoff, he evidenced great interest in several novels we had in our possession, including Steinbeck's *Of Mice and Men*. We tried to convince him of how embarrassing it would be when his superiors found out that he was wrong, that there was nothing subversive about the map. Finally, as much out of spontaneity as shrewdness, we gave him the Steinbeck book and two others. He smiled, and let us pass into Hungary.

That summer, I also lived in Germany, with a family at Überlingen on the Bodensee, and tried unsuccessfully to learn the German language in six weeks. I spent Christmas in Bethlehem and Jerusalem, and New Year's Eve I was in Jordan with a group of off-duty U.N. soldiers from Australia and Scandinavia who were patrolling the Jordanian-Israeli border, which would become a tripwire for war in less than two years. In Jericho, three Palestinians outside a refugee camp elaborated in great detail on the pain of the Palestinian diaspora. In Damascus, after I had shown a certain polite (I felt) interest in a young Syrian woman whose backyard lay right below our hotel window, I was warned by a representative of the hotel that under Islamic law the father could have my hand chopped off for such boldness. Whether or not that was true I wasn't willing to find out. I stopped waving to her.

I had friends during these years who motorcycled from Beirut to Baghdad, who lived as Peace Corps teachers in Tunisia, who began to trade in African tribal art. For me and many of my contemporaries, the world seemed to be ours for the exploring. We were Americans, and we took so much for granted. Yet there was no denying the value of those years of wandering, listening, and learning.

Today, when I read in a public-opinion poll that foreign affairs are important to only 15 percent of the American people, I realize how greatly the times have changed. What transformed me into a citizen of the world—even more than the wanderlust of a small-town boy or the open-endedness of the Oxford experience—was Vietnam. For my generation of Americans, the cold war between the United States and the Soviet Union was on a level of abstraction that Vietnam was not. Being stationed in Germany or England on call as a part of NATO was not significantly different from life back home. After all, Elvis served in Germany. Vietnam was something else. When the draft notice came, you went to a shooting war in a strange country with a different worldview on the other side of the globe. And you might never come back.

Foreign affairs had a tangible effect on my generation in our college years. In my junior year at Princeton, Madame Nhu (Vietnam president Diem's sister-in-law) visited and a year later George Kennan gave the first of many brilliant speeches, raising troubling questions about the war. Vietnam, of course, was a subject of constant discussion among undergraduates. The first order of business was always to decide whether one had an obligation to serve or not. Some said you had no such obligation, because it was an unjust war. A few said that patriotism required you to put aside all questions of justice and serve your country. There were those who thought it was a war of imperialism that should be resisted by violence, if necessary. Others said that the war's morality was sufficiently gray that obligation to country outweighed any personal hesitation. Still others claimed that whether the war was just or unjust, you could use any means available to escape any kind of military service in order to pursue your own interests, the country be damned. Many said that if you ever wanted to enter elective politics—as it appeared a third of the senior class at Princeton contemplated—then you had to be a veteran, preferably a decorated veteran. I participated in some of those discussions, but at the time I failed to appreciate how much this war would affect me. I was too isolated, both by my minifame as a basketball player and by the prospect of Oxford. And after all, that spring Lyndon Johnson had said, when he substantially raised the U.S. troop commitment, that our troops would be home soon. At some point I knew I would be subject to the military draft, but as I watched LBJ's speech in the middle of writing my senior thesis on Harry Truman's 1940 senatorial campaign, the implications of this troop deployment simply did not register with me.

At Oxford, the Vietnam debate became a great deal more pointed. I remember a Protestant student from Northern Ireland saying to an American friend of mine, "You'll be the best-educated corpse in Vietnam." Some of my Princeton classmates had already lost their lives in Southeast Asian jungles. Discussions with friends and strangers became intense, even heated, and forced me to read about Vietnam in the context of Asia. I found myself wanting to understand the country that impinged so strongly on my future. It seemed to me that the role of communism there, though prominent in most analyses, did not begin to compare in importance to the historical, ethnic, and religious tensions in Vietnam. Americans had to know more—not only about American interests and intentions but about the internal dynamics of Asia itself. Only Kennan, whose containment theory of fighting communism had guided a generation of U.S. policy makers, saw that the 1965 anticommunist coup in Indonesia had invalidated the belief that Asian countries were a stack of dominoes ready to fall.

In the meantime, a former British Foreign Office intellectual, Harry T. Willets, my tutor in international relations at Worcester College, probed and challenged and questioned enough to keep me reading and thinking long after the tutorial was over. I wrote papers on the prewar Japan–East Asian co-prosperity sphere, on Germany during the postwar occupation, on the roots of the cold war, and on the Suez crisis. A lecture on the Cultural Revolution in China depicted that society as being in the middle of changes that were so bizarre as to be unbelievable. The ossification of the Kremlin—something I had seen firsthand in encounters with its police apparatus the previous summer—was simultaneously sobering and laughable, fundamentally uninteresting, and profoundly threatening. And Vietnam became a metaphor for much more than a certain kind of misguided military strategy. Different people, I could see, had arrived at different conclusions about America's role there. In America, the media and the intellectuals were the first to see the futility and wrongheadedness of our endeavor. Most Americans never did. Richard Nixon, who in his 1968 election campaign said he had a secret plan to end the Vietnam War, won re-election in 1972 with the war still in full force. But whatever the politics surrounding the war, no one could assert that what happened eight thousand miles away from the continental United States had no relevance to life here. Among a certain age group, the war still arouses the old feelings with an intensity that the passage of time has not diminished.

I was not an early opponent of the war. There were powerful psychological forces in me that gave people in authority the benefit of the doubt. In the international intellectual hothouse that was Oxford, I found myself frequently attacked for being an American. When another American criticized President Johnson or American policy in Vietnam, I listened, and often I agreed. But when an Englishman or a Pakistani or a Frenchman lambasted LBJ and our involvement, my visceral reaction was to defend the actions of my country. I felt that I couldn't make a judgment about Vietnam until I knew as much as the war's proponents and opponents did. As usual, I expected the unexplored nuance to be the decisive factor.

By 1968, however, the error of our involvement had become evident to me. To make a commitment and never review it was an impossibly narrow interpretation of the word "commitment." As the economist John Maynard Keynes once said when asked why he had changed his position on an issue, "When circumstances change, I change my view. What do you do?" I came to believe that the conflict in Vietnam was a civil war, that victory would never be clear-cut unless Vietnam were made a colony or leveled, that we had erred in turning Ho Chi Minh away when he sought American counsel in the struggle against French colonialism and the imperial Chinese, that Ike was right about not getting involved in a land war in Asia, and that President Kennedy had been reckless with his talk about the Green Berets' ability to handle virtually any circumstance. The war belonged to JFK and LBJ, but their actions were consistent with a long-standing mindset that put too much faith in the Pentagon and its cost/benefit military and political analysis. The analytical error of our involvement was the failure to understand the depth of Vietnamese nationalism or to make distinctions among governments labeled "communist." Above all, the war raised a red flag about any future military action that did not enjoy, after an open national debate, the full backing of the American people and support from the international community.

In 1967, my Oxford idyll was coming to an end. I contemplated joining the Army for a tour of four years, with a possible teaching position at West Point forming a part of it. I thought about taking my chances and waiting until I got a draft notice. Ultimately, I joined the Air Force Reserve and competed successfully with other, nonreserve recruits to enter Officer Training School at Lackland Air Force Base, in San Antonio, Texas, followed by Personnel Officer Training at the Air Force base in Amarillo. My reserve unit's home was McGuire AFB, in Wrightstown, New Jersey, and I served on active duty for nearly six months in 1967, joining the Knicks in midseason. For the next five years, my reserve unit met one weekend a month and two weeks in the summer, augmenting the Military Airlift Command's active-duty forces. (My old reserve unit kept planes in the air twenty-two hours a day during Operation Desert Storm in 1991.)

My interest in politics was growing, and on one of my weekend tours I ordered all the men in my wing to the base theater, where I showed them Leni Riefenstahl's great movie about Nazism, *Triumph of the Will*. At its end, I asked the men to ponder what we could do to assure that such a right-wing coup never took place in the United States. Full of coffee and cannoli, courtesy of Sergeant Joseph Ferrara of Brooklyn, they offered no new theories.

I didn't see myself as a budding secretary of state, even though in high school I had answered "Diplomat" to questions about career choice, but in my off season with the Knicks, I continued to travel. After an eight-month season with a hundred and twenty games—sixty on the road—I would sometimes spend the summer on the road abroad. During the basketball season, with the help of acquaintances at the U.N., or the State Department, or various professors at universities, I would compile lists of interesting people in Kuala Lumpur or Bombay or Kabul. These were journalists, government officials, academics, businessmen, social activists. When I arrived in town, I'd call their offices, usually giving a mutual friend as a reference, and ask if I could meet them. Often they said yes. Sometimes the meeting would end after fifteen minutes, but occasionally it would extend into lunch or dinner. I kept notebooks of these travels, and by the time I entered politics, I had spent a decade working hard to broaden my international horizons.

My enthusiasm for new places and different people grew. The Bamian Valley in Afghanistan, with its huge Buddhas carved into the mountainside, reminded me that before Islam there was Buddhism. The island of Bali in Indonesia introduced me to the Hindu story of the Ramayana and showed me how animism still shaped lives. While I was flying around the U.S. with my Knick teammates, they used to joke that if someone in an airport wore a turban, they would find me talking with him. A basketball friend in Prague, traumatized by the events of 1968; the colored South African political prisoner in exile at Oxford and in despair about apartheid; the Italian businessman who described in detail how he had bested the clumsy communist-run markets of Eastern Europe; the young Chinese graduate student in Singapore who said in 1970 that China was a building wave—these and countless other people filled in my picture of the world. I agreed with Carlyle that the great individual could shape events, and with Tolstoy that chance played an important role in every historical event, but most of all I agreed with the French historian Fernand Braudel that geography formed a people.

In the Senate, geopolitics became a special area of interest.

My work on the Senate Select Committee on Intelligence, to which I was appointed in 1985, went a long way toward furthering my knowledge of the world, particularly in the areas of defense and foreign policy. Before I joined the committee, I knew little about the intelligence business. Whenever I had brushed up against it, the results had been partly offensive, partly comical. Once during my Oxford years, after I had worked out in the gym at the U.S. Air Force base at Upper Heyford, an Air Force officer asked me to come by his office. When I walked in and sat down, he asked me if I would be willing to inform him about antiwar activities among Americans at Oxford. I said no, got up, and walked out. A couple of years later, after one of my postseason trips to Asia, I was invited for a drink at the apartment of a retired admiral who was on the board of Madison Square Garden. He told me that he had heard I went abroad every year in the off season, and he suggested that on future trips I might function as an intelligence agent on the streets of Asia. Promoting a six-foot-five Caucasian as an undercover agent in Asia did not strike me as the wisest of moves. I accepted my assignment to the committee in a state of low expectations.

Unlike other committees, the members of the Intelligence Committee in both the House and the Senate are appointed by the party leaders. When the committee was established, in the wake of the CIA and Watergate scandals of the mid-1970s, the Congress limited membership to a time period not to exceed eight years: terms were for four years, six years, or eight years. I asked and was appointed for six years by Robert Byrd, and my appointment was extended to eight years by George Mitchell. The purpose of the term limitation is to avoid a cozy relationship between the intelligence community and those charged with holding it accountable, but new members, though they may guarantee the committee's independence, don't bring much knowledge to the job. In every Congress they have to go through the equivalent of a course in Intelligence 101.

The committee has two major responsibilities. It approves the top-secret budget for the entire intelligence community: the CIA, the NSA (National Security Agency), the NRO (National Reconnaissance Office), the DIA (Defense Intelligence Agency), and the intelligence sections of the FBI and the State Department. It also oversees covert intelligence activities, for which it seeks both success and full value for taxpayers' investment.

The CIA monitors and assesses events worldwide for the president and the Congress. The Defense Intelligence Agency works primarily for the Defense Department. The NRO manages the worldwide satellite system that (among other things) allows the NSA to monitor telephonic messages. The bulk of the intelligence community's money is spent on satellite reconnaissance systems, which can photograph virtually any place in the world or tune into any electronic signal moving through the earth's atmosphere. The people who work in the CIA are divided into analytical and operational divisions. The analytical side of the CIA takes all the information that flows in from all worldwide sources and with it answers critical questions. What did Soviet troop movements in the vicinity of Afghanistan mean? What methods of concealment did the Soviets use to hide their long-range missiles? How would a change in China's leadership affect its military strategy or its economic policy? How vulnerable were Soviet offensive missiles to U.S. strategic defenses? What did missile tests by China and by the Soviets imply about their technology? Could Soviet sensor systems track our nuclear subs? How far along were Pakistan, South Africa, Israel, Iran, or Argentina in attempting to develop nuclear capability?

The operational side of the CIA, on the other hand, is made up of traditional spy-handlers. They are the undercover agents of John le Carré and Tom Clancy novels, who during the cold war sought to penetrate the decision-making processes of the adversary. They pursued and enlisted people in the Soviet or Cuban or Chinese political systems to give us information on what their governments were planning, how they interpreted U.S. policies, what their assessment of our military capability was, and how they would be likely to attack us in the event of war.

On rare occasions, the operational division went "proactive," seeking to support, covertly or indirectly, opponents of a regime that was conducting activities hostile or threatening to U.S. interests. Unlike the days before the creation of the Select Committees on Intelligence, when CIA disruptions led to Salvador Allende's murder in Chile, Mohammad Mosaddeq's overthrow in Iran, and comically ineffective attempts to assassinate Fidel Castro with exploding cigars, the proactive moves of the late 1980s were conventional. What were new and disturbing were what I called overt/covert wars in Nicaragua, Angola, and Afghanistan. Essentially, these were efforts to supply rebels with military aid ranging from tents to missiles. Shrouding U.S. involvement in secrecy was sometimes seen as a convenient way to limit our liability if things turned bad. And things turned bad all too often, in part because intelligence operatives were not as publicly accountable or as professionally skilled as U.S. military officers. The overt/covert wars had mixed results.

I thought we were making a colossal blunder in Angola. I had no sense that Jonas Savimbi, our client guerrilla warrior, was any more committed to democracy than was the country's dictatorial leftist leadership. When Gorbachev pulled the plug on Soviet aid to the Angolan government, we had absolutely no reason to persist in aiding Savimbi. But by then he had hired an effective Washington lobbying firm, which successfully obtained further funding.

In Afghanistan, however, I thought we had a major opportunity to respond to blatant aggression by the Soviet Union. I had been an advocate of helping the Mujahedin since 1980, and I felt that the Soviet invaders would not succeed where everyone from Alexander the Great to the British in the nineteenth century had failed. The mountains of the Hindu Kush were nearly impenetrable to an invading army, and the Islamic fundamentalists who inhabited them were fierce guerrilla fighters. In 1985, with three other U.S. senators—David Boren (D.-Okla.), Chic Hecht (R.-Nev.), and Orrin Hatch (R.-Utah)—I visited refugee sites outside Peshawar, Pakistan, and nine miles from the Khyber Pass. The camps there were full of sick and frightened women and children, who had fled south from such Soviet atrocities as giving children toys that exploded. After a tour of the camps, we sat at a table under an open-air tent before three hundred active and former Mujahedin freedom fighters in turbans and flowing pants. As Hatch, our delegation leader, was introduced, the guerrillas began chanting, the chant growing into a roar. Men whose legs had been lost to Soviet land mines sat in the front row, next to men who had only one eye and no patch over the bad one. Some of them held rifles. We told them that America was committed to helping their cause, and they listened to us through an interpreter, cocking their turbaned heads to the side as if they were birds on a perch.

As I sat there, my mind raced back fifteen years to a visit I made during the basketball off season to the Hindu Kush in search of the blue-eyed Kafirs who had remained deep in these mountains since Alexander's day. I was accompanied by two Afghan men from Kabul and three guides wearing ammunition belts over their shoulders and carrying rifles. One of them, Mr. Schpoon, was a poet. The following fall, he was accepted at the Iowa Writers' Workshop, and I got him a job waiting tables in Central Park on his way to Iowa City. The other, Mr. Amin, later became an information officer for a group of the Mujahedin and came to see me several times in Washington. Whether we were squatting together in a mountain village in the Hindu Kush having tea amidst the flies or sitting in my office having coffee amidst the Senate buzzers, our easy familiarity—like our common desire to expel the Soviets—masked a vast difference in our assumptions about what was possible or even desirable in politics and in life. Getting beyond those differences in worldview and values was the key to a deeper bond.

The U.S. involvement in a place such as Afghanistan, so far from our borders, was problematic, but the aid created a certain irony. It placed us in the same relation to the Afghan rebels as the Soviets had had to the North Vietnamese—that of supplier and adviser to soldiers who needed no motivation. Orrin Hatch, on the same 1985 trip, had put into motion steps that would lead to giving the Mujahedin handheld Stinger missiles, which could shoot down Soviet helicopter gunships and fighter bombers. That action stopped what the late President Zia of Pakistan feared would have been the easy advance of Soviet forces through Pakistan to the long-desired Russian and Soviet dream, a warm-water port. By the end of the eighties, on trips to Moscow, I sensed that the cost of Soviet occupation had become too much. I saw officially tolerated films of Afghanistan veterans who sounded like Vietnam veterans—demoralized and angry, unable to see what they had been fighting for, and shocked by the hostility of the native people. More Russians were being killed. An organization called Mothers Against the Afghan War attracted members as more Russians came home in coffins. Soviet rock groups began to sing protest songs about the war.

On our side, the problem with our supply effort to the Mujahedin was our inability to know whom to trust. There was little unity among the various Islamic groups. Supply lines for sophisticated missiles were constantly in jeopardy, and on occasion we couldn't keep track of where the missiles were. But on the whole, our effort did speed up the withdrawal of Soviet troops, with its attendant loss of face for the Soviet military. Along with the deployment of Pershing II missiles in Europe, the growing deterioration of the Soviet economy, and his own sense of historic opportunity, it convinced Gorbachev to seek accommodation with the West.

The trouble with the intelligence business was how it often changed those who practiced it. Suspicion, control, and secrecy dominated where curiosity, flexibility, and openness should have ruled. Though the CIA had, person for person, the brightest people in government, most of whom were hardworking and dedicated (in Vietnam, during another era, it was the only government voice arguing that no amount of bombing would stop the North from seeking to win the South and that U.S. withdrawal would not harm our basic security interests), it failed to reward the contrarian view. Over the years, this tendency hardened. Like any giant bureaucracy of the old mold, it rewarded the company line, which during the cold war was a rigid demonization of the Soviet Union. There was plenty wrong with this communist totalitarian state, but when you spend your whole life finding ways in which it threatened our way of life without ever asking why the hostility existed in the first place, or how religious faith and the yearning for freedom could survive communism's onslaught, it is not surprising that you couldn't tell an olive branch from a poisoned arrow. The CIA counted missile silos and assembled enemy battle plans from thousands of bits of information, as if its analysts were jigsaw-puzzle champions. But it missed what was in people's hearts and minds and what gave their lives meaning and how that shaped their worldview and sense of the possible. It missed the Iranian Revolution in 1979, and the rise of Solidarity in Poland. It didn't see the collapse of Soviet communism coming. The failure to anticipate the crumbling Soviet Empire—a mistake of monumental proportions—prevented us from even thinking in advance about a strategy for helping to move a failed communist society into the world of democratic capitalism.

Because of compartmentalization, one section of the agency often couldn't know what another part was doing. Instead of interacting freely with your colleagues, you were supposed to do your job, pass information up the line, and trust someone else to draw the connections. Such secrecy, over time, became a normal way of working, and it distorted the agency's collective judgment. It also left the spy-catching to the agency's internal police. Removing the incentive and opportunity for each analyst to keep an eye out and report suspicious activities made the counterintelligence function less robust. The attitude that took hold was "It's not my responsibility," the intelligence community's version of the old bureaucratic excuse. The Aldrich Ames case was the most serious example of betrayal that went undiscovered for years, but there were several other examples in the 1980s. Spies in our government operated because they thought they could get away with it—and they could, because the agency didn't know its workers well enough to insist on adequate safeguards. The astonishing aspect of these betrayals is that no one in any real authority has been punished and no one has stepped forward honorably to assume responsibility for the failures. The verb "to stonewall" comes from the cloak-and-dagger world, in which deniability can erase the facts.

The agency's continuing problem is that a big part of its mission runs counter to the best of American ideals. Open speech, not secrecy, is America's strength. In the legitimate need to protect ourselves from a real threat coming from the Soviet Union, we deadened the nerves that make us special. An atmosphere of spying breeds distrust among neighbors and between the state and its citizens. Intelligence operations that guard a free democratic society must always include a refusal to go beyond a certain point, or there will no longer be freedom for the intelligence community to protect. Operatives who break the law to safeguard American interests in fact subvert those interests.

During its budget discussions with the Intelligence Committee, the CIA, acting as the lead intelligence agency and sometimes on behalf of the other agencies in the intelligence community, treated committee members like assets, which in the spy trade is the lingo for an agent whom a case officer is trying to "run," or control. In battles over the budget, the CIA was rarely, if ever, denied a surveillance system or covert activity it labeled as critical. The key to the agency's lobbying success was its great effort to make the chairmen of the House and Senate committees into advocates rather than overseers. During my eight years, the Senate committee was chaired by the Republican David Durenberger and the Democrat David Boren, both of whom had a different kind of power from the chairman of any other Senate committee. They were in the loop on all top-secret decisions. No presidential administration wanted to be accused of bypassing Congress on a matter of national security, so the gang of four—the chairmen of the House and Senate Intelligence committees, the Senate majority leader, and the House Speaker—were informed of breaking developments by the CIA almost simultaneously with the White House. Often, the ranking members and the minority leaders were also included. Our chairman was invariably flattered by calls from the agency about small nuances of policy changes. He was constantly asked for his opinions. He was invited to breakfasts, lunches, and top-secret briefings. A chairman would slowly become molded by the community; he molded the community hardly at all— though Boren made a valiant effort. A chairman increasingly saw himself as part of the policy-making apparatus, championing and defending "his" agency. Moreover, while the cold war was on, who would say no to the latest technofix, even if it cost three billion dollars? Any expenditure could be justified as essential if it gave us a real or imagined edge over the U.S.S.R. in virtually any respect.

Our oversight of the CIA's special clandestine activity and its covert actions was more successful than our efforts to trim the overall intelligence budget. Periodically, the CIA would come before the Senate Select Committee with a list of proposed clandestine actions after the entire community's budget had already been approved. If we wanted to end an action at that point, the only way was to cut the discretionary budget, which amounted to a contingency fund used for covert actions. In my eight years on the committee, we made frequent attempts to cut the discretionary budget, all of them to no avail. Though senators failed to cut off funds, they nonetheless could have an impact on policy by remarking that a proposed covert action was colossally dumb. Laying out objections powerfully, senators could convince the agency to postpone, alter, or even cancel the action. These kinds of exchanges were how oversight was supposed to work, in principle. In practice, the intelligence community had to be candid and the senators had to be fully knowledgeable—a rare combination.

The committee met on the second floor of the Hart Senate Office Building, in a large air-conditioned vault that was impenetrable by hostile intelligence services and was much smaller than the usual hearing room. There were fifteen of us on the committee, and we sat on a dais, as in ordinary hearing rooms, with a bench for staff behind us. In front of the dais was a table that could seat six witnesses, and behind the table were chairs for staff accompanying the witnesses. On one wall was a map of the world, and the other walls usually held pictures from the state represented by the chairman. It was an intimate setting in which to review the government's most sensitive activities. No information that came close to exposing an intelligence source could be discussed outside the room. Every word spoken was recorded on tape. Sometimes, the clerk would interrupt a witness in order to replace a used cassette with a new one. In the beginning, I couldn't imagine what importance these records would have to anyone except the eccentric historian. Then a series of actions that came to be known as Iran-contra burst on the scene. Teams of staff researchers and lawyers pored over every word. Questions that had been asked in secrecy were now available to hundreds of people, and I was pleased that there was sufficient information on the record for an aggressive prosecution. I believe that some of the principal players, especially Oliver North, escaped conviction on technicalities. (Senator Chuck Robb—a Democrat from Virginia—in the closing days of his successful 1994 Senate race against North, summarized many people's feelings about the colonel in one of the all-time great partisan blasts: "My opponent is a document-shredding, Constitution-trashing, commander-in-chief-bashing, Congress-thrashing, uniform-shaming, Ayatollah-loving, arms-dealing, criminal-protecting, résumé-misrepresenting, Noriega-coddling, Social Security–threatening, public-school-denigrating, Swiss-banking, law-breaking, letter-faking, self-serving, election-losing, snake-oil salesman who can't tell the difference between the truth and a lie!")

In my first two years as a member of the committee, I spent fifteen hours a week in the vault learning the structure of the intelligence systems and the personnel who ran them. I visited the NSA, the DIA, the CIA, and talked with many of their analysts. I visited the covert-action centers and the disguise-and-magic-tricks house. My second two years were dominated by events in the Soviet Union and by Iran-contra. I believed and still believe that the Iran-contra cover-up went right to Ronald Reagan and was one of his administration's most significant accomplishments. The whole episode raised basic questions about the relations among the executive, legislative, and judicial branches of government, questions that are never finally answered in our democracy.

I also oversaw the contra war for the committee. I had once supported aboveboard military aid to the contras, until I saw that many of the recipients and much of the process had been corrupted by a lack of accountability. But part of my responsibility, since I had voted for the one hundred million dollars of military aid, was to do everything possible to see that it was spent properly. Every week, the agency would explain what had happened the previous week, what goals had been set for the next several weeks, and how they analyzed the evolving political and military situation. Every week, I asked countless questions, trying to assure myself that actions taken were pursuant to established guidelines and that the operatives were doing no more or less than Congress had authorized. Such in-depth oversight taught me that unless you asked a detailed, direct question, even responsible public officials would not volunteer their true concerns or reveal their ultimate motives. In addition, amidst swirling events, it was difficult to know whether the response was the truth, a partial version of the truth, or a figment of some-one's imagination.

Before I traveled anyplace officially, I always sought an intelligence briefing (which included military and national security dimensions as well as economic and political assessments) about my destinations, and I tried to meet with U.S. or foreign officials in each country who I thought could give me further insights. After I became familiar with how the in-telligence system itself worked, I focused on the five countries that I be-lieved were most important to our future: Japan, China, Russia, Germany, and Mexico. I visited all but China on a regular basis, and I met in Washington with visiting politicians from each. Gradually, I began to be more aware of how power flowed in each country. I began to form my own hunches about what would happen there, and I tested these hunches against events over time.

More than ever, I saw that what happened in foreign policy affected domestic policy. Preparing for war had shaped our budget priorities and scientific-research efforts for two generations. With 20 percent of our national income dependent on exports and our deficit being financed by foreign capital, what happened to our living standard was being deter-mined every day by foreign investors and consumers. But domestic pol-icy also affected foreign policy. Just as after the Second World War American affluence at home provided the material and psychological basis for the use of American power abroad, so today a loss of affluence would endanger our role in the world. In addition, domestic politics, with its vulnerability to television images, may well make it impossible to deploy U.S. power overseas in the event of the death of even one American soldier—a situation that threatens to cripple our diplomatic efforts. A diplomacy without a perceived willingness to use force or a diplomacy tied more to polls and television images than to long-term na-tional interest invites failure and opens the way for bullies to swagger across the globe.

From my first trip to the Soviet Union as a senator in 1979, I realized the importance of something rather mundane—a good interpreter. On that trip, our group met in the Kremlin with Premier Aleksei Kosygin, whose blue eyes were like laser beams shooting across the long, green-felt-covered table. After several questions and answers, our congres-sional delegation leader, Senator Joe Biden, said skeptically, "Mr. Premier, be careful what you say to me. Where I come from we have a saying—you can't shit a shitter." Later I asked the American interpreter, Bill Kreimer, how he had translated the statement. The veteran of all the Nixon and Carter summits replied, "Not literally." In 1990, I was part of a delegation led by Majority Leader George Mitchell. In a meeting with Mikhail Gorbachev, our group raised the prospect of independence for the Baltic states. When we began discussing the situation in Lithuania, then under the presidency of Vytautas Landsbergis, a former professor of music and a particularly dedicated democrat, Gorbachev responded through his Russian interpreter that if Lithuania persisted in pushing for independence on a fast track, the Soviet Union would take steps that conveyed to the Lithuanians that their efforts would be fruitless. Two days later, the delegation's State Department interpreter sidled up to me as I was walking across the Kremlin grounds and said that the Soviet interpreter had exercised what I had come to call the Bill Kreimer option. What Gorbachev had actually said, when asked about Lithuania and Landsbergis, was an old Russian peasant expression: "If Landsbergis fails to do exactly what I demand, I will skin him like Sidor's goat." Not all interpreters are as skillful and diplomatic as Kreimer. In 1992, I led a delegation consisting of Senator Bob Kerrey and Congressman Jim Leach from the farm states of Nebraska and Iowa, respectively. In St. Petersburg, we met with the head of the largest private chicken farm in Russia. I broke the ice by saying, "In our country we have a saying: 'Those who raise chickens raise hell.' " The faces of Kerrey and Leach seemed to say, "We do?" But the Russians' faces went sullen. Later our interpreter from the embassy said that the chicken farmer's interpreter had translated my opener as "Those who raise chickens go to Hell."

WHEN THE COLD WAR ended, we were left with a giant intelligence apparatus targeted at the U.S.S.R. On the face of it, there was much less need for this massive investment, but bureaucracies don't self-immolate. They seek to perpetuate themselves. What happened was predictable. The old monolithic military threat was replaced by a variety of ambiguous threats: military, economic, ethnic, environmental. The intelligence community surveyed the world for that evil force whose activities could endanger our future. Japan was a possible target. Nationalism was resurgent there, and they were often untrustworthy, predatory traders. Islam was another potential enemy. After all, Muslim countries controlled the world's oil, and some fundamentalist regimes had declared their implacable hostility to the West. Given a few dashed expectations about progress and a predictably entrenched ethnic awareness, a Russian and Slavic Orthodox threat was not impossible to imagine. China, with its burgeoning economy, proud national traditions, modernizing military, and enormous population, also merited close scrutiny. The intelligence community started selling a menu of needs that only they could meet. Whether it was information on terrorism or trade negotiations, ethnic consciousness or economic secrets, refugee migrations or religious fanaticism, nuclear nonproliferation or the formation of new governments, environmental pollution or technological breakthroughs, the intelligence community argued that it alone was capable of gathering the information necessary for prudent, farsighted policy makers. Few questioned whether the CIA was the institution best suited to gather, analyze, and coordinate information on a world infinitely more complex than the old bipolar world.

For forty-five years, our leadership in the world had come primarily from our ability to protect other nations against an obvious military threat coming from the Soviet Union. Now that threat is gone, perhaps forever, and no equivalent threat, notwithstanding the CIA's view, exists. The new question that needs to be answered today is: what now is the nature of America's leadership in the world? In some places, such as East Asia, there is a continuity of role for the U.S. Our military strength remains crucial. Japan has huge wealth but much difficulty communicating to the outside world. The U.S. presence remains a balance wheel and the best insurance against an arms race between China and Japan. In Europe our role is less central, in part because of European integration and Russia's desire for peace. But, more than ever, I believe that our leadership will come from the power of our example: the strength of our economy and the dynamism of our society. The most appealing aspects of America relate to our pluralism as a multiracial, multiethnic nation; our democratic form of government, in which people not only vote but actively participate; and our economy, which, when it works well, offers unparalleled opportunity. The real question posed for an American president is how to take advantage of these strengths without self-righteous proselytizing.

Once a year for the last fourteen years, I have held seminars in New Jersey for the state's high-school students. For that day, the students become senators, grappling with such issues as how to reduce the budget deficit or how to define America's role in the world. Many of the sons and daughters of new immigrants attend these seminars, and they offer unique perspectives. One day, in a discussion on America's role in the world, a particularly glib, predictably liberal, suburban kid was arguing that whether a country was communist or not was simply a matter of how its economy was organized. Then a student, a Cuban American from Union City, just across the Hudson River from midtown Manhattan, described the routine workings of the totalitarian society he had escaped from at age ten. He remembered block committees that monitored the movements of his parents and the parents of his schoolmates, taking note of when they left home and when they returned. He talked about his sisters' and brothers' being unable to study what they wanted; about being denied food for speaking out against some aspect of everyday life; about being forbidden to start a social club because the authorities considered it counterrevolutionary; about being unable to travel; about being harassed constantly by the police. The room became silent. Many of the aspects of daily life that the other students had taken for granted appeared to be privileges in this light. Everyone in the room, including me, felt the power of the Cuban American's personal experience. It wasn't theory— it was real life. Pollyanna-ish views of communism were as off the mark as mindless puffery of American virtue. Above all, sunny convictions about the perfectibility of man had to be regarded skeptically. After hearing the stories of people who fled tyranny in many countries, I had to temper a belief in progress and peace with a record of humankind's evil deeds.

I've met frequently with first-generation New Jerseyans. They usually detested the government in power in their old country. Often, that government was communist or authoritarian. I listened to their stories of oppression, depravation, torture, and expropriation. A survivor of the Ukrainian famine of the 1930s described Stalin's officially sanctioned starvation of four million people. I learned about the Sandinista technique of placing an unclothed prisoner in a cell built entirely of metal. A survivor of the Holocaust showed me the number that had been tattooed on his arm in a concentration camp, and a survivor of the Cultural Revolution in China told of the knock on the door in the middle of the night, and of how the next day she was on her way to a re-education camp thousands of miles away, where she would live in solitary confinement for long periods of time. When the foundations of totalitarianism began to give way, I thought of these stories and the thousands of others that could now be told. We need to lay out the record, so that these deeds will not be repeated. Memory is the current that lights up the new world.

A German friend of mine was put in charge of the files of the East German Stasi (secret police) in Berlin, after East Germany ceased to exist. I toured the archives one winter afternoon in 1994. "That's the Stasi smell," an assistant to my friend said, as we walked through the narrow, low-ceilinged corridors in the five-story gray stone headquarters, whose odor seemed to mix the aroma of old paper with the stench of disinfectant. "We can't seem to get it out." We came to a room that was full of giant card catalogues, which were in turn full of cards for tens of thousands of people. Each card had a person's name on it, some brief information about his or her life, and a number referring to a more complete file somewhere else in the complex. In another room, notebooks were stacked four feet high on shelves. I opened one at random and read the report of a Stasi agent monitoring the movements of another East German from the time he left his house—to work, to lunch, to the store, and on through the day—until he returned home. We got into a small elevator, went up a floor, and walked up some concrete steps, until we came into a room in which there were rows and rows of shelves. On the shelves were small jars, each containing a felt strip suspended from the lid. The assistant director explained that, when people were interrogated by the Stasi, they were forced to attach the felt strip to the back of their trousers or their skirt and sit on it during the questioning. Afterward, the strip was removed and placed in a jar with the person's name on it.

"Why?" I asked.

"So that, if the police ever wanted to find this person, they had his scent, which they could give to a dog to help track him down," the assistant director replied.

Seeing the Berlin Wall fall gave hope to people around the world that they too might someday achieve freedom. The end of communist rule in the Soviet Union ratified the policies of nine U.S. presidents, twenty-three U.S. Congresses, and three generations of foreign-policy experts. The end of the U.S.S.R. itself was an equally momentous shift. With the success of democratic revolution in many Third World countries, the end of apartheid in South Africa, the Palestinian-Israeli rapprochement, and the Jordanian-Israeli peace, the world appeared to be changing radically almost overnight.

For some Americans, the end of the cold war was disorienting. I remember in 1988 talking with a team of Army officers who had just come back from observing a Soviet Army exercise pursuant to an agreement arrived at during Gorbachev's *perestroika*. They were slightly depressed. What bothered them was how easy the intelligence information was to gather. These officers had spent their careers compiling pictures of the enemy's strength from fragmentary evidence gleaned from a multitude of sources. Now they could see it all for themselves. The challenge and the stakes of their professions were diminished, and they felt it.

Archibald MacLeish once wrote, "A people who have been real to themselves because they were *for* something cannot continue to be real to themselves when they find they are merely *against* something." During the forty-five-year cold war, we had a politics that was primarily "against something." It deformed our political debate. It deadened our intelligence and idealism. Now, with communism a diminishing force, we are uncertain about our place in the global politics of the future, even as we are relieved and energized. Will we once again be able to sustain ourselves by being "*for* something"?

Although this loss of a villain has affected everyone in the political process, it has probably affected Republicans more than it has Democrats. I remember sitting on the edge of a bed at the Hyatt Hotel in Key West early on New Year's Day in 1992, unable to sleep. I flipped on the television, turned to C-Span, and found Frank Fahrenkopf, the former Republican national chairman, saying that the economy would hurt President Bush's re-election chances but what was more ominous was the fall of the Soviet Empire. He went on to explain that anticommunism was the foundation of the modern Republican coalition. It gave the Republican internationalists a cause, allowed the old right, in the tradition of Senator Robert Taft, the excuse to accept bigger government, and brought the far-right, John Birch Society types into the mainstream.

As it was for many Americans my age, the nuclear threat had always been a part of my life. When I was twelve years old, I made a diagram of my own bomb shelter. I had a place for my cot, my favorite foods, my favorite books, and my basketball. (The assumption behind my selection of possessions was that even after a nuclear holocaust there would still be basketball.) I and millions of other Americans had lived every day with the threat of nuclear war. Now it was all over. The world, while not able to live as one, was a safer place.

But peace has its price in jobs as well as throw weight. I saw that firsthand in 1992, during one of my campaign visits to Missouri. There were five days left in the presidential campaign, and I went to St. Louis to attend a thank-you breakfast for local Democratic fund-raisers, which was given by the Democratic gubernatorial candidate, Mel Carnahan. After the breakfast, I went to what was billed as a labor rally for Mc-Donnell Douglas workers at a UAW hall in Bridgeton. The giant aircraft manufacturer had seemed invulnerable to the business cycle in the 1980s, when the Reagan defense buildup kept orders for planes high. Then the cold war ended, just at a time when worldwide competition in airplane manufacturing increased. Thousands of McDonnell Douglas workers lost their jobs.

When I arrived at the union hall, only twenty people were present, and by the time I was due to start speaking no more than thirty had appeared. The overheated hall smelled of stale cigarettes. The union organizer was apologetic, saying that he hadn't gotten the final word that I was coming until two days before. I had to do something, so I turned the "rally" into a talking-and-listening session. What did they think, and what did they want? Health care? Jobs? What were their expectations of a Democratic president?

These workers weren't formally educated. They combined the patriotism of the cold war with the parochialism of a small place in a big country. They questioned little, worked hard, and counted on the promise of a pension tomorrow. On and off, they had worked two jobs in order to give their kids a better life. They ate what they pleased, slow-danced to country-and-western, and occasionally bought *Playboy*. They were the children of the Depression and the Second World War, a few years from retirement—and now they were unemployed. One of the men in the hall was Lucky Cantrell, who had once been convicted of misappropriating union funds. In 1972, according to long-forgotten rumors, he (then a local pol) was going to run against me if I had returned to Missouri to stand for state treasurer. On this union hall visit, he was especially insistent that Democrats should point out how Reagan and Bush used government to enrich their economic class: "welfare for the rich," he called it. The rest listened and nodded. Their faces expressed anxiety. America was full of people with faces like that in 1992. They were too skeptical to believe in politicians and too tired to be inspired by celebrity, but they thought Clinton would be no worse than Bush.

Beyond partisan advantage and more than economic or social issues, the loss of the cold war's negative organizing force would change American politics in unpredictable ways. Many historians have said that America seems prone to see its politics in terms of a simple struggle between good and evil. Evil usually takes the form of some aspect of American society. If only that particular aspect were eliminated, America would again be pure. At different times, this "evil" role has been played by the Catholic Church, by gold-standard advocates, by big business, foreigners, Mormons, corrupt politicians, liquor, and for forty-five years by communists. With the collapse of communism, the domestic political process is at a watershed. It can scurry around looking for the next enemy, foreign or domestic. Or it can improve what we have by moving toward a more mature polity—less xenophobic, more generous, more tolerant, more able to cultivate and lead and play to the best impulses of the American people.

A key to our world leadership as a pluralistic democracy with a growing economy is our knowledge of other cultures. Americans can travel to other nations to learn about them, and they can learn from Americans of different national backgrounds. What is essential is that we now look outward and avoid being consumed by inward-looking, shortsighted, ethnocentric politics.

More immigrants have come to America in the last fifteen years than arrived in the previous fifty years. The new wave has brought to New Jersey Poles, Portuguese, Chinese, Koreans, Russian Jews, Egyptians, Filipinos, Colombians, Asian Indians, Turks, Ecuadorians, and Palestinians. As one who grew up in a world that was white and black, Catholic and Protestant, urban and small-town, I find in the ethnic diversity of New Jersey a microcosm of the world. Different languages challenge. Different customs enrich. Different political ideas broaden. Different attitudes about the world surprise. Different perceptions of American reality enlighten. Simply by doing my job representing the state, I learn a great deal about many countries.

I had traveled the world for thirty years, it occurred to me—seeking insight and understanding, fascinated by all that was different from the norm of a small Missouri town. Now America, and New Jersey itself, was offering some of what I had traveled to find. If we can absorb these new influences that make us a world society, even as we take note of the perspectives they offer about who we are as Americans, we can truly show the world the future. Ironically, all the years of travel had done little more than bring me home.

7

The Media Burn

JOHN GLENN is a good friend. He comes from a nonpolitical background. Before he ever ran for the Senate he had already established his celebrity as one of America's first astronauts. He is thorough and exudes integrity. He combines the openness of a small-town boy with the worldliness of a Marine general. He is not glib or flashy; he has tenacity, a sense of purpose, and, above all, courage. When the political process disappoints him, it is usually because of the failure of others to do what they said they would do. He rarely dodges. He never lies.

When Michael Dukakis was considering him as a running mate in 1988, Glenn and I talked often. His sense of humor and perspective about the selection game struck me as the hallmark of a man secure within himself, with just enough invested in the process to be pleased if he was chosen and not enough to be crushed if he was rejected. John treats politics with the detachment of a man who has literally and figuratively rocketed into space. His achievements both in space and on land allow the Senate to fit into his life but not to dominate it.

In 1984, Glenn ran for president without thinking it through. He ended up with a gigantic debt (the bulk of it to Ohio banks) that, under the law, he was prohibited from paying off personally. In raising money to reduce his debt, he accepted contributions—which were perfectly legal—from a savings-and-loan operator named Charles Keating, an Ohioan who had moved to Arizona, where, unbeknownst to Glenn, he had milked the Lincoln Savings & Loan (of which he was the principal stockholder) of millions of dollars for his own interests, and had invested his depositors' money in a series of grossly speculative enterprises.

In April 1987, Glenn attended two meetings in the office of Senator Dennis DeConcini of Arizona. The first meeting, on April 2, was with Ed Gray, then the chairman of the Federal Home Loan Bank Board, which regulated savings-and-loan institutions. It concerned a problem that Lincoln Savings & Loan was having with Gray's agency; Keating was reluctant to abide by a recent ruling limiting the amount an S&L could invest directly in nonresidential projects. Glenn urged that the Federal Home Loan Bank Board promptly carry out its examination of Lincoln on the nonresidential-projects rule, but he did not advocate a particular outcome. A week later, Glenn, DeConcini, and three other senators met with four officials from the San Francisco Home Loan Bank Board, again in DeConcini's office. During this second meeting, on April 9, one of the regulators said that Lincoln was under review for possible criminal conduct; afterward, Glenn and his staff had no further contact with the FHLBB on behalf of Lincoln, and Glenn subsequently declined a fundraising offer from Keating. Nevertheless, his attendance at the two meetings included him with the four other senators there (besides DeConcini, they were John McCain [R.-Ariz.], Don Riegle [D.-Mich.], and Alan Cranston [D.-Calif.] as the so-called Keating Five.

A special Ethics Committee investigation found in September 1990 that Glenn and McCain had done nothing wrong, and the special outside counsel recommended that their cases be separated from those of the other three senators. However, the three remaining senators were all Democrats, and the committee, which was under Democratic leadership, decided to lump the five together to keep the scandal bipartisan. Accordingly, Glenn had to wait until the investigations of all the senators (only Cranston's had lasting substance) were complete to have his lesser involvement—which, besides attendance at the April 1987 meetings, consisted of arranging a lunch between Keating and House Speaker Jim Wright—described and criticized in the committee report. To most of the public, the senators were equally culpable. The Ethics Committee's decision hurt Glenn, tainting him by association. It also cost him four hundred and fifty thousand dollars in legal fees to defend his character, which was unimpeachable.

In 1992, I campaigned for Glenn's re-election. Toward the end of the campaign, as I settled into an Ohio hotel room late one night, I turned on the television and was greeted by one of his opponent's commercials. Keating's face was splashed across the screen in a mug shot with a convict number under it (Keating had been convicted of securities fraud), and the voice-over charged that John Glenn had taken money from this "jailed S&L kingpin."

The most important thing you have in politics is your reputation. John Glenn prizes his. Yet the Keating Five ordeal had tarnished it. Glenn saw his 1992 race as a way to eliminate the stain of innuendo and guilt by association and to put behind him the judgment error of setting up the luncheon in the first place. But in the campaign his opponent made Glenn's character the target of scurrilous attacks. I knew how much pain Glenn was in, and I felt for him. Ultimately he won, and in so doing he provided the sharpest answer to those who thought the low road would take this good man out of the Senate. Glenn and McCain are still senators; the other three of the Keating Five chose not to seek re-election.

Campaigns have always been dirty, but today the scope of inquiry and the depth of scrutiny would make even a religious ascetic nervous. Anyone running for office confronts an ugly reality, compounded of sophisticated surveillance techniques, the fierce appetite of the media, instantaneous and ubiquitous communication, ambiguous campaign regulations, and slash-and-burn campaign tactics. If you become a candidate for high office, whether elective or appointive, don't expect that any part of your life will be kept private. For a political appointee, the selectively leaked FBI report can make life a nightmare. For the political candidate, it's the wide net of "Did you ever . . . ?" questions. In both situations, an army of journalists will dig relentlessly to find the one fact or confirm the one rumor that will give their stories an edge over the competition. The reporter knows that the more personal the fact, the more appealing it will be to the public.

If today's circumstances had existed in 1978, I probably would never have become a candidate. I wanted to serve the public and make America a better place. I did not want to see dirty linen washed in public—my own or anybody else's. Having lived for many years in the public eye, I had become preoccupied with privacy. I went to great lengths to preserve it. In retrospect, I sometimes took absurd precautions. For example, throughout the 1978 campaign I never allowed the college students who drove me to bring their cars to our house, whose location I kept private. I met them instead at a local gas station.

In that first campaign, I ran against the Democratic machine as the archetypal Mr. Clean outsider. I expected to play by a clear set of honored rules, and I wanted to avoid the character attacks that sometimes discolored political campaigns. In 1978 in New Jersey, my hopes were realized. In the primary, Governor Brendan Byrne, all the big-city mayors, and most of the county chairmen supported my principal opponent, Dick Leone, who was a decent man and a good public servant. Although many of these career politicians resented what they saw as my audacity in running for the Senate without having held prior political office, they didn't engage in dirty tricks. Beyond my suffering the viselike handshake of a machine thug, being physically barred from a rally organized by the Hudson County machine, and having some of our poll workers in Jersey City intimidated on primary day by uniformed city police officers, it was a civilized campaign. Leone focused only on the issues. In the general election, my Republican opponent, Jeff Bell, was equally issue-oriented. He wasn't interested in my family, my childhood, my investments, or my social life; he was interested in advocating a 30-percent tax cut.

During the campaign, Bell made a highly visible conversion to Roman Catholicism. New Jersey is 42 percent Roman Catholic. I thought it a suspiciously convenient conversion at the time, but I never dreamed of raising the issue in the campaign context. Religion was off-limits. I didn't parade my own religious convictions, and as far as I was concerned an opponent's religious views were his business and no one else's. If I couldn't make our differences on the issues into a winning strategy, I was prepared to lose. Jeff, who became a friend out of the campaign experience, told me years later that he and his staff had thought I would use his conversion, which was genuine, to brand him a political opportunist, and were very surprised when I didn't.

One potentially painful invasion of privacy for me related to trying marijuana. Several times in the early 1970s, I had taken a few puffs of marijuana, but I didn't consider it anyone else's business; nor did I consider it a disqualification for public office. But any answer a candidate gives to the drug question other than "No" lends itself to misinterpretation. Unlike alcohol, marijuana use—however innocent or minuscule—

is surrounded by the fact of illegality. An admission of use connotes other drugs and regular use or even addiction in the public's mind. Each evening after work, when my father would drink two bourbons-and-water, he would say, "Everything in moderation." I am my father's son. Two gin-and-tonics or three beers hit me harder than a few drags ever did, but once you crossed the threshold of admission, people wouldn't believe how limited your use had been.

No one asked me the drug question in the 1978 Senate campaign or in the 1984 re-election campaign. In 1990, a reporter looking to be first to subject me to a tough "presidential" probing, asked the question. I told her that I didn't answer "did-you-ever" questions. She duly reported her question and my response, positing that my desire for privacy made it unlikely that I would ever run for president.

Another subject I felt uneasy about addressing in the public arena was money—my money. Our family lived comfortably, but money was a taboo subject while I was growing up. My father's comments about money generally related only to the importance of saving it. ("If you put your money in the bank, it works for you while you sleep.") From age five, I had a piggy bank. From age ten, I had my own bank account, into which I would deposit the money I earned from delivering the *Daily News Democrat*. I had no idea what my father's income was. It was something that no one ever spoke about in our house. When I began earning my own money as an adult, I never talked about it either. During my Oxford days, I was paid to be a CBS radio reporter and to play basketball in Italy, but I didn't broadcast either salary. The advance I got to write *Life on the Run* remained undisclosed, and my lawyer said that I even whispered when I talked to him about the salary I made playing professional basketball. When I signed my first Knick contract, I insisted that the exact amount be kept out of the papers. I wanted it that way, not so much to avoid the potential jealousy of teammates as to avoid what from early childhood I had come to associate with having money—namely, embarrassment.

When you are a small-town banker's son, you constantly have to demonstrate that you are one of the guys. Sports did that for me in large part, but silence regarding my so-called wealth was also a "get-along" tactic. This attitude complemented my father's inherent reticence. He fiercely defended himself against his neighbors' curiosity—not simply about his money but about his health problems and the details of his family life. The result of this upbringing was that when it came to money, I was a stone wall. In 1978, therefore, it was with a sense of personal trauma that I labored over my Senate financial-disclosure statement, required of every senatorial candidate as well as every senator. Going beyond the legal requirement, I offered a summary of my previous three years of income taxes. I realized that financial disclosure was appropriate for someone seeking the public trust, and I had nothing to fear. Still, my income was a private matter, something I regretted revealing. Invasion of personal space was what discomfited me.

As a public figure, I believe that people are entitled to know my views on the issues of the day and why I hold them; they are also entitled to a full disclosure of what I own and some basic biographical material. The public has a right to know if you're a crook, but they do not need to know if you're a sinner, since we all are. They're not entitled to an answer to every possible personal question about you and your family. Elected officials have to be able to preserve an area in which to regenerate, away from the glare. They have to be able to wall off some things from public view—to protect a part of their lives while at the same time giving their lives to public service. This is the irony of successful service: Without some time and space in which to be alone and free from anxiety and constant guardedness, your life withers. You become a robot. Then your job, and not your humanity, defines your life. Some privacy is essential to maintain healthy emotions. The candidates who reveal their medical records since childhood, how many people they have slept with, or how many times they have seen priests, spiritual advisers, marriage counselors, or psychiatrists offer too much, simultaneously demeaning their offices and catering to sensationalism. Privacy is also indispensable for soul-searching and considering new options. If the press demands more, it should be told no, politely but firmly. Supreme Court Justice Louis Brandeis once said, "The right to be let alone [is] the most comprehensive of rights and the right most valued by civilized man." On some levels, that applies even to politicians.

Does a person's private life reflect on the ability to serve? Except in the most extreme and universally obvious cases, such as theft, alcoholism, drug addiction, or other past criminal offenses, I believe that the clues to future public behavior that might be found in past private behavior are paltry. Only private behavior that is truly pathological—such as wife beating, persistent and flagrant lying, sexual abuse—has public implications. Individual quirks, such as preferring Bach to blues, suffering from fear of heights, choosing certain kinds of sensual pleasures, having difficulty relaxing after a period of intense work, waging a vendetta, working at a messy desk, having nightmares about death, being unable to sleep for more than a few hours at a time, cannot be correlated to one's ability to perform public service. Armchair psychologists who extrapolate from such tidbits to predict a candidate's performance in office don't know what they're talking about.

A politician's life has the same complexity as any other person's. His or her personality is shaped by countless influences. The information gleaned from snippets of biography—the comments of a childhood friend, the assessment of a teacher, a paragraph in a piece of writing, the analysis of a defeated opponent—cannot provide an adequate psychological profile, much less determine that someone is unfit for public office. Something that happened ten or twenty or thirty years ago is most often of no predictive value and ignores the fact that most people, if not wholly perfectible, are capable of growth and the achievement of maturity.

The 1992 presidential race raised all these questions anew. Instead of reporting the problems and opportunities confronting the country and Bill Clinton's plan to deal with them, the press went for titillation. Did Clinton or didn't Clinton smoke marijuana twenty years ago? Did he or didn't he inhale? What did his discomfort and reluctance to talk about it mean? Investing such rite-of-passage behavior with Wagnerian dimensions of interpretation seems misplaced and fundamentally unfair.

Did Clinton have an extramarital affair? Did Bush? It seems to me that the only people to whom those questions are relevant are a man's wife, his lover (if there is one), his family, and himself. Are we to imagine that if a man is unfaithful to his wife he will therefore also (and the "therefore also" is important, because on it alone rests the arrogated right to know) commit political acts of disloyalty? Since history is full of many great men and women (including American presidents) whose private lives would not have withstood the same scrutiny as their public deeds, must we deny or invalidate their public deeds? No, their great public achievements raise questions instead about the relevance of private behavior to public life. For the press to persist, going to extraordinary lengths—staking out a home, obtaining telephone logs, buying secretly tape-recorded conversations, paying off a potential source for a story, following someone anonymously with a hidden camera—in trying to discover the dark side of someone's life, is more an indictment of the press than of the maligned candidate.

When the red-hot media burn is in progress, it seems that nothing escapes its flames. The reporters are waiting at each stop on your campaign schedule. Just to see them, let alone to hear them, shortens your breath, dries up your voice, turns your face hot, tightens your chest, and makes you feel like an average guy about to be hit by the heavyweight champion. Depending on how much money a newspaper or a television network puts behind a developing story (how many reporters assigned, how much travel allowed, how big a research budget set aside), there is little factual information about your life that can't be acquired. Any misdemeanor conviction can be found at county or state courthouses. A speeding ticket will be unearthed in a computer search of the records in a state's motor-vehicle department. Any mortgage- or property-tax records or liens against property can be discovered in the county clerk's files. Financial records such as brokerage accounts, or even income-tax returns, are obtainable if they were laid on the public record in the course of a litigation. If the candidate was ever an officer or director of a corporation, all corporate records are available at either the Securities and Exchange Commission or the offices of state secretaries of state. A rumor about a candidate's health that made its way into one newspaper story ten years ago will turn up in a name search in any number of computer files. An ex-girlfriend's reportedly salacious comments can be checked with cold phone calls to her, catching her off-guard; or in some cases she can be intimidated or bribed to repeat them on the air. Academic transcripts and military records are accessible to the skillful sleuth. If all that fails, there is always a detective agency or its high-tech equivalent, the "deep-research firm." If reporters don't find the embarrassing fact, the research team in the opponent's campaign is likely to discover it, and when they find it, they will give it to the press, ingratiating themselves and trying to destroy the opponent at the same time. A firm working for a candidate who is ruthlessly in pursuit of the "killer fact" about his opponent might even skirt legality by attempting to access telephone toll records, credit information, and bank statements, or even by rummaging through the opponent's garbage. Sometimes I feel that I'm living during a political era in which what I value most, character, is endangered; what I admire most, humanity, is devalued; and what I feel most sensitive about, privacy, is denied.

Most candidates for major office will bring no real change to this kind of invasive yet trivial media coverage. Those few politicians who have no dark chapters in their lives will either brag about it or, more likely, put it in the political bank and move on, with an enhanced feeling of personal invulnerability. Very few candidates will attempt to shrink the importance of the personal by enlarging the importance of the substantive. Instead, almost as if to avoid drawing attention to themselves, candidates will adhere to the cautious conventional wisdom that to win you need to capture the center, nothing too drastic right or left. The musical equivalent of a political campaign headed to the center is an orchestra in which all instruments play the same note; both produce boredom in their listeners. When two candidates refuse to offer a real choice and neither will risk being a truth teller, the campaign debate is reduced to minor policy disagreements and to differences in "style." Grand designs for policy succumb to gossip and rumors, which are then blown out of proportion. You might expect such behavior in a small-town mayoral race, not in a run for the presidency of the United States.

America would have an impoverished democracy without a free press. A clash of opinions is the essence of liberty. From the viciously partisan press of Jefferson's day to the thorough investigative journalism of the mugwumps and progressives to the tenacity of the press during Vietnam and Watergate, America has benefited from open public expression. But if your personal life is the target of the focus, the experience of a free press can become very painful.

"Never get into an argument with someone who buys ink by the barrel or deploys a truck full of minicams"—that is the advice always given to young politicians, based on the beliefs that reporters are bullies and that the press has the ultimate advantage. To make an enemy of the media is fatal for a public figure. That statement is true not because the press will print lies—although some newspapers do, without hesitation—but because so much depends on where reporters want to put the emphasis, or on how they want to see events that are often subject to several interpretations.

If you're honest, the press gives you the benefit of the doubt for being honest. If you're a pain in the neck, the press treats you as such. Like the IRS, the press can get anyone. All they have to do is to decide—sometimes, it seems, almost subconsciously—that they will make the extra effort to cast a negative light on you. My own experience offers the following sampling: The press can report that a magazine named you one of the five most overrated senators but omit the fact that in previous years the same magazine named you among the most respected members of the Senate. They can criticize you for taking official work-related trips at taxpayer expense and study trips abroad paid for by universities, or they can criticize you for having a limited perspective on the world. They can criticize you for holding to a policy position of your party or fault you for showing independence from party. They can criticize you for being a cautious senator or question your motives for speaking out. They can criticize you for not paying attention to your state because you deal with national issues, or they can criticize you for not being a national leader because you're focusing on New Jersey. They can scold you for missing votes in D.C. while you were in New Jersey, or chastise you for missing events in New Jersey when you were voting in D.C. They can criticize you for keeping staff too long, or criticize you for getting rid of staff too quickly. They can criticize you for raising too much money for TV ads to tell people what you've done as a senator, or criticize you because people don't know what you've done as a senator.

In an interview for a job as a schoolteacher during the Depression, and desperate for work, LBJ is reported to have been asked whether the world was round or flat and to have answered, "I can teach it either way." Similarly, the press can cover it round or flat—but either way the message too frequently will be a barb.

ONE LATE NOVEMBER EVENING IN 1992, I flew to Chicago to put in a campaign appearance for Carol Moseley-Braun. Carol was preparing to conduct a closed-circuit town meeting with audiences on thirteen Illinois college campuses, and I was to be her guest. When I arrived at the campus of the University of Illinois, in Chicago, one of her aides was waiting at the door and rushed me downstairs to a TV studio. Several Illinois political reporters who traveled with Carol everywhere she went were sitting in the first rows on the left. When I joined Carol backstage, she told me that her relationship with the press in the last three weeks of the campaign had been tense.

Coming off an upset victory in the primary over the incumbent, Senator Alan Dixon, Carol had become an instant celebrity. Dixon was a competent legislator, but he had calculated wrongly that a vote to confirm Clarence Thomas as a justice of the Supreme Court would help him in conservative southern Illinois. His usually astute political judgment went askew. He so outraged women with his vote that Carol, a former state legislator and Cook County recorder of deeds, came out of nowhere to win a tough three-way primary. Propelled into the race by her own outrage over the Anita Hill–Clarence Thomas hearings, she became the most dramatic example of the hearing's repercussions: a black woman, a political unknown, who had slain Goliath in the primary and was destined to become a U.S. senator in the Year of the Woman.

Carol Moseley-Braun grew up with a father who was a sergeant in the Cook County jail and who on occasion beat his wife and children with a police belt or a wet rope. At the same time, Carol remembers him as a remarkable musician who played seven musical instruments—most notably, tenor sax, with a local bandleader named Red Saunders. Her father took responsibility for introducing Carol to many religions—visiting synagogues, black Protestant churches, Baha'i gatherings, and the mosques of the Black Muslims. He told her stories of his youth, including his mother's recollections of the Chicago race riots in 1919, when "blood ran in the streets like water." Carol's mother was a devout Catholic who worked as a medical technician in an animal laboratory. When Carol's parents were finally divorced, her mother had an extremely hard time supporting four kids. From her mother Carol got her set of values, her sense of fairness, and her capacity for hard work. From her father she got her tolerance and abiding awareness of human frailty.

After her primary victory, Carol became swept up in the excitement of being a famous figure. At first, it was refreshing, as a rain always is after a long drought, but the rain of fame didn't stop. It kept coming harder and became a storm. The iron law of celebrity went into effect: the faster and more intense the stardom, the quicker and more inexorable the backlash. People demanded her presence, not because she was bright, attractive, and approachable, or even because she was the party's nominee, but because she was "a star." She quickly sensed the darker side of celebrity. She could not have met all the demands even if she had been as organized as Operation Desert Storm, which she was not. Many men had difficulty taking her candidacy seriously, much less the prospect that she would wield the power of a U.S. senator. That summer, a well-educated, liberal, professional woman bad-mouthed Carol to me for canceling appointments with well-known Democratic fund-raisers. Another Illinois politician predicted that there would be some explosive revelations about her before the campaign ended.

Backstage before the closed-circuit town meeting, Carol was livid. The press had just revealed that Carol's mother had given a $28,750 inheritance to Carol and her siblings even though she was living in a nursing home paid for by Medicaid. Heedless of the political storm that would ensue, Carol behaved as if this were only her mother's business. (Later she donated her share of the inheritance to Medicaid.) "Don't they ever stop prying?" she asked me. She told me only in 1994 that the press, having somehow gotten access to the autopsy report, had also revealed that her brother died in 1986 of a drug overdose. The news had so traumatized Carol's mother, who had thought her son died from a heart aneurysm, that she didn't speak for two weeks.

Most journalists simply report what happens; they furnish straightforward descriptions of statements and actions by the candidate. Some engage in analysis. But for the political candidate those kinds of reporters are not memorable, they are just doing what they're supposed to do. They're like the air you breathe—taken for granted. The reporters who loom large in the mind of a candidate are the ones who pry, who look for the cheap shot. They are the ones who stick in a candidate's craw. The word "detest" has new levels of meaning when you're a candidate in that position. Sooner or later, a politician runs into such reporters and situations. Then, the more you struggle to escape the preconceptions of the press, the more you find yourself in the middle of the spotlight. For Carol, it was happening the night I arrived. "They just won't leave me alone!" she fumed. "How do you handle all this?"

Carol and I left the backstage room, with its catered table of cheese and fruit and desserts, and made our way to the stage. The auditorium was about two-thirds full, and the television lights were at full glare. We were announced, and took our seats at a coffee table with the moderator between us. I spoke first, introducing Carol and talking about the need for America to lead the world as a pluralistic democracy whose growing economy would take everyone to higher ground. Carol opened with a version of her stump speech about fighting for Illinois and bringing change to the Senate by her very presence. Both of us then answered questions for an hour from the predominantly youthful audience:

"What will you do to make it easier for us to go to college?"

"How can we control health-care costs?"

"What about an AIDS cure?"

"Can we ever conquer racism?"

"What are you going to do to help small business?"

"I got a degree in environmental science because I thought it was a booming industry, but now I can't get a job. What should I do?"

Carol spoke clearly and to the point on most questions. She didn't try to evade. The audience got involved, applauding at several points. The show, I felt, was a great success—highly substantive and marked by candor and responsiveness, both in the audience and onstage.

As soon as it was over, I took my lapel microphone off, congratulated the moderator, and gave Carol a kiss. The stage swarmed with kids from the audience, who thanked us and asked further questions about subjects we had covered. Then the TV crews and reporters closed in on us, and something like a feeding frenzy ensued.

"Your opponent says you support child pornography, Carol. Didn't you support a bill in the state legislature that encouraged child pornographers?"

"Isn't that pornography question a legitimate one for your opponent?"

"Is there any difference between his charge and yours two days ago that he belonged to an all-white country club?"

I stepped in. I was incensed and I showed it. I pointed out that we had just spent an hour answering questions that the people of Illinois wanted answered, and now the press was trying to manufacture sensational issues. "Why don't you report on what questions were asked, and the answers Carol gave, and offer a critique of those answers?" I snapped. I turned to Carol and told her not to answer the kind of questions they were asking. The reporters looked startled, and one said sheepishly, "But that's our job."

That's what's wrong with the process. Too many reporters think the search for the lurid and the sensational is their job, and in some selfish sense it is—after all, it catches the eye of their editors, and increasingly editors are being asked by publishers to sell more papers rather than simply report factually on events or educate their readers. Doing both seems rare. Some of the brightest people in America work for newspapers. Editors struggle daily with how to be thorough and truthful. Some political journalists are fair, even incisive. They understand how they shape opinion through what they choose to emphasize (television often follows the lead of a print story), and most of them avoid the cheap shots available to anyone in their position. When they support big-picture reform, they improve its chance of passage. But as a group, political pundits in this country command more respect than the quality of their work deserves. Too many of their observations and stories are superficial, providing little context, little historical insight, little enlightenment of any sort, and reveling in hyperbole. They wouldn't do that if the public didn't buy it, but if we're not careful, we could be on a race to the bottom, with the lowest common denominator determining airtime and newspaper coverage.

Coverage of political personalities and issues is further complicated by the entrance into the field of radio talk-show hosts, many of whom employ no standards to distinguish legitimate news from malicious gossip. Some talk shows qualify as a marketplace of ideas; others reveal the human and often humorous side of people in the news. Too many, however, lead nowhere. There is a difference between mere utterance and a civilized conversation among citizens. A Democratic congressman from the state of Washington who lost in the 1994 midterm elections told me that conservative talk-show hosts had broadcast six hours of attacks on him daily, with no comparable rejoinder possible. These attacks went on for months, and early in the process civility crumbled and journalistic standards disappeared.

Many reporters have begun to treat politics as though it were a sporting event: What's the score today? Just how did you win this game? What's your strategy for tomorrow? How do you feel about where you are in the standings? Others, in the name of balance, give the bizarre and the mainstream equal time. For some, substantive campaign issues are of much less importance than controversies involving the press itself: Was this reporter justified in revealing a candidate's extramarital affair? Did that columnist unfairly interpret the views of another columnist? More and more of the campaign coverage on television consists of one reporter interviewing another about how he or she "perceives" the campaign or the government.

Press secretaries know that although the press's appetite may be voracious, it will accept its daily feeding only in a certain way. News releases must be ready by 3 p.m., television "standup shots" by 4 p.m., or the media often won't even cover an event—unless, of course, it involves sex, drugs, or crime. Write a thoughtful analysis of the American predicament and it will be reduced to thirty seconds, if it makes the TV news at all. The ebb and flow of a campaign, unfolding with all the unpredictability and richness of American life, cannot be squeezed into a headline, or a two-minute segment on the evening news, or the video tabloids. Democracy by ad slogan prods but rarely satisfies. Rather than pursuing an independent course informed by shoe-leather reportage, a point of view, and a set of values, too many reporters and writers wait for participants in a campaign to define the news of the day. An openly partisan press is better than one that claims objectivity but delivers pap aimed to offend no one or succumbs to sensationalism aimed at its readers' basest instincts.

Politicians themselves are not without shortcomings in this area. Every politician wants to shape opinions and determine the way the press treats him or her. A major goal of every officeholder, from president to mayor, is favorable news coverage. There is nothing wrong with that, as long as flash doesn't replace substance or public relations substitute for effective governance. If politicians become totally unresponsive to legitimate press inquiries and instead attempt to maintain a self-serving surface, then the politician joins the game.

The generating of news stories that advance a politician's interests—legislative or partisan—is also part of the press/political game, and it requires a strategy. Sometimes the strategy is inoffensively organizational, as in the placing of op-ed pieces in certain papers on specific dates, followed by TV and radio appearances and a direct-mail campaign. Such an effort requires coordination and a goal, such as ensuring that the people in your state know that your interest in education is one of your ways of caring about them. Often the strategy is no more than allowing a politician who has a nice manner to interact with the press unofficially. The techniques are numerous. Flattery often succeeds. ("That was a great story!") Candor succeeds, too. Saying, "I blew it," "I made a mistake," "The president looked bad," bolsters your credibility with the press. To deny an obvious error by concocting an elaborate justification raises more questions than it answers and turns off the public as well as the newshounds. Most politicians have discovered that what succeeds above all is making a reporter look good professionally—and that means giving the reporter a story no one else has. A substantive breakthrough mitigates a refusal to offer up gossip.

Newspapers and radio and television networks are in the business of making money. They are not so much intellectually opposed to intelligent political coverage as they are aware of the importance, as news organizations discovered in the 1980s, of pandering to what their market-research gurus tell them the public wants—and buys. High-mindedness seems to have a small audience. What passes for independent thought follows the ratings. Like the U.S. government's attitude toward tobacco (the surgeon general warns that it's dangerous to your health, while the tax code subsidizes tobacco advertisements), television's attitude toward violence yields panel discussions and public-service ads decrying it, followed by programs full of violent acts. The two-million-dollar salaries of television news anchors (some of whom are serious journalists) are paid by networks whose earnings derive in part from sponsors of programs celebrating violence without context. The "news" itself is equally violent. (In Washington, D.C., the local television news brims over with mayhem and murder, the more bizarre or sex-related the better.) The dual credo of local television news seems to be: "If it bleeds, it leads; if it thinks, it stinks."

"Simulated" news is the new escalation. Actors re-enact a real event, so that the public can experience all aspects of it as if it were another episode in a soap opera. With the miniaturization of video cameras and the invention of day/night videotape, documentaries also invade more places, capture more versions of reality. I have often wondered how many times I've been filmed without my consent. The TV news shows solicit taped "news stories" from their viewers, and some TV programs consist literally of these home videos, bought because they have captured sensational or embarrassing moments. Sometimes, as in the videotape of the Rodney King beating in Los Angeles in 1991, they can play an important role in achieving justice. Sometimes the amateur videos add up to nothing more than raw titillation. In both cases, the amateur camera-man's desire for money or a measure of celebrity dovetails with a network's appetite for docudramas of often brutal reality, revealing the rawest aspects of American life.

The power of those who control television news is greater than the responsibility they show in exercising it. (I'm not referring here to the "liberal bias" that so many conservatives have exaggerated out of all proportion.) They rarely seem to use any restraint, if restraint means loss of money or viewership. Ask a media executive to tell you when he lost money for principle, and you'll wait a long time for an answer. Some news programs reserve a five-minute segment, at the end of a thirty-minute broadcast otherwise filled with catastrophes, for good news about America. But by and large, the news on television is bad news or frightening news or pandering news or lurid news or trivial news. Rarely does it make the human spirit soar. America isn't as bad as it looks on the television news. I know; I've seen it from the road.

8

Money Is Power

ONEY IS WOVEN through American politics like a pattern woven into fabric. Money spent by the federal government represents 20 percent of the annual gross domestic product. Millions of jobs and thousands of millionaires depend on these government expenditures. In our democracy, where so much money is taken in and spent by government and where decisions about how to spend that money are made by majority votes in Congress, efforts to influence legislators are predictable.

Politicians need money to get elected and re-elected. More than ever, individual politicians are responsible for raising their own campaign funds; since the 1970s, the party no longer delivers large sums of money to candidates. And only a relatively few Americans contribute money to campaigns. The people who do often want to direct governmental money in a particular way, either for their own personal benefit or for the benefit of causes dear to their hearts.

American government has been susceptible to the influence of money for a long time. Modern political fund-raising began in William McKinley's campaign for president in 1896. It was an innovation of Marcus Alonzo Hanna, a successful Cleveland entrepreneur who made his money in the coal-and-iron business. After Hanna was rejected for service in the Cleveland Civil Service Reform Association, he opted for the world of politics. He was a Scotch-Irish man of action, a politician who scoffed at the bookish and preferred the company of men with money.

Mark Hanna loved sweets, eating hard candy by the bowlful and chocolates by the boxful. He disliked smutty stories, refrained from drinking even a glass of wine until he was over thirty-five, and believed that government existed to serve business, in whose terms he judged all men and measures.

As the Republican boss of Ohio, he controlled a state that had produced Supreme Court justices, cabinet members, three presidents (Grant, Hayes, and Garfield), and a senator of national stature (John Sherman). In the tradition of the Albany regency of the mid-nineteenth century, and before that the Virginia presidents of the nation's founding period, the Ohio political dynasty was leaving its imprint on the country. To govern Ohio meant learning how to meet the needs and aspirations of the Yankee north, the former Virginians and Kentuckians in the southern part of the state, and the yeomen of the broad, flat farmland in between, which resembled the central Illinois of Abe Lincoln more than it did Cleveland or Steubenville. Ohio was also a mixture of religions and ethnicities. It embraced the industrialism and feverish production pace of the modern age, with all its acquisitive energy, and the agriculture of the old America, with its emphasis on "family, land, and community." Ohio politics was a perfect training ground for national politics.

Hanna backed former U.S. Congressman William McKinley for governor in 1892. In 1893 he rescued the governor from bankruptcy proceedings by raising a hundred and thirty thousand dollars to pay off a note that McKinley had become liable for when the business of an old friend failed. Three years later, having left his businesses in the hands of a younger brother, he worked full-time as McKinley's campaign strategist and chief fund-raiser when the governor ran for president. Hanna used every social connection and political cajolement to get McKinley, whom he genuinely admired, the Republican nomination, and in the process, according to his biographer Herbert Croly, he spent a hundred thousand dollars of his own money.

As the presidential election got under way, Hanna—then the newly appointed Republican national chairman—had positioned McKinley perfectly. The country was not ready to deal with the growing class divisions, the intensifying urban poverty, or the continual cycles of boom and bust. Republicans had successfully blamed the Panic of 1893 on Democratic promises to cut tariffs, and all Hanna had to do was promote McKinley as "the advance agent of prosperity." The American historian James MacGregor Burns has written of McKinley in 1896, "an air of predestination hung about his apparent victory. But he and Hanna insured that destiny with years of hard work, cultivation of mass opinion, and close attention to a new, widened industrial constituency."

Hanna was the precursor of the modern media consultant, who controls the candidate's schedule to fit it to the message and strategy of the campaign. He insisted that McKinley simply sit on his front porch in Canton, Ohio, receive delegations of well-wishers from around the country, and occasionally issue a carefully worded public speech. Railroads cooperated by reducing fares for Canton-bound Republican delegations. In one day, McKinley spoke to nearly eighty thousand people who paraded up North Market Street to the candidate's house to exchange greetings and profess loyalty.

Meanwhile, the campaign—with its fourteen hundred orators, including the likes of former President Benjamin Harrison, House Speaker Tom Reed, and former Senator Carl Schurz—crisscrossed the country on campaign-paid trips, spreading the word of the new Ohio Republican. Hanna approved every itinerary and all the invoices. To argue the case against McKinley's Democratic opponent William Jennings Bryan, Hanna sent Theodore Roosevelt, the young police commissioner from New York, to shadow Bryan as he traveled across Illinois, Michigan, and Minnesota. Bryan, conjuring up his famous "cross of gold" speech, would inveigh against the gold standard, and within hours Teddy would show up to refute the "boy orator" with an array of parables and props such as gold coins and loaves of bread. The campaign also countered Bryan's positions by printing and distributing in closely contested states more than a hundred million documents, many of them in German, French, Italian, Swedish, Danish, Dutch, Hebrew, Spanish, and Norwegian, in addition to English. Country newspapers reaching over one and a half million people were provided three columns of preset material every week.

For a Republican presidential campaign, the message was fresh. On the surface, McKinley—a former lawyer, who once had represented striking miners in Massillon—appeared to have moved to the political middle. "Labor," he said, "is indispensable to the creation and profitable use of capital, and capital increases the efficiency of and value of labor.

Whoever arrays one against the other is the enemy of both." The acknowledgment was a big political gesture with little substantive impact. Like his espousal of an eight-hour day for federal employees (but federal employees only), it allowed him to ask for workers' votes as if he were a different kind of Republican.

The union of a new Republican message with pamphleteering methods on such a vast scale cost more money than had ever been spent on a presidential campaign. Reports had it as high as twelve million dollars, but the audited accounts of the Republican National Committee showed three and a half million, half of which went to state parties to get out the vote and half to the fueling of the communications machine. Most of the money came from New York financial circles, through an assessment on banks, which benefited from continuance of the gold standard. They kicked in amounts equal to 0.25 percent of their capital. Hanna pointed out that under Republican rule the rich had done well. His appeals to the rich were based on his expectation of their gratitude and an implied promise of continued protection of their interests. Wealthy Americans responded. For example, John D. Rockefeller's Standard Oil Company contributed two hundred and fifty thousand dollars. Life insurance companies also made big donations. Hanna's competence and businesslike demeanor complemented his conviction that by pursuing individual economic interests one could pursue the public interest. He believed fervently that the market should remain unfettered by state controls of any kind, and only private charities should care for the poor. Both his personal honesty (no grafter he) and his beliefs brought an avalanche of money into Republican coffers. The result was an overwhelming victory for McKinley and for the strategy and methods of Mark Hanna.

Teddy Roosevelt himself, while aggressively campaigning for McKinley in 1896, had been revolted by Hanna's way of managing the message. "He has advertised McKinley as if he were a patent medicine," he said. Biographer Edmund Morris reports that Roosevelt also blanched at Hanna's fervent solicitation of the rich. At a luncheon after the 1896 election, he realized that half of those in attendance were moneymen. "I felt as if I was personally realizing all of [historian] Brooks Adams's gloomy anticipations of our gold-ridden, capitalist-bestridden, usurer-mastered future," he wrote to a friend. With the assassination of McKinley in 1901 and the ascension of Roosevelt, America got its first progressive president. Hanna, on the other hand, who regarded Roosevelt as an impulsive idealist, served the moneymen to the end. As 1904 approached, Hanna, by then a seven-year U.S. senator, encouraged speculation about his own candidacy for president. Though it was an unlikely prospect, he seemed to want to give the New York moneymen a chance to decide whether to wage a battle against the young president in Roosevelt's first effort to get the nomination on his own. Whatever the motivation, nothing could have stopped Roosevelt.

When I was a senior in high school, a reporter from the *St. Louis Post-Dispatch,* in researching a profile about me as a basketball player, asked me who my heroes were. The answer was an incongruous threesome: evangelist Billy Graham, basketball star Bob Pettit, and kingmaker Mark Hanna. I knew about Hanna because I had written a paper on the 1896 presidential election. (A few years ago, my high-school history teacher reminded me that its theme had been "Money is power.")

As I made my way in politics, I never forgot the story of McKinley. For a time, I searched for my own Mark Hanna, who could meld organization and money into an unbeatable political machine. Then, again, I knew there was another standard. Twelve years after McKinley's assassination, Woodrow Wilson, the second great progressive president, assumed the nation's ultimate elective office. When it came to political money, Wilson was naïve. Biographer August Heckscher points out that upon obtaining the Democratic nomination for governor of New Jersey in 1910, he called a meeting at Prospect, his official residence as president of Princeton University. The New Jersey bosses, such as James Smith of Essex County, James Nugent of Newark, and the Democratic leaders of Mercer County, came to assess their new candidate. Wilson told them that he intended to pay for his gubernatorial campaign with his own money. He reasoned that he could make enough from three post-election lectures. Since he expected to borrow a car to move around the state, he calculated that five hundred dollars was all he needed to win the governorship. The local bosses didn't know whether to laugh or cry. As it happened, by Election Day, Smith alone had spent more than fifty thousand dollars.

Wilson may have been naïve, but he had the right impulses. He won the governorship because he had given a ringing endorsement to progressive policies such as workmen's compensation, utility commissions, and direct election of U.S. senators by the people instead of the state legislatures, and because he had demonstrated a willingness to challenge bossism even as he benefited from it. He identified money flowing into campaigns as a threat to democracy. Moreover, he acted on his conviction. When he ran for president in 1 9 1 2, he was aware that if he won he would be lambasting monied interests. Because he was determined to avoid the charge of hypocrisy, he instructed his finance committee chairman, the financier Henry Morgenthau, to accept no corporate contributions. Whenever one arrived anyway, Morgenthau sent it back.

Both Teddy Roosevelt and Wilson saw the power of money in politics and sought to lessen it. Lyndon Johnson saw the same thing, but he was drawn to it like a moth to a lightbulb. LBJ's rise to prominence as a congressman rested largely on his talent for raising large sums of money, and this talent in turn rested on his willingness and his prodigious abilities to deliver taxpayer dollars to his contributors in the form of contracts, special tax benefits, and favorable government rulings. When he came through with the Marshall Ford Dam for his district in his first term as congressman and arranged for one of his contributors, the construction firm of Brown & Root, to get the contract to build it, he began an association that would help bring power and wealth to both of them. After procuring the dam, he tried in 1 9 3 9 to get part of the Corpus Christi Naval Air Station contract for Brown & Root. He failed, because Brown & Root had very little experience in the construction of buildings. Roads and dams, yes; buildings, no. Yet Johnson persisted.

As 1 9 4 0 began, it looked as if FDR would be challenged for the Democratic presidential nomination by his own vice-president, John Nance Garner, a Texan who had most of the cattle-and-cotton money locked up. FDR needed help in Texas. An ambitious Johnson called his friend Herman Brown of Brown & Root, who said that anything Lyndon wanted Lyndon would get. Brown went to his suppliers and subcontractors for contributions and put together a campaign fund for the president. As soon as Brown came forward with money for FDR, a Brown & Root attorney, Alvin Wirtz, was appointed to the number-two position at the Department of Interior, which awarded giant dam contracts; shortly thereafter, the Navy, also at White House direction and without bids, "negotiated" a large part of the forty-five-million-dollar Corpus Christi contract for Brown & Root.

Robert Caro points out in his biography of LBJ covering the congressional years that during the late 1 9 3 0 s there had emerged another force in political giving—the independent oilman. These were men such as Sid Richardson and Clint Murchison, who had discovered a giant oil field in East Texas. These entrepreneurs had virtually no competition, because the major oil companies, such as Standard Oil, Gulf Oil, and Sun Oil, had focused on West Texas. Their geologists had advised them that in East Texas there was no oil beyond isolated pockets. But below the dried-up cotton fields lay a reservoir of oil some fifty miles in length and at an easy-to-reach depth of thirty-five hundred feet. With a production that exceeded in volume that of any oil-producing nation on earth, the East Texas field, dominated by wildcatters, became a target for acquisition by the majors. By the end of the decade, many independent oilmen had sold out to the majors and in the process become multimillionaires. At a time when a three-bedroom house cost ten thousand dollars and a car cost seven hundred dollars, Sid Richardson's income in 1940 approached two million dollars. Independent oilmen now had the means to compete with the majors—particularly with the help of friends in Washington, D.C., who guaranteed continuance of a 27.5-percent depletion allowance. When the risk-taking independents hit oil in East Texas, 27.5 percent of their income came off the top for tax purposes, which meant that only 72.5 percent of their personal income from oil was subject to income tax. The only politician that the new breed of oilmen trusted was their fellow Texan and newly elected Speaker of the House, Sam Rayburn, but he didn't recognize their fund-raising potential. Johnson, on the other hand, realized that their wealth was directly related to decisions made by the federal government, such as tax and regulatory policies. Where others saw constituents with needs, Johnson saw contributors.

A few months after getting Herman Brown of Brown & Root to bankroll FDR's Texas campaign, Johnson saw an even bigger opportunity to enhance his power and his friends' wealth. He set his eyes on the chairmanship of the Democratic Congressional Campaign Committee. But Rayburn, who had been caught in the middle in FDR's facedown of Garner and was still smarting over Johnson's attacks on him at the White House during the Garner struggle, refused to appoint Lyndon. As the 1940 congressional sessions lengthened and became more contentious, congressmen couldn't get back to their districts. Unable to campaign, Democratic incumbents, who held 60 percent of the seats, saw their Republican challengers gaining ground. There was a good chance that the House might go Republican. Concern grew at the White House that without a Democratic Congress, FDR would be damaged in his third term. Rayburn had assumed his powerful position of Speaker after twenty-eight years in the House, and he feared that the efforts of a life-time might be lost. Only money could prevent it.

Rayburn turned to his former protégé. He still refused to make John-son the chairman of the Congressional Campaign Committee, but he did set him up with a separate office in the Munsey Building in downtown Washington, and he gave him a mandate to marshal sizable resources, and do it in short order.

Johnson's first call was to Herman Brown, whom he asked to raise money in five-thousand-dollar chunks from as many people as possible. (Most House races in 1940 cost less than five thousand dollars, many less than a thousand.) A week later, forty-five thousand dollars had come in from Texas. Johnson also turned to independent oil, using Rayburn's credibility and friendships and his own drive and insight into oil's need of government. Rayburn's friends came through, and in the process made a new friend in Johnson, who always took care of his friends. Toward the end of the campaign, Robert Caro writes, Johnson and Rayburn went back to the contractors and the oilmen. Many contributed above the legal limit—and did it in amounts of cash that are still unknown. Telegrams were flying back and forth between Johnson's office and more than a hun-dred grateful congressional-campaign headquarters around the country. On election night in 1940, the frenetic fund-raising was seen to have paid off. Democrats retained control of the House.

While Johnson was collecting cash for endangered House Demo-crats, Senator Harry Truman of Missouri was running for re-election to the U.S. Senate. Truman's opponents in the Democratic primary—the important race, since Missouri was heavily Democratic—were the state's starchy governor, Lloyd Stark, an apple-orchard magnate, and Maurice Milligan, the Kansas City district attorney who had sent Kansas City Democratic boss Tom Pendergast to jail on charges of income tax evasion. Neither of these men had any trouble raising money. Truman, by contrast, had virtually no money for his re-election effort. For cam-paign funds, he sent letters to constituents asking each for a dollar. His only radio exposure came during the last week of the primary campaign, in one program, which was paid for by the St. Louis Democratic organi-zation. Without much money, Senator Truman took his case to the peo-ple. He drove across the state, speaking to the people where they were. He pointed to his record. He appealed to labor and to blacks and to farm-ers. He talked plainly to group after group. Milligan faded and Governor

Stark made some tactical errors, such as floating his name for vice-president and for Navy secretary in the same year he was seeking the Senate nomination. The result was a Truman victory.

Even if he could have raised the money, one doubts that Truman would have felt comfortable accepting it. Having matured politically in the cesspool of Jackson County politics, where the Pendergast machine had built roads and paved creek beds with concrete bought from the boss's own concrete company, and having seen his friend Tom go to jail for not reporting as income bribes from insurance companies, he knew the pitfalls. He had seen the points where gratitude flowed beyond proper boundaries. He had benefited from the support of a corrupt machine, but he had always kept his distance from corruption. Later he admitted to a biographer, "I was always very particular about where my money came from. Very few people are going to give you large sums of money if they don't expect to get something from it, and you've got to keep that in mind."

Republicans, from McKinley on, have never had much trouble raising money. Many of these Republicans have been very wealthy to begin with. Political contributions from party loyalists, ever since Mark Hanna explicitly legitimized protecting the rich, were similar to dues at the country club. You gave to maintain your class. Within the party, there was the old money of the Eastern aristocracy and the new money of Western entrepreneurs. In between was the small-town money from the big fish in hundreds of small ponds.

Richard Nixon came from the West. His only serious rival in 1960 was Nelson Rockefeller, the prototype of the Eastern establishment. Beyond the stylistic differences, the West was more conservative, particularly in its anticommunism and its zealous opposition to federal expenditures (except when they subsidized Western economic development). But Nixon was not wealthy. He was small-town and of modest means, and he had a correspondingly intense desire to defeat the establishment candidate, as well as the fear that entrenched money could deny him the prize he thought his abilities merited. Nixon got the nomination and enough contributions to run a national campaign, but he believed that Kennedy money bought the election in Chicago, as it had in the Democratic primary in West Virginia. The irony of the Republican candidate, whose party was a mouthpiece for the wealthy, seeing himself as a "little man" against "big money" was not unique to Nixon. Bob Dole felt the same resentment about money and class in 1988, when he ran against

George Bush, and in countless Senate debates in which his adversary was Ted Kennedy.

By the time Nixon got a second shot at the presidency, eight years later, he had attained personal financial security from his lucrative New York law practice. Perhaps that gave him greater political confidence. Perhaps the Republican establishment believed that he had paid his dues. Whatever the reason, money flowed into his campaign. In fact, Republicans threw buckets of money his way. After his election in 1968, and with his purchase of an estate in San Clemente, Nixon symbolically unified the West and the East and guaranteed himself access to the national wealth of Republican loyalists on both coasts and throughout America. By the time he ran for re-election four years later, money was as easy to gather as ripe apples from a low-hanging branch. Maurice Stans, his finance director, frequently left contributors' offices with briefcases full of cash, which he would deposit in his desk drawer in a "secret fund" that eventually totaled nearly two million dollars. The New Jersey speculator and international investor Robert Vesco, then under investigation by the SEC, contributed two hundred thousand dollars, in hundred-dollar bills. Stans and his staff urged wealthy Californians to give 0.5 percent of their net worth. Large businesses were assessed 1 percent of their profits (shades of Mark Hanna and the banks), and small businesses were asked for a hundred thousand dollars each.

When the Watergate scandal exploded, much of the financial murkiness came to light. In October 1974, Congress passed and President Ford signed a campaign reform law that among other things set strict limits on the amount of money that could be given by individuals to a political campaign, required full disclosure of contributions, and limited the amount that a candidate could contribute to his or her own campaign. A year later, in *Buckley* v. *Valeo,* the Supreme Court threw out the limitation on a candidate's spending of his own money, arguing that it was an infringement on the right of free speech. Though this ruling opened a giant loophole in the campaign-finance reform law, enough restrictions remained to change the way money flowed into politics. No longer could rich individuals or the corporations or accused felons pass political money in brown paper bags full of cash. The post-Watergate era had begun.

————

IN MY FIRST CAMPAIGN, I spent about 40 percent of my time raising money. I made a list of all the people I had known in my life who I thought could afford to contribute money on any scale to my campaign. I then either visited or called them to ask for a contribution. Finding the person who would raise money as well as give it was important, and not easy. After about four months of these attempts, a few things were clear. People whom I had pegged as sure contributors because of an association with me over many years became elusive. One man with whom I had had business dealings as a Knick for ten years said he would like to help, but his help would be more generous if I shared his interests, such as the new Broadway play he was financing. I invested seventeen thousand dollars of my own money in the play, which failed shortly after its opening, and the man responded by throwing a cocktail party in New York that raised eight thousand dollars. With this kind of balance sheet, I'd go broke before the campaign was financed.

In 1978, I was known as a basketball player, not as a politician. Though my celebrity might attract two hundred people instead of fifty to hear me speak, the result would be that I had two hundred people before whom I could fail if I had nothing to say. Giving money to a basketball player who was running for the U.S. Senate was not something most people were eager to do. As I often noted in my speeches in that first campaign, "I took a different road to the U.S. Senate." To most potential contributors, the road was often so far off the beaten track that they couldn't find it.

I would stand before twenty or thirty or eighty people in a living room and pour my heart out. If they liked what they heard, or they felt that I answered questions competently enough, they would make a contribution. For a while, I felt that contributors were as cold as the ice that encased New Jersey month after month in that winter of 1978.

Slowly, the lifetime-association list began to yield results. A call, a second call, a third call determined whether a friend would put his money where his mouth was. The results were sometimes surprising. I raised more money from NBA players than from Princeton alumni. I was told so often that "the check is in the mail" that I could only conclude that an amazing number were being lost by the post office. The leaders of the organized Jewish community, with several notable exceptions, told me candidly before the primary that they were supporting the Republican incumbent, Clifford Case, who had been a friend of Israel for twenty-four years. Acquaintances who had long professed undying admiration for me begged off by saying, "But you're a Democrat!" Surprisingly, I found that California, fertile from the Laker-Knick rivalry of my basketball days, yielded an impressive amount.

There were also journeys that ended in failure. On one particularly disastrous trip, a luncheon organized by a self-described old friend did not yield enough to pay for the food. Thereafter, the worst fund-raising event of any trip received an award called "The Ernie," named after the host of that first negative-cash-flow luncheon.

On another occasion, an oilman basketball fan offered to host a fund-raiser at his Fifth Avenue apartment. On the day of the event, there was a blizzard. He insisted that the event go on anyway. I will never forget how the vast oak floor of his apartment gleamed, as only a few people were scattered around it during my pitch. My original finance committee of twenty-one, who were primarily personal friends of my finance chairman, had raised all they could raise in the first three months of the campaign. After that, it was one phone call and one coffee visit and one luncheon visit at a time.

Two factors helped me with money in 1978. Politics is full of talkers, not doers. My major primary opponent, Dick Leone, couldn't parlay Governor Brendan Byrne's support into contributions. Byrne backed him, but he didn't dislike me. Besides, rarely did Byrne make fund-raising calls. Without more pressure, the fund-raisers and contributors associated with state politics, whom my opponent had counted on to raise his money, took a pass. Leone was competent, honest, predictable, and not at all well known to the public. I was a newcomer to politics, and much more widely known. On top of that advantage was the loophole created by the Supreme Court's decision in *Buckley* v. *Valeo*. I could contribute and/or loan my own campaign an unlimited amount of money. I determined, given what I had made playing basketball, that I could provide up to two hundred and fifty thousand dollars—part loan, part contribution. That was about 19 percent of my whole budget, and, more important, it assured me that I could compete even if I didn't raise as much as I had hoped. With the existence of that self-generated cushion, I was able to raise more. When potential contributors see a campaign with money, they assume it's well run, and they are more likely to make a contribution. Everyone likes to be with a winner, whether in basketball or politics.

The *Buckley* v. *Valeo* loophole had given me a shot at victory even before I declared. In the years ahead, the loophole would become as wide as a barn door for others. Four years later in New Jersey, Frank Lautenberg, a wealthy computer executive with no elective experience, would spend over three and a half million dollars of his own money to win a U.S. Senate seat. In Pennsylvania, the son of the Heinz Ketchup fortune spent more than three million dollars of his own money to get elected to the Senate. In West Virginia, the great-grandson of John D. Rockefeller spent ten million two hundred and fifty thousand dollars of his own money to get three hundred and seventy thousand votes. In Wisconsin in 1988, Herb Kohl promised to spend primarily his own money in his Senate campaign; seven and a half million dollars later, he won. Michael Huffington was one candidate of immense wealth who fell short of joining the "rich caucus," composed, not so facetiously, of senators who "bought" their seats themselves. In 1994, Huffington spent an unprecedented twenty-eight million dollars of his own money trying to win a U.S. Senate seat from California, unsuccessfully.

Whereas a candidate could contribute as much of his own money as he chose, he could accept individual contributions of only two thousand dollars from others—one thousand of it for the primary and one thousand for the general election. Pat Moynihan used to joke that under the old fund-raising system a politician risked being obligated to twenty rich people who gave him one hundred thousand dollars each, but under the new system a politician risked obligating himself to a whole class of people who could afford to give two thousand dollars each.

Money was raised in the new system by personalizing your candidacy to rich people. The sequence of the hoped-for events always began in the same places—a living room in Summit, Cherry Hill, Chevy Chase, Evanston, Scarsdale, Short Hills, Scottsdale, Beverly Hills, Portola Valley, Ladue, River Oaks, Bloomfield Hills, Shaker Heights, Bryn Mawr, Palm Beach, Nantucket, Easthampton, Palm Springs. The activity was usually the same. A group of well-dressed guests awaited your arrival. After saying hello to the hostess, you ducked into the bathroom to straighten your tie, and then gradually moved around the room exchanging pleasantries with individual guests and snatching vegetables or shrimp from the buffet. The host would call the people into the living room or onto the patio, and you would stand in front of the fireplace or next to the pool as the host introduced you, to make a few comments and answer questions. Once you had impressed a house party, you hoped to use that base to build support for future small breakfasts or larger luncheons, and finally to attract an expanded group of supporters who would run a big dinner with a thousand tickets at a thousand dollars per person. Often in the chase for campaign money you met bright, talented people; occasionally, a friendship developed. But just as often the people who attended fund-raisers blurred in your memory and events and locations began to look very much the same.

For their part, many of the people in these living rooms met fifteen, or even twenty, candidates in one political season. As they observed more politicians, their standards rose, their questions became more pointed, and their demands intensified. Many of them wanted more than competence in the candidate. Increasingly, they looked for commitments. An hour in front of a group of insistent fund-raisers became as challenging as addressing a group of newspaper editors. Politicians who go through this process have to get used to people looking them over as if they were a piece of meat in the supermarket.

Many hosts had a den in which one wall was covered by pictures of the host with an array of Democratic presidential aspirants and well-known senators or congresspeople. I always enjoyed seeing who had preceded me on the hotspot in front of the fireplace. Some hosts were cause oriented. They raised money from fellow believers. Whether the bond was the whales, the environment as a whole, capital gains, gun control, fiscal prudence, oil, Israel, India, Greece—unless you shared the group's views on a particular issue, it was unlikely that you would raise much money. Other hosts, whose walls were covered with paintings, opened their homes out of friendship. They were kindred spirits in a nonpolitical sense—old friends and business associates, basketball fans, lovers of art, those in search of a new experience; they all raised money without implied conditions, and they were my preferred fund-raisers. My goal was to find what I came to regard as "monogamous" fund-raisers—people who asked others for money only on my behalf and who had friends untapped by other politicians.

In the nineteenth century, senators were on the payroll of the railroads and the power companies. The historian Henry Adams referred to American democracy as "government of the people, by the people, and for the benefit of senators." There were scandals such as Crédit Mobilier, in which congressmen (including future president James Garfield) made money out of investments in railroad construction that their votes had helped to finance. The Crédit Mobilier revelations brought only censure from the Republican Congress. Then there were the distillers who bribed Treasury officials in order to evade taxes on whiskey. William Belknap, Grant's secretary of war, was impeached on charges of accepting bribes from traders at Indian reservations and resigned. In these cases there was little pretense of serving the public interest. President Grant could lead an army, but he couldn't tell a rogue from a saint in his own presidential administration.

Today, the flow of money into politics is more complicated but equally destructive. Its biggest channels are the contributions of political-action committees, or PACs. There are corporate PACs, funded by the voluntary contributions of a company's employees; union or trade-association PACs funded by the contributions of members; and free-standing or cause PACs, funded by those who believe in the cause. PACs are a loophole in the 1974 law. Each can give a candidate five thousand dollars in the primary election and five thousand dollars in the general election.

Corporate PACs have replaced the corporate sinecures for senators and congresspeople. In some campaigns, they represent 50 percent of total contributions. The five-thousand-dollar limit for PACs allows corporate interests to have a bigger impact on campaigns than individuals, with their thousand-dollar limitation. Many PACs buy access as insurance against changes in law adverse to their corporate interest. The contributor assumes that the corporation's Washington representative, who oversees the PAC allocations, can get an audience with the elected official, or at least with the official's staff, to make the special-interest case. Occasionally, that meeting results in report language that accompanies passage of a bill, or a colloquy on the floor between two senators, with the intent of directing the regulators to interpret a section of the law in a way that favors the special interest. In rare instances, the meeting produces an amendment that alters an effective date for a tax provision or a regulation in favor of the corporation. To assure a willing ear whatever the elective outcome, corporate PACs frequently give to both parties, like prudent businessmen hedging their risks. Those who control PACs are often blunt in their quest for any information that might affect their interests. Once, at a big PAC fund-raiser for the Democratic Party, a Washington PAC representative came up to me and said, "Senator, you've lost a lot of weight. What's the matter? Have you got AIDS?"

Occasionally, a politician will raise money through direct-mail solicitation aimed at targeted mailing lists. This approach yields many small contributions, but it takes time and a big investment up front. If 3 percent of those mailed to actually respond, the mailing is considered a success. Once someone contributes, you can probably get that person to contribute a second or third time during the campaign, but, as with compound interest, it takes time before big money builds up. The greatest returns come from strident appeals to large but narrow constituencies. Jesse Helms and Oliver North have raised gigantic amounts of money by appealing to a dedicated base of right-wing Americans who give when buttons marked "communism," "big government," "abortion," "homosexuals," "birth control," and "secular humanism" are pushed.

Jesse Helms's National Congressional Club hovers over North Carolina politics like a specter. It has sizable direct-mail fund-raising capabilities established over twenty-three years. The tactics are transparent: Helms offers an outrageous amendment in the Senate and insists on a vote. The Congressional Club puts that vote in a direct-mail piece targeted at ultraconservatives, and the money rolls in. Liberals, such as Ted Kennedy and Barbara Boxer, touch different buttons: "abortion rights," "right-wing fanaticism," "civil liberties," "gun control." Helms uses Kennedy and Kennedy uses Helms to energize the direct-mail contributions of the right and the left. They are like partners in a dance for dollars.

A more recent innovation is telemarketing, but the targeted blind solicitation by a telemarketing firm is not as successful as an appeal by the candidate. A Democratic Senate challenger in 1994 proclaimed to me in October that he had a shot at winning because of his fund-raising prowess on the telephone. He claimed that for six to eight hours every day for nine months, with two fund-raising assistants handing him names, he had sat in a room calling people he didn't know and asking for money. He told me that he had made more than four thousand calls since the first of the year. (He lost.) Usually, however, the financial base of federal legislators comes from PACs and the rich. To have enough money for a statewide campaign in New Jersey, I had to raise an average of twenty thousand dollars per week for six years. I raised more than double that amount for my 1990 reelection.

My wife has a theory about politicians. Ernestine maintains that a politician's greatest strength often becomes his greatest weakness. President Clinton's impressive facility with language confines him in a prison of glibness and makes citizens who are less verbal suspicious that he is too smooth. George Bush's personal reserve and dignity enhanced his presidential command, but also prevented him from making a connection with average people struggling to make ends meet. Ronald Reagan's nonoperational leadership style, which focused only on the biggest picture and then only through carefully crafted scripts, gave people a clear sense of what he stood for, but it also led to the grotesque mismanagement of the S&L crisis and the corruption of Iran-contra. Jimmy Carter's impeccable personal morality and religious conception of public service reassured people after Watergate, but also allowed opponents in the rough and tumble of politics to say that he was soft and out of touch. Richard Nixon's penchant for secrecy and for shaping his historical image led to his re-emergence as a presidential candidate in 1968 and to his reputation as a foreign-policy sage in the 1980s, but it also accounted in part for the Watergate break-in and cover-up and the decision to tape visitors in the Oval Office. LBJ's skills as a political manipulator who often shaded the truth helped to bring about his legislative triumphs, but also made him unable to lead a nation yearning for candor in the midst of an unpopular war.

In my 1990 campaign, money proved to be my Achilles' heel. When I first thought about running for elective office in New Jersey in a 1974 congressional race, the question of money loomed very large. Consultants and advisers reiterated the point that, without enough money, good people had lost. I didn't run that year, but I remembered the advice. In my first Senate race, I didn't need sizable amounts, because mainstream Republicans felt no strong affinity for my opponent, who was a newcomer and had upset the incumbent. I had sufficient funds, with my own seed money and the help of friends. The total I spent in 1978 was close to one and a half million dollars. In 1984, I raised four and a half million dollars, in a contest against an unknown opponent, and I used the money chiefly to pay for television ads. As I went into the six-year 1990 cycle, I started raising money in 1985 with the goal of building up a huge campaign war chest.

First of all, I believed that if I had millions in the bank I would draw a weak opponent—a pre-emptive strategy that had worked in 1984. With approval ratings of nearly 80 percent or more and an apparently unlimited fund-raising capacity, I felt that most potentially difficult opponents would pass, thereby allowing me to save resources in the long run. A large war chest is part of an incumbent's armor.

Second, raising a large war chest would give me the flexibility to run for national office. If I had several million dollars in the bank and drew a weak opponent in 1990, I could bank the surplus for a potential 1992 presidential run. Walter Mondale won the Democratic nomination in 1984 because the more than eighteen million dollars he raised allowed him to offset the bump that Gary Hart got from his early victory in New Hampshire. Dick Gephardt told me after his 1988 presidential run that he had concluded that money was without question the most important component of a presidential campaign. I was far from decided on a run, but as someone who wanted to keep options open, I considered this a cost-free strategy.

Third, I went along with grandiose recommendations by my staff that I build a polling-and-computer infrastructure that could be transferred to a national effort. In 1987, we started polling in markets other than New Jersey. The purpose was to help me understand what constituencies certain colleagues had to deal with, so that I could garner wider support for my legislative initiatives in behalf of New Jersey. In addition to that legitimate rationale was the ambitious goal of charting the country with our own "typologies." We had developed a set of voter types into which we classified people. These categories were value-based—that is, we asked questions that defined the respondent's values—and after polling in this way we could target our communications to a particular group based not on issues but on shared values. If we honed this communication-and-polling technique, it would become an advantage few other politicians could boast. In addition to the polling, we made an investment in a large, secure computer system that could quickly be expanded in a national effort. These two investments together cost nearly two million dollars.

Fourth, I wanted to be prepared for the unforeseen. If my preemptive strategy failed and I found myself running against a wealthy opponent who would spend personal money, I couldn't match this overnight. A rich candidate could write a check for a three-million-dollar TV-ad buy in October and run a strong race. I had to raise that amount over nearly two years. Never wanting to be unprepared, I raised the money.

Fifth, in the years leading up to 1990, I began to realize I could no longer be personally indifferent to money. My family's relatively comfortable circumstances when I was young, and my generous salary with the Knicks, had created a life in which I rarely thought about money. Combined with my natural frugality—my teammates joked that I had kept the first dollar I'd ever earned, which is one of the reasons they called me Dollar Bill—my income had always been enough for me to do what I wanted. After I became a senator, however, the bulk of my annual income consisted of my Senate salary. Nearly all assets that I owned I had owned when I became a senator. Since I felt there were no acceptable ways to make investments without conflict of interest, I didn't invest in stocks and I refused to buy real estate other than a Washington home. The only financial assets I owned or acquired were some government bonds and notes. Far from amassing wealth, I was liquidating assets just to pay ongoing bills. I once calculated that being in the Senate, as opposed to holding another job in New Jersey, cost me more than half my Senate salary. After subtracting the expense of living in Washington and New Jersey, with the accompanying two sets of cars, homes, and electricians, I had little left. I suppose I could have shared a one-room bachelor apartment in Washington and commuted from New Jersey to the Senate, but I wasn't prepared to do that to my family. Because I wasn't, the expenses mounted quickly. The normal impulse to count up your assets was for me a painful one. I was watching them decline. It was as if my assets were grains of sand streaming from the top half of an hourglass. This personal financial pressure had implications for the campaign. Unable to dip into personal funds to support my campaign in a crunch, as I had in 1978, I needed a large campaign fund in the bank to cushion against the unknown.

Sixth, fund-raising became a challenge, a game played in competition with myself. By the end of 1988, I had raised as much money as I had spent in the 1984 campaign. I still had no opponent on the horizon. The New Jersey Republicans regarded as tough opponents by conventional political thinkers chose not to run. Still I kept raising money. If we pulled in fifty thousand dollars, I wanted seventy-five thousand dollars at the next event. If we succeeded with a two-hundred-and-fifty-thousand-dollar dinner, why not a five-hundred-thousand-dollar dinner? Everyone felt triumphant when we surpassed our goals. Other senators regarded me with envy. The fund-raising ability became a part of a generally perceived political strength. How could you have too much money?

Fund-raising in 1989 and 1990 took less of my time than it had in 1984 and much less than it had in 1978. The campaign fund-raising operation was led by Betty Sapoch, a friend of twenty-five years. If the effort was not the best in the country, it was close to it. Betty made thousands of people feel good about giving more to a politician than they had ever anticipated they would. In that sense, she had a little Mark Hanna in her. She paid attention to details, insisting on stylish table decorations at dinners and quick thank-you notes afterward. She was an extraordinary networker, always available to listen, and over time she developed a unique capacity to field complaints in a way that made a caller feel better about me after the call. One night in 1989, with a dinner at the Waldorf-Astoria in New York, she directed an effort that raised a million dollars. She collected six hundred thousand dollars at a dinner in Los Angeles a few months later. In both places, I had good and influential friends who were willing to ask their friends and associates to contribute, but Betty put it all together. I traveled to Austin, Dallas, Houston, and El Paso to raise money. I visited Chicago several times, for fifty-thousand-dollar events in people's homes and a two-hundred-and-fifty-thousand-dollar event in a hotel. Friends and interested supporters hosted luncheons or cocktail parties in Palm Beach, Miami, Jacksonville, and Fort Lauderdale. Other friends offered to organize smaller fund-raisers in Baltimore, Atlanta, St. Louis, Kansas City, Denver, and Seattle. The country became dotted with Bradley fund-raisers, and money kept pouring in.

Only 10 percent of it came from PACs. The largest amount came in contributions of two hundred and fifty dollars to two thousand dollars from individuals all over the country. Contributors from New Jersey, New York, and Pennsylvania formed the core of my support, with California close behind. Ultimately, we raised a total of $12.9 million. But it did not make me invincible. Instead, it became a string that almost undid my political career when it was yanked.

SETTING UP the administrative pieces that could be transferred to a national campaign and maintaining an active fund-raising operation for five years yielded a very high "burn rate," meaning that although we were raising a lot of money, we were spending a lot on polls, offices, fund-raising staff, and computer programs and hardware. The fund-raising and political infrastructure became so expensive that much of what we raised was sopped up by it. Once we had raised the money, few people focused on the net—the amount we needed to spend after Labor Day in 1990. This insouciance led to some wasteful expenditures. For example, in the early summer of 1990, to counter the charges of my opponent, Christine Todd Whitman, that we had too much money, we ran public-service television commercials warning about lead poisoning in the environment. Some in the campaign felt that the commercials might save people's lives, and perhaps they did, but they produced little goodwill and resulted in less money in the bank.

People gave money to my campaign for different reasons. Many contributed because they were personal friends who wished me well. Many contributed because they had known me from my days on the road playing basketball, or from a particular legislative effort such as tax reform or Third World debt. Some admired speeches I had made on Russia, Japan, or trade policy. Some gave because they had followed my Senate service and supported my overall voting record. Others contributed because my personal friends asked them to and they wanted to please those friends. Finally, there were some contributors who wanted to get in on the ground floor of a presidential campaign. I mistook their support of me as being a more personal commitment than it was. During 1992, I discovered that virtually every person of significant means who was a Democrat and had supported me in 1989–90 had given to Bill Clinton or Bob Kerrey or Tom Harkin or Paul Tsongas in their presidential campaigns. So much for monogamous fund-raisers.

When it comes to what people get for their political contributions, I'm more Harry Truman than LBJ. Those who have given out of friendship, a sense of values, or admiration of my record have never asked for anything. I tried to make sure that no one gave money with expectations of receiving a favor. When it comes to fund-raising ethics, I'm similar to a friend who, in a response to a CIA lie-detector test, answered the question "Do you advocate overthrowing the government of the United States?" in the negative. The alarms went off, indicating that he had lied. The question was asked again. Same response. The question was changed to "Do you advocate overthrowing the government of the United States *by unlawful means?*" This time when my friend said no, he passed the test. I, too, had become hyperconscious of fine distinctions. I often saw potential conflicts of interest in harmless circumstances.

Like many of my colleagues in the Senate, I go to great extremes to ensure that no one can ever sustain a question of ethics about my service. In the 1990 campaign, this obsession with rectitude translated into having a full-time campaign accountant and bookkeeper, two law firms on call for specific legal questions, and a campaign manager whose greatest strength was his honesty and financial-accounting skills. All of this cost money.

Contributions were meticulously logged in the new computer system. Biographical data, such as hobbies, education, and children's names, were quickly entered—or, for those with biographical gaps, obtained in follow-up calls. With more than seventy-five thousand contributors, such information would assure more personal communication in mailings to a larger number of my supporters. The nightmare of my public service is that someone on my staff to whom I have delegated authority will make an ethical error out of ignorance or fatigue, such as failing to record the name of a contributor or the correct amount of the contribution. Most campaigns are run out of a shoebox—that is, contribution cards and financial records are not well ordered or computerized. Though I took every extra precaution, politics is full of trapdoors.

My desire to be super-clean made me vulnerable to any hint of criticism about fund-raising. Like Woodrow Wilson, who worried about criticism of his perfectly legal professor's pension, I had tried to set a high moral tone in my campaign. I had seen no theoretical conflict between idealism and raising money. Now, in a kind of political judo, the money was what my opponent was using against me.

By the summer of 1990, the press had begun to depict the race as David against Goliath. When I started in politics, every time my name was mentioned it was "Bill Bradley, former New York Knick." Now it was "Bill Bradley, the candidate who raised twelve million dollars." The press did not focus on what I stood for or what I had accomplished; the money overshadowed everything else. In isolation and without explanation, the amount looked embarrassing. When I supported campaign-finance reform, my opponent's campaign said that it was "similar to someone eating giant éclairs and saying they're observing Lent." But it was too late to do anything about it. I had raised too much money for a New Jersey Senate campaign, and in that campaign I could hardly allude to the money's potential national purposes, or to the five-year burn-rate problem. As with the state-tax revolt I was saddled with, I just had to get through it.

When the fall campaign began, of the nearly twelve million dollars we had raised up to that point, only five million remained in the bank. Over the next eight weeks, we spent three million dollars on television advertising alone. The money that had been laboriously raised over five years poured out in days. After the narrow election victory, a college friend of mine who had raised more than a hundred thousand dollars for the campaign complained loudly that we had ended up with less than a million dollars in the bank. He and his friends had thought that the goal of all the fund-raising was a presidential war chest.

The 12.9-million-dollar lesson was indeed expensive. I had started out with the highest of motives and had followed every rule in the book. I had lived my life so as never to have a blemish, and yet somehow I felt tarnished by the fund-raising success of 1985–90. It was as if I were walking around with a scarlet dollar sign on my chest. At a minimum, it made me see the folly of the fund-raising strategy. The antidote, I realized, was twofold: a holiday from fund-raising, and fighting for campaign-finance reform with a new sense of urgency.

With the decline of the parties as sources of funds, individual congresspeople must raise their own money. There is no Lyndon Johnson delivering rescue money for Democrats in the final weeks of the election. The quest for money for the next election begins only months after the last one. It is constant. It drains time and energy from the lives of many elected officials and opens doors to unending speculation about corruption, influence peddling, or, in my case, misguided conceptions of what constitutes preparedness. One senator complaining to me about the current system recalled how he ran into a colleague at 4 A.M. in the Dallas airport. Both were changing planes, having come from fund-raisers in different cities, and both were waiting to get an early-morning flight back to Washington for a day of Senate votes.

Certain interests do attempt to buy off congresspeople with contributions—not overtly but by ingratiating themselves. I've actually been visited by cause PACs urging that I not support campaign-finance reform if it impedes their use of money in the political process. It's a mark of how bad things have gotten that they make these requests without blushing. When corporate PACs displace parties as funding sources, politicians answer to such interest groups more than to their party leaders. After all, the political leaders don't help them when they're in the greatest need. What is threatened is not only any sense of loyally serving a party's interests but also the sense of serving even the "public interest."

Finally, there are the independent PACs, which don't give money to a candidate but spend their own money to champion a specific issue. For example, the National Rifle Association has a PAC that runs negative TV commercials against candidates who disagree with them on gun control. If one candidate opposes gun control and the other one supports it, an anti-gun-control commercial can make a difference, even though the campaign and the independent PAC are technically separate. Policing the contacts an independent PAC may or may not make with a friendly candidate is virtually impossible.

Beyond PACs, big money enters politics through something called the "coordinated campaign," which is supposedly a party effort to register voters and to get them out to vote for all the candidates on the party ticket that year in a particular state. The candidate at the top of the ticket usually controls the expenditures, which means that the candidate's campaign manager usually places as many campaign workers as possible on the payroll of the coordinated campaign. That way the candidate's campaign war chest can be saved to buy TV ads. There are no limits on the amount of money that someone can give to a coordinated campaign, and in a national election there is one in each state. Wealthy individuals who want to help a presidential nominee have given more than five hundred thousand dollars in one year to separate state-coordinated campaigns. And that is after the campaign reform of 1974.

Senator Fritz Hollings says that his Senate colleagues aren't corrupt, the system is corrupt. Fundamental campaign-finance reform must be comprehensive and embodied in an amendment to the U.S. Constitution. TV and mail costs should be dramatically discounted to reflect the public ownership of the airwaves and the public interest in an informed electorate. There should be voluntary taxpayer funding, but no PACs, no big contributions to special committees, no unaccounted-for money for state parties to use in behalf of candidates, and no rich candidates able to buy an election with their wealth. The amount of money candidates get should depend on how much the citizens of their state give them through a non-deductible check-off of up to five thousand dollars above their tax liability on their federal tax returns. The money from the tax check-off would go into a fund that, eight weeks before the general election, would be distributed equally to Republican, Democratic, or qualified independent candidates. Candidates would have to live with what the people of their

state gave them. If that means that there will not be enough money to inform voters about the views of the candidates (money for the presidential
check-off is dropping), it will be the voters themselves who will suffer.
But at least it will be their choice; the point is that the citizens will be in
charge. If candidates in different years are given different amounts for a
campaign, their circumstances will be no less uncertain than those most
Americans face every day. Some senators have suggested a combination of
spending limits based on population and media costs in a state and a national lottery dedicated to public financing of federal campaigns. At least
as another form of voluntary citizen financing, a lottery would also effect
change. Money in politics is similar to the ants in your kitchen. Just when
you think you've got them blocked, they find another way to get in. Only
hermetically sealing the kitchen off will work—which means total voluntary public funding of campaigns encompassed by a constitutional amendment. Anything less means that democracy can still be corrupted.

THE FUND-RAISER in Seattle in 1992 was similar to hundreds of
others I had attended over my fourteen years in the Senate. The candidate this time was Patty Murray, running for the Senate to succeed Brock
Adams.

Patty was the daughter of the manager of Meredith's dime store in
Bothell, Washington (population one thousand). From the time she was
twelve, she worked the cash register in the store; on a great day she took
in six hundred dollars and on an average day two hundred. Along with
her six brothers and sisters, she lived "across the river and over the
tracks," as she puts it—on the poor side of town. Her father, the son of
an asparagus farmer from Kennewick, had gotten his education on the GI
Bill and had worked six-day weeks in the store for years. He gave up the
store when his multiple sclerosis made full-time work an impossibility.
Patty was fifteen then and remembers her mother budgeting down to the
last penny to get by. Her mother, who still had five kids at home, had
never held a job, but with the assistance of a federal education program
she got a degree in accounting from Lake Washington Vo-Tech College
and went to work for Black Ball Transport, Inc., which operated ferries
between Port Angeles, Washington, and Victoria, British Columbia. For
twenty years, she held down a job without complaining, raised a loving
family, and took care of her increasingly invalided husband.

Patty paid her own way through college, where she earned a degree in recreational therapy. She wanted to work with the handicapped, but the best-paying job she could find was as a secretary. With shorthand facility and hundred-word-a-minute typing skills, she worked at different times for the H. H. Robertson construction company, Rainier Bank's international division, and Washington State University. With the money she made, she put her husband, Rob, through Washington State, where in 1975 he received a degree in economics.

Rob and Patty moved to Seattle, where Rob worked for the General Steamship Company and then Stevedore Services of America, overseeing the movement of cargo in and out of the Port of Seattle. Their first child was born in 1977 and their second in 1980. Rob loved computers; as early as 1975 he had bought a Sycom System, which he taught himself to use. Quickly he became a computer problem solver for his employers, fielding calls in the middle of the night from people on the docks who had misplaced cargo in the computer. He would work them through the steps without looking at a computer screen and then roll over and go back to sleep. He had a structural mind and he easily developed suitable skills for the advancing information era, but he worried that if Patty won the Senate seat and the family moved to Washington, D.C., the East Coast ports might not offer jobs in his specialty.

In 1979, Patty was lobbying the Washington state legislature to keep funds for parental education in the budget, when a legislator referred to her derisively as merely "a mom in tennis shoes." Patty recalls saying to herself, "This mom in tennis shoes is going to beat him." She did, and the proposed cuts were defeated. A few years later she was appointed to the Shoreline school board in Seattle and then became its president. When she decided to run for the state senate in 1988, she was regarded as a "hope candidate." The antiwoman bias pervaded the language of male legislators. She was told to forget her candidacy, but did not. She persevered and she won. In her second term, against the opposition of the chemical industry and the farmers, she introduced a bill to control pesticides and meticulously lined up a coalition of consumers, environmentalists, and health-conscious businesspeople and won. Then, in 1991, the Anita Hill–Clarence Thomas hearings propelled her to a decision to run for the U.S. Senate. "Being short, four feet eleven," she says, "people underestimate you."

I arrived a few days after her last debate with her Republican opponent, Rod Chandler, a five-term incumbent congressman. In her closing statement, Patty had talked about the buildup of the budget deficit and the neglect of domestic affairs in the 1980s, and then she criticized Chandler for voting to raise his congressional pay. In response, Rod inexplicably spouted lyrics to Roger Miller's "Dang Me"—"Dang me, Dang me / Oughta take a rope and hang me / high from the highest tree / Woman, would you weep for me?"—a song about a man who leaves his wife and baby at home to go out with the boys. His tone and his facial expression reeked of condescension and chauvinist glee. He had misjudged Patty, who shot back, "That's just the attitude that got me into this race, Rod."

All that went before in the debate was now irrelevant. Patty had the advantage. With two weeks left in the campaign, she didn't have to retell this story. Instead, people came up to her at almost every stop, expressing their outrage at Chandler's response. A candidate yearns for something like this to happen in the campaign—something that underlines its main theme. Patti's opponent now could not avoid being labeled as a male insensitive to women who strive for excellence. He was finished.

The fund-raiser I attended for Patty was in the home of Thurston and Catherine Roach, Arkansas natives, who were friends of the Clintons. The living room looked out over Lake Washington, and it was raining, as it often is in Seattle. There were about sixty people in the Roaches' home when I arrived. The routine was the same as it always has been. I walked in with Patty and Seattle's mayor, Norm Rice. I began "meeting and greeting" the attendees. Three women congratulated me on the floor speech I had made in defense of Anita Hill. Two said they had wanted me to run for president this year. One man recalled watching me play for the Knicks. No one said anything about tax reform, Third World debt, or the Central Valley Project, the esoteric triumphs of my legislative record. One of the guests recalled a sports banquet at which I had spoken in 1979, at the request of Scoop Jackson. Another remembered when I was in Seattle campaigning for Senator Warren Magnuson in 1980, and yet another recalled my appearances for Brock Adams in 1986 and Mike Lowry in 1988. All were hopeful of a Democratic victory in the presidential race, and all were dedicated to the mom in tennis shoes.

The host called the room to order and introduced Mayor Rice, who introduced Lynn Cutler, of the Democratic National Committee, who would introduce me. Lynn began by noting that I had been campaigning for women for a long time. I had campaigned for her, she said, when she had run for Congress from Iowa in 1982. I stood against the wall and thought, "That was ten years ago!" I had been doing this for fourteen years—fourteen years of living-room fund-raisers, party dinners, tarmac press conferences. That was longer than I had played pro basketball.

During my first few years in the Senate, when candidates wanted me to campaign for them they asked me because I was a draw as a former basketball player. I was regularly taken to a gym to shoot baskets with the candidate, for the local television news. Then, when I was intensely focused on tax reform, trade, exchange rates, and international-debt issues, I became a draw because of my views on business and finance. I appeared before businesspeople and bankers to give my perspectives on the economy. By the late 1980s, I had begun drawing people as a national party figure and a potential presidential candidate.

I was in demand for more than a decade, and I complied with many, many requests. I went to Idaho for Church; Missouri for Eagleton; Indiana for Bayh; Iowa for Culver; Iowa for Harkin; South Dakota for Mc-Govern; Delaware for Biden; Tennessee for Sasser; Maryland for Mikulski; Maryland for Sarbanes; Washington for Magnuson; Washington for Adams; California for Cranston; California for Boxer; California for Feinstein; New Mexico for Bingaman; Nebraska for Kerrey; Nebraska for Exon; Colorado for Hart; Colorado for Wirth; North Carolina for Sanford; Ohio for Metzenbaum; Ohio for Glenn; Vermont for Leahy; Louisiana for Long; Kentucky for Ford; Kentucky for Huddleston; Maine for Mitchell; Connecticut for Dodd; North Dakota for Conrad; Montana for Baucus; Nevada for Reid; Nevada for Bryan; Wisconsin for Feingold; Wisconsin for Kohl; Virginia for Robb; and West Virginia for Byrd. I also went to the other states for twenty other Democratic challengers who never made it to the Senate, and to countless congressional districts where Democrats invited me. I appeared at events that raised many millions of dollars in total. The only place I knew I'd never be invited back to was South Dakota, after I had proposed returning a part of the Black Hills to the Sioux. There I was persona non grata.

With experience, I had grown more comfortable with speaking, even though my improvement had been marginal. I was more spontaneous. I invested less preparation time. I organized trips so that I didn't spend a whole weekend of travel just to appear at a two-hour event on Saturday night. But the same patterns of activity persisted. Nothing was fresh, much was predictable.

Year after year, I traveled, and now I asked myself why. I wasn't running for president. I wasn't lining up delegates. I didn't build lists of party activists with whom I stayed in touch. I had made more than a few friends along the way. I did get to know colleagues better by seeing them in their home-state environments. But the chits I was supposed to be collecting could be cashed only rarely.

During Truman's 1940 Senate campaign, three senior U.S. senators came to Missouri to endorse him in his contested primary. It helped his confidence, but it did nothing for his election. The issues were too local. That's the way it is with most visiting senators. They give the candidate a boost through heartfelt flattery, but they do little for the outcome of the campaign.

If you have loyal supporters and if you're doing your job thinking about the country's direction and sharing your conclusions with your constituents, then a guest senator adds little to your luster. Few additional contributors give five hundred dollars just to hear a senatorial celebrity. Fund-raising depends on the home-state candidate more than on the candidate's guest. Only the right comment by the right visiting senator in the right campaign situation can make any difference. It happened to me once. In my first campaign, Pat Moynihan came in to campaign for me. In his comments to the press and to my contributors, he quoted Woodrow Wilson, who wrote in *Congressional Government,* "Men of ordinary physique and discretion cannot be Presidents and live, if the strain be not somehow relieved. We shall be obligated always to be picking our chief magistrates from among wise and prudent athletes—a small class."

Too often senators go on the road with the expectation that it will benefit them more than the person running. Or they go on the road just to be on the road, like aging entertainers in search of one more crowd. In either case, they are of little significant help to the candidate and rarely help themselves in any permanent way. Still, the ritual goes on, as if it were a pilgrimage or some sort of team requirement.

How did my presence in Seattle help Patty Murray? She was the epitome of the outsider running against the male-dominated system. To have me there seemed to say that the Senate club, in which I served, would welcome the "outsider." I'm not sure that helped. Prior to the living-room fund-raiser, we had held a press conference in front of her campaign headquarters, in the Pioneer Square section of Seattle. Norm Rice stood on one side of her and I stood on the other. Patty stood on a box, which added a foot to her height. "Patty," a reporter said, "last week you had Senator Biden. Two weeks ago Senator Rockefeller, and now Senator Bradley. How are you going to take on the Senate when so many senators are campaigning for you?"

As I stood in the big room above Lake Washington in this fourteenth year on the political road, I slowly realized how far my political perspective had shifted. After 1990, I had begun to speak out more forcefully on highly charged and divisive issues, such as race, on which the country needed candor, healing, and leadership. This had been a liberating experience for me, and it had touched other people. For example, in the wake of the acquittal of the Los Angeles policemen who beat Rodney King, I went to the Senate floor to speak and found myself grabbing several pencils and hitting the podium fifty-six times in two minutes to simulate the fifty-six blows that they had delivered in two minutes to Rodney King's body. The response to that spontaneous act with the pencils surprised me. Many people attacked me, but many others praised me. One composer in Philadelphia wrote a symphony he entitled *56 Blows*. What differed from previous public expressions toward me was the intensity.

A senator's job is to pass laws, and much of my legislative efforts had gone to righting wrongs through big reform, but the job has another dimension—using the platform of the office to speak, to challenge, to lead. In that latter category, I had failed, because until after the 1990 election I had not used the potential of my office to confront Americans with the tough choices of our day. I had not waded into turbulent waters by defining my views clearly, preferring instead the comfort of ambiguity or silence. Ambition had fueled a desire to please, and had choked my leadership impulses. For much of my career I had no authentic political voice. I had been campaigning all over the country not to change the world or shake up my audiences but to please the roomful of people to whom I was speaking. The issues I championed did not move people. I had mounted no crusades for abortion rights or against TV violence; there were no calls to protect American jobs or to confront greedy big business or to provide all Americans with health care; no urgency expressed about middle-class economic stress; no call for policies to ease our entry into the information age; no candor about wealth distribution and the national debt, or the real spending cuts and tax increases that it would take to right our national course. My friends, staff, and a few specialists who followed the legislative process knew my values and what I strove to uphold with every vote, every speech, every committee hearing, but to the public at large I was a blank slate. Occasionally, I broke through momentarily, but then I quickly returned to playing the inside game of legislating, getting things for New Jersey, and using my senatorial celebrity only to raise money for colleagues. Most fund-raisers involve a mixed Republican and Democratic audience, so frequently the pitch is not even supposed to be partisan. The less ideological and more personal the approach, the better. That individualized, nonthreatening manner had become my style. I was trying to make them like me.

It was a successful style for fund-raisers. But what was my purpose? I had reasoned that if I didn't polarize people, I could more easily build a legislative coalition. But passing laws and mobilizing a country require different styles. Until 1991, when I began to speak from my gut as well as my head, I had been content to follow a nonconfrontational strategy that had always allowed me to achieve my goals. I was smooth, not sharp-edged; bland, not "exciting." Understatement was my trademark. Intellectual analysis was my approach. The modest format of a town meeting or a small fund-raiser suited me better than delivering the partisan stem-winder or the prophetic jeremiad. I wore discretion as a badge. I almost never assigned blame for our predicament, or knowingly offended an audience, even if I thought they were dead wrong. As a result, my words rarely had the ring of truth to the nonpolitical observer.

The event in the Seattle living room was a perfect occasion for the same old stuff. Lynn Cutler finished her introduction. I took a few steps out of the corner toward the center of the room and started to talk. Picking individuals in the room, I elaborated on anecdotes each of them had told me about Patty. I spoke about her record in the state legislature and the status of her campaign. I said that Patty's opponent had raised $3.4 million to her $1.3 million. I said how difficult it was for a woman to raise money—there were organizations, such as Emily's List or the Women's National Political Caucus, that gave money only to women, but rarely did a woman's hardest efforts result in a war chest equal to that of her male opponent. I pointed out that most of Patty's money had come from women in small contributions of, on average, forty-seven dollars. I thanked them for coming to this five-hundred-dollar-per-person fund-raiser. They laughed, since the tickets were a hundred dollars. I told them to make their individual contributions as close as possible to five hundred dollars by the end of the campaign, and to do it just for me. They laughed again. I urged them to think of the historic nature of this race, telling them that good candidates sometimes lose when they haven't been able to raise enough money to get their message out. I said that over time I'd learned never to take anything for granted. I pointed out that Patty's opponent had made a grievous gaffe in the last debate, so we had a chance against his superior financial resources, if Patty could just raise enough to remind people about it. I suggested that Patty's race was an advertisement for the need for campaign-finance reform. I said that we needed her vote for reform and her voice for women. I said to give more now so that Patty would be in the Senate for them and for the state of Washington. I said that of all the things someone could give, time and money were the two most important. And at this stage in the campaign, what Patty needed was money, money, money. So give, give, give.

As I spoke, I couldn't imagine Woodrow Wilson saying what I was saying. For LBJ, the gathering would have been too insignificant. Harry Truman would have frowned at the direct solicitation, and Mark Hanna, the man who started us down this crazy fund-raising path—well, Mark Hanna was popping a chocolate into his mouth and smiling.

9

Night Thoughts

ODERN PRESIDENTIAL DEBATES are very diffi-
cult to win. They have become the arena of the big mistake.
Richard Nixon forgot to use makeup in 1960. Gerald Ford
forgot that Poland wasn't a member of the free world in
1976. Michael Dukakis forgot to defend his wife's honor by challenging
the questioner in 1988. Debates don't test comprehensive knowledge,
wisdom, courage, steadfastness, moral strength, or honesty. They provide only a glimpse of the human being who is the candidate. They reward glibness, aggressiveness, and attractive physical appearance. To do
exceptionally well requires spontaneity, but that means taking risks. Few
politicians take risks.

Most candidates plan their responses and regurgitate them on cue.
Even apparently spontaneous moments are often scripted and practiced
assiduously. I believe that it's easier to get candidates to reveal themselves and their abilities in a series of nonconfrontational hourlong interviews. A journalist once told me that he got better interviews when he
acted like the sun; if he came on like the winter wind, his interviewees
covered up. I agree. Debates give people more information than most
would have without them, but make no mistake, during debates there is
little sunshine.

Be that as it may, refusing to debate is no longer an option for a candidate. Nineteen seventy-two was the last year without presidential debates. Richard Nixon, having lost the most important of his 1960 debates with John Kennedy, sat on his lead in 1972 and allowed his campaign staff to destroy George McGovern. Today the candidates have yielded to the sizable TV audience and the presumed drama of a debate, and in 1987 a Commission on Presidential Debates, whose sole job is to plan and execute this series of ninety-minute encounters, was established by the two major parties. The debate buildup parallels those of major sporting events, but in place of public discussions about player matchups and team scouting reports there is argument over the format. Should it be similar to the Lincoln-Douglas debates, in which the candidates had ample time to develop ideas and respond to each other's views? Should candidates at least ask each other questions? Should the candidates respond to questions put by a panel of journalists, in a glorified joint press conference? If there is to be a panel, each side will want to make certain that no panelist will be hostile to its candidate. The geography of debates is also relevant, and in particular the location of the first debate, which is by far the most important. After the first encounter, the stakes and the audience decrease substantially. There is never enough time for complex issues, but there is still time enough for the big mistake.

In 1992, the Bush campaign began the predebate speculation by exaggerating Clinton's rhetorical skill, so as to dampen the reaction to a possibly poor performance by the president. The rule in sports is "Don't give someone an incentive to play beyond his normal ability." The psychological gamesmanship was particularly important in 1992, because a third candidate, the billionaire Ross Perot, who detested George Bush, figured prominently in debate preparations. After dropping out of the presidential race in July and battling the fear that Republicans would disrupt his daughter's wedding, he returned to the presidential fray about ten days before the first debate, in an unprecedented attempt to buy the presidency with his own money. His presence created even greater unpredictability. In such a three-ring circus, Bush and even Clinton preferred to dampen expectations.

In 1988, the Dukakis campaign had asked me to be their chief TV spokesman. As the Dukakis campaign's spin doctor, I was more interested in promoting my candidate than in giving a candid appraisal of his performance, but the campaign staff offered no guidance on what should be said. After the first debate, in Winston-Salem, North Carolina, I simply claimed that Dukakis had won. The morning after the second Dukakis-Bush debate, in Los Angeles, I appeared opposite Senator Phil Gramm on the *Today* show. The polls showed Bush ahead by nine points. After the show, Gramm said to me, "You did as good a job as possible with the material they gave you in this candidate." His condescension toward Dukakis made me burn with anger, but I didn't show it.

In 1992, I was asked by the Clinton campaign to attend the first Clinton-Bush-Perot debate, in St. Louis. This time the campaign staff would be suggesting a line of comment in advance. When the debate was three-fourths over, Clinton's staff would decide what the final message ought to be; they would print it out and give it to those of us who were partisan commentators for the postdebate radio, TV, and print interviews. Everyone would say the same thing. That way a consistent message would have a chance of getting through.

On the flight out to St. Louis, I talked with some reporter friends, who felt that unless Bush did something to change the course of the campaign, he would lose. All through the previous spring, these reporters had felt that Clinton could never win: the so-called character issues had seemed too debilitating. Now they were amazed at how unimportant these issues had become in the general-election campaign. For one thing, the draft issue had sputtered. Clinton's lack of military service in the Vietnam War years seemed almost irrelevant; that was a time most Americans apparently wanted to forget. Admiral William Crowe, the sixty-seven-year-old former chairman of the Joint Chiefs of Staff under Reagan and Bush, had just endorsed Clinton, and his comment on the draft stories was "One of the things about being my age is you discover you want to be judged on your life and not on when you were twenty-three years old. And some of the things I did when I was twenty-three I'd prefer not to remember." Polls showed that most people agreed with him.

Bush and his team hadn't been able to formulate or execute an effective campaign plan. The Republican convention was an unmitigated disaster—so much so that former Secretary of State Jim Baker and the team he brought with him from the State Department to take over the campaign were using the convention as an excuse for Bush's problems. *The New York Times* quoted one White House official as saying that "the hostility expressed at the convention toward homosexuals, feminists, welfare recipients, and women who identify with Hillary Clinton was a strategy that was poorly managed and consequently ran amok." In other words, the tactics themselves weren't repulsive—they were just not executed properly. It was process, not principle; timing, not content. But the Republicans were running out of excuses. First, they had said, "Just wait until the convention." Then it was "Just wait until the TV ads." Then "Just wait until Jim Baker takes over as campaign manager." The vaunted Republican presidential machine was collapsing. Clinton was ahead by thirteen points in the polls, and I hoped to appear with Phil Gramm again after the St. Louis debate, so that I could say, "You did as good a job as possible with the material they gave you in this candidate."

The debate site, Washington University, was familiar ground: within two miles of the St. Louis Museum of Fine Arts and the St. Louis Zoo, where I first encountered lions and pythons and George Caleb Binghams; nine miles from the site of the old Sportsman's Park, where as a kid I drank Mountain Valley Water and watched in amazement as "Stan the Man" Musial practiced his craft as a clutch hitter for the Cardinals; one mile from the Municipal Opera, where my high-school girlfriend used to sing and I would wait for her after performances on summer evenings; a half mile from the house where, in 1964, for my senior thesis, I interviewed a still bitter Lloyd Stark, Harry Truman's chief opponent in his Senate re-election campaign of 1940; six miles from Kiel Auditorium, where as a kid I had attended pro-basketball games and rock concerts, and seven miles from the St. Louis Public Library, where I had sought out books for particularly important high-school papers, sharing the reading room with homeless men, who filled it in the winter even then.

The debate took place in a familiar building, too—the Washington University fieldhouse, which from 1956 to 1962 was the site of the Missouri High School Basketball Tournament. As a high-school junior, I drove from Crystal City to this fieldhouse twice a week in summer to play in pickup games with college and professional players. It was in this building that Zelmo Beatty, a six-foot-nine, two-hundred-forty-pound professional center, split my face open with an elbow so effectively that the St. Louis Hawks' doctor had to stitch it up. In this building, in the summer between my freshman and sophomore years at Princeton, I would come to work out every day, after my French classes at Washington University's summer school; and in this building I ended my high-school basketball career. In 1961, Crystal City played St. Louis University High School for the state championship, in a classic big-city/small-town matchup. If we won, we would take our place with Puxico and Fruitland in Missouri and Herrin and Galesburg in Illinois as a wonder team from a small high school who beat the big-city team. We had beaten St. Louis University High by two points earlier in the year, at home; we lost the championship by one point.

The Clinton campaign had put out an all-points bulletin for prominent Democrats to attend the first debate as a sign of support for the candidate. A large turnout would mean a lot to Clinton personally, and a large turnout he got. Those who came were some of the cream of the Democratic Party: Governors Mario Cuomo and Ann Richards, Admiral Crowe, Mayor Richard Daley of Chicago, Majority Leader Dick Gephardt, Representatives Dave McCurdy, Nancy Pelosi, Maxine Waters, and Bill Richardson, Senators Joe Biden and Jay Rockefeller. The Bush side may have made a comparable effort, but the only notable Republican I saw was Senator Alan Simpson.

The Democratic group assembled in a VIP room under the bleachers—a long, drab hallway, with frosted windows high up along one wall and at the far end a curtain separating us from the Clinton staff operation. A large buffet of the usual cold cuts and raw vegetables was laid out. Three TV sets had been placed on portable platforms, so that we could see the debate, and folding chairs had been set out. It looked more like a potluck supper in a church basement than the venue for viewing a crucial encounter in the race for the leadership of the Western world.

Most of the politicians in this unprepossessing room thought of themselves as could-have-been presidents or someday-would-be presidents. If asked, they would say that they were there to support the candidate, but deep down each of them knew that if Clinton won, their chances would likely be in the deep freeze for eight years. Biden joked with Daley and Pelosi, but he was probably still dreaming of allowing his considerable talents a second chance at the presidency, after the 1988 debacle and a brain aneurysm had almost ended his career and his life. Mario Cuomo told a small group of us that Clinton was riding the wave of something bigger than his own candidacy. Ann Richards eyed Cuomo warily. These were the two best orators in the party. In 1988 and 1984 respectively, their keynote speeches had invigorated the convention. This year Cuomo had tantalized the party with his prospective candidacy up until the last moment, and then backed out again. Richards, as chairwoman of the convention, had executed an active, make-as-many-friends-as-possible convention strategy that was preparation for her own rumored bid in 1996. Tonight both of them must have sensed that their time was passing. Dave McCurdy and Bill Richardson were full of a younger ambition. Richardson, of New Mexico, was a Latino politician to whom Anglos could relate. McCurdy, of Oklahoma, who was an early supporter of Clinton's, had floated his own candidacy in 1991 so that he would be ready next time if Clinton were to stumble. Rockefeller and Gephardt treated each other with an easy familiarity that covered their considerable differences. Ambition and friendship are the Cain and Abel of American politics.

In a strange sort of way, despite our differences, we all looked alike. We wore the same dark suits or well-tailored dresses. Our hair was meticulously styled. We were in good shape; obesity was a political liability we knew we could avoid with a little exercise, a moderate diet, and the regular sight of ourselves on TV. Seldom had so much political ambition been cooped up in such a small space. Many in attendance volunteered what they had told Clinton to do in the debate. I thought to myself that if he had listened to half the advice, he was going to be confused and tense. In 1988, Clinton and I had worked separately with Dukakis on daylong sessions of debate preparation. With each hour I was there, Dukakis got tighter. This was not the way to do it.

There were several hundred people in the studio audience by the time the show began. Jim Lehrer, of the MacNeil/Lehrer NewsHour, introduced the three candidates and the panelists—Ann Compton, of ABC News; John Mashek, of the *Boston Globe;* and Sander Vanocur, an unaffiliated television journalist. The podiums were set at the right height, with a glass of water and a notepad on each; the set's blue background would show each candidate at his best. We settled ourselves onto the folding chairs, and I felt a heightening of the tension in the room—there was a lot at stake for the country, the party, and for many of us.

Clinton was nervous at the beginning—short of breath—but he threw a punch early, by remarking that Bush, in attacking Clinton's opposition to the Vietnam War, wasn't even true to his own father's legacy as a defender of civil liberties. It was a blow just above the belt, and it landed. Bush, for his part, was not connecting. Ross Perot was doing exceedingly well. He was clear, concise, funny, colloquial. He kept referring to the economy as if it were a car and he a mechanic who knew how to get under the hood and fix it. Clinton, like the good student he is, hit all the points he had practiced, but I thought he lacked spontaneity and passion; I wondered whether the national television audience would think so too. Bush was almost incoherent. Whether the question was about the economy, education, or the environment, he continually failed to give any context for his comments, sounding more like a government bureaucrat than a leader who knew what was troubling his people.

Afterward, the press declared the debate a draw. Bush had needed a win. He didn't get it, so he had lost. I made my swing through the press room in an adjoining gym, which was full of hundreds of print reporters and other media people. I was ready to give them the campaign message from the staff-prepared printout, but most had no interest in talking to me, turning instead to campaign manager James Carville or major campaign spinner Paul Begala. I went into the radio studio behind the field-house and recorded my scripted analysis for radio interviews in six different cities in America. Unfortunately, I never saw Phil Gramm.

Twenty minutes later, I was back in my hotel room. Crystal City was only thirty-two miles away, but it seemed a lot farther than that. My parents were sick and retired in Florida; many of my beloved relatives were dead; only a few friends remained. It was unnatural to settle down for the night at a hotel in a place that was so close to my childhood home. The campaign journey to St. Louis became a journey of self-discovery. On that night, in that town, I reflected on my decision not to run for president.

FOR ME, as odd as it sounds, the whole issue of running for the presidency is related to my days in basketball. It was through sport that I initially received public acclaim and press attention. Americans often attribute to successful athletes qualities that are unrelated to athletic performance. When reporters began questioning my friends about my nonathletic interests, my friends didn't just say that I wanted to be a diplomat. They said I'd be secretary of state. My high-school principal, like all high-school principals touting their stars, said, "Bill might be president someday, with the help of his friends, and without it he still might make it." That quote appeared in story after story. Why write about jump shots if you could engage in hyperbolic speculation at little apparent cost to the athlete and great benefit in reader interest?

Throughout the years with the Knicks, my second nickname, after "Dollar Bill," was "Mr. President"; the appellation was 95 percent sarcastic, but many people focused on the other 5 percent. When I decided to enter politics, the wave of presidential expectations, narrowly subscribed to as they were, had been building for about fifteen years. After I'd spent nearly a decade in the Senate, the expectations increased. The last time I had reviewed my own attitude about running for president was in October 1991, when it was clear that a Democrat had a good chance to beat President Bush, and not through a four-year campaign ordeal but in a one-year burst of activity. Still, I passed.

I believe that there are four requirements for a presidential run. These were criteria I had laid down for myself and repeated publicly time after time from 1987 until 1992: (1) You need to have firsthand knowledge of as much of the country as possible, which means that you have to have traveled to many, many places and talked with thousands of different people. That way you can feel the country's rhythms and absorb its contradictions. (2) You need depth in foreign policy—not just slogans attached to briefing papers but knowledge tested against events over time. After all, a president is commander-in-chief of the Armed Forces, and America is more than ever inextricably bound to a wider world. (3) You need a team to govern, not just to win a campaign—a team that shares your values and has worked together on other issues at other times. (4) You should be able to communicate your ideas clearly, in everything from a fifteen-second sound bite to a full-fledged lecture, and you should be able to handle questions in a debate or a TV interview.

I knew that if I wasn't confident of having mastered all four areas, I would feel inadequate. While one part of me said I was ready, on another level doubt persisted—something beyond the sense of incompleteness that most people feel when facing a large job. To those who inquired seriously, I would explain that my reluctance to run wasn't a matter of success or failure but of what I owed this country. Obviously, I owed it my best.

As I gave that explanation over and over between 1987 and 1992, I knew it said what I needed to say. Yet I knew the answer wasn't totally candid. It ignored my skepticism about what any president could accomplish at our current national moment. It ignored my concern for my family's well-being—a teenage daughter, whom I had never elbowed into politics, and a wife, who simply by virtue of being born German would probably have to endure speculation about her father's possible Nazi connections, even though none existed. It minimized my own natural antipathy to the invasion by the press of all the aspects of my life. It disregarded my continuing stage fright, and my inability to rouse people as a speaker. It missed my ingrained assumption (in refutation of which lay a lifetime of achievement) that this small-town boy could never win the biggest contest of all.

And, finally, I was afflicted by an ambivalence that made these kinds of life decisions difficult. Was I a public or a private person? Could I integrate my deep desire for privacy with the urgency of my commitment to serve? Even to admit to such hesitations publicly would be to disqualify myself in the minds of some people. So I kept silent, but that's how I felt.

I have never allowed myself to luxuriate in ambition. It was always something to be denied, even when it burned deeply. For years, I had been pulled by other people's ambitions for me. When the national moment, my performance as a senator, and other people's expectations of me converged in 1988 and 1992 and made my presidential candidacy a possibility, I said no. My vanity was as large as the next person's. I enjoyed being thought of as presidential material. Yet it wasn't enough to get me to run. Besides, during 1991 I was regaining my political balance from the close call in 1990.

I began to understand more clearly in that Missouri hotel room what I had to do if I ever wanted to stand before people and claim to be their national leader. It dawned on me that there was a fifth requirement for a presidential run, beyond the ones I'd been stating for years. It related to the inner knowing that allows one to assume a special task. Self-examination can be excessive and even self-indulgent, but sometimes it's a necessary prerequisite for strong leadership. Strength and clarity both flow from it.

For me, leadership is tied to self-knowledge. The examined life has become one of my ideals. To lead a people, you have to know who you are, where you come from, what you believe and why, what you're prepared to fight for or even die for, where you draw your strength, why and how you share yourself, and, finally, where you would want to take the nation. What is important is not power per se, but using power to alter national self-perceptions when the moment is right—using it, if necessary, to forge a new national identity, to help the country arrive at a more expansive sense of what is possible. Above all, a leader's abilities and sense of national direction must in part reflect what is best about America and in so doing give people hope. As I sat in my room and watched the debate replayed, I had no pangs of regret. I saw the play. It was in slow motion.

Two weeks before the 1992 election, my campaign path would cross Clinton's again, in Seattle. By now he had a ten-point lead in the polls. At my hotel, a phalanx of Secret Service personnel was posted in the lobby awaiting his arrival. In my room, I composed a note to him. I told him that he should enjoy the campaign's remaining days, which would be unlike any he would ever experience again. The warm gush of popular approval and affection would crest during this period. He would appear before cheering crowds of ten thousand, twenty thousand, thirty thousand, who would hang on his every word. Grateful Democrats would submerge their divisions in anticipation of victory. Enthusiastic independents would sense generational change and new possibilities, and thousands more who were only faintly political would come to see the new celebrity that the convention, the bus tour, and the national spotlight had created. The moment was fresh and full of possibilities. "Absorb it all," I wrote to him. "You deserve it. You've worked hard. You've won."

The next morning at 6:45, I gave the letter to a member of Clinton's staff. Then I ran into Clinton himself in the lobby, as he was about to go jogging. I told him the contents of the letter. He asked about New Jersey. I said that he would be fine, but it would be close.

A mist was falling. The air was cold. I walked to the car that would take me to the chartered plane that would fly me from Seattle to Bozeman and Kalispell, Montana; Fort Collins, Colorado; and Milwaukee, Wisconsin. I looked back and saw Bill Clinton in his baseball cap surrounded by Secret Service agents, walking out of the hotel toward a special, bulletproof car in the motorcade that would escort him to a place where he could jog. As I saw him duck into the car, I wondered whether he ever thought about how different his life would be as president.

I can't imagine what a president's life is like, and I've tried. I've read presidential biographies. I've read cabinet officials' memoirs. I've read novels about presidents. I've talked with Walter Mondale about it. I've talked with Jimmy Carter about it. But I still can't comprehend what it means to be a guaranteed historical figure. You can be a failure or a success, depending on what you do and how the press and the people view what you do. But you cannot fail to be a part of history. Whatever you do will be remembered. There is no historical anonymity for a president.

In all likelihood, in two weeks Clinton would dedicate his very life to his country and would thenceforth live in a luxurious prison. His life as an independent being would close. He would be asked every day to give of himself so as to embody, symbolize, and represent America, and there would be no time to replenish. Televised town meetings and working prescreened rope lines would not be sufficient to recharge him.

Unlike senators or Supreme Court justices, presidents rarely change while they are in office. Only the very best show a capacity for intellectual growth. To read how Holmes or Brandeis changed over time points up a striking difference between the judicial and the executive branches. Even senators can shift interests or expertise or passions or parties and evolve over many years. A president doesn't have the time.

When they take office, most presidents are as formed as they'll ever be. They will acquire few new experiences of life. New abilities, yes. New pressures, yes. New experiences of statecraft and politics, yes. New dimensions of their own personalities, maybe. But there will be no more wandering into the unknown of an urban neighborhood, small town, or forest. No more privacy in the middle of a crowd. No more unhurried observation. No more smells and sights and sounds that come from being physically in a new place, with time to absorb it. Almost no opportunity for relaxed reflection. There will be no more room for ambiguity.

A president is there to execute policy, not to deliberate. A president's purpose, ideally, is set before the campaign. Presidents must lead every day. Those who haven't thought before they run risk taking meaningless or contradictory action after they have won. There is no substitute for a solid conceptual framework.

As president, you do not have one day left in your life when your office and title don't dwarf your individuality. That's just the way it is. The presidency is an honor that the people bestow, and a genuine contract that only forty-one politicians have been allowed to sign. I think of how different life is for Tom Harkin, Bob Kerrey, Jerry Brown, Paul Tsongas, Bob Dole, Howard Baker, Joe Biden, Jack Kemp, Jesse Jackson, Bruce Babbitt, Gary Hart—or for that matter George McGovern, Barry Goldwater, or Walter Mondale. They tried and missed. A few harbor dreams of rebirth. Most have recognized their passing celebrity and settled into another, different life. Those who failed in their presidential runs may have lost a chance to lead their country, but what they have retained is the possibility to define themselves apart from others, to continue to grow intellectually and spiritually, and to have time for their families. In short, what they have gained is the chance for a normal life.

In 1984, at the Democratic National Convention in San Francisco, I saw Gary Hart get out of his limousine surrounded by Secret Service agents and enter the St. Francis Hotel, with screaming supporters chanting, "Gary! Gary!" He turned rather stiffly and waved—part JFK, part Warren Beatty, part Jimmy Swaggart. Less than a year later, after Walter Mondale got the Democratic nomination and lost in the general election to Ronald Reagan, I saw Hart leave a political dinner at the Washington Hilton alone, pulling out into Connecticut Avenue in a beat-up Ford Mustang. No crowd. No staff. No adoration. No stiffness. Just a gas gauge and a bad muffler. Twelve blocks away, the Republican president sat behind infrared fences and security guards, with a black briefcase never far away. One had the power. The other had the freedom.

THERE ARE events more important than the presidency, which put ambition in perspective. My decision not to run for president in 1992 turned out to be a godsend for my wife, Ernestine, and me, but at the time neither one of us had known what the future would bring. In the spring of that campaign year, she discovered that she had breast cancer. I will never forget the moment in the hospital when we learned that the lumps were malignant. As she persevered through a mastectomy and six months of chemotherapy, each day was filled with new agony: the trauma over the invasiveness of the surgery, the sense of loss, the deliberate poisoning of the entire body so as to kill any mobile, errant cancer cells. I coped with my great anxiety by reading scientific articles about the disease and the various regimes of treatment. In between sessions at the Democratic convention, my wife and I sat in our New York hotel room talking to an oncologist about chemotherapy options. I wondered whether a hundred years from now medical science might not look upon chemotherapy as it does now upon the medical blood-letting of the eighteenth century.

To see this happening to the one I loved made me reassess what was important in life and what was unnecessary clutter. I thanked God that I was not running for president. I valued friends who wrote or sent flowers, and especially those who sent food and tried to do something practical. I realized that being a friend was an achievement every bit as important as organizing and executing a work life. I vowed to reduce stress and live life as what it was—a grant of time—rather than what it wasn't: an endless schedule of events to make, obstacles to overcome, achievements to amass. The great deception of life is to assume that what is so today will be so tomorrow. History reveals the folly of such thinking for nations, but as individuals we continue to take for granted the predictability of our lives—a predictability that presumes good health, the absence of war, and relatively stable personal finances. Only a severe jolt moves us out of our routine to contemplate a different life. Cancer, like all serious sickness, changes lives. What is hardest to realize is that you are dealing with a condition that could be terminal.

The chronic nature of the disease, with its five-year deadline for recurrence before you can breathe more easily, posed a new but eternal question. If these were your last days, what would you do differently? If you were among the lucky few to get off the cancer road, the answer to such a question could only enhance the rest of your life. Going through all this in the spring and summer of 1992 made me reflect particularly on the career of a wonderfully engaging and competent former U.S. senator, Birch Bayh. Now I had greater appreciation for the stress Birch had experienced, and the courage he had demonstrated in his last senatorial campaign.

In 1980, Birch Bayh was fighting for his political life in a re-election bid he would eventually lose to a young congressman named Dan Quayle. Nineteen eighty was the year of the Reagan landslide. It was the year the Senate also lost Frank Church, Gaylord Nelson, George McGovern, John Durkin, Bob Morgan, John Culver, and Warren Magnuson to the conservative tide. Still relatively young, Birch was a leader on the Judiciary Committee and a strong proponent of abolishing the electoral college in favor of popular-vote election of the president. The antiabortion people picketed most meetings that year, including a fundraiser for Birch at which I spoke. The antiabortion movement was dominated by zealots, who had yet to recognize that a call to conscience was stronger than confrontation. Still, Birch didn't have much of a chance.

Quayle was aggressive in his attacks, coordinating them with the emerging religious right, the Moral Majority. They said that Birch was not a true Hoosier but a liberal-Democratic friend of Ted Kennedy. In particular, Quayle hammered away at Bayh's missed votes, even though Quayle himself had a mediocre voting record in the House. Quayle's relentless attack attained some credibility, because Bayh refused to explain and in explaining politicize his wife's death.

Marvella Bayh died in April 1979, right before the 1980 campaign got under way. She had been an active political wife. She had campaigned, counseled, and traveled. She was a valuable and active half of the Bayh political team. In 1971, she developed breast cancer. She started crusading and talking about it publicly, at a time when many women kept the illness hidden. During the last months of her life, Bayh missed many votes so that he could be at his wife's side. To Quayle, the reason for the missed votes appeared to make no difference: the record was the record; Bayh had missed votes important to Indiana. The people agreed. Quayle won. During his tenure as vice-president, when his wife, Marilyn, became a genuine champion of finding a cure for breast cancer, I recalled the 1980 campaign with a sense of bitter irony.

"I don't know if Birch will ever recover if he loses this way," a Bayh aide had said to me. Though defeat can be overcome by another victory or by developing a new perspective or by going on to another profession, the character assaults and personal injuries of politics too often leave permanent scars. A political campaign is an arena where there are no rules beyond a candidate's internal moral compass. It can be very cruel. The object is to turn your opponent's strength into a weakness—to take what he views as his finest moment and then to attack it and demean it. The advice to those who use this tactic is clear: never give the opponent any benefit of the doubt as a human being, full of contradictions, healthy idiosyncrasies, and both good and bad impulses; simplify his humanity until it is reduced to a negative slogan. That's the way to win a modern slash-and-burn campaign.

Some of our greatest presidents—Thomas Jefferson, Andrew Jackson, Abraham Lincoln—felt the sting of untruths that were spread about their lives, of everyday facts being spun into a web of nefarious implications. Newspapers made little pretense of objectivity. They were arms of partisan battle and treated as such by the general public. But each of these men had loyal party members, for whom he could do no wrong. Today there is less loyalty among party members, and there are fewer of them. Independents are the fastest-growing "party" in the United States. People vote person, not party, more frequently than ever. A party can't convince independents; only the candidate can win them over. Therefore, more and more, the candidate stands alone.

In a world in which personality dominates and party plays less of a role, narrow, ideological groups can have a real impact. The best example of that is Jesse Helms's National Congressional Club. Helms, as a colleague, is considerate and courtly. He is also dedicated to his family, especially to his basketball-playing granddaughter, but in a political campaign, as my Knick teammates might say, "he takes no prisoners." The National Congressional Club has no respect for the views of the traditional opinion leaders, in the press or on television. Helms, a former television commentator himself, maintains that the traditional opinion leaders are part of the problem. The Congressional Club targets its voters with hard-core gut issues and ignores all the other issues a senator must deal with. The premise of its strategy is that campaigns are war. There are a few simple rules: don't attempt to use free media, keep control of your message by means of television advertising, stop at nothing to tar your opponent, and expose yourself to direct questions by the press as little as possible.

For nearly two decades in North Carolina, the National Congressional Club used any attack necessary to win. When Governor Jim Hunt challenged Helms for the Senate in 1984, the National Congressional Club labeled him soft on communism in Central America. In 1990, Helms refused to appear on the same stage with his black opponent, Harvey Gantt, much less debate him—thus sending the message that he was putting Gantt "in his place." During the last weeks of that campaign, in which Helms had charged Gantt with being an apologist for homosexuals, a "tool of Hollywood," and an advocate of abortions in the third trimester, a new Helms television commercial appeared: The hand of a white man (with a prominent wedding band) was shown submitting a job application. The voice-over informed viewers that even though this man was "best qualified" he lost the job to "a minority because of a racial quota," and then it asked, "Is that really fair?" Then the faces of Ted Kennedy and Harvey Gantt filled the screen, and we were told that Gantt supported Kennedy's racial-quota bill, a bill that according to Helms made "the color of your skin more important than your qualifications." The final picture showed the hand of the white job applicant crumpling the job application, throwing it away, and clenching into a fist, while the announcer intoned, "For racial quotas—Harvey Gantt; against racial quotas—Jesse Helms."

In 1992, I went to North Carolina to campaign for Senator Terry Sanford, the Democratic incumbent, in his contest against Congressional Club candidate Lauch Faircloth. Faircloth's television ads were claiming that Sanford wanted to give taxpayer dollars to welfare cheats. The press, seemingly paralyzed in their attempts to appear objective, asked about virtually every charge that Faircloth made, however outlandish. The Congressional Club knew that the more extreme and sensational a charge, the higher the visibility awarded to it by the press. Such allegations sold papers. Are you giving welfare cheats taxpayer dollars? Why do you support communists in Nicaragua? Why do you promote homosexual lifestyles? The press would amplify the charge by asking the opponent to respond; then the opponent's response would necessitate a restatement of the charge and a second day's story: "Mr. Sanford yesterday denied he was for welfare cheats, saying . . ." Those who stuck to the issues and ran a traditional campaign became boring—or the press presented them as boring, while simultaneously complaining about the nastiness of campaigns.

Sanford had just had heart surgery to replace an infected valve. His doctor had told him that he needed the surgery immediately, otherwise he risked dying at any time. So he went into Duke Medical Center in mid-October for the operation. Two weeks later, he was out of the hospital, but he was tired and he looked older than his seventy-five years. Far from suspending the campaign, Faircloth had attempted to exploit Sanford's surgery, actively campaigning while Terry was in the hospital. (Senator Paul Douglas of Illinois, although he was in a tough contest, suspended campaigning in 1966 when challenger Chuck Percy's daughter was murdered.) Faircloth also ran a commercial featuring a picture of Sanford looking horribly gaunt, with the slogan "Terry Sanford is confused"—a clear implication that Sanford's health was poor. It was a wretched tactic, but I had seen other politicians do it. Al D'Amato had used the same contemptible slur against Jacob Javits in the New York Republican primary in 1980. When it comes to the pursuit of victory, many politicians fail to heed the caution light of decency.

The cruel part of a U.S. senator's life, consisting as it does of political campaigns and legislative sessions, is the toll it takes on his or her family. Not only do the character attacks and slurs of a campaign hurt a senator's spouse and children, but the job itself leaves big holes in a normal family life. It is always uncertain when a day's session will end, thereby making even the family dinner contingent on the whim or needs of the majority leader. Separation is constant. Late-night sessions are frequent, and travel to your home state takes you away from Washington on weekends. Travel to another state to help a colleague comes with seniority or fame and takes you away on the remaining free weekends. The constant fund-raising, with all that implies about spending time and getting comfortable with people who have money, requires sizable segments of what should be the public's time or your family's time. Everything in your life is scheduled. Now you have four hours for personal time, so be personal; now you have an hour and a half for a personal dinner, so eat; or an hour's time to see your daughter's play, so enjoy it. More work always waits. The in-box never empties. Each week I get fifteen hundred letters, four hundred speaking requests, and twenty-three hundred telephone calls. I work about fourteen hours a day, every day, and I'm not unusual in the Senate. There is little time for anything but work. When you are away from the Senate, you take the issues with you. Despite what reporters say, politicians do give their lives to public service.

Then you get into a campaign and an opponent seeks to make all the hours, days, months, and years of commitment count for nothing, and a few perceived or drummed-up failures count for everything. That's when an election loss can become a painfully personal verdict.

The possibility of defeat pervades politics. Few politicians have never lost. When a loss occurs, it can define a career. To lose after serving in office for many years usually means the end of a political career. The feeling you are left with is that the public knows you well enough to reject you—that the loss wasn't a fluke. The hardest thing in politics is to know when to quit. Often politicians stay long after they've lost a zest for the job. Then the public senses unconcern on the part of the politician and rejects him.

For some who were the presidential nominees of their parties, a defeat is particularly bitter. Walter Mondale once asked George McGovern, "When do you get over a presidential defeat?" McGovern replied, "Never."

To lose in midcareer is the major test of a politician's strength of ambition and personal resilience. The reaction to loss offers drama and reveals character. Whoever is down today in politics can be up again tomorrow, and anyone who is up today will sooner or later experience the inexorable pull of going down. The iron rule of celebrity again: the hotter you are today, the faster the negative forces will go into play tomorrow to balance your good fame with bad fame. Stories about strength and character and wisdom are inevitably followed by stories about peccadilloes, campaign tensions, and personal limitations. Only the very best or the very lucky can avoid it. The question is: where will you be on this scale of ups and downs at election time?

Every politician who loses comforts himself or herself with the thought of revival and regained victory. The public loves the political comeback. Dukakis, Clinton, and Reagan all used it well. And it plays in many countries. Winston Churchill and Charles de Gaulle knew it. The "new Nixon" rising from the ashes of successive defeats for president and for governor of California is the most salient example in recent political history. Over the years, I've learned never to underestimate a politician's ambition—particularly the ambition of one who has tasted the power of office. The phoenix remains a politician's favorite choice for national bird, and the political comeback is another example of America's general fascination with a second chance.

Early in 1992, I flew with Birch Bayh to Indianapolis for a fund-raiser in honor of his son, Evan Bayh, the young governor of Indiana. As the plane made its way through the night sky and I watched Birch working on his remarks, I thought back to his 1980 senatorial campaign. I wondered if he still hurt from the attacks leveled at him then. After his loss, he had moved easily into a Washington law firm, and in a few years he remarried, fathered another child, and saw his and Marvella's grown son elected governor. But how had he made peace with that campaign and its result?

I also wondered how Birch, as a father, felt when he saw his son follow him into elected office. If the family business is politics, can you separate the pride you take in your children's accomplishment from the knowledge that there will be certain pain ahead for them? Can you assume that the chance to do great things will be more likely than the chance to be destroyed? Birch must pause when he sees Evan in the same tumult, subjecting his family to the same pressures, so obviously following in his father's footsteps. Yet there is an understandable satisfaction in seeing a child do well in your own chosen profession. (Although sometimes the well-known father has to make an adjustment. I thought about what Calvin Hill—Yale, Dallas Cowboys, for ten years vice-president of the Baltimore Orioles—said when he saw his son Grant become a great basketball player at Duke University: "I read in the sports section 'Hill did this, Hill did that.' 'Hey, wait a minute,' I thought, '*I'm* Hill.' ")

The Governor's Starry Night Ball was held in the Indiana Roof Ballroom, a renovated theater that looked like a movie set of seventeenth-century Seville, including a built-in starlit sky. Evan Bayh, a slight, angular thirty-six-year-old, and his wife, Susan, a lawyer with rich blond hair and a glistening smile, had met when their mothers were both dying of breast cancer and talking publicly about it. Tonight they moved about the room effortlessly, giving each person they met a smile, a special word, or a willing ear. A thousand people attended, wearing tuxedoes and expensive dresses. They were corporate executives, lobbyists, state legislators of both parties. The mood of the evening was upbeat; the guests seemed to feel that they were investing in a growth stock.

Most political dinners have the same problem—so much noise that you can't hear the person next to you. It was not easy to talk in the Indiana Roof Ballroom. Every sixty seconds, someone tapped me on the shoulder and I stood to say hello. In between, I took a bite of dinner. This is what politicians enjoy; it might be tiring, but it's better than no one tapping you on the shoulder. "Thanks for coming," people said.

"Thanks for taking on Bush for what he said about Clinton's trip to Russia."

"I remember when you came to Vincennes in 1988 for the Democratic congressional candidate."

"I really enjoyed your speech at the convention."

"Senator, I represent the realtors. Will Bush sign the tax bill?"

"I remember seeing you play basketball in high school in Missouri."

"Do you think Russia will hold together?"

The dinner chairman introduced Birch. He walked up the steps to the stage, the spotlight on him, and in his aw-shucks manner he began to talk about his son:

Like most fathers, I was interested in my son's future goals in life. We talked about it in general terms, but we really didn't talk about specifics. Later, when I asked him just what he thought he wanted to do with his life, he responded quickly that he thought he'd like to be involved in public service and perhaps run for public office some day.

I must confess that as a father, believe it or not, my advice to him was rather conservative. I gave him advice to go slow, get his roots down, think of his financial security, think of his family. In fact, it is fair to say that I gave him the same advice I ignored when I received it at his age. Of course, he had a better feel for what he was doing, made his own decisions, and because of your help is now your governor.

. . . Each of us who have had the good fortune of carrying public trust understands that this is not an easy responsibility. It is really a very difficult life.

If there was one prayer I had for him, it was that God would keep him safe and give him wisdom and courage, help him to always understand that to truly be worthy of public office, he must be prepared to lose it in order to do what is right.

Whatever else happens in politics, full as it is of moral traps, self-delusions, pain, hilarious moments, mind-numbing work, soaring possibilities, and human frailties, the finest kind of public service boils down to this very simple proposition: do what's right, as you see the right, and then stand by it honestly.

10

The Closed Frontier

FOR SEVENTEEN YEARS, I have been a member of the
Senate Energy and Natural Resources Committee. Before 1976,
it was known as the Interior Committee. It has jurisdiction over
nearly one-third of the land in America: the so-called public
lands, including the resources under or on those lands, such as timber,
oil, gas, hard-rock minerals, and water. Most of the public lands are west
of the Mississippi River. In New York State, only 1 percent of the land is
owned by the federal government. In North Carolina, it's 6 percent; in
Michigan, 9 percent. But 35 percent of Colorado and New Mexico, 50
percent of Wyoming, 65 percent of Idaho, and 90 percent of Nevada are
public lands. What happens on public lands affects the people of the seventeen states of the West disproportionately. Senators on the committee
are, in effect, federal governors; they have a bigger say over more land
in many Western states than the state governors. That is why the committee has been known as a "Western committee," even though its
charge is to guard the patrimony of the nation. As I experienced in my efforts to reform the Central Valley Project, a non-Westerner with different ideas is deeply resented. At any one time, only a few of the twenty
senators on the committee represent states east of the Mississippi.

When I sought to secure a seat on the committee, my interest was energy, not natural resources or the West. I had worked as an unpaid aide to the commissioner of the New Jersey Energy Department for a few months in 1977, before I started running full-time for the Senate. The natural-gas shortage that year had hit New Jersey hard, and the effect of the 1973 Arab oil embargo still reverberated in a state that imported most of its oil from abroad. The flow through the international financial system of the billions of petroleum dollars that the West paid OPEC for oil was of interest to me both as a financial and a foreign-policy problem. Only after several years on the committee did I become interested in problems peculiar to the West.

My impressions of the land west of Missouri had been shaped by the movies and the popular literature of my childhood—the conflict between cowboys and Indians, farmers and ranchers. The West had seemed one great big adventure, where the personal desire for unbounded land matched the nation's desire for territorial expansion, and where striking it rich was a measure of your self-worth. It was clear who the good guys were—those who facilitated westward expansion and made it as safe as possible. They were the trappers and traders, the scouts and wagon masters, the sheriffs, railroad detectives, homesteaders, and ranchers, who brought structure to chaos, defeated savagery, promoted civilization, and carved livelihoods out of wilderness. The bad guys were the Indians, the Mexicans, the bloodthirsty outlaws, and the crooked bankers, and they had names: Jesse James, Billy the Kid, Calamity Jane, Sitting Bull, Geronimo. The Oregon Trail, the Santa Fe Trail, Dodge City, cattle drives, and gold rushes provided the settings for the good guys to win, every time. These were the people and places of the West I learned while I was growing up in Missouri.

As a member of the Energy and Natural Resources Committee, I came to know a different West. I listened to countless corporate and individual witnesses present their cases—for development of oil shale in Wyoming and Colorado, offshore oil in Alaska, deep-sands natural gas in New Mexico, coal in Montana, uranium and gold in Nevada, silver in Idaho, logging in Washington, Oregon, and Alaska, and water projects in Arizona, Utah, Nevada, California, Texas, Oklahoma, Oregon, Washington, Colorado, Idaho, and South Dakota.

In my work on the committee, I talked a lot with Westerners, both in Congress and, equally important, in the states. I was determined to learn more about this America that was so far from New Jersey and so different from Missouri but so much a part of our national consciousness. I heard miners, ranchers, and loggers defend the exploitation of nature as being a part of their job, while environmentalists celebrated a spiritual journey that required greater stewardship. I visited wheat farmers in South Dakota and fruit growers in California, Indian reservations in South Dakota, Nevada, Arizona, and Washington, and national parks in fourteen Western states.

I had always loved Seattle, where temperatures annually averaged between thirty-nine and sixty-six degrees Fahrenheit. I had no experience of extreme conditions like those in North Dakota, where there were stories of annual temperature swings of a hundred and eighty degrees, or in Montana, where the temperature could drop a hundred degrees in twenty-four hours, or in Spearfish, South Dakota, where in 1943 the temperature, as if fired by a blowtorch, skyrocketed forty-nine degrees in two minutes. Storms moved across the plains slowly, a heavenly procession announced by lightning bolts. Storms in the mountains appeared suddenly and then passed. The air seemed purer, the light shone brighter in these western landscapes. In the spring even the desert shimmered with color. Slowly, the region came alive for me, more subtle and various than one vast empty stretch of arid land.

In 1893, Professor Frederick Jackson Turner delivered his famous lecture, "The Significance of the Frontier in American History." "So long as free land exists," he said, "the opportunity for a competency exists, and economic power secures political power." The premise of the Turner thesis was the old Jeffersonian belief that the work of yeomen on the land was a virtuous activity and renewed the human spirit. It provided independence, guaranteed subsistence, and promoted democracy. It suggested that American inventiveness developed, in part, when an immigrant people were forced to work the land in the face of harsh weather and hostile Indians. Professor Turner concluded his 1893 lecture by announcing the closing of the American frontier: "And now, four centuries from the discovery of America, at the end of a hundred years of life under the Constitution, the frontier has gone, and with its going has closed the first period of American history."

As we approach the eve of the twenty-first century, we can ask: Did the frontier, as Turner portrayed it, ever exist? Was the "frontier" a wave of self-reliant farmers braving the elements to generate a living from the soil, even as they gave all America a mythic passage west? Or was the frontier simply a process—the result of people's flight from congestion and disease (such as the cholera epidemic in St. Louis in 1849, which killed 6 percent of that city's residents) in order to breathe the clean air, shoot the prolific game, fish the clear waters, and lay claim to the piece of "free land"? Was it a place where middle-class dreams could become realities for the thousand dollars it took to put a wagon in the train? Was it a paradisal place of second chances, where "lighting out for the Territory," as Mark Twain put it, was an act of personal liberation? Was it another New World, offering material success and religious freedom? Was it the central image-setting story of "American history"? Or was the history of the American West something else, something more complex?

When Turner delivered his lecture a hundred years ago, the federal government had already given away one billion acres to private individuals and corporations. Railroads alone owned an area nearly the size of the states of Washington and California combined. Half the land in the West remained in the hands of the federal government, but even in these areas absentee corporate interests obtained virtually full access to the minerals, timber, range, and water. The historian Charles Wilkinson has collectively dubbed these policies governing westward expansion "the lords of yesterday." Many other people profited from furs, banking, transportation, merchandising, real-estate speculation, prostitution, and saloons. Being a small farmer was only one possible livelihood among many in the West. In fact, the small farmer was a minor part of the overall economic activity.

The self-sufficient frontiersman, as personified by Daniel Boone and Davy Crockett and depicted in the *Leatherstocking* novels by James Fenimore Cooper, was a figure in the early settlements east of the Mississippi. It was possible to imagine a Kentucky or Ohio or Illinois frontiersman, with his coonskin cap and long rifle, going into the forests to kill his food, cut logs for his house, clear and plow the fields with his family, and draw water from the lakes and rivers. But those images of wooded land, abundant water, and plentiful game were not characteristic of America west of the hundredth meridian, where there was scant water and geology limited possibilities. The myth of the frontier as embodied by a white male in buckskins had little to do with the West of the second half of the nineteenth century.

The frontier myth left out so much—the power of non-Western

economic interests, the role of women, the racial and ethnic diversity, the xenophobia that accompanied Chinese immigration, the outrage over Mormon apostasy, and the richness and variety of the Native American cultures. The unspoiled land was rarely protected for its beauty. More often it was a source of speculation and an object of exploitation. The political historian Richard Hofstadter pointed out in his 1955 book *The Age of Reform* that Westerners evoked the Jeffersonian ideal to justify their acceptance of federal assistance. Most Westerners were more interested in money and property values than in the agrarian ideal, and the federal government was viewed as a source of wealth.

From the beginning of our nation, the land west of the Mississippi was a federal province, shaped by federal initiatives. When President Thomas Jefferson purchased Louisiana in 1803, he soon sent Meriwether Lewis and William Clark on an expedition to explore and map the region. Jefferson believed that rationality and science should shape the new nation, and from Lewis and Clark he wanted every detail, from assessments of natural medicines to specific information on Indian tribes. Even earlier, the federal government had begun surveying, selling, and registering public lands. It acted as broker between its vast holdings and the desire of people to own a piece of land. The local land office was where you got information, and the land agent was no high-minded public servant steeped in Locke and Rousseau but often a speculator using inside information to buy and sell tracts, and more dedicated to profit than to public service. In her exceptional 1987 book, *The Legacy of Conquest,* the historian Patricia Limerick has pointed out:

> Even with more dedicated public servants to administer it, land law bore little resemblance to the simple Jeffersonian ideal. From 1789 to 1834, Congress passed a total of 375 land laws—laws adjusting the size of lots for sale, shifting the price per acre, altering the requirements for cash payments or adding the option of credit, and granting rights of preemption in specific regions. A great burden fell on the Land Office simply to keep up with those laws, while congressional parsimony guaranteed understaffing and inefficiency. At one point, the Land Office commissioner did not have money to provide his field officers with copies of federal land laws. Into the last half of the nineteenth century, variations in land law—the Homestead Act [of 1862] and its variations, the Timber Culture Act, the Desert Land Law— kept matters as complex as ever.

After the Homestead Act, which gave a settler a hundred and sixty acres of public land if he farmed it, the corruption and inefficiency continued:

> The use of "dummy entrymen" permitted speculators, or mining, timber, or cattle companies to acquire land under falsified claims. In a variety of ways—huge grants to subsidize railroad construction, grants to states, the distribution of land warrants to veterans, the sale of tracts made available by further reductions of Indian reservations—much desirable land was taken from the reach of homesteaders. Moreover, much of the land made available to them was beyond the line of semiaridity, in regions where the 160-acre farm and the methods of conventional farming could produce little except frustration.

In 1878, Major John Wesley Powell, founder of the U.S. Geological Survey, published his Report on the Lands of the Arid Region of the United States, which described the land west of the hundredth meridian. Powell was concerned that much of the land being given away under the Homestead Act was too dry to support farms, and that small farmers who went west expecting to make a living growing crops in a desert would go bankrupt. Powell wanted to ensure homesteading only on land that could be irrigated, and he believed that irrigation should be facilitated by the federal government. Not a wild-eyed conservationist by today's standards, he also suggested that trees should be cut down so there would be more runoff for irrigation. But above all, he warned against unrestricted development and urged awareness of the uniqueness of this vast, dry, open space. A decade later, he urged that a hydrological mapping of the entire West, and especially the seven major river basins, take place before more land was given to homesteaders. Powell's caution and professionalism were ignored. The water survey was ultimately done, but politicians rejected the slower, more planned development that its conclusions called for. Instead, the land was poked for gold and silver, drilled for oil, gouged for coal and uranium, clear-cut for logs, and by the 1930s parts of the West had been "homesteaded" into a dust bowl.

With the passage of the Taylor Grazing Act in 1934, the Westerner's sense of entitlement took a different form. The unrestricted use of the public domain for grazing by the livestock interests, and the unfettered homesteading and "sodbusting" of free land by individuals, gave way to a new policy of gentle federal regulation that preserved the economic power of those cattle ranchers who were already exploiting the range. The current users saw little change in their circumstances and much more stability. They paid almost nothing for the new entitlement (federal grazing leases) and continued to use the public lands for their personal profit and at their personal whim. There were no provisions in the act for the protection of wildlife or the range itself. Ranchers went on poisoning eagles, wolves, and coyotes, shooting wild horses, mule deer, and burros, and putting too many cattle on the land.

From the beginning of Western settlement, it was "first in time, first in right." Whether one was a squatter or a legitimate homesteader, a miner, or a water user, one got the right to the property by being there first. As Patricia Limerick has pointed out, the only difference between you and a thief was time.

If free land drew people to the West, the discovery of gold there set their imaginations on fire. Over two hundred thousand people rushed overland to California from 1848 until 1852. They were joined by thousands more who came by clipper ship from the East Coast and from Australia, China, and Europe. Like Francisco Vásquez de Coronado in the sixteenth century, they came expecting to find enormous riches. Most were disappointed, even though by the mid-1850s California was producing almost half the world's gold. At the end of the Civil War, a third of Nevada's population were miners. In Montana that figure was 25 percent, and in Idaho 30 percent. (In the more cosmopolitan state of California, only one person in twenty was a miner.) Five years later, the individual with his pick and pan wandering the Sierras had been all but replaced by the corporate miners, who employed dynamite experts from England and imported the cheapest labor from China.

Conservationists such as John Muir, Gifford Pinchot, and later Aldo Leopold saw a mystical dimension in the West which diminished with increasing exploitation of the region's natural resources. As the onslaught against nature accelerated, it became apparent that if the West was not protected, it would be further ravaged without remorse. Gradually, non-Westerners realized their stake as Americans in stopping the West's despoliation. The creation of national parks saved the gems of our natural heritage, and the 1906 Antiquities Act did the same thing for historic and prehistoric landmarks. As a committed conservationist, President Theodore Roosevelt also issued a series of executive orders protecting vast areas of land from the ravages of mining companies, timber cutters, and cattlemen. Then, in 1907, Western politicians amended an agricultural-appropriations bill to prohibit any further removals from public lands without an act of Congress. Roosevelt knew he couldn't defeat the amendment, so, shortly before the act went into effect, he huddled over maps in the White House with Pinchot and issued a series of "midnight" executive orders establishing sixteen million acres of new forest reserves.

In some cases, efforts to control exploitation came too late. The inconsistently administered land offices closed only in 1946 and that year consolidated with the Grazing Service to create the federal government's Bureau of Land Management, which took control in perpetuity of thousands of square miles. Today it controls a hundred and seventy-eight million acres—excluding Alaska. Although the huge dams built in the twentieth century gave some order to the economic development of Western river basins, the primordial character of deserts and plains was gone and the power of the wild rivers was transformed. Ask anyone who experienced the quiet stillness of the canyons now flooded by Lake Powell, or who climbed the mountains now obliterated by open-pit mining in places from Arizona to Montana, and you will hear the notes of sadness for something irretrievably lost. The land seemed more for profit than for preservation.

In the mid-1970s, oil entrepreneurs drove their drill bits eleven thousand feet down into parts of the so-called overthrust belt in northeastern Utah and southwestern Wyoming, where geologic action had trapped vast pools of oil and gas far underground. In Colorado and in other parts of Wyoming and Utah, in the early 1980s, entrepreneurs unearthed layers of shale, and heated them to extract the oil. Modern boomtowns, conjuring up memories of Sutter's Mill and Cripple Creek, sprang up in remote places like Gillette and Evanston in Wyoming and Rifle and De Beque in Colorado. In the Evanston area alone, with oil prices expected to quadruple in a decade and oil reserves just north of town thought to be worth five hundred million dollars at 1980 prices, oil companies reportedly spent over two hundred million. Four thousand newcomers arrived from 1978 to 1981, overwhelming this single-movie-house town of forty-five hundred people. It was an old story in the West. As Mark Twain wrote in *Roughing It* about miners in the fictional boomtown of Unionville, Nevada, "We were stark mad with excitement—drunk with happiness—smothered under mountains of prospective wealth." It was a wealth that rarely lasted and frequently didn't materialize. The money always ran out, and the newcomers moved on. What remained was the land, pockmarked by abandoned shafts and split open by wide gashes. The land could not move on and would never be the same.

In order to guarantee access to federal public lands and state resources, the various "interests" had to be able to influence the federal and state decision makers. Such a pattern is not a recent development. Montana politics in the 1890s was more a contest between copper-mining magnates who were buying state legislators than between political parties seeking votes to enact their views of the state's future. In New Mexico, the Santa Fe Ring of lawyers and businessmen controlled the territory's politics and made big money. By the late nineteenth century, U.S. Senator William Stewart of Nevada symbolized the age. A commanding figure, known for intimidating witnesses when he was a trial attorney, he served in the Senate from 1864 through 1875 and again from 1887 through 1905, shaping legislation in such areas as land reclamation and railroads. His biographer Russell R. Elliott refers to him as "a servant of power." As a lawyer, he had represented major mining companies; while in the Senate, he drew financial benefits from the Southern Pacific Railroad. As Wallace Stegner has described him:

> Robust, aggressive, contentious, narrow, self-made, impatient of "theorists," irritated by abstract principles, a Nevada lawyer, miner, Indian-killer; a fixer, a getter-done, an indefatigable manipulator around the whiskey and cigars, a dragon whose cave was the smoke-filled room, Big Bill Stewart was one to delight a caricaturist and depress a patriot. But he was also, in his way, a man of faith: he believed in Western "development" and he believed in the right of men—himself among them—to get rich by this "development."

Until 1866, there was no federal mining law. Miners were free to go onto public lands, mine whatever they wanted, and pay Uncle Sam nothing, no matter how much gold they extracted. Senator Stewart wrote the 1866 law, which, with minor revisions, became the General Mining Act of 1872. These laws did not change what had existed before, which was essentially local control. The legislation stated: "The mineral lands of the public domain, both surveyed and unsurveyed, are hereby declared to be free and open to exploration and occupation by all citizens of the United

States . . . subject also to the local customs or rules of miners in the several mining districts." Virtually all of the public lands of the West were thrown open to mining as the "preferred use."

The 1872 law, with modest changes, still governs mining in the West. Whether you are a lone miner prospecting for silver with pick and shovel or a corporate giant—such as the Canadian company American Barrick, which expects to make three billion dollars in profit from a gold mine in northeastern Nevada—any American or American subsidiary of a foreign company can enter most areas of federal lands at will, file an unpatented claim, and take valuable minerals without making any royalty payment to the United States (although, as they are for any U.S. corporation, income taxes are required). Companies can also obtain a patent—full title not only to the minerals but also to the overlying land—for a song. For example, on March 15, 1995, the Interior Department, for fees that totaled less than five thousand dollars, issued patents (deeds) for minerals and land worth over two hundred million dollars. There are today some sixty-five thousand such patents, covering nearly three million acres. A patented property falls under state law and remains exempt from any future establishment of a federal royalty.

Patenting a property, however, has some drawbacks—the patent-holder has to pay more taxes to cover the cost of public roads to the property, as well as shoulder zoning and regulatory burdens (especially environmental ones)—so many miners don't bother. The unpatented claim has most of the advantages of the patent and none of its liabilities (except that it is subject to regulation by the U.S. Forest Service and the Bureau of Land Management). Generally, a miner can stake such a claim only on a property up to twenty acres in size; however, there is no limitation on the amount of unpatented claims any one person can assert. According to the 1872 law, the unpatented claim can be maintained indefinitely, as long as the claimant spends one hundred dollars per year "improving" the property. The fulfillment of this requirement is established by filing a one-page form with the Bureau of Land Management. Charles Wilkinson points out in his book *Crossing the Next Meridian:* "The requirement begs, and receives, widespread fraud: federal agencies can hardly take the time to disprove a notarized affidavit alleging a day or two's work, perhaps coupled with a bulldozer scrape or the purchase of a shovel."

If there has been no discovery of valuable minerals, an area being prospected can be taken over by the federal government without compensation—as wilderness land, for example. But when a miner discovers a hard-rock mineral, he automatically obtains an unpatented mining claim—a property right to the minerals, which cannot be seized by the U.S. government without compensation and which he can sell or transfer or pass on as inheritance. The establishment of a "discovery" requires only a "prudent person" test—that is, a prudent person would decide that there was a reasonable chance of developing a mine successfully and marketing the mineral for a profit. The public lands of the West are dotted with over a million unpatented claims, comprising some twenty-five million acres, and ninety thousand new claims are staked each year; in such circumstances, enforcement becomes laughable. Without question, the 1872 law has facilitated the greatest grant of public goods in American history. The historian Vernon Parrington has referred to the spirit of the era in which the law originated as "the Great Barbecue."

John Wesley Powell had hoped for federal leadership in the development of Western water resources, and with time it came. By 1944, the federal government had invested billions in the seventeen Western states for irrigation and hydropower projects and, almost incredibly, the pace picked up after the Second World War. The first water project was the 1903 Newlands Project, which harnessed the Truckee River in Nevada and diverted a portion of it for farming outside Reno. Since then, the Bureau of Reclamation has built 254 diversion dams, 348 reservoirs, 1,460 miles of pipeline, and 54,535 miles of canals and drains. It delivers nearly ten trillion gallons of irrigation water and industrial and municipal water annually to more than thirty million people. In addition to irrigation, the bureau has built fifty-two power plants generating forty-eight billion kilowatt hours of electricity annually. Water rights stir deep emotions; American Indian water rights and state water rights occupy center stage in Western courts and law schools and among the bar. Disputes over water in Western history have affected sovereignty and influenced borders. In the West, as people say, whiskey is for drinking, water is for fighting.

IN MY YEARS on the Energy and Natural Resources Committee, I've seen that what happens in Washington determines the future of many small water districts and inefficient mines in the West as much as advances in technology do. The irony is that most of those who petition for federal support consider themselves conservative politically. Many Western senators are shameless in advocating more federal water for their crops or less tax on their ore, all the while opposing help for the poor or cleanup of older environments, such as industrial rivers and dumps in New Jersey. They fail time after time to see the natural resources of America as the patrimony of all Americans, not just their state's private preserve. They see the value in preserving Yosemite or Yellowstone, the Grand Canyon or the Grand Tetons, but they also regard the coal and the copper and the forests and the water in their states with a possessiveness that connotes ownership, notwithstanding the effect that development of these resources has had on the environment all of us share, as well as on the lives of those who did the developing. They like to assume that they are protecting the environment, when they are destroying it. They often delude themselves into believing that they can have both unlimited development and a clean environment.

Political fund-raisers representing Western natural-resource interests consider themselves pragmatists. They exert great efforts and spend much money to counter the views of public-interest advocates, whom they label as radical. Their objective is clear: expand their subsidies and send the bill to the American taxpayers. In a 1990 study, resource development industries were the largest source of political money in seven Western states. When I became chairman of the Water and Power Subcommittee, a subcommittee staffer asked me if I wanted him to set up a fund-raiser with some "water boys" in the West. I got rid of him instead. Hearings on an obscure mining provision would pack the hearing room with industry lobbyists, whereas a hearing on a major national-park acquisition would attract only a few environmental lobbyists. It was clear that the federal government not only governed the rules of private development but, with the guidance of well-paid Western lobbyists, passed out billions of dollars each year to mining, agriculture, timber, and cattle interests.

When the Great Depression forced thousands of families to leave the plains for the chance of better work in California, the myth of unrestricted utilization of the land was refuted powerfully. Wallace Stegner writes that when Congressman Taylor's grazing bill, which had been precipitated by overuse of the land, came to the Senate floor, "winds from the West carried soil from the dust bowl states clear to the East Coast, and the air of the capital was thick with the presence of what one senator called 'the most tragic, the most impressive lobbyist' that had ever come to Washington." There are times when I feel that it would take a catastrophe the equivalent of another dust bowl to slow the petitions of those who want to squeeze more and more from the land.

Ironically, the senators from many states in the West are known as natural-resource senators. They promote the exploitation of a particular natural resource that has historically formed the backbone of their state's economy. Ideology rarely makes a difference: a liberal Democrat and a conservative Republican will often unite when the issue is grazing fees, mineral royalties, or water charges. The advantage that natural-resource senators have is that they can trade their votes to other senators on many issues that have a peripheral effect on their states. In return, they get the support of those senators on mining or grazing or water issues. In economic terms, the narrower a state's economy is, the more vulnerable it is to collapsing commodity markets and economic cycles, but in political terms the more likely it is to win federal subsidies.

Western Republicans and Western Democrats scuttled the Mining Law Reform Bill of 1994, which would have been the biggest change in the laws governing mining since 1872. When the bill passed out of the Energy and Natural Resources Committee and through the Senate, it was heavily weighted toward the mining industry. Reformers, myself included, had agreed to that procedure, because we anticipated a more environmentally oriented, pro-taxpayer version of the bill to come out of the House, and we expected that the House-Senate conference would compromise between the two. We wanted reform—a federal royalty on gross revenues, minimum federal environmental standards for mining reclamation, and, above all, an end to federal patents for mineral lands—and we thought that with a new administration, and with Bruce Babbitt, a geologist and reformer, as secretary of interior, we had a chance. Then the snows of the 1993–94 winter melted, the azaleas bloomed in Washington, and the mining interests from Idaho, Wyoming, Nevada, Arizona, New Mexico, Utah, Colorado, Montana, and Alaska descended on the Capitol.

Bennett Johnston of Louisiana, a lover both of the outdoors and of oil exploration, and then the chairman of the Energy and Natural Resources Committee, wanted a bill that balanced economic and environmental interests. At the same time, he wanted a conference agreement that would pass the Senate. Always fearful of the chits that Western natural-resource senators held, he preferred to get an agreement with them, instead of a fight. There were four Democratic senators and three Republican senators on the Senate half of the House-Senate Conference Committee. Johnston and I were members, and the two other Democrats were Dale Bumpers of Arkansas and Dan Akaka of Hawaii. None of us were natural-resource senators. Even though Johnston, our chairman, came from an oil state, on the issue of hard-rock mining he was a reformer. Bumpers had fought the mining interests for the last seven years and had lost every time. The three Republicans were from Idaho, Wyoming, and Alaska. Negotiations between supporters and opponents of reform focused on the amount of royalties that should go to the federal government from the sale of a mined mineral, the size of environmental buffer zones around any mining operation, and whether the states or the secretary of interior would be the ultimate arbiter in disputes. In the Senate as a whole, a few Western senators said that they were willing to give on patents—although most were implacably opposed to any change—if we reformers gave on virtually everything else, which, of course, made the price too high. The three Republican senators on the conference committee, in consultation with Democratic and Republican Western senators both on and off the Energy and Natural Resources Committee, delayed, double-checking with the mining interests in their respective states and nitpicking every draft of Chairman Johnston's various proposed compromises.

After weeks of meetings, the Republican members of the conference committee asked Johnston if he would meet with all the Western senators, Republican and Democrat alike. In that meeting, the Westerners echoed the mining industry line, demonstrating anew that the unrestricted right to exploit natural resources is upheld by both parties equally. Summer turned into fall. Time was running out. Elections were approaching. Now, even if an agreement could be reached, a filibuster might stop the conference report.

The Western senators on the conference committee denounced the various drafts, with the familiar charges:

"You're not from the West, you don't understand."

"Why are you trying to tell us how to run our affairs?"

"Why doesn't the federal government just give the land back to the states and let them manage it?"

"People in my part of the country are tired of Washington dictating our affairs to us."

They launched into faulty analogies about what a similar intrusion of federal power would mean in Arkansas or New Jersey. One senator said that he could not go with a compromise that kept even a net royalty (which meant that after most of the mining company's expenses were deducted, a portion of what remained would go to the federal government), because it would put small miners out of business. As small farmers once served as unwitting frontmen for large corporate subsidy-seekers, now the small miner was evoked to tug at our heartstrings.

In response, we said we would agree to a hardship clause, whereby a small mine in bad financial shape would pay a smaller royalty. That wasn't enough. The Republicans on the conference committee then had a problem with the methodology of determining profitability. Every move they made was checked out by the mining industry, led in Washington by Jim McClure, a former chairman of the Energy and Natural Resources Committee and now a high-priced Washington lawyer. "My people say" was a frequent justification for rejecting a modification. Finally, one Western Republican senator said that the pending compromise on royalties would cost two hundred jobs in one of the towns in his state—a town where there had already been layoffs because of falling mineral prices and competition from South America. He needed guarantees that there would be no further job loss. Many of these senators had opposed the bailout of Chrysler, had railed against government spending for worker retraining, had blamed the federal government for urban unemployment, and had ignored the thousands of lost jobs from corporate downsizing, but when it came to mining they insisted on no loss of jobs. In fact, they were doing the industry's bidding and hiding behind the solitary miner. It was an old game.

After two more drafts, the Senate Republicans on the conference committee rejected the final proposal, and the bill died in conference, with the Senate never even making an offer to the House. The natural-resource senators had played the clock skillfully. Big Bill Stewart would have been proud of them.

After the midterm election, there were more Western senators than ever on the Energy and Natural Resources Committee. Any additional reform seems unlikely. The new cry is for greater compensation of property rights that have been limited or curtailed by federal regulations. Some committee members even want compensation for any loss of water subsidies, so that taxpayers face a lose-lose proposition—pay the cost of the subsidy or pay the cost of compensation. The lords of yesterday ride again.

THE WESTERN ARTIST Charles Marion Russell lived in Great Falls, Montana, where he drank a lot and painted a lot. Once, in 1923, he was asked to address the Great Falls booster club. After several speeches by local dignitaries championing the virtues of the town and the admirableness of the pioneer spirit, Russell tore up his prepared talk and said, "In my book, a pioneer is a man who turned all the grass upside down, strung bob-wire over the dust that was left, poisoned the water and cut down the trees, killed the Indians who owned the land and called it progress. If I had my way, the land here would be like God made it and none of you sons of bitches would be here at all."

The West on the eve of the twenty-first century is a world apart from the West on the eve of the twentieth century, yet the political process lags woefully behind its—and the nation's—urgent needs. Though the Homestead Act was one of the most successful land-distribution schemes in history, and the railroads needed generous incentives to make sizable investments, and the desert needed water to farm it, each of these subsidies, in the absence of regulation that kept the taxpayer interest paramount, became excessive, and this way of operating ignored the long-term consequences of unplanned development. The very complexity of existing regulation often gave the lawyers representing mining, timber, grazing, and irrigated agriculture the room to carve out special deals. The imperative to preserve the environment and to create jobs cannot be a zero-sum game. Sustainable development must replace unfettered exploitation of natural resources as the desired ethos. The region's future will depend on management and planning, so that man and mining and nature can coexist. The focus must shift from interest in a specific resource to concern about a complete ecosystem; not this or that piece of the West, but the entire region; not the Old West but the Whole West. To worry about the pit of a strip mine but not the stream or aquifer that its runoff pollutes is shortsighted. To see clear-cutting of forests as only a "tree problem" and not a habitat problem is wrong. Extractive industry must now be balanced by recreational, scenic, and spiritual uses of the land.

Even though ninety-five million acres have been declared official wilderness, the frontier as a place is long gone. In 1945, eighty thousand people lived in Phoenix. Today it is a metropolis of over two million. The same kind of explosive growth has taken place in Denver, Salt Lake City, Seattle, Tucson, Albuquerque, San Diego, Las Vegas, and Reno. There are more city dwellers as a percentage of the total regional population in the West today than in any other part of the country. People who live in these cities have little at stake in extractive industries. Many came for the climate and the informal Western lifestyle. They need water and power, but they couldn't care less about minerals, grazing, or timber. They oppose the growth of these industries if it is at the expense of the environment they came to enjoy. But there is also self-delusion going on. Lawyers wearing boots and cowboy hats arrive for work every day in Denver's highest skyscrapers, as if headed for the range. The practice of their daily profession tells them that the West has changed, but their imagination and self-concept remain rooted in the Old West. The tension between the two is fought out every day in lawyers' minds, as well as in courtrooms. The outcome of the struggle will determine not just the West's politics but also its future. Yet whatever conflicts rest in the psyche of Westerners, if people continue to stream into Western cities, environmental problems will worsen. It is not that individual miners or ranchers or lumbermen who came west and despoiled the land were evil; many were simply doing a job to support their families and didn't think of much else. But times have changed, and new imperatives shape our future. The land of what Bernard De Voto called "the plundered province," if it is to avoid population controls, must be managed to protect its waters and way of life, or that way of life will be destroyed by the developers who converge on the region from West and East as if they were part of a pincer movement bent on conquest.

The sustainability movement asserts that one generation must be the trustee for the next. It attempts to provide both job creation and environmental value by increasing the productivity of the land through application of knowledge and technology. It begins by determining the natural and cultural legacy that must be sustained and then plans how, for example, a stream can be used as a commodity in mining or power production and still be a blue-ribbon trout stream, or how a forest can provide lumber and still preserve habitat. At the core of the sustainability movement is the commonsense observation that the right of a property owner must be balanced against the needs of society.

Pyramid Lake sits in a Nevada desert. You reach it by driving east and north from Reno. As you come over the crest of a hill, the lake appears, stark and surprising. A vast blue body of water twenty-seven miles long and up to nine miles wide, surrounded by mountains, boulders, and sagebrush, it confounds expectations. Pyramid Lake is fed by the Truckee River, which originates in Lake Tahoe and falls twenty-four hundred feet, as if it were flowing down a spiral staircase, until it reaches the valley floor, eventually emptying into what was once the second-largest natural lake in the West. For nearly four thousand years, the area around the lake has been the home of the Paiute Indians. When General John Charles Frémont first saw the lake, on his way to California in 1844, he was astounded by its size and the succulence of its fish, the Lahontan cutthroat trout and the cui-ui, a species of sucker unique to Pyramid Lake. By the 1870s, the Lahontan trout of Pyramid Lake were being eaten throughout the country. The Indians lived at the southern edge of the lake, where the Truckee flows in and the fish were easiest to catch as they headed out of the lake to spawn.

South of Pyramid Lake is the Carson River. It flows northeast from the Sierra Nevada and empties into the Carson Sink; at its delta is a web of wetlands comprising Stillwater Marsh, Carson Lake, and the Lahontan Valley wetlands, which ultimately disappear, absorbed by the surrounding desert. These two rivers, the Truckee and the Carson, together once formed an expansive lake-and-wetland complex with a unique habitat at the western edge of the high desert that is the Great Basin of Nevada.

In 1905, as a part of the Newlands Project, the Derby Dam was built on the Truckee, thirty-five miles upstream from Pyramid Lake. It diverted Truckee water through the Truckee Canal into the farm area around Fallon and Stillwater. With less water making it to Pyramid Lake, a vast marsh known as Lake Winnemucca dried up, since its existence depended on an occasional overflow of Pyramid Lake. The level of Pyramid Lake itself fell seventy feet, and its surface shrank by 25 percent. The Lahontan trout died out, flapping to death on the mud flats or slamming against the Derby Dam in a vain effort to reach their spawning waters upstream. The sturdier cui-ui became an endangered species. In addition to Lake Winnemucca, birds lost another significant stopover on the Pacific flyway: over the years, the runoff from agricultural pesticides turned the Stillwater Wildlife Refuge into a poisonous pond. If more water was allotted to Pyramid Lake, there would be less water to dilute the agricul-

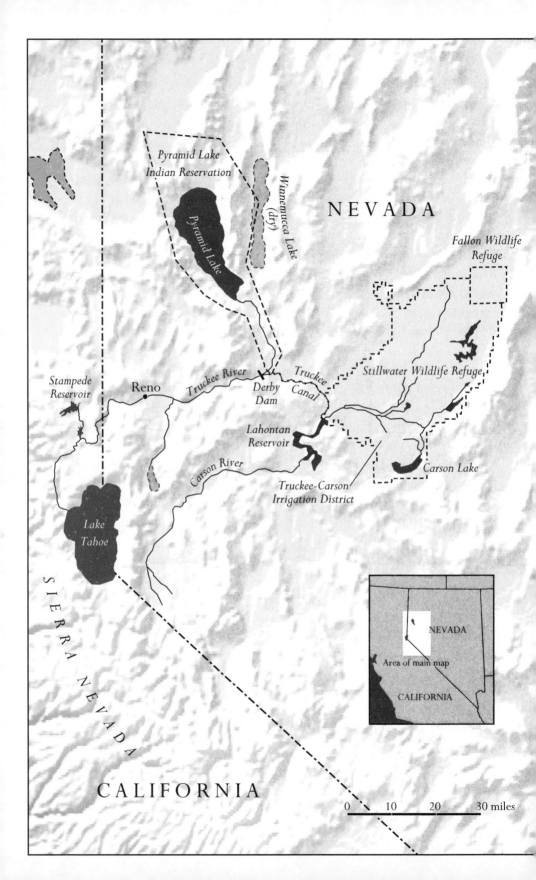

Pyramid Lake
Indian Reservation

Winnemucca Lake (dry)

Pyramid Lake

NEVADA

Fallon Wildlife
Refuge

Stampede
Reservoir

Reno

Truckee River

Truckee
Canal

Stillwater Wildlife Refuge

Derby
Dam

Lahontan
Reservoir

Carson River

Carson Lake

Truckee-Carson
Irrigation District

Lake
Tahoe

S I E R R A   N E V A D A

CALIFORNIA

NEVADA

Area of main map

CALIFORNIA

0   10   20   30 miles

tural runoff, and therefore the amount of selenium and mercury at Stillwater would become more concentrated. But the less water that flowed into Pyramid, the more threatened was the remaining cui-ui population. It was a classic double bind. All this was occurring as Reno, like other Western cities, was booming. From a hamlet of easy divorce and thirty-two thousand people in the 1950s, it grew to a tourist city of nearly three hundred thousand in the 1990s.

The Fallon-Paiute-Shoshone and Truckee–Carson–Pyramid Lake Water Settlement Act of 1990 is the first water-settlement bill ever passed in which ecosystem needs became an integral part of the Great Basin's water resources management. In the mid-eighties, I blocked attempts to settle the water dispute on the cheap, as if it were simply a disagreement between California and Nevada that two former governors, President Ronald Reagan and Senator Paul Laxalt, could now resolve, given their positions in Washington. There were larger issues, which I insisted that any settlement address. The act attempts to balance ecosystem needs, Native American claims, and burgeoning urban-sector demands, while at the same time assuring the continued viability of agricultural communities long dependent on reclamation-era water. The act was the result of a two-year negotiation, spearheaded by Nevada Senator Harry Reid and preceded by years of legal battles and stalemate. It involved all parties, not just the states, and sought compromise from each. Reno agreed to conserve water, thereby allowing more water to flow into Pyramid Lake. The Sierra Pacific Power Company agreed to reduce its flows through upstream Truckee River dams, thereby preserving more water for fish in the Stampede Reservoir, high in the mountains, which could be released during the spawning season. The Pyramid Lake Paiute Indians, after securing access to Stampede Reservoir water in a court decree, agreed to put on hold their other lawsuits against the U.S. government and the farmers. The original users of the nation's first reclamation project—the vegetable and alfalfa farmers—agreed to sell some of their water rights as reserve water to preserve wetlands in the area east of Reno fed by the Carson River and the Truckee Canal. This action by the farmers means less water has to flow down the Truckee Canal away from Pyramid Lake.

In many ways, the Pyramid Lake Settlement Act is a model for future ecosystem reclamation efforts. If it succeeds, the water level of Pyramid Lake will rise and its Anaho Island will remain an island, thereby safeguarding from predators one of the largest white pelican rookeries in North America. The agreement will restore the cui-ui fisheries and also a new species of Lahontan trout, developed by the Fish and Wildlife Service, both of which will ensure the livelihood of an ancient people. Reno will make the water it gets last longer and go further. Finally, pollution of the Stillwater and Carson wetlands will abate, and there will be enough water for birds. The key concepts in the framework of the law are balance, sustainability, and cooperation.

In December 1993, I held a hearing in Reno on the implementation of the Pyramid Lake Settlement Act. (A few weeks earlier, a Bureau of Land Management office in Reno had been bombed by radical Nevadans opposed to any federal control of "their" property rights. Luckily, there was no one in the building at the time.) The hearing began at 8 a.m. on a Saturday and more than three hundred people attended. As each of the groups testified in the cavernous convention hall, I sensed that most of them had accepted the changes embodied in the legislation, and I felt that the envisioned balance could work. The threat to the ecosystem today comes from the agricultural users of the Newlands Project water. If there had never been a Newlands Project, the Truckee would still be a natural trout stream, and birds at Stillwater would not be deformed and dying from the selenium in irrigation runoff. The bill forces these primary water-right holders to adjust their operations to accommodate the needs and rights both of Indians and of fish and wildlife—the forgotten players in the water wars of the Old West. But the water reserved in Stampede Reservoir for the Paiutes' fish can also be used for Reno. Today the farmer will get less. Tomorrow I think that Reno may want more.

I have no evidence for my concern, except that Reno's users have the most economic clout. I remember an old saying in the West that water does not flow downhill but toward money, and I worry that it's been all too true. The balance so precariously struck depends on continued goodwill. What the law will never be able to do is create more water, and no matter how great the efficiency and goodwill, if the people keep coming to Reno (and towns like it) from East and West, there will be a time when the water supply will reach its limit. Charles Wilkinson worried, too: "What will happen to Pyramid Lake, the tribe, the river, Stillwater, the fish, and the birds in twenty-five years, when the [Reno-Sparks] population reaches 500,000?" he wrote in *Crossing the Next Meridian*. "Were not Powell and Stegner right, after all, about their central point—that the aridity and terrain dictate a finiteness beyond the 100th meridian? Is not the finite in view?"

The only thing that will guarantee the West (and America as a whole) a brighter, if proscribed, future is the recognition that the goodwill offered by all the participants in the Pyramid Lake Settlement and the longer-term time horizon of the sustainability movement must become the norm. The old economic and political power cannot improve the current circumstance. The get-in-and-get-out mentality of the miner looking for gold must give way to thinking on a different time scale. Even senators from as far away as New Jersey have the obligation to point out that the vast public lands and their resources belong to all of us.

11

Getting to Billings

MONTANA WAS the last of the fifty states I have visited. I went there in the fall of 1987, to speak to the Montana State Democratic Party at the invitation of my Senate colleague Max Baucus. Up to then, I had known the state primarily through the work of another Montana senator, John Melcher, with whom I served on the Energy and Natural Resources Committee. John was a veterinarian by training and a monotone by choice. He kept several cats in his Senate office. They were given free rein. When he lost his Senate seat after years of cat breeding, the new occupant of his office told me that he had to not only change the rugs but sand the concrete floors, to get the smell out. Senator Melcher was a proponent of MHD, a special additive for low-sulfur Montana coal which made it burn cleaner and more efficiently. When he began to tout its attributes, you could leave the room, because he would give new meaning to the term "extended debate."

Phil Jackson, my Knick teammate, is a summer resident at Flathead Lake, in the northwestern corner of the state, and for years he had been telling me about Montana's beauty. When my plane landed at sunset at the Bozeman airport in the Gallatin Valley, I remembered those descriptions. For a person not accustomed to Big Sky country, the mountain ranges surrounding the valley—the Bridger Range, the Madison Range, and the Tobacco Roots—provided comforting limits to the vast expanse. Like the rivers of the valley—the Gallatin, the Madison, and the Jefferson, which join at Three Forks to become the Missouri River—they were named by Lewis and Clark on their journey west. After the dry heat of the plane, the September evening air was brisk and fresh, like the water in a good Montana trout stream.

After an airport press conference, Max and I headed to a reception given by the state Democratic chairman at the home of a prominent local Democrat. At the reception, a cocktail party for the significant contributors and workers, a man named Frank Cikan introduced himself and said that he wanted to thank me.

"For what?" I asked, whereupon he told a story that began more than twenty years earlier. In the winter of 1965–66, at Oxford as a Rhodes Scholar, I was doing a minimum of academic work. Besides reading novels and histories that I had not had time for at Princeton, and traveling extensively in Europe and the Middle East, that year, as noted, I also played basketball for Simmanthal of Milan, in the European Cup competition. Shortly after Valentine's Day, our team traveled to Prague to play Slavia, a good club that we had beaten by eighteen points two weeks earlier in Milan. In Prague, we lost by nineteen points, and therefore lost the series with the Czechs (in European Cup competition, teams play each other twice, once at home and once away, with the winner being the team with the highest combined point total for the two games.) The Italian press roasted me for being out of condition. This was the first real press assault of my life, and I felt stung. "Who does this fat American think we are?" one newspaper said, in a distillation of the prevailing view. "He doesn't care about his commitment enough even to get into shape." (I had put on thirty pounds.) For the remaining three months of the season, I buckled down, and we won the European Cup, beating in the semifinals the same U.S.S.R. team that had represented the Soviet Union in the 1964 Olympics.

Frank Cikan remembered my visit to Prague in early 1966. He was seventeen at the time. He had also seen me play a year earlier, when he had sneaked into the practice of the touring American team on its way to represent the United States at the World University Games in Budapest. He did the same thing when Simmanthal came to Prague.

I stayed behind to practice after my teammates had left. My practice routine was to end by making fifteen baskets in a row from each of five spots on the floor. While watching, Frank decided he was going to be a basketball player. He became a good guard. He made the club team in Prague, and in 1968 he made the national team.

In December 1968, Vladimir Hager, coach of the Sparta Club and the Czech national team, brought a group of Czech players to America for a basketball tour sponsored by an organization called People to People. The Prague Spring of 1968 had been followed by the Soviet tanks in August. Soviet and Czech hard-liner repression had replaced Alexander Dubček's "socialism with a human face," and the dreams of spring vanished. Some of my Czech basketball contemporaries accepted less freedom and became depressed. Not Frank; he decided to leave the first chance he got.

When the Czech basketball team got off the plane in New York, no one met them. They were stranded, with little money. I got a call from Coach Hager, whom I had met in 1965 and kept up with ever since. I contributed some of the money necessary to get the team back to Czechoslovakia, and I also arranged for the Czechs to play a preliminary game at Madison Square Garden on January 21, before the Knicks played the Seattle Supersonics.

That was a memorable night. I had not yet broken into the Knicks' starting lineup. I was failing as a guard; I was just too slow. Still, I refused to admit it, even to myself. In the January 21 game, the Knicks' starting forward, Cazzie Russell, broke his ankle. That gave me my chance to switch to forward, and, as they say in sports biographies, "the rest was history." It was also a memorable night for Frank. One week earlier, in Lancaster, Pennsylvania, another member of the Czech team had come to him and proposed that both of them defect. Coach Harry Pappas of Brandywine College in Wilmington, Delaware, had offered them scholarships. The two boys quit the team and went to Wilmington. Pappas had arranged for a former Czech defector to meet with each of them individually and talk to them about the consequences of defection, such as never being able to return to Czechoslovakia or see their families again. After his one-on-one meeting with the defector, Frank's teammate changed his mind and decided to return to Czechoslovakia. Frank announced that he would stay in America and build a new life for himself no matter what the consequences.

On the 21st, Frank came to Madison Square Garden to say goodbye to his teammates, who refused to speak to him. He suited up and sat at the end of the bench throughout the game, waiting for the chance to play in the Garden, but Hager never gave it to him. Afterward, he dressed and left with Pappas for his new life. In Delaware, he played for Brandywine, cleaning bathrooms and sweeping floors after classes to earn money. His first paycheck in America was for $49.37. He had never seen so much money, and he sent the entire amount to his parents in Czechoslovakia.

Frank wanted to pursue a career in architecture, and Montana State University, in Bozeman, was the only place that had an architecture school and would offer him a basketball scholarship. So he left Brandywine and, like the immigrants of old, made his way across the continent to the land of the Big Sky. Over the next three years, he worked all night in a dairy, went from work straight to classes, and ended the day with basketball practice.

By the time the Iron Curtain had collapsed and Czech national identity had triumphed over communism, Frank had become a successful architect with a bright future in a booming area of the American West. In 1991, he went back to Czechoslovakia, out of curiosity and ethnic loyalty. From the Czechs who had not fled he encountered strong criticism for being a "rich American." Taken aback, he realized that there was a difference between him and his friends. He had become more optimistic and more tolerant. He was, in fact, now more an American than a Czech, and he wanted to thank me for the part I had played in this transformation when I was taking those postpractice jump shots in the deserted gym in Prague.

After the state party chairman's reception, Max Baucus and I went to the Democratic rally, on the second floor of the Montana State University Activity Center, a renovated barn big enough to play basketball in. The Montana Democrats sat on folding chairs along the wall and crowded around buffet tables covered with buckets of chili, bread, and soft drinks. There were kegs of beer anchoring each end of the barn. We worked the room before the speeches, saying hello, shaking hands, and listening to people's stories. One of the people I met was a tall dark-haired woman named Dorothy Bradley. She was a lawyer by training, state representative by avocation; she had run for Congress in 1978, at age thirty-one, and lost. It was thought that she had statewide ambitions. That night our futures would mesh because her last name was Bradley.

Finding a way to identify with a local audience is one of the techniques of a political speaker. There are many ways to do it. You can talk about the food, as in "It sure was great eating those grits" or that barbe-cue, or that apple pie, or that tandoori chicken, or that lobster stew, or that ravioli, or those chiles rellenos. You can recognize and praise major officeholders: "Lieutenant Governor such-and-such, who works eigh-teen-hour days, has done so much to ensure that the elderly will be housed and clothed." You can simply acknowledge the politicians pres-ent, the more the better. At a big political dinner in New Jersey in 1984, I memorized the names of all twenty-seven politicians in their seating order on the dais, and when I began to speak, gazing straight ahead with-out looking right or left, I led off with the sequence as if it were a rap: "Thank you, Chairman Durkin, Freeholder Jones, Senator Lipman, Con-gressman Roe," and so on all the way to the end. At first people paid lit-tle attention, then they began to laugh, and finally, hanging intently on each additional name until I finished, they burst into applause. Another technique is to adapt a standard joke to a local politician. Once, in North Carolina, I told a story about the machine politician who got votes from graveyards and I tied it to Liston Ramsey, a powerful Democratic state legislator from western North Carolina, who was happy to be singled out by the visiting speaker. Finally, you can create a story out of the raw ma-terial you get at the event, stitching together a series of observations and comments people make to you. That's my favorite technique, because it's the most memorable when it's right. When it's wrong—well, it's also memorable.

In Bozeman that night in 1987, I decided to be creative and have some fun. Senator Baucus introduced me. I talked about the state chair-man, using generic humor applicable to state chairs in any state, and then I turned to Dorothy Bradley, who was standing to my left at the edge of the crowd. Without explanation, I walked over to her, gave her a kiss on the cheek, returned to the stage, and said that I was particularly glad to be in Montana because it gave me a chance to see "my first wife, Dorothy Bradley." I said I had to confess that I had missed her, and never did I re-alize that more than I did right now. Seeing her in this old barn, I said, had made me re-evaluate the relationship, and I hoped she was doing the same thing. So I wanted to thank the Montana Democratic Party for get-ting us back together.

A gratifying hush had fallen over the audience, which was in a state of bemused doubt about where I was going. I asked Dorothy to come up on the large wooden platform that served as the stage. I gave her another kiss on the cheek and embraced her. By now the crowd had begun to catch on—there were scattered chuckles, a few Montana hoots, and then wild laughter. Dorothy laughed too, for which I will always be grateful.

Since that foolish rally talk, I have followed Dorothy's political career with avid interest. She remained a state representative for the next several years, rising to become chairperson of the Appropriations Human Services Committee, with jurisdiction over the largest part of the state's budget. In 1992, she ran for governor against a former Democrat named Marc Racicot, who had turned Republican several years earlier, after the Democrats gave him the brush-off when he expressed interest in running for the nomination for state attorney general, and who became well known when he successfully prosecuted the mountain-man kidnappers of the Olympic biathlon star Kari Swenson. Dorothy was the first female nominee for governor from any party in the state's history. On her campaign postcards was a line from country-western singer Garth Brooks: "Our lives are better left to chance. I could've missed the pain, but I'da had to miss the dance." In late October of that year, I flew back to Montana to campaign for her.

Dorothy Bradley is the daughter of a geologist from Madison, Wisconsin, and an archeology student from New York. She grew up in Bozeman, where her father was a professor at Montana State University. Her mother, a Bryn Mawr graduate who had relinquished her career in archeology, was a "full-time mom" who occupied herself with a regular dose of *The New York Times* and many good works.

Dorothy's ancestors included a deaf grandmother who learned to lipread from Alexander Graham Bell, a great-uncle who had served as postmaster general in President Rutherford B. Hayes's cabinet, and a doctor who as a medical missionary once saved the life of the king of Siam. There was a flintiness about her family's history. The family made no concessions to her deaf grandmother's disability. Her father found a way to join the Army during the Second World War, even though he was too old. Her mother fought a twenty-year battle against breast cancer that doctors said would kill her in five. In addition to a mastectomy, she had (in Dorothy's words) "every possible mutilating operation a woman can have: hysterectomy, gall bladder, appendix removal—you name it, she had it. But her spirit never died. She felt that every moment had to be lived as if it were the last."

By age thirteen, Dorothy had a horse, and after that she "never wanted to leave Montana." But after high school she went to Colorado College, in Colorado Springs. "During my first year, I felt intimidated and overwhelmed, and I wanted to transfer to Montana State, where I could get lost in a big student body," she told me. "But my father said I had to learn to live with my own shortcomings. And he was right. You know, we so desperately want to be better than we are. We want to be brilliant, insightful, and all of those things. You can do the best you can, but not better. You must forgive yourself after that."

After graduation from college and a brief job in Germany, Dorothy applied to the University of Wisconsin for a graduate program in anthropology and environmental sciences, but in the meantime she began working for an activist group called the Bozeman Environmental Task Force, which sought to ensure mine reclamation, groundwater quality, and proper siting of thermal energy facilities. One thing led to another, and "a couple of friends lured me into running for the Montana legislature," she said. "So I turned down a fellowship I had just won at Wisconsin. I had never had a fellowship before. I was very proud of myself." Her father told her that she was embarking on something crazy. Dorothy ran for the legislature and won. She was the only woman in the Montana House.

Dorothy met me at the airport in Missoula. She seemed as steady as ever. Her candidacy for governor was heading into its final phase and only four points separated her from her opponent that day. She thought she could close the gap by the election and win. We went into the airport terminal for what turned out to be a perfunctory press conference, before an audience of about forty people carrying banners that read "Clinton-Gore, Bradley for governor." Then we headed back out to a small private plane that would take us to Kalispell, just north of Flathead Lake, for a fund-raising luncheon.

On the plane, I glanced at Dorothy's face, with its high cheekbones, strong jaw, and incipient crow's feet at the edge of the eyes. I thought of what William Kittredge once wrote about Western women—that they "wind up looking fifty when they are thirty-seven and fifty-three when they are seventy. It's as though they wear down to what counts and just last there. . . ." Shoulder to shoulder in the tiny propeller plane, we talked. I asked her about herself. She said that she was divorced, no children. Her work was her life. She had poured herself into the state legislature and Democratic politics. In 1971, two years before *Roe* v. *Wade*, she had introduced a bill to legalize abortion in Montana. It was one of her first acts as a legislator and, predictably, it failed. She had alienated the AFL-CIO by pushing for a sales tax and by agreeing to support

Burlington Northern's effort to close poorly manned railroad stations in towns with fewer than one thousand people. She had entered politics to change Montana, she said, and she had had some successes and some failures, but no one doubted that she was still trying. In the campaign, she had decided to tell the people the truth: that the state government had to raise taxes. Her Republican opponent, whom she debated nearly fifty times, agreed. The difference was that Dorothy wanted to take half the revenue and use it for education and aid to local governments. But she said that in her first year as governor she would hold a referendum on whether to do that and also on which tax to raise, promising to abide by the results. She radiated integrity, candor, and modesty. The more we talked, the more I wanted her to win.

As we flew into Kalispell, we could see Flathead Lake, nestled against the mountains dusted with newly fallen snow; it was one of the great sights of the fall of 1992. In an upstairs room of the Lighterside restaurant, about fifty local businesspeople had assembled. I didn't know what to expect. Phil Jackson had told me that, before his time with the Bulls, he once considered staying the whole year at Flathead Lake and coaching at the local college, but after a newspaper interview in which he made it clear that he would recruit black athletes, Kalispell's booster fund dried up. That day in the restaurant, a local lawyer, who had himself run in a Republican primary for governor years ago, introduced me, and after I finished speaking, he praised Dorothy. Her clear statement of the need for transportation and education investment had won him over, as it had also appealed to other businessmen in this summer-resort town. Dorothy had done her homework.

In the saga of the American West, women have largely been left out or idealized or marginalized. In the great paintings of the West, women are usually absent. Whether the artist is Charles Marion Russell, Frederic Remington, Albert Bierstadt, or George Catlin, the white women who bore and raised the children of the frontier are rarely seen in paintings. And except for the occasional painting of village life, and a few portraits of Native American women by the great photographer of North American Indians Edward Sheriff Curtis, nonwhite Western women seem never to have existed. Yet it was the labor of Mexican American and Native American women, who were bearing children and raising families of their own, that made an extremely hard life a little less so for many white women of the West.

The traditional view of women in the West turns them into innocents or victims. In the few paintings in which women figure, they are usually in the protective shadow of their husbands. The stereotype has the Western wife going meekly wherever her husband's ambition took them. In the process, she would either break emotionally, unable to cope with the rigors of the frontier, or she would become the indispensable helpmate who stood by her man. She worked hard—very hard—bearing children, caring for the brood, tilling the garden, running the house. Her pain was her loneliness and her lack of comfort in living among "brutes and savages." Rarely was she portrayed as having strong opinions that were listened to, or being capable of action independent of her husband. But whether fragile or strong, the wife was trapped on her pedestal.

At the other extreme were the "fallen women"—prostitutes or saloon girls who were there essentially for the physical initiation of teenage boys and the pleasures of soldiers in military-post towns or miners in mining towns. Imagine you were a single woman, a divorced woman, or a widow, and ended up in Dodge City, Kansas, or Virginia City, Nevada, without money or hope. Jobs for these unattached women were not easily available or even conceivable. Many such women did indeed become prostitutes. It was often a short life, and suicide was a common way to retire. There was very little money in it, particularly if you lived in a group house and wore reasonable clothes and ate well. You could barely get by. If you had your own house and operated independently, you had no security from violence. In both cases, you had to pay off the local police authorities. As Patricia Limerick has written:

> The history of prostitution restores the participants of Western history to a gritty, recognizably physical reality. Testifying as a witness in a Nevada case in 1878, Belle West was asked to identify her occupation. "I go to bed with men for money," she said. A century later, Belle West's frankness will not let us take refuge in sentimental and nostalgic images of the Western past. Acknowledge the human reality of Western prostitutes, and you have taken a major step toward removing Western history from the domain of myth and symbol and restoring it to actuality. Exclude women from Western history, and unreality sets in. Restore them, and the Western drama gains a fully human cast of characters—males and females whose urges, needs, failings, and conflicts we can recognize and even share.

The picture of the wife going to church and living behind a white picket fence and of the prostitute swilling liquor and servicing the men is the Western version of the dichotomy of saint/sinner found in many Christian and pagan cultures. Again, it misses the complexities—in this case of women's experience in the West. Rather than being passive participants or workers in the male venture of settling the frontier, many women were themselves active and independent seekers of a better life.

Existing along with the submissive, hardworking wife and the beleaguered prostitute was the crusader for social justice. In the pre–Civil War days, that moral and emotional outlet for women found expression in the abolitionist effort. After the Civil War, the temperance and suffragette movements became women's causes. Every schoolchild reads about Carry Nation going into saloons, her ax flailing, outraged at the demons of alcohol. Countless other women started homes for unwed mothers. Some became suffragettes and led the efforts to get women the vote. Women succeeded in the oddest places. Utah, where polygamy was practiced until 1890, was also a state where women had the right to vote in state and local elections in 1896, the year it achieved statehood. Thousands of other women headed West alone, but with a signed contract to teach in the schools or to care for children in homes of widowers. Sometimes they married. When they didn't, they remained respectable spinsters locked in Victorian rectitude. Western reality was different from the picture we get from historians such as Frederick Jackson Turner or artists such as Remington or writers such as Zane Grey. Women were more individualistic, and they had more power, than the portrait (or nonportrait) that has come down to us. Possessing diverse interests and full of talent, energy, daring, and strength, women in the West were often movers and shakers in their communities. You had only to listen to Dorothy Bradley to sense a connection between her and the pioneer women of the nineteenth century.

Dorothy lost the 1992 gubernatorial race by 11,473 votes out of 406,309 votes cast. She ran ahead of Bill Clinton, but she didn't have the benefit of a third candidate such as Ross Perot to drain votes from her opponent. I dropped her a note after the election. There was no reply. I kept tabs on her. She was on a short list for U.S. attorney for western Montana. I heard that she was considering a run for the U.S. Senate in 1994. Finally, I called her, as the idea for this book took shape. I told her I wanted to talk with her the next time she was in Washington. That con-

versation took place in the spring of 1994, in a conference room at the
Sheraton Woodley Hotel.

"Election night I had to pull out more strength than I thought I had,
to endure the pain of the concession," Dorothy began. "We could not believe we had lost. I had only thought for a week that it was even a possibility. . . . It never crossed my mind that we would lose. So that was a
readjustment. I was pretty devastated. Not by the experience—it was
one of the best experiences of my life, and I would not have missed it.
We accomplished things. But I know my team was more equipped to do
the job than the team that won. The first pains in losing were all the
friends who wanted to tell me the things we did wrong. I didn't want to
hear it anymore. I knew a million things we could have done differently.
Then there were the wonderful letters saying that there will be something better for me.

"I was so afraid of people being discouraged at the political process
because of the defeat, and I didn't want them to feel that way. I don't feel
that way! I wanted people to feel the same way I did about what we had
done—the gift of it all, and the opportunity that it was. The positive
thing that it was. So we had dinners all over the state in November and
December, meeting groups of volunteers—groups of eight, ten, twelve
in restaurants—to confirm for them and for ourselves that their involvement was a worthwhile endeavor and tell them not to be discouraged.

"As I was having those meetings, I began to think about what I personally would do next. I knew myself well enough to know that I had to
get away. To divert myself from thinking about the defeat, I had to do
something constructive. I could go into law, but I wasn't in the mood for
the courtroom. I had friends who were moving into the Clinton administration, but I didn't want to be a part of someone else's administration—I had been too set on having my own. I'd always romanticized
about working at a small rural school, so I started checking with some
colleges that train teachers and that had their antennae out to small public schools where teachers might be needed. Finally, I found a vacancy. It
was in Ashland, a town of two hundred and fifty people across the
Tongue River from the Northern Cheyenne Reservation. A third of our
kids were Indians; some were bused to school from as far as forty miles
away. The school district said they couldn't pay me a teacher's salary, because I wasn't certified. But they would take me as a teacher's aide. From
gubernatorial candidate to teacher's aide! At first, I did everything a

floater can do. I even coached the cheerleaders. I ran the academic olympics and the geography bee. I substituted when a teacher was out. Finally, three months into it, they trusted me enough so that when a teacher left on maternity leave and I asked about her class, they gave it to me.

"My little mission there—besides devoting myself to the children, which was wonderful, even though at first they gave me a wary eye—was to heal myself. I lived in a teacherage, as in 'parsonage'—a little apartment built for the school. I slept on a mattress on the floor. I didn't want to move a bed in, because I knew I'd have to get a U-Haul and all of that. I had a chair and a kitchen table, my music, and a nice living room with no furniture at all. The only news I had about the whole four-month legislative session was on the Northern Ag Radio Network. That was what I needed. If I had had a TV, I would have sat and watched the news every night, I would have watched the governor's announcements on everything. I would have sat and thought of all the things I could have done differently if I had been there. I didn't want to put myself through that torture. So, for the whole semester, I listened to my radio music, I wrote, and I read. I wrote about what I was going through, and about what I was reading. I read a whole set of biographies. I had never been interested in biographies. Now I love them. Sam Houston was my favorite. I read quite a bit about political people and about women, such as Katharine Hepburn. There was no rhyme or reason to the pattern of reading. I read novels. I read about the West—Wallace Stegner all over again, Aldo Leopold all over again.

"The community of Ashland was very upset that I had come in. It's a Republican community, whose partisanship hadn't entirely ended with the election. Thirty people actually attended the January school-board meetings—in this tiny, out-of-the-way school with one hundred and ten students K through eight. Some said they didn't know why I was there, and they didn't want me to stay—'What's she doing here? She's not qualified. Couldn't we hire one of our own? Why didn't we advertise all over the state?'

"The controversy came to a head one bitterly cold night, when it was thirty degrees below zero. I was sick with pneumonia. For three weeks, I had been wrapping myself in an Ace bandage, because my rib cage was sore from coughing. I had never been sick before in my life; I had always thought that sickness was a state of mind—I was my mother's daughter.

But that night at the board meeting I felt terrible. I sat there as these people again questioned my presence in town. They were taking me apart right in front of my eyes. I thought, This is going to be the final blow! First, I had lost the election and now the papers would carry the story that I was fired as a teacher's aide in Ashland. Finally, a big rancher got up. My heart just sank. I figured he was going to do me in. Instead, out of the blue, he said to the complainers, 'All of you ought to be ashamed. I've never been so ashamed of a community in my whole life.' Suddenly, the tone of the meeting changed, and all of my friends decided that it was time to get up and give testimonials for Dorothy Bradley. It was a pretty emotional moment for me.

"Before the meeting was over, the rancher got up and left. I made a mad dash to the parking lot, without a coat. The wind was whistling, so it was much colder than the official thirty degrees below. I said, 'Mr. Mobley, I just wanted to come out and thank you.'

" 'Why?' he asked.

" 'You don't know me from Adam,' I said, 'but you stood up and defended me, and I feel very grateful, and I just wanted to tell you.'

" 'Well, I didn't vote for you,' he said.

" 'I know you didn't vote for me,' I said. 'Nobody here voted for me.'

"Out of that exchange, we became good friends. I had some good Sunday dinners at the Mobley ranch. What I developed unexpectedly in Ashland was a community of friends. Because I was there and my presence forced people to deal with each other, I like to think that the community came closer together. In any case, I certainly found whatever I was needing.

"Being a woman in politics, I want to show that I know the issues and repay my debt to society. At this point in my life that is what drives me. The personal side of my life . . . I simply have not had much of one since my divorce. When you run for governor, there's no time. Sometimes I feel quite angry that I have nothing else in my life. But I think it's also what I've asked for—it's no surprise. I made the commitments. I chopped everything else off. That's what I chose. How do I balance it now? I have a wonderful set of friends, but I don't see them much now. With my dual jobs—as director of the Montana State University Water Resource Center, where I supervise research and education on drinking-water quality and water supplies, and as chairperson of the Health Care

Authority, where we are thinking through a health plan tailored for Montana—I spend a lot of time working. But I've tried to find a few hours to grow flowers in my garden.

"I wasn't afraid when I lost the race for Congress at thirty-one. When you're thirty-one, you still have a long future. What I fear lately, and wonder about, is whether I have the energy now, at forty-six, to do a respectable job again. I have good people helping me now, but I don't know if I can live up to their expectations, or my own. What kept gnawing at me after the 1992 election were the letters that said there was a reason for the defeat—that it was supposed to be this way. I felt it was *not* supposed to be this way. But I also learned in Ashland that as human beings we can lay something out for ourselves to make even defeat worthwhile. We have the ability and fiber to do this. I am not going to say that what I do now in health care and education is better than being governor, but I know that I can find things to do that are meaningful contributions. Let me illustrate where I am by a story. Once, my running mate was flying home to Billings late at night in a small plane, so that he could grab some time the next morning with his kids. Suddenly, all the lights in the plane went out. They began to fly off course in this vast Montana wilderness, because they couldn't see the instruments. Then, the moon came out, and they found their way to Billings by following the Yellowstone River. These days I feel like I'm flying without instruments. I can see the Yellowstone River in the moonlight, but I don't know if I'll get to Billings."

12

Trouble with Unions

MARTINS FERRY, across the Ohio River from Wheeling, West Virginia, is in a region of Ohio that was developed because it was close to iron and coal. The great furnaces that melted the iron, and the coke ovens that mixed in the coal, were at first centered in Pittsburgh, the home of U.S. Steel. Gradually, steel factories dotted the shores of the Great Lakes, in places such as Chicago, Cleveland, Erie, and Buffalo. They also moved down the Ohio River from Pittsburgh to Beech Bottom and Weirton, West Virginia, and Yorkville and Steubenville, Ohio, and many other river towns, where land was cheap and coal was nearby. The giant steel mills employed fifteen hundred, four thousand, even ten thousand workers at a site. The men took pride in making steel, which formed the backbone of the American industrial revolution. They knew that their work had made the United States into a world power and helped it to win two world wars. From the days of the great industrialists like Andrew Carnegie to the days when steel's corporate leadership resisted John Kennedy's jawboning, the industry has symbolized American economic power.

The steelworkers of the Wheeling-Pittsburgh Steel plant in Martins Ferry could trace their ethnic ancestry to countries in central and southern Europe: Czechoslovakia, Austria, Yugoslavia, Hungary, and

Italy. They had arrived in America in the early twentieth century and had come directly to the cities along the river, where they worked long hours under dangerous conditions. They learned their roles in the production process and performed them over and over, year after year. They gave their loyalty to their union and their company in exchange for a wage large enough to support their families. They rarely had to think about their work. They didn't even talk about it often. They just did it. Talk was for sports. When Bill Clinton said that he was the candidate of "those who work hard and play by the rules," he was talking about these people.

A few times when we played basketball in Detroit during my years as a Knick, I would go with my roommate, Dave DeBusschere, to his family's bar across from one of the large Chrysler plants. It was a spacious, dark room with a long bar on one side covered with bowls of pretzels, jars of pickled eggs, boxes of beef jerky. A mirror behind the bar had beer ads plastered to it: *Molson's Best. Budweiser, the King of Bottled Beers. Pabst Blue Ribbon. Schlitz, the Beer That Made Milwaukee Famous.* In the back of the room was a pool table with a green-shaded lamp hanging from a string over the center. In the front were small wooden tables, where customers ate burgers or chili. DeBusschere's father had run the bar before he died, and now his mother and his two sisters ran it. The crowd was heavily composed of displaced Southerners, who had come north for the factory work and saw the Lycast Bar as a place to soak their sorrows or bolster their courage. Before the eight-hour shifts at the Chrysler plant changed, the bar would fill with autoworkers, who listened to country-and-western tunes on the Wurlitzer jukebox and chugged a few beers or a couple of shots before going to work. Shortly thereafter, the men from the homeward-bound shift stopped in. Whether it was seven o'clock in the morning or eleven o'clock at night, the talk was the same and so was the quantity of alcohol consumed. Most of the autoworkers knew Dave, the basketball star, who played the game the same way these men approached their jobs: Work hard and get it done. Give a few blows and take a few. No complaints. Dave could consume six cans of beer to my one—whether on the team bus or in a bar, I wasn't much of a drinker. But no one seemed to care. I was Dave's friend, and a player too. That was good enough. Besides, in such places the whole world is welcome.

The steelworkers of Martins Ferry, like many of the autoworkers in the Detroit bar, lived in a macho culture, but one in which women had to work, too, in order to make ends meet. Their lives centered around the job, the bar, the union, the church, the local school, sports, and the family. Not that they never blew their paychecks. Not that divorce was unheard of or adultery unknown. Not that they were saints. But they did feel a part of something larger than themselves. And they believed in America—the America that was different from the Europe of their ancestors; the America that won wars and gave them a chance to put food on the family table and clothes on the backs of their kids; the America that respected religion and wasn't too proud to kneel. They gave deep and primary loyalties and made harsh, direct judgments. They either liked you or they didn't. Their greatest dignity derived from their capacity for hard work. To produce a tangible, eminently useful product gave their work meaning and made it understandable, both to them and to others. They weren't ready for the 1990s.

By 1994, this whole area of southeastern Ohio had been in a ten-year decline. Steel jobs were disappearing. The companies had failed to invest in new technology or even in new equipment. When thousands of men brought home paychecks working in the smoke and dirt of a steel mill, people overlooked the pollution. Now, with the jobs going, the grime seemed grimier. Few houses were painted white. The curbs were broken, and weeds grew out of sidewalk cracks.

In many ways, this town reminded me of the one-company towns along the Mississippi, with plants such as St. Joe Lead, Mallinckrodt Chemicals, Monsanto, Pfizer, and Pittsburgh Plate Glass lining the banks like passengers waiting for a giant river steamer. Before the 1970s, companies along America's industrial rivers—the Ohio, the Mississippi, the Wabash, the Cuyahoga, the Delaware, the Hudson, the Connecticut, the James, the Penobscot—did pretty much what they wanted. They dumped unknown quantities of dangerous substances into the rivers; they spewed unlimited particles and pollutants into the air; they paid no heed to the health or safety of their workers. By the 1990s, the Occupational Safety and Health Administration (OSHA) and strict environmental laws had stopped much of that, but by now the economy had changed as well.

Since the early days of the republic, there had been a lead plant at Herculaneum, five miles up the river from Crystal City. Even Karl Bodmer, in his mid-nineteenth-century sketches, caught the site. Just as steel plants sprang up along the Ohio because of nearby coal and iron, a lead plant originated in Herculaneum because of the town's proximity to the largest deposit of lead in America, the leadbelt of Missouri. Some people say that during Civil War days, lead shot had been dropped from the bluff at Herculaneum to cool in the river water below. It was easier to imagine St. Louis without a Budweiser brewery than Herculaneum without a lead factory.

On many days during my childhood, when the wind blew from the north, the smell of sulfur coming from the St. Joe Lead Company burned my throat when I took a breath. That was the "Herky smell"—a smell like rotten eggs, but sharper. Imagine the intensity of the fumes in the factory if five miles away it burned one's nostrils and made one's eyes water. My Uncle Cecil Partney, who was married to my Aunt Bub, the would-be Jefferson County assessor, worked in this dangerous open-hearth lead factory for forty years. His job was to ensure the flow of molten lead into lead pots and then to operate a trolley that moved the pots from the furnace to the refinery department. It was hard, physical work. Calluses padded his hands. Every morning, he carried his lunch to work in a lunch box. Every afternoon before he left the factory, he showered to wash off the toxic lead dust. My Aunt Bub would pick him up from the plant with his hair still wet from the shower and perspiration running down his face. But no matter how vigorously he scrubbed, he brought the sour odor home. Occasionally, he'd tell me about a worker who had been badly burned or injured, or who had broken his leg or lost a finger.

When I was thirteen, I decided to forgo my parents' annual two-month winter vacation in Florida. It required me to transfer to a school whose winter sport was soccer. I wanted to stay in Missouri and play basketball. My aunt and uncle moved into our home in Crystal City during those months. They were like a second set of parents to me, and their cheerful raffishness was a welcome contrast to the frequent silences and somewhat staid moralizing of my parents. My uncle had captured my imagination long before with stories about Mickey McGuire, an imaginary (I think) dead-end kid, who lived in a culvert under the railroad tracks along the river. Mickey did bad things. He skipped school, smoked marijuana, and hung out with the bums who rode the rails. My uncle also told me of violent fights in his youth between "Herky kids" and the kids of Crystal City. The only fight I had ever been in outside of athletic competition was in the third grade, when I pinned the hands of Howard Buff, one of the school bullies. I had no experience of Herky boys waiting outside the movie or the pool hall and warning me never to date a Herky girl or to set foot in town again. I had missed the golden age of the early

teenage gangs. Cecil's stories had all the romance and allure of the vanished frontier. In fact, his life was anything but romantic.

My Uncle Cecil married Bub (my mother's younger sister Elizabeth)
when they were both in high school. A child followed within a few
months. Bub and Cecil lived with my Grandpa Crowe and took care of
Riverside. After my grandfather's death and the sale of the big house,
they moved down closer to the river and rented an old switchman's
house on a gravel road at the intersection of two lines of the Missouri Pacific Railroad. It was a white, three-room, wooden frame house, consisting of a big kitchen, a bedroom, and a living room. They lived in the
kitchen and the bedroom. Their daughter had left home at age eighteen,
before I started making visits. In winter, the wind whipped through the
house as if its walls were sieves. In spring, the smell of creosote on the
railroad ties and oil on the gravel trackbeds merged with the Herky smell
to blot out the fragrance of grass and flowers. By August, this mixture of
chemical aromas was joined by the odor of drying river mud in the
sloughs that bordered the channel, less than a mile away. Inside the
house, in all seasons, the smell of fried eggs and bacon mixed with
the sulfur smell from my uncle's work clothes.

When I was a small boy and my mother would leave me with my
Aunt Bub for a day, I used to snuggle under the covers in their double bed
to watch television. Bub was a big fan of Arthur Godfrey, in his radio days
and later on TV. Her firmest conviction in life was that someday she and
my uncle would hit the jackpot in Las Vegas. Until she died, she spent
more money on lottery tickets each week than she spent on food.

My uncle always worked a second job. For twenty years, in addition
to his factory job, he operated what used to be called the St. Joe Lead
Company golf course, and later, more grandly, the Joachim Golf Club,
named for the creek that ran behind the third hole. For ten years, Aunt
Bub ran a noon hamburger joint across from Herculaneum High School.
When the railroad company tore down the white frame house, they
moved to a small trailer behind the golf-course clubhouse. The trailer
boasted a tiny living room, a kitchen, and a bedroom that was filled by
their bed. It reeked of cigarette smoke, cigarette butts, and the sulfur
smell from my uncle's clothes. At age sixty-two, after suffering
a heart attack and several bouts of cancer, my uncle retired from the
lead plant on a minuscule pension and without a company-paid health-
insurance plan. It was 1972. He had been exploited and discarded, yet he

didn't see it that way. He got a few thousand dollars a year in Social Security. The local doctor was a friend of the Crowe family, so Cecil was never turned away. A well-off relative who operated a successful restaurant on Route 66 took Cecil and Bub for an all-expense-paid vacation to Las Vegas every few years, where Cecil claimed to make money at the craps tables.

When I asked him why he hadn't organized a union at the plant, he said that a union didn't always guarantee a better situation. He admitted that union members got better wages, benefits, and working conditions, but he was a shy man. He had lived a lifetime of shame heaped upon him by Bub's sisters for his teenage mistake of impregnating Bub. He hung on to what he had. He knew that "rabble-rousers" at the factory lost their jobs. At core, he distrusted his fellow workers. He said a union organizer, usually from St. Louis (which he pronounced as if it were a big-city disease), got people to step forward and say they wanted a union, and then, when the company squashed the effort, the organizer left town and the key union supporters got fired. Too often, unions were what he called "Teamster corrupt."

Right across from Riverside, on the site of Hummelzimer's old apple orchard, the Teamsters had built a health resort in the late 1950s. To my uncle, the Teamsters—whether under the tenure of a good man locally, like Harold Gibbons, or a bad man nationally, like Jimmy Hoffa—could be expected to swindle the average worker. He pointed to union bosses—and probably not just in the Teamsters, he said—who were collecting big salaries from the local union, the international union, and the union pension fund, while the rank-and-file workers got the equivalent of a day at the health resort. He also feared the intimidation and the threat of job loss that accompanied any deviation from the union line. He resented the fact that workers in most unions had no say in who represented their union at the international level; it was all done through conventions or indirect votes, which assured control by a small number of bosses. Even the election for leaders of locals he felt was full of rampant corruption—stuffing of ballot boxes and threats leveled at members who put up an alternative to the bosses' candidate.

Ironically, Uncle Cecil would rather take his chances with a company that paid him poorly and could fire him on a whim than with a union that would cut into his independence and command his total loyalty. He felt that he had less to lose dealing one-on-one with the company than with a complex and arbitrary solidarity. He told me that every weekend at the health resort some poor slob lost his union membership and his job because he had had a few beers and started a fight. There was no appeal, no legal recourse, no democratic redress. Break the union rule and you'd be out of a job, and with it health insurance and a pension, no matter how long you had worked. For the street brawler from Herky, the creator of Mickey McGuire, that was too much. Besides, he was a Republican.

AT MARTINS FERRY, the steel town on the Ohio River, one cold October morning during the 1992 presidential race, the Democratic county chairman and I went to the union hall headquarters at 6:45 a.m. The high roof of the Wheeling-Pittsburgh Steel plant loomed above the town. The union headquarters was over a bar, a half-mile from the plant. At the top of the stairs, to the right, was the union hall, where a few members had already begun to gather for the rally a few hours later. We went to our left, into the union office, which was jammed with desks and file cabinets. Every flat surface was covered with Styrofoam coffee cups, packages of cookies, documents, pamphlets, ashtrays that needed emptying. The smell of pencil shavings, old newspapers, and stale cigarettes filled the air. I said hello to John Saunders, the president of the local, and his secretary, and passed up a cup of coffee. We walked back down the creaky wooden stairs and out into the morning cold to Saunders's car and a van that would take us to the plant. Besides the county chairman and myself, there were four union members, another Martins Ferry Democrat, my aide, a friend, and a reporter in the expedition. When we got there, there weren't enough helmets for all of us, and while we waited for someone to scare them up, Saunders told me the plant's story. He asked if I could get any help for them in dealing with the Pension Benefit Guaranty Corporation (PBGC), which had been set up by the federal government in 1974 to guarantee workers' pensions and which was now proposing to guarantee less of the pension than the union wanted. Saunders was middle-aged and sharp-eyed, with a cock of the head that reminded me of a guy in a pool hall who is smarter than his years of formal education indicate and unskillful in covering up that fact. He knew his union, its negotiating positions, and its history. He understood the industry's position internationally; and he knew that he needed federal money from the PBGC if he was to assure all of his workers— past and present—an adequate pension.

The plant was one of several owned by Wheeling-Pittsburgh, and even though the production line was decreasing, it continued to make flat steel sheets. In the 1980s, the Reagan economic policies of keeping interest rates and the value of the dollar high hurt the steel industry. High interest rates made it difficult for manufacturing firms to get capital, and the high value of the dollar gave foreign steel a significant price advantage in the U.S. market and acted as a tax on our exports. Though the public-relations departments of steel companies would try to explain the decline of jobs by pointing to high wages, the cost of labor actually accounted for only about 25 percent of a company's total costs. Capital costs were much more determinative, and during the 1980s, because of high interest rates, they were prohibitive. These macroeconomic blows came after fifteen years of cartel pricing, in which U.S. steel companies had manipulated production to keep prices artificially high. The effects of this monopolistic action hid the industry's underlying weakness, but while it lasted, prosperity was sweet and the success was shared with the unions. By the late 1970s, many steelworkers were making forty thousand dollars a year, along with Cadillac pensions and full health benefits. At Wisconsin Steel, in Chicago, for example—according to labor lawyer Tom Geoghegan in his moving book, *Which Side Are You On*—the median income was thirty thousand dollars.

The union feasted on its material success, and in the process its vitality was sapped. With the Experimental Negotiating Agreement of 1977 between the steelworkers and the steel industry, the union gave up industry-wide strikes as a weapon. Labor and management had almost become one. Pension promises and good wages lulled workers into believing that their union leaders and the industry's management knew what they were doing. Yet investment was not being made. Management and labor alike had become giant bureaucracies, operating out of different Pittsburgh skyscrapers, unable to see the future at their feet because they could not see beyond their giant stomachs, fattened at the table of cartel pricing.

Management had failed to invest in new materials research or to develop new products. Management had ignored the entry of plastics and aluminum into markets formerly dominated by steel. For twenty years, with very few exceptions, the steelworkers' union did not strike, yet when things began to fall apart because of management's failure to modernize, it was the workers who lost their jobs. An industry determined to save jobs and meet the new competition might have survived, but the

Reagan years were not the time for community meetings, much less true company-oriented solidarity. Instead, person after person, business after business, looked after number one, took the money and ran.

American management often did not care about anything but the quarterly bottom line. If the numbers were manipulated well by the financial vice-president, the company was a success, whether or not it really sold anything or produced anything. Too often, management saw itself and its future as separate from that of the workers. Too often, arrogance and disdain governed the executive suite. The gap that exists between the lowest-paid American worker and the highest-paid executive in American corporations is the biggest in the world.

The Wheeling-Pittsburgh company, after going into bankruptcy in 1985, changed owners three times in the next five years. The bankruptcy occurred when the company, in a rare but bold attempt to modernize its equipment and diversify into the production of wide-range beams, got caught by high interest rates and the collapsing steel market. The union, which had given wage concessions in 1982, became infuriated in 1985, when the company asked it to give up more wage gains. The union struck—the first time a union had ever struck a company in bankruptcy—and its action precipitated the ouster of Wheeling-Pittsburgh's chairman. These developments paved the way for a takeover by the company's largest shareholder, Allen Paulson, the CEO of Gulfstream Aerospace, who, in exchange for giving the union a bigger voice in operating the company, obtained not only further wage concessions but union agreement to assign the company's pension liability to the PBGC. That cleared away company obligations but left the taxpayer holding the bag. Paulson held 34 percent of the company until the last week of 1986, when he sold his holdings for a hundred thousand dollars.

The reason that stock Paulson had purchased for nearly fifty million dollars three years earlier, in a company with fixed assets worth half a billion dollars, could be sold for such a meager amount demonstrated the extent to which decisions in the manufacturing sector had come to be driven by tax considerations rather than production potential. Paulson had a large income gain in 1986 from his other properties. To pay less tax on that gain, he needed an offsetting tax loss. The tax-reform bill of that year would disallow, beginning in 1987, passive losses against unrelated business income. To take advantage of the more generous subsidy before the law did away with it, Paulson sold his Wheeling-Pittsburgh stock for peanuts to Lloyd Lubensky, a friend and the president of American Jet Industries, which he had bought from Paulson in 1982. Paulson got the loss to offset his other income, and his friend got the seventh largest steel company in the country for a hundred thousand dollars. When reporters asked Paulson why he had sold his shares to his friend, Paulson replied, "I queried various people. . . . But who wants to buy shares in a bankrupt steel company? After a while, it seemed that a private sale was the best way to do it."

One group Paulson didn't "query" was the U.S. steelworkers. John Saunders recalls that the first time the union members at Martins Ferry knew of the sale was when they read about it in the newspaper.

Two years later, Lubensky sold his 34 percent of the shares to Goldman, Sachs & Company for $13.8 million. In 1985, a bankruptcy judge in Pittsburgh had allowed Wheeling-Pittsburgh to sign a joint venture with Nisshin Steel of Japan for a modern plant in Follansbee, West Virginia, fifteen miles up the river. By 1989, steel prices were recovering, and Wall Street saw an opportunity for gain. Two other Wall Street investors started hovering over the carcass of Wheeling-Pittsburgh. Oppenheimer & Co. bought some of the stock and assumed some of the company's debt. Private investors Ronald LaBow and David Hains began buying incrementally, taking over increasingly larger amounts of the company debt. The bankruptcy judge stopped the scramble of the vultures by ending the competition and awarding control of the company to the LaBow group in 1990, and weeks later Wheeling-Pittsburgh came out of bankruptcy.

Paulson received gigantic offsetting tax breaks from his eighteen-month ownership. Owner Lubensky walked away with nearly fourteen million dollars for his two-year ownership. Owner LaBow not only obtained a company that had shed its debt and pension liability but he also got a union accustomed to understanding the company's plight from the vantage point of a board member. LaBow, with the best of intentions, invested some capital in new equipment and made a lot of money. During 1994, the price of a share rose in value from thirteen dollars to twenty-three dollars, making his group thirty million dollars wealthier.

While all these moneymen were passing the company around as if it were a tray of candies, the steelworkers were losing their jobs. Wheeling-Pittsburgh went from eighty-five hundred employees in 1982 to forty-seven hundred in 1994, and the responsibility for most of the

workers' pensions now rested with the PBGC. It was not a tale of triumph for average people; rather, it was a typical story from the swash-
buckling 1980s, when the American manufacturing economy went
through wrenching change and government sought to reward speculation more than solid production, when greed went unchecked and mutual obligation diminished, when the "creative destruction" that
economist Joseph Schumpeter attributed to capitalism was at its most
obvious, and when notions about what a company owed its workers as
human beings were ignored.

As we walked through the plant, I thought of steel factories I had visited in China and Ukraine. This factory resembled them. The equipment
was old; the working conditions appeared to be unsafe. The flux tank
where the steel was prepared for galvanizing, the water tank where it was
washed, and the pulpit and galvanizing pot where a molten zinc coating
was added all groaned with age. The noise of the conveyors, compressors,
and rollers was deafening. The men who worked the line appeared to be
in their fifties. Indeed, the average age of the plant's workers was fifty-
two. Very few were young. Saunders said that no young people were developing the skills that these jobs demanded. Many workplaces in America
were similar: young, unskilled Americans were not being trained at a pace
that replaced people who retired. But I wondered aloud whether there
would be jobs for them even if they did have the requisite skills. The information age seemed as far away from this plant floor as the Renaissance.
"Hell," Saunders said, "everyone can't be a computer operator."

What will happen to places like this plant? It can't compete with the
new steel factory in Perth Amboy, New Jersey, that makes fresh steel
from steel scrap, or with the new Nisshin-Wheeling joint venture just up
the river, which guarantees its product's quality with computers, not the
human eye. That was one of the ironies of the 1992 presidential campaign. Clinton campaigned on the need for change, yet large segments of
his voting bloc wanted no change. The fear of change was persistent and
deep. These workers liked what they did in their jobs less than what their
jobs gave them. If they lost the job, they lost health and pension benefits.
Above all, they were afraid—at average age fifty-two—of being forced
to change the way they earned their living; what they really wanted was
stability.

Because union leaders often became apologists for a status quo that
couldn't last, their power was destined to diminish. The American economic future was not the assembly line or any other traditional industrial

process. Making things, in the sense of performing repetitive tasks to turn out a standardized product, could be done in many places, but over time customized production would diminish the demand for these goods. It was deciding what to make and how to make it that determined the future.

When Ronald Reagan fired the air-traffic controllers in 1981, organized labor got the message. It quaked and kept quiet. Reagan's act made palpable what every labor lawyer knew: the advantage in a labor dispute rests with the employer. It isn't even close. The law can be manipulated. The Wagner Act had no significant sanctions against companies who violated the law, and fair enforcement of its purposes depended on having a prolabor National Labor Relations Board, which would then petition the U.S. Court of Appeals for enforcement. The Taft-Hartley Act of 1947, enacted when Southern Democrats and the Republican majority overrode Harry Truman's veto, denied labor the tools of its heyday—the secondary strike, mass picketing, and sit-downs. It also effectively reversed the Norris–La Guardia Act, by putting the federal courts back into the business of enjoining unions from striking, through the imposition of an eighty-day cooling-off period. Most important, it made the process of organizing and settling labor disputes difficult and complex, requiring hearings, secret ballots, and the filing of legal briefs, so that running a union became a lawyer's game and the sense of mission got lost. Ruthless firing, hiring of scabs, and the passage of time were the tools of the trade for labor consultants, who helped companies with deep pockets get rid of unwanted employees. John L. Lewis's mission to "organize the unorganized" had by the 1980s become a challenge greater than climbing Mt. Everest.

Gone for many union leaders was the idealism that made the trade-union movement a moral force. The labor movement had contributed to America's becoming a more humane, democratic place. Ask any miner, dockhand, or garment worker. The labor movement demonstrated that ordinary working people, if they stayed together, could successfully counter the owners of capital. It stood for individual dignity and for justice. Although its objective was blatantly material and its means openly communal, its leadership and its mission were infused with righteous conviction in the face of often rapacious, inhumane conditions. To see a force so focused on changing what was self-evidently evil inspired generations of Americans.

I keep a photograph on my office wall of a young American girl—a child, really—who stands on the floor of a garment factory, exhausted, wan, afraid, and alone, with deep circles under her eyes. The photo was taken in 1913. Times have changed, and now the factory children are Chinese or Mexican or Indonesian or Polish or Moroccan, but for me she remains alive—a testament to the national policies that took her out of the sweatshop and put her in school. Every time I look up at her eyes, I'm reminded of the labor movement's moral claim on all of us.

When the problems were poverty, child labor, and exploited workers, labor could feel assured that common sense and fair play were on its side. When it fought for health care and pensions, even nonunion citizens identified with labor's demands. It was always one of the forces fighting to make America more humane and more just. It never forgot the poor. Then something happened. The movement became rigid, bureaucratic, without imagination, and out of touch with the living circumstances of nonunion America. The civil-rights struggle was labor's last great public crusade, and even that was not a wholehearted effort. Unions often opposed environmentalism and failed to promote gender equity. They became less of a mirror in which America could see itself, and more a group predictably interested in its own members and little else. Yet there they stumbled too. After 1978, when attempts to reform labor law failed, the unions didn't even persist in arguing the general-interest case for making organizing easier. Opportunities for reviving membership faltered.

When the Clinton administration backed the North American Free Trade Agreement (NAFTA), the trade unions could have supported it on the condition that the administration add a provision to the implementing legislation making it possible for unions to be certified (as in Canada) if 55 percent of the workers in the company assented. Such a change would have short-circuited the legal delays that employers were allowed at the NLRB and made organizing easier. Instead, the unions ignored the opportunity and blindly opposed the agreement. Like politicians grown rusty and soft, many trade unionists appeared to have forgotten why they did what they did.

To meet the rising expectations of its membership, labor was forced to demand higher and higher wages, more benefits, and tighter work rules, even if economic productivity no longer justified such things. The intensity of labor's demands belied the relative prosperity of the American worker. When stagehands in New York got ninety thousand dollars a year for flipping four light switches a night, or dockhands in New Jersey got lifetime wages for allowing containerization of a port to supplant their jobs, or schoolteachers refused to be held accountable for student results, or public-employee unions kept asking for more money regardless of the size of a polity's budget deficit or the tough times in the private sector, the public concluded that unions were becoming more of a problem than a solution. As wages stagnated and unemployment rose, high-wage, high-pension union members became the target of resentment. The union leadership itself fell victim to its own success. Its executivelike salaries and benefits, summer homes, New York apartments, drivers, and cars were all paid by union dues. Its corruption was the same as its promise to its members—the "good life."

Not all labor leaders were like this, but too many were. Some of those who were socially progressive, concerned about the poor, and involved in the movement for idealistic reasons were embarrassed by the narrow focus on protecting benefits for the more senior members and repulsed by the self-interested compromises of their colleagues. More than one union has purged corrupt leadership; witness Ron Carey's election as head of the Teamsters. But a more subtle corruption remained, wherein the worker put his own interests ahead of a genuine solidarity with his fellow worker.

I'll never forget a Labor Day breakfast in New Jersey during the Reagan years, when what a couple of the union officials at my table wanted to talk about were real-estate tax breaks, especially for their summer homes at the Jersey Shore. Part of the trade-union movement railed against banks and Wall Street, but another part followed the financial pages avidly. With billions in their pension funds and annuities, the unions themselves became big players in the market, even though laws severely limited their control of the funds. The more the leaders realized the financial interdependence between labor and management, the less they could attack class privileges. Often their pension funds were invested in computer companies, whose success cost workers their jobs. Many members could not follow the financial details of their pensions or even their health benefits. They had to trust their elected leadership, who in turn had to trust some financial professional. The gap between knowledge and responsibility widened. Any number of times, men in the shops came to me with questions that had been written out by lawyers and that they themselves would never have asked. It was a situation ripe for further deterioration. Without a set of conditions to better or a moral outrage to quell or some purpose more distinctive than consumption, the labor movement was moribund.

From 1960 to 1992, union membership dropped from 35 percent to 16 percent of all workers in America, even though individual benefits went up. Aggressive organizing in the public sector hid the fact that private-sector union membership had dropped to 11 percent and private-sector organizing had virtually disappeared. Computerization, foreign competition, Reagan's economic policies, a hostile legal structure, the decline of labor's idealism: all had taken their toll. What would happen when labor had 10 percent or less of all workers? Change was sweeping our economy. Without a union, who would look after the workers when the economy turned down?

The peculiar irony was that Ronald Reagan had some union leadership in his corner. Not because they were drawn by social issues such as abortion or prayer in the schools—they were not. Nor was it because he consulted with labor and took its recommendations for appointments to the National Labor Relations Board or OSHA. He did neither. He approached labor leaders with implacable hostility. Many union members, on the other hand, liked Reagan, because of his macho anticommunism, his willingness to use military force, his frequently expressed view that too many welfare recipients were trying to get something for nothing, his promotion of the American conviction that anyone could strike it rich. These were largely gut reactions from people who saw the world as something of a battleground and Reagan as a warrior. Reagan never apologized. When he failed, he denied it. He was the embodiment of the nineteenth-century belief that those who make money possess a moral superiority. Bluntness about core convictions came across as strength, even when it was a confrontational position toward labor itself. Like the guys in the platoon or in the gang or on the team, union members responded to strength.

The labor movement must find a way to revive, if it is to remain a positive, or even a relevant, force in American life. Defending the old ways offers little hope. Labor needs to identify the new industries and explore ways to organize them not only around wages or pensions but around quality-of-life issues—child care, privacy, new health threats in a computerized workplace. Labor, unable to get even a hearing from Republicans, needs to push a Democratic president and a Democratic Congress (when there is one again) to make it easier for employees to certify a union, and a Democratic Congress needs to push labor toward greater union democracy—more rank-and-file elections, with strong federal oversight. Above all, with the world becoming more interdependent, we need to export the American labor experience of the 1930s through the 1950s. Countries where workers make next to nothing cry out for honest, idealistic representation by trade unions. Trade unions need a government that sees their future as a part of its foreign policy. Unions, like the rest of America, need to see their future in an international as well as a domestic context.

To compare hourly wages and say we'll never be able to compete against Mexicans or Chinese or Brazilians or Indians ignores the necessity for Americans in all workplaces to work "smarter"—in the vanguard of technology. In a world of two and a half billion workers, it's only the smartest who will make the high wages. We owe these workers who form the backbone of America an explanation of where we're headed and why. Millions of Americans need not lose their jobs as the pace of global change accelerates. We must show them that customized production in a domestic plant, not abroad, will be the dominant form of the new economy and will generate new jobs. Far from the assembly line of Henry Ford, where the uniform Model T was produced for a market whose size was guessed at, companies will have assembly lines producing many different kinds of goods to individual specifications, delivered twenty-four hours after the order is placed. Above all, workers and managers need to see that lifetime education, like good health care and pension security, is not a luxury. It is a necessity—if we want to have a robust economic future.

Companies need to utilize the country's entire talent pool. Women in the workplace are here to stay. The number of working mothers in this country has gone from 20 percent of all mothers with children under eighteen to 60 percent in just twenty years. Yet our institutions haven't adjusted. Parental leave will be a necessity, and it should be measured in years, not weeks. Genderless positions will become the norm. Corporate day care will become accepted. Female CEOs and female union leaders will raise issues the male leadership hasn't thought of. The greatest loyalty will come from workers who enjoy their work and one another.

And unions will continue to be necessary as long as management remains stingy, possesses little social conscience, and controls its rubber-stamp board of directors. Without a union, an employee still has no protection against being fired without cause. Solidarity, community, and long-term strategic planning cannot encompass both worker and management in any lasting way without a union.

The members of the Wheeling-Pittsburgh steelworkers' local feared for their future. They wanted to continue working; they wanted security for their pensions and adequate health coverage. John Saunders told me that he didn't really believe that Clinton could do any good against the larger economic forces in play. He said he'd settle for some guaranteed security.

We headed back to the union hall at 11 a.m., where about sixty people were waiting for us. Congressman Doug Applegate, a well-coiffed man in his middle sixties, was there. Saunders spoke first, about his hopes for Clinton, the Democrats, and the election. He said that the last twelve years had been a disaster, that the Republicans and the foreigners were responsible. The true believers at the rally nodded their heads. Congressman Applegate introduced me, and I talked about the election, and said I was glad to be in the home territory of my old adversary on the Boston Celtics, John Havlicek, who wasn't, I said, such a bad ballplayer. Then I gave the Clinton message about slowing the loss of good jobs, getting wages moving up instead of down, and cushioning people from the starkest effects of rapid change with health care and lifetime education. The audience had heard it all before, but they liked it, and they undoubtedly would vote for Clinton.

After the speeches, Saunders introduced me to his daughter, who was fifteen and a basketball player for St. Cecilia. Some of the union members slapped me on the back and said, "You're all right." Even though they had said they wanted change, I wondered whether they were ready for it. The congressman's wife smiled her approval of the event. I downed another Styrofoam cup of union coffee with a lot of sugar and milk, grabbed a chocolate doughnut from the table, walked down the creaking wooden steps again, and got into the campaign van to go to Steubenville and an event for the local Democratic organization, and then on to Youngstown to rally campaign workers for a big Election Day effort. As the wheels of the van hummed along the interstate, the local reporter accompanying me asked, "Do you think Clinton will be able to do anything for those steelworkers, or is he just promising the moon?"

13

The Scotch-Irish Nation

NTIL THE LATE 1970s, when Alex Haley's book *Roots*
became popular, I had never wondered much about my own origins. For most of my life, my interest in my ancestors was similar to that of Abe Lincoln's, who once joked that his Puritan
forebears had settled in "a place [called] Hingham—or perhaps it was
Hanghim. Which was it, judge?" I had always thought I was just an American or a Missourian or a New Jerseyan. I had little curiosity about my
bloodlines. In America, it always seems more common and more profitable to be interested in today than in yesterday. If you look, you never
know what you will find in the past—a scoundrel, a thief, a murderer, a
religious fanatic, a bore, a small forward, a senator.

The ethnic sensitivity that *Roots* triggered in me has heightened during my years in the Senate. Representing New Jersey, I noticed that ethnic group after ethnic group seemed to draw strength from its heritage.
What was mine? I wondered. Who were these people, the Bradleys and
the Crowes, and why did they end up where they did? I would get part
of the answer on my last campaign trip of 1992, which would take me
first to Kentucky, and then to Tennessee, North Carolina, West Virginia, Ohio, Illinois, Michigan, and New Jersey, all in two days.

From the air, eastern Kentucky, with its hills and valleys jammed tightly together, looks a little like an old-fashioned washboard. As our six-passenger, twin-propeller plane circled the Paintsville airport, which was located on a truncated mountaintop, you could see deep gashes in the hills and broad gouges distributed randomly across the countryside—old strip mines, partly covered by trees and landfill.

Coal barons ruled this region for a hundred years. One writer called them "men of vision, faith, courage, and skill" who transformed a "veritable wilderness into one of the world's richest coal fields." In his 1982 book, *Miners, Millhands, and Mountaineers,* Ronald Eller presents a different view:

> Entering upon a region of serried hills matted in a dense forest of virgin hemlocks, poplars, oaks, and laurel, they left the land scarred and barren, covered with the black residue of coking ovens, coal tipples, and slag piles. Finding few established communities, they became the feudal lords of closed company towns in which mountaineers exchanged their traditional independence for an existence characterized by "dependency, powerlessness, and a lack of autonomy."

The people who live in these hills reacted in different ways to the dominance of coal. There were the backcountry Scotch-Irish, who arrived from southwestern Scotland, northwestern England, and the north of Ireland and transplanted their clannishness, ferocity, religion, and medieval English to the New World before the discovery of coal. There were the immigrants from Poland, Austria-Hungary, and Italy, who came on trains directly from Ellis Island to a life underground, toiling for the coal boss and living under the thumb of the coal boss's sheriff. There were coal-industry suppliers, whose livelihood depended on the coal operators' good fortune. There were union organizers and union members, who fought the exploitation of big coal and the political corruption of local political machines. There were doctors, schoolteachers, and ministers, who in their own various ways tried to promote self-respect and meet human needs in a world that didn't always conform to their values. And there were the families and corporations who controlled the bulk of the wealth. As recently as 1980, in eighty Appalachian counties, 1 percent of the population, along with absentee corporate and government owners, controlled more than half the land. Local individuals owned less than a quarter of it.

Popular history has painted this part of America as a region of the rich and the poor. Although the contrast remains sharp, it is overlain by a common attachment to place and a fierce dedication to family. The rhythms of life in the mountains are deeper and the shared experience is richer than either appears at first. To see the region as a place whose inhabitants have been exploited is to ignore not only their fortitude but their rootedness and their desire for an uncomplicated life. Many have had the opportunity to leave but have chosen instead to stay. To see it as an area of rapacious capitalists is to ignore the generosity often expressed by those who succeed here and the ambivalence they feel about their wealth because of the lives that have been damaged in the mines in order to guarantee it.

Though there is a vast difference in economic circumstances between rich and poor here, the changes in energy policy worldwide affect all residents. Since the 1970s, mining coal has been more constrained by environmental concerns, and competition from other energy sources has grown. No longer are the operative questions how to get the coal and with whom to share the proceeds. Rather, without new technology, one wonders whether coal has much of a future at all.

The Democratic congressional candidate, John Doug Hays, and the local county prosecutor met me at the airport. Eastern Kentucky's government is rooted in its counties. There are a few Republican counties, but most of them in this part of Kentucky are Democratic. These are the "yellow-dog" Democrats, who were raised Democrat and saw to it from the days of Andrew Jackson to those of Jimmy Carter that their kids were Democrats, too. "I don't care if a rattlesnake runs for office; if he's a Democrat, we'll support him," a local said to me once during dinner in his home. This kind of loyalty held together the region's clans for two centuries. (It also produced the feuds between the Hatfields and the Mc-Coys.) Whoever controlled the county government ruled the lives of people in ways that were hard for an outsider to imagine. To begin with, the government was the region's largest employer. To get a job in a public agency or even to teach school, one had to follow the party line. To sell a piece of real estate often required a zoning change, and the approval came only with the intervention of the local political boss. For wavering supporters, the boss's lieutenants gave advice, then gentle guidance. If both of those failed, there was always overt intimidation, even threats of job loss. Even so, John Doug was in trouble, because his district had eastern Kentucky's strongest Republican counties. I was told he did not have a good chance to win against the Republican incumbent, the likable Hal Rogers, who acted more as a spokesman and promoter of the area than as a partisan politician.

John Doug and the prosecutor both remembered the April day in 1964 when LBJ had flown into Paintsville's mountaintop airstrip to publicize his War on Poverty. "We are not going to be satisfied until we have driven poverty underground and until we have found jobs for all our people," he said, and the Great Society's alphabet of government agencies began to appear: OEO, HUD, ARC, VISTA. Community-action groups pushed welfare departments and school boards to be more responsive to the needs of the poor. Other groups fought for better roads and against strip-mining. Idealistic young volunteers (among them West Virginia's senator-to-be Jay Rockefeller) came to Appalachia to work for VISTA (Volunteers in Service to America), with visions of wiping out poverty in the region.

Political activists and social scientists believed that with the power of the federal government behind them they could change the living conditions here. The local people, however, were not altogether impressed. One chronicler of the period observed that in the average Appalachian family there was "one mother, one father, a brood of children, and a resident sociologist." The inhabitants of these hills had attracted the interest of outsiders before. In the late nineteenth century and then again in the 1930s, reformers, many of them from families along the Eastern Seaboard, had set up schools and medical clinics. A few mountain residents had benefited, and the do-gooders had felt better, but the underlying conditions created by isolated geography and the limits of an economy based on coal remained unchanged.

In the 1960s, too, things would get marginally better. And in fact the Great Society's programs accomplished significantly more than private generosity had delivered in the 1930s. Coal miners and their families received black-lung benefits to compensate for the damage done to them by the coal dust. Community colleges were established to give mountain residents a chance to further their education. Medicare and Medicaid paid for the poor and the elderly to get health care. Low-income housing sprouted in a few communities. But economic development never took root in the topsoil of these rocky hills, even when the oil shock of the 1970s created another boom for coal. During 1974–76, Kentucky became the nation's leading producer of "black gold," and the money rolled in again, but the people harbored suspicions. They had known booms before, and the booms were always followed by busts. That was the history of coal. Besides, with greater efficiency there always came job losses. The new methods of mining coal, such as contour stripping, which allowed more automation, were safer, but they required fewer miners.

To some observers, federal assistance in Appalachia was little more than a form of tokenism. Harry Caudill, author of the hugely influential 1963 book *Night Comes to the Cumberlands,* said that the measures of the Great Society amounted to "pouring mercurochrome on cancer." Many Appalachia residents tired of giving interviews. After countless visits from reporters and researchers, and after TV crews had promised that their documentaries would raise the nation's consciousness about the terrible living conditions in the mountains, little had changed. A number concluded that despite poverty they still had their independence and their pride, and they dreamed of a better day on their own terms. "I know a man, his wife, and his family who live up a holler called Happy Holler," a local person told me on one of my visits. "Outsiders think that's funny, but the family *is* happy. It's a family holler. They know the history. All their family lives up there. They may be poor, but they're very happy. But if you bring a television crew in and you take pictures and you want to point out certain little things about Happy Holler, you can make fun of it. And nobody likes to be made fun of. So a healthy response to people making fun of you is to ignore them."

But too many others, after trashing their own people and their heritage as a prerequisite for help, seemed to have lost their self-respect, becoming just what the outsiders told them they were—the unlearned poor. In that sense, their relation to do-gooders was similar to their relation to the coal companies. The coal companies controlled their physical circumstances—where they worked, lived, and relaxed, and whether they got health care and an education. Now a new group of people were saying they were dumb and backward and therefore "exploited." The do-gooders were inadvertently trying to control the very essence of the mountaineers' self-perception.

FROM THE Paintsville airport in Johnson County, our group headed south into Floyd County, to Prestonsburg Community College, founded during the heyday of the Great Society, twenty-eight years before. Floyd County, Kentucky, is an economically distressed county. Thirty-one percent of the people live in poverty. Only half the adult county residents have finished high school. The county's actual (not official) unemployment rate—calculated by the University of Kentucky's Appalachian Center in the early 1990s—is 40 percent. The lung-cancer death rate—for males in all of rural Appalachia—is the highest in the nation. The number of Appalachian women who die from cervical cancer is twice the national average. But heart disease is the biggest killer in Floyd County, taking one-third of all who die here.

We were on Route 23, known as Old Country Music Highway, and in Johnson County as Loretta Lynn Highway, in recognition of the singer's childhood home. It wound through narrow valleys, beside rock bluffs and roadcuts, with a creek running along one side. Small houses were scattered in the valleys, and occasionally a gas station and convenience store stood off the road, between the blacktop and the mountain. That day the road was being repaired, and the Highway Department made it a stop-and-go one-way passage. When we arrived in Prestonsburg, the county seat (population 3,558), it reminded me of a more remote Crystal City. The water-treatment plant occupied a piece of choice real estate along Route 23. Several pizza and hamburger franchises sat opposite the college, which consisted of single-story, gray, ranch-style school buildings clustered in the center of forty-eight acres of flat land. There was a welcoming committee at the college, and I was taken to meet its president, an attractive educator named Deborah Floyd.

Deborah grew up in Longview, Texas, a hundred and twenty miles east of, and a world away from, Dallas. Her father taught her to be self-reliant. Her mother used to say, "Take lemons and turn them into lemonade." Her mother and father loved her, but fought each other "like cats and dogs," Deborah said. She feared that the constant acrimony would pull her down, so she left at the first opportunity, going to East Texas State University, in Commerce, where she graduated with a double major in speech and English.

Deborah possessed an iron determination and great self-confidence. The most striking example of her single-mindedness was her visit to Washington, D.C., to seek the counsel of her senator, John Tower. She had finished a master's in education at East Texas State, and now she had to decide whether she would go for a doctorate or go to work, and whether she would leave Texas. She decided to seek advice from Tower, whom she had never met, "because I voted for him and because he was my senator. Because he was on the television, and because he sent my family letters all the time. And because my dad said he was a good senator. I put him there, and it was his job to pay attention to me." Deborah arrived in Washington (her first airplane trip out of Texas) on a ticket paid for by her father. She had arranged to stay with a sorority sister, for whom she brought a case of Coors beer as a house gift. She thought Washington would be similar to Austin, with the Capitol dominating the horizon. After taking the wrong bus and circling the Pentagon in it four times, she (perhaps understandably) attracted the attention of a policeman, who helped her get to the Russell Senate Office Building.

"I remember looking down that Senate office hall," she said. "I had never seen anything like it. It was huge, and the ceilings were huge. I just took a deep breath and thought, Here you go! Wearing a sundress and high-heeled sandals and carrying my white gloves and a briefcase with my portfolio and letters of support from some state representatives, I walked down the hall. I arrived at his office, and I said to the receptionist that I was here to see John Tower. She said, 'Well, are you here for a gallery pass?'

" 'What's that?' I asked.

"And she said, 'Well, a Senate pass. You know, so that you can watch the Senate.'

" 'No,' I said, 'I didn't come here for that. I came to meet with Senator Tower.'

" 'Well, do you have an appointment?'

" 'No, I don't have an appointment.'

" 'Well, I'm sorry, you can't see the senator unless you have an appointment.'

"And I said, 'Wait a minute! I came all the way from Texas to see this man. Nobody told me I had to have an appointment to see him. This is very important, because this man is supposed to help me figure out what to do with the rest of my life, and you have got to let me get in and see him.' I didn't want to be rude to her, you know, but it was getting—I mean, it could have gotten a little heated. About that time, this little guy came up to me and said, 'Can I help you?'

"I said, 'Yes, sir. I'm here to see John Tower, and this woman says I have to have an appointment. I didn't know that I had to have an appointment.'

" 'What do you need to see him about?' he asked.

" 'What to do with the rest of my life,' I said. 'I came all the way from Texas.'

" 'Come on in here,' he said, motioning with his hand. At that point I realized who he was. I had never met him. I had only seen him on television. I had no clue he was a little short guy. We went into his office. I remember what it looked like as if I had been there yesterday. Huge desk. *Humongous* desk. And he had the Texas flag and the American flag. That was real impressive. Then he went behind the desk, and the desk swallowed him up. But then he emerged from it. You know what I mean? He just emerged from it. I mean, he was a tough little guy.

" 'Well, how are you?' he asked.

" 'Well, I'm fine.' I said. Then I said, 'I don't mean to tell you how to do your business, but that lady out there was a little bit rude. She really didn't treat home folks real well. I can tell that you're a good person, and that you would want to treat the people from home well.'

"He said, 'Yes, I do,' and then he said, 'Now, tell me, what brought you to Washington?'

"I said, 'I came here to get your advice and counsel about what to do with the rest of my life. I'm at a turning point. I'm from Texas. And I'm made of Texas. You can see my credentials. You can see my background. I have to decide what to do—and all I know is Texas. I want to learn.'

" 'Well, how can I help you?' he asked.

" 'I'm either going to go to school and get a doctorate,' I said, 'or I'm going to get a job outside of Texas. And I figure, if I get a job outside of Texas, the best place I'm going to do it is right here in the nation's capital. Then I can learn about the country.'

"He said, 'I think I can help you with that.'

" 'Well, good,' I said. 'Do you have a listing of all the jobs here, and I'll apply for them?'

" 'It doesn't work that way,' he said. So we talked a little while, and then he asked me if I knew Jimmy Turman, who was a former Speaker of the House in the Texas legislature. I said, 'I don't know him. . . . I do know of him. I know his parents. I spent some time with his parents. And his parents really love him a lot. But he needs to go see them. They're really lonely and they really miss him. They talk about him a lot, and he doesn't go home very much. If you talk to him, would you tell him that?' And he said, 'Yeah, I will, because I'm going to call him and see if he can see you. He may have a job that you might be interested in.' I said, 'That would be very nice.' So he picked up the phone and he called Jimmy Tur-man, who must have been a lobbyist. Then he's reading to Jimmy Turman over the phone from my portfolio, sounding like he has known me my en-tire life. He said, 'Lived in Longview, Texas, and worked in Odessa, Texas.' Said I came from good stock and good family, and that he knew I was good stock. The man hadn't ever met me before in my life. And I just sat there and thought, Now, Debbie, you're just really smart! If you go straight to your senator, he'll take care of you. And it worked. It really did. I met with Turman's wife, and she said, 'You'll have a job, and we'll figure out what it is that you can do to work in this organization.'

" 'Well, are you telling me this is not a real job?' I asked.

" 'It'll be a real job,' she said, 'but we don't have a job description. But we can utilize your talent.' Then she got me aside and said, 'Why are you really doing this?'

" 'Because I'm trying to figure out what to do with my life,' I said. 'I'm either going to do this or I'm going to go to graduate school.' And that's when she said, 'Do whatever you want to do, but I recommend that you look into going to graduate school. Because, honey, this town will eat you alive!' "

As it turned out, Debbie did not take the job with Jimmy Turman in Washington (she said she didn't want a handout), but the next day she flew to Blacksburg, Virginia, where Virginia Tech gave her a job as a re-search associate, which they supplemented with a scholarship. She got her doctorate in education from Virginia Tech in 1979.

The one thing that never changed was her accent. She had failed a speech test necessary for graduation from East Texas State University—a test that required her to speak with a Midwestern accent. But she had persuaded the professor to pass her anyway by promising to pursue a master's in education and not speech. In eastern Kentucky, however, her accent proved to be a tremendous advantage. Residents of eastern Ken-tucky and East Texas sound remarkably similar: "nice," for example, is pronounced "nass," and iced tea is "assed tea." There is a factual basis for the connection. In the 1890s, after one of the periodic coal busts, a large group of miners from eastern Kentucky moved to the East Texas area. Over time, the eastern Kentucky accent came to dominate, and it be-came the accent of East Texas. Part of the reason for the ready acceptance of Deborah in eastern Kentucky was that people thought she was one of them. She certainly sounded that way.

Now Deborah, who had held administrative positions at community colleges in Iowa and Texas too, told me that 46 percent of undergraduate college students in America attended community colleges, yet community colleges got only 20 percent of the money spent on higher education by all levels of government. The land-grant colleges, the state universities, and the private research universities all received much more per student. Still, upwards of 70 percent of the Prestonsburg Community College students received some financial aid, and 68 percent were women, ranging in age from seventeen to seventy-four. Most of these women, she said, managed a home and a family while they were going to school. In Floyd County, people still had big families—12 percent had four kids or more. During the 1980s, as the mines closed, men lost their jobs, but more and more women went to work. There were 23 percent more women working in 1990 than a decade before.

Deborah follows her vision for the college as tenaciously as she sought her senator's advice. She wants to improve the health of the people of eastern Kentucky. Kentuckians were the most sedentary people in America, she said, rattling off statistics: 69 percent of them reported no voluntary physical exercise; 29 percent were big smokers; 44 percent never got their cholesterol checked; 29 percent were obese. Nearly half the deaths in Floyd County were directly related to these poor health habits.

She talked about how the college had looked when she arrived: "The hallways were full of smoke. There were cigarette butts all over the place. The environment was such that your eyes watered. I mean, how can you learn in that environment? . . . The first thing I did was to try to clean up the place. Physically. A clean house—it's real important! We painted the walls white. We cleaned up the floors. We planted flowers. I saw people walking down the hallway—I'd say, 'Hello, how are you?' They wouldn't look at me—people with their heads down and their shoulders down. They just didn't walk like they had confidence in themselves. They didn't. Now, if you're going to succeed and compete in anybody's world, inside the mountains or outside the mountains, you have got to have confidence in yourself. Because you're going to get beat up. There's no way around it. The world is not going to give you everything you want. One thing I figured I could do to help people help themselves was implement a health-and-wellness program."

Deborah said that if she could get a few hundred thousand dollars, she could start a health center emphasizing preventive medicine—health education, diet, and exercise. She could serve a broader community interest—and, after all, that was her mandate as the leader of a community college. Her toughest job was to convince the community that the college should contribute to the community. She fixed on a simple idea: build a walking track that goes through the campus and along the Levisa fork of the Big Sandy River and encourage local residents to use it. If she succeeded, the health of the community would improve as well as her chances of building a health center. She got the materials for the track through donations. When the county government was slow to help, she announced that enough donors had come forward so that a sign with their names on it would be unveiled three weeks before the county election. The local political boss's contribution arrived a few days later, and Deborah, true to her word and looking to the future, gave him a conspicuous role at the very popular dedication ceremony.

Deborah Floyd is an extraordinary educator. She can make friends with all kinds of people. Decency, order, clarity, and community are the watchwords of her life. She is extremely disciplined in pursuit of her vision. She knows her way around the Kentucky statehouse, getting the governor to back a three-hundred-fifty-five-thousand-dollar grant from the Appalachian Regional Commission (ARC) for an interactive-TV health network. She plays her congressman and Kentucky's two U.S. senators with skill. She also expressed a desire to begin a systematic effort to find private donors who would make large contributions.

Deborah is not only intelligent but she is astute in subtle ways, too. To counter Prestonsburg's gossip about her imagined personal life as a single woman, she rented an apartment next to the Methodist church and befriended a well-known senior citizen who had always wanted a daughter. The woman would be both her early-warning system and her promoter. Deborah also followed the advice of the Floyd County sheriff who said, "If you trade locally and pay your bills on time, you'll have a good turnout at your funeral." By working hard, inviting local residents to participate in college activities, and joining community parades, Deborah achieved local acceptance. The Chamber of Commerce gave her a public service award, and the local hospital applauded her health network.

After my brief visit with Deborah in her office, I entered a large, overheated room in the college's main building, where about two hundred students sat waiting to hear me. I went to the microphone and began talking about the fall campaign, Bush's record, Clinton's promises. The audience was respectful and quiet, and slowly they got involved. I caught a few eyes that didn't drop when I looked at them. A few heads nodded assent, especially when I talked about the need for more infrastructure in the region. These hollows never got their share of road dollars; the old roads just got repaved. To do it any differently—requiring a hundred tunnels to be dug or a hundred mountains to be leveled— was too expensive.

When I talked about Clinton's call for more federal assistance for college tuition, I received a predictably positive response. The need was palpable. I could see the urgency in their faces. These people saw education more as a meal ticket than as a path to self-fulfillment. You had to eat before you could dream. I could almost hear the conversations over kitchen tables—conversations ending with, "I don't think we can make it and still have enough money for you to go to college."

The biggest audience response, however, came when I began talking about the need for some form of national health care. Some of these young people did not look well. The mines, the diet, the lack of exercise, the bad drinking water, the shortage of hospital beds—all of these had combined to sicken the population. The last thing these kids wanted was for you to feel sorry for them, but their needs pressed in, compelling me to confront how government had failed this part of America.

These Kentucky towns reminded me of the towns in the Missouri leadbelt of my youth. There, too, the region's wealth lay underneath the ground. There, too, miners and smelter workers coughed and wheezed their way to an early death, courtesy of a disastrous diet and a company that gave them a job in the most toxic working environment imaginable. In the seventies, the emergence of the environmental movement fundamentally challenged the way things were being done in the Kentucky coal fields. Put simply, the environment was a disaster. In her 1979 book, *The Big Sandy,* Carol Crowe-Carraco provides a vivid description:

> The removal of the overburden [the land above the coal seam] leaves ugly scars on the face of the mountain; the benches [flat horizontal shelves] are eyesores and present the danger of mudslides in rainy periods. The eroding silt from the bench can also cause pollution of waterways, damage to recreational areas, and the likelihood of flooding.

Furthermore, after the easily removed coal is taken away, a thin layer of dust and mineral fragments is left exposed to the elements. Rainfall and standing water react with the residual coal to form toxic sulfuric acid, which seeps into the creeks, killing vegetation and destroying fish and wildlife. A native folksinger, Jean Ritchie, aptly laments,

> Sad scenes of destruction on every hand;
> Black waters, black waters run down through the land.

Environmentalists waged war on the coal companies. In particular, the focus fell on strip-mining, which accounted for the overburdens, the benches, the eroding silt, and the dripping sulfuric acid. I remember one slide presentation in the Energy and Natural Resources Committee that portrayed the effects of strip-mining in pictures so revolting that you wanted to send the coal-company executives to prison. In 1977, the Congress passed a national strip-mining law, and by 1989 the pits were being filled and replanted. Nonetheless, the coal companies did their best to co-opt the local professional talent so that their opponents could not do battle effectively. Many good men got trapped, compromised by coal-company retainers, and then they looked away from what was happening around them; after a while they were hesitant to challenge the company, even from within. Mirroring the mercenary instincts of the companies and their local accomplices, a few local lawyers became millionaires, milking the trust fund established by the federal government to compensate victims of black-lung disease. Most people in the mountains came to terms with the way things were done; only a small number of people fought for change over a lifetime. If you stayed, you accepted the customs.

People lived isolated lives here. A community organizer who came to the mountains thirty years earlier would still be referred to as "the guy from New York." Even television didn't get through, unless you had a satellite dish. If you left the mountains of eastern Kentucky and then returned with a broader point of view, you were said to be "gettin' above your raisin'." People got stuck; they couldn't beat the coal companies. The weak local governments and the fallow land offered no hope. Many were incapable of realizing that their lives were being shortened by forces that could be challenged.

Deborah Floyd tells a story of a man who approached her after one meeting, in which she had talked about hope and opportunity and what the college and the people of the mountains could achieve by working together. She had said how wonderful and smart and full of potential were the people she had met in eastern Kentucky. She had talked about where she had come from and what odds she'd overcome. The man asked her if she meant it when she said that the children in the mountains could be what they wanted to be. She said yes. He asked if she was a psychologist. No, Deborah said, but she was a trained counselor. He looked away, and then blurted out another question: "So do you think our kids are genetically inferior?" Deborah said no, and he sighed in relief and asked her if she would come to his area and talk to the parents there. "You're from the outside," he said. "You're not from here, and you believe we can be somebody. Will you come and tell them that?"

After I finished my speech, congressional candidate John Doug Hays began to speak, in a slow, deliberate manner. I stepped out the back door to meet some of the press from the local cable-TV station and the newspaper. They were all kids who appeared to be in their twenties. The reporter from the *Floyd County Times,* a hefty blue-eyed brunette, in slacks and a windbreaker, asked a few questions about the campaign and gave me her card—Susan Bradley Allen.

"Oh," I joked, "we're relatives."

"Maybe," she said. "There are a lot of Bradleys around here."

THE EARLIEST RECORD that I can find of my Bradley ancestors is in Loudoun County, Virginia, in 1785; in that year, a Jonas Bradley, who probably had moved south from Pennsylvania, leased a hundred acres on the eastern Blue Ridge from a George Fairfax, who stipulated in the contract everything from price to placement of trees, from the design of the house to reservation of mineral rights. After being asked to withdraw from the Episcopal Church for some unknown reason (maybe he was really Presbyterian), Jonas and his sons made the journey over the mountains into what is now southern Ohio. One son was James Bradley, who was my great-great-great-grandfather. He shared his land with Indians when peace was made with them, and he fought in the War of 1812. He is buried in Madison County, Ohio, in what is coincidentally called the Billy Bradley Cemetery—named for another of my ancestors. His son, Jonas, my great-great-grandfather, married Elizabeth Davis in

1828. One of their children was Hugh M. Bradley. Hugh was raised in Ohio and got his education at Delaware College (later Ohio Wesleyan). In 1857, he went to Dubuque, Iowa, to study law and entered the bar in Louisiana, Missouri, in 1859. In the Civil War, he raised two companies for the Union side—the 10th Regiment Missouri State Militia Cavalry Volunteers and the 47th Missouri Volunteers.

As a captain, he fought in military engagements at Morse's Mill and Pilot Knob, Missouri, and Patterson, Louisiana. In the last encounter, he was wounded seven times; a miniball passed through his thigh, and his left hand was shot to pieces. For the remainder of the war, he served as provost marshal for Ironton, Fredericktown, and Columbia, Missouri. After the war, he signed a contract to carry the mail between Pilot Knob and Pocahontas, Arkansas. In addition, he ran three mercantile stores and helped build the Iron Mountain Railroad. He settled in Ironton in 1873, where he practiced law and engaged in the claim-agency business, representing two insurance companies, Phoenix of London and Niagara of New York. I keep the Civil War discharge papers of my great-grandfather Hugh Bradley on my office wall.

I remember my father's mother occasionally saying to me, "You're Scotch-Irish." As I searched for my ancestors, I could go no further back than the mid-eighteenth century in Virginia, but many of the Bradleys came from Yorkshire. To me, Scotch-Irish had seemed a nondescript ethnicity, lumped into WASP in the contemporary ethnic stew, but as I started to investigate, it began to take on a distinct character. Of all the English-speaking people who came to America between 1607 and the Revolution, the Scotch-Irish arrived last and remain the least known as a group. They were different from Yankee stock, the Puritans of New England; different also from the Anglican Cavaliers and indentured servants of the South, who built or worked on the great plantations; different still from the people they first settled among, the Quakers of the mid-Atlantic colonies.

In the British Isles, only a few of the Scotch-Irish had been gentry. Some had been independent yeomen, but by far the greatest number were tenant farmers. For centuries, they had lived in the borderlands between Scotland and England, buffeted by invasions from each, often living outside the law of either. In this no-man's-land, danger was omnipresent and trust was given only to family. After the union of Scotland and England in 1707, they could no longer play one country off against the other. Many of them were arrested and shipped to the north of Ireland, which occasions the Irish of Scotch-Irish. Instead of prospering there, they found themselves, like the Scots who had preceded them, squeezed between Anglicans and Roman Catholics, the two branches of an old ecclesiastical argument. Professionally, they worked in a linen trade that was, by the early 1770s, in a state of rapid decline.

Those who remained in the borderlands found themselves under increasing financial pressure. The absentee English landlords became ever more demanding, extracting more labor and more rent from their tenants. Many sold their lands to English merchants. Famine struck in 1727, 1740, and 1770. Epidemics took lives. The people of the borderlands and northern Ireland were required to pay taxes to the Church of England, even though they were overwhelmingly Presbyterian. The landlords and the British government instituted a policy of pacification to subdue the independent-minded tenants, who resisted exorbitant rents—a campaign that grew increasingly violent, with gallows erected on many borderland hilltops. The poorer the Scotch-Irish became, the higher the level of violence; and the greater the violence, the poorer they became.

The families who emigrated to America—farmers, small traders, and semiskilled craftsmen—did so for economic reasons, not to build (in John Winthrop's phrase) a "city upon a hill." Their English landlords encouraged them to leave, referring to the Scotch-Irish as "the scum of two nations." Actually, they were a mixture of the many ethnicities who once occupied the north country: Romans, Saxons, Vikings, Irish, Normans, English, Scottish, and, of course, the original Celtic tribes. They were a hybrid people with no rigid social rank or official religion, and especially without "pure" ancestry. But they were not poor in the sense of being dispirited or without pride. The Scotch-Irish were possessed of a deep appreciation of freedom. Very few of them emigrated as indentured servants. Most of them hated organized religion, in its Roman Catholic as well as its Anglican form. They despised curates with a passion. They believed in "free grace" and practiced their religion by meeting in open fields. To their way of thinking, nothing was to come between the individual and his God.

When the Scotch-Irish came to America, they didn't mesh with the Quakers. They did not yield to official direction. Urged on by letters from family members and friends who had already come to America, about two hundred and fifty thousand Scotch-Irish emigrated between 1718 and 1775. The migration itself was horrendous. Passengers occasionally starved, and on one ship resorted to cannibalism, even of their own family members. An independent farmer emigrating to the United States with his family in some decades of the eighteenth century had about as much chance of arriving alive as did a slave chained in a slave ship.

Most of the Scotch-Irish immigrants disembarked at Philadelphia. Historian David Hackett Fischer reports in *Albion's Seed,* a groundbreaking history of the various waves of emigration from the British Isles,

> These new immigrants dressed in outlandish ways. The men were tall and lean, with hard, weather-beaten faces. They wore felt hats, loose sackcloth shirts close-belted at the waist, baggy trousers, thick yarn stockings, and wooden shoes "shod like a horse's feet with iron." The young women startled Quaker Philadelphia by the sensuous appearance of their full bodices, tight waists, bare legs, and skirts as scandalously short as an English undershift.

The Scotch-Irish brought with them their hostility to other ethnic groups as well as the belligerent habits they had practiced for so long. One Pennsylvania official complained that settling five Scotch-Irish families "gives me more trouble than fifty of any other people." The Quakers encouraged them to head west to the frontier, where by the time of the American Revolution they had peopled an eight-hundred-mile swath of Appalachian forests from Pennsylvania through the Shenandoah Valley to Georgia and from the mountain ridges to the valleys of rivers that flowed into the Mississippi.

The Scotch-Irish settlers of Appalachia engaged in savage warfare with Indian tribes, who were unwilling to yield the backcountry. They battled, among others, the Shawnees in the north and the Cherokees in the south, in some of the bloodiest fighting to take place on the American continent. Even the names of their settlements reflected their love of freedom and their proclivity for violence: Liberty and Soldier's Delight, Bloody Rock and Scuffletown. In the mountains of Appalachia, as Fischer points out, there were no Puritan names such as Concord and no Quaker names such as Contentment. The times were rough and raw. Survival considerations dominated.

The biggest obligation was to family. In some cases, whole families had transplanted themselves from the severe terrain of Cumberland, Yorkshire, Westmorland, Lancashire, Derry, or Donegal to the mountains of Appalachia. Bonds of mutual dependence were taken for granted. Everybody had to do his or her share of the work. Pretense was not tolerated. Women worked; sensuality was open, prenuptial pregnancy common. The frontier bred a kind of fatalism; its violence and its uncertainty called for a remarkable toughness. There was a kind of self-sovereignty; one saying went, "Every man should be sheriff on his own hearth." This kind of folk justice became the norm and explained in part the emergence of the "regulators" of the eighteenth century, the vigilantes of the nineteenth, and the night riders of the twentieth. There were no soft edges among the Scotch-Irish. They had little use for Puritan learning and they disdained the social pretensions of plantation Cavaliers. Only power and wealth were respected.

The vast inequalities of wealth that had plagued the British borderlands in the eighteenth century arose again in nineteenth-century America, as the Calhouns, the Bells, the Jacksons, the Grahams, the Bankheads, the Polks, and the other Scotch-Irish elite known as the Ascendancy dominated the economics and politics of the region for a century. According to Fischer, by 1850, in eight counties of eastern Tennessee, "more than one-half of all adult males (free and slave) owned no land at all. The top 20 percent owned 82 percent of improved land and 99 percent of the slaves." Few bothered to worry about the poor. If your family couldn't care for you, no one else would.

Above all, what the Scotch-Irish of the Appalachian highlands hated most were disloyalty and clerics. They prized honesty—a man's word was his bond—and they gave more weight to oral testimony than to written expression. Their original Presbyterianism appealed to both reason and emotion, but with the passage of time it gave way to variant religious experiences full of ecstasy and extreme interventions by God in an individual's life. For a week in August 1801, in Cane Ridge, Kentucky, there was a remarkable revival that rejected the stiffer sort of Calvinism and hastened the emergence of a violent personal faith, with inner grace manifested by shaking and shouting and wallowing in the grass. Twenty-five thousand people came to Cane Ridge. That was twelve times the number of people living in Kentucky's largest city. They came as isolated frontiersmen who found just being in the presence of so many other people simultaneously transforming and disorienting. They found communion and conversion, in the great camp-meeting tradition of America.

It was impossible to see the Scotch-Irish as advisers to a king or bankers to a court, or as in any way supplicants to power. They cherished their autonomy too much. They wanted independence from taxes, and if another infringed on their treasured liberty, they reserved "the right of the revolver." Fischer writes:

> To the first settlers, the American backcountry was a dangerous environment, just as the British borderlands had been. Much of the southern highlands were "debatable lands" in the border sense of a contested territory without established government or the rule of law. The [Scotch-Irish] were more at home than others in this anarchic environment, which was well suited to their family system, their warrior ethic, their farming and herding economy, their attitudes toward land and wealth, and their ideas of work and power. So well adapted was the border culture to this environment that other ethnic groups tended to copy it. The ethos of the North British borders came to dominate this "dark and bloody ground," partly by force of numbers, but mainly because it was a means of survival in a raw and dangerous world.

Because they are the people who settled the first American frontier, it is easy to romanticize their toughness, self-reliance, earthiness, sheer drive, and loyalty to one another, but alongside these attributes lay the intolerance toward people different from their kind, the violence that became an act of first resort and a storied virtue, the dispassionate pursuit of self-interest, the unwillingness to think beyond region, and the pettiness, vindictiveness, and score-settling that colored their self-image and dominated their relationships. They were at once parochial and restless. They showed a fierce dedication to personal advancement and a disquieting belief in their own righteousness.

President Andrew Jackson was the epitome of Scotch-Irish backcountry success. I have always found him to be an ambiguous figure. There are two ways to view a life such as Andrew Jackson's. He was the skillful and decisive leader, fierce Indian-fighter, hero of the Battle of New Orleans, champion of the small capitalist and yeoman farmer, and defender of the common man's political rights. This was the Jackson I had learned about in high school. He was, among our great presidents, the historical stepping-stone between Jefferson and Lincoln in the stream of our national life. He was also the Anglophobe, suspicious of great plantation owners, Eastern financiers, and masters of commerce; the provincial, who stymied American prosperity by opposing the national bank; the crude backwoodsman, who knew nothing of learning or art or science; the owner of slaves, who as president ordered the forcible removal of all American Indians east of the Mississippi to what would become Oklahoma, Kansas, and Nebraska. This was the Jackson I was shocked to discover upon a more thorough reading of history, a Jackson whose misguided politics amplified his personal shortcomings. Yet at times I think the impulses of both Andrew Jacksons live in each of us.

There are also two ways to look at the Scotch-Irish moguls of Pittsburgh, who were the descendants of the first Scotch-Irish whom the Quakers had pushed toward western Pennsylvania. They were the frugal and wise investors who built their industrial city with hard work and discipline, and the egalitarian Ulstermen who kept the political process open to participation by succeeding waves of immigrants, while endowing libraries and community institutions available to all. But they were also anti-Catholic, anti-Semitic apologists for economic privilege—hardcore, old-money Republicans, who exploited the labor of the later immigrants and preached that godliness and material success went hand in hand. The Scotch-Irish legacy remains contradictory and reflects an ambivalence that is very much at the core of my feeling about being Scotch-Irish. Their views on the economy were consistent over time, from the clear imperative to acquire land in the eighteenth century to the imperative to acquire business success and industrial wealth early in the twentieth. These materialistic people seemed insensitive to inequality, although they were otherwise unpretentious, and comfortable with the consumption ethic of modern America. Riches were a symbol of God's approval—marks of the elect, not goods to be flaunted. Wealth was to be reinvested or saved, not enjoyed.

The Scotch-Irish showed an interest in politics from the beginning. They peopled the American Revolution when British armies invaded the backcountry, and, in 1800, they gave Jefferson his army of locally rooted egalitarian Republicans. By 1992, the nation had had nineteen presidents of Scotch-Irish ancestry. Over time, these people of the political center who cherished personal loyalty and championed hard work kept American democracy going forward. They may have been xenophobic, but they were above all democratic. They held intense grudges, but they respected the vote. They were not authoritarian by nature. Their personal values drove them to succeed as individuals—to become rich, to "make it"—as well as to leave open the route for participation and redress of grievances for those who had failed in the economic sphere. By the end of the nineteenth century, they had swept across Kentucky and Tennessee into the Ozark plateau of Missouri and Arkansas and into Oklahoma, East Texas, the Southwest, and finally southern California, led by men who were selected not by bloodlines but by strength of personality and achievement. The wealthy landowner, the magistrate, the surveyor, the banker provided leadership, and within a limited range people followed.

S O T H E S E S C O T C H - I R I S H were my ancestors, too, I mused, waving goodbye to John Doug and the prosecutor as the plane circled over the filled coal pits and wooded mountains of Johnson County and headed toward North Carolina. Yet what emotional bond did I share with these people—these hardworking, independent, unlearned landgrabbers? In what ways was I characteristically Scotch-Irish?

I have seen the strong bonds of other ethnic groups. Their common experience as immigrants held them together. A new language, new customs, and cold economic reality pushed them back into their own religion and customs for nurturing even as they were learning the ways of their adopted country. After a few generations, some of the connections to the past weakened, but they still thought of themselves as Italians, Poles, Jews, or Chinese. They had a sense of what it meant to be Italian, Polish, Jewish, or Chinese. Sometimes it was no more than a family celebration around a special holiday, or an identification with their ancestors' struggles, or the inflexibility of strong judgments, or the warmth of unquestioning acceptance. How am I, in those senses, Scotch-Irish? What rhythms of life, what habits of mind and feeling, what rituals of family and faith have imprinted themselves on me through the generations?

The English and Scottish liberal traditions formed the basis of American government and political habits. One hundred years before the American Revolution, most colonies had parliaments and on most matters were governing themselves. America's gift to the world was showing how a belief in reason, rooted in the Enlightenment, could be translated into political institutions. But abstract ideas meant little to the

Scotch-Irish. No Scotch-Irish man played a significant role in the Constitutional Convention. Their belief in freedom bordered on anarchism. Still, they pushed the frontier west to the Mississippi and beyond, and in so doing bequeathed to the world the image of the rough-hewn, independent American adventurers who settled the land of liberty and allowed tamer souls to follow. Other ethnic groups would make contributions to American society through their genius, their sacrifice, their industry, their religious observances, their manner of living and habits of mind. They would all shape how we thought about ourselves as Americans. But the United States in its first two centuries cannot be separated from what it means to be Scotch-Irish.

The Scotch-Irish individual of today, disconnected from family and surrounded by strangers, is as lonely as—perhaps more so than—the Scotch-Irish clan in the eighteenth-century wilderness surrounded by Indians, forbidding forests, and raging rivers. The clan lived apart. Now the individual lives apart. There are no nurturing groups of Scotch-Irish, no society of Scotch-Irish, but also no social stereotypes to confront in adolescence, no difficulty in melting into a crowd. This loneliness can be full of existential angst, but it can also provide room to rest.

For me, there is a connection between the collective loneliness of my ancestors and my yearning for personal space today. Just as Daniel Boone needed elbow room and got it by moving on to a new frontier, so many Americans of the late twentieth century, buffeted by assorted alarms, schedules, and growing pressures to make a living, need time to themselves—time away from the exigencies of every day. Solitude amid the clatter and conformity of modern life is not loneliness. To read a book, to walk in the woods, to reflect on your dreams, to gather your thoughts, to keep a diary—these are the modern equivalents of Boone's quest. This need for aloneness—time alone today and time apart in yesteryear—is a continuum.

The land, the space, the solitude shaped a state of mind that persists. Over the years, the Scotch-Irish have been great haters, disliking, at different times, planters and abolitionists, Yankees and Confederates, communists and capitalists, with equal fervor. Today that suspicion of strangers applies more generally. At its extreme fringes, it can turn into xenophobia; usually it simply argues for self-reliance. Big groups of strangers are considered unwieldy; they reduce your room for maneuver. The brotherhood of man, the masses, the proletariat never meant much to the Scotch-Irish. Grandiose social movements never took root with them. The Scotch-Irish championed few objectives that required collective action, other than war.

Doubtful that mass movements could remake human nature, the Scotch-Irish rejected what they did not know firsthand. A human being was a double-crossing, lying, deeply disappointing creature who would shoot you as soon as look at you. Besides, the best-laid plans could go up in a puff of smoke. Nothing was for sure. Too many children had died from disease. Too many fortunes had been lost. Too many flatboats and too many wagon trains never reached their destinations. In the words of Ecclesiastes, "I returned, and saw under the sun, that the race is not to the swift, nor the battle to the strong, neither yet bread to the wise, nor yet riches to men of understanding, nor yet favour to men of skill; but time and chance happeneth to them all."

That awareness is some of what being Scotch-Irish means to me. The Scotch-Irish lived with the vagaries of time and chance for centuries in ways that more settled peoples did not. Their experiences moderated a rigid Calvinist concept of predestination, and they brought this spiritual dexterity to America. Their violent natures thrived in the competition of politics and business. Where others saw danger, they saw opportunity, and they moved across the continent armed with a materialist ethic and committed to one another. Whereas others could not leave the warmth of settled family or the familiarity of place, the Scotch-Irish took the risks and lived with the consequences. Being Scotch-Irish is to prefer moving to sitting still. As the eighteenth-century ancestors used to say, "Never argue with the wind." Being Scotch-Irish is always to assess your chances before you strike. "He that fights and runs away will live to fight another day." Being Scotch-Irish is to recognize that once or twice or several times in your life defeat will seem certain, but never to give up when faced with this moment, instead to persevere, to advance. Being Scotch-Irish is to gain courage from the forebears' example. Being Scotch-Irish is to recognize—even as beholden as we are to each other—that only you, the solitary individual, will make your own way in this world.

14

The Original Americans

A D A   D E E R is the assistant secretary of interior for Indian affairs. I first met her when she was a Democratic congressional candidate in 1992 for the district that includes Madison, Wisconsin. She is a sixty-year-old, powerfully built, mixed-blood Menominee woman with short-cropped brown hair and full cheeks and a set of eyes that bores through you from behind her dark-rimmed eyeglasses. She grew up on the Menominee reservation in northeastern Wisconsin, in a one-room log cabin beside the Wolf River, with no electricity and no running water. Her father, Joseph Deer, known as "Joe Buck" to his friends, was a nearly full-blooded Menominee who worked for thirty-five years in the tribal lumber mill in Neopit. Her mother was born Constance Stockton Wood, a Caucasian from a Philadelphia Main Line family possessed of social conscience. Her mother's father was an evangelical Presbyterian minister, and his father, a deviant Quaker, had been a great friend of revivalist Dwight Moody. The family seemed to breed missionaries. As a young woman, Constance became a nurse and went to work among the poor in Appalachia. From there, she moved on to the Rosebud Sioux reservation in South Dakota, and then to the Midwest, working among the Menominee for the Bureau of Indian Affairs. Along the way, she met Ada's father. As Ada said at her father's funeral, in 1993, "Riding there among the Sioux people my mother came to love horses. She came to Wisconsin looking for horses and found a man."

They were married in Oshkosh in 1934, and afterward they lived on the Menominee reservation in Wisconsin. Over the next fifteen years, they would have nine children, of whom five would survive. Ada was the oldest. When the Second World War broke out, Ada's father was drafted and her mother took the children—Ada, Joe Jr., Robert, and Ferial—to Milwaukee and enrolled those old enough in a public school. Later, when they returned to the reservation, her mother insisted that Ada and her oldest brother and sister attend school off the reservation, in Shawano. The tribal officials were against it, but Ada's mother convinced the principal of the Shawano elementary school to take the kids. For nearly three years, she drove her children the ten miles to school each morning. Ada recalls her mother saying, " 'You have a brain—use it!' If she said, 'Read one book,' I'd read five. If I had a science project, she would go to the library and get ten books, and I would feel obligated to read them all and do the project. I don't want to paint her as a saint. She was very stubborn: right is right; wrong is wrong. There was no gray area." Ada's mother was the single most important influence in her life. She would say, "Ada Deer, you were put on this planet to help people, not to indulge your own personal pleasures." Ada feels that she is carrying out the agenda her mother planted in her mind years ago.

Ada's father was a handsome man, who loved to hunt and fish. "He would have been much happier a hundred years ago," Ada says, "because in my opinion he got caught in the culture clash." He had had a sad childhood, in which he was taken from his parents and placed in a Catholic boarding school, where his Indian culture was literally beaten out of him. Years later, he would often beat his wife and children. Ada attributes his actions to alcoholism and frustration. "The world of the Indian had been decimated," she told me. "I think a lot of his anger was directed at us because of the conditions imposed on the Indian people."

Ada first met her mother's family when she was four or five. She recalls a large shiny blue car pulling up in front of their cabin on the reservation. A man with white hair and a woman who looked like Ada's mother got out—this was her Aunt Ada, her namesake and her mother's identical twin. The woman wore a beautiful flowing silk dress and smelled of perfume. The man, Ada's grandfather, wore a gray suit and a tie. They were there to convince Constance to put Ada and her brother

Joe in an orphanage and return with them to Philadelphia. After voices had been raised in anger, Ada heard her grandfather say, "Constance, you just stay in the backwoods with your half-breeds." Curious, Ada approached her aunt. "I was smelling the perfume," she recalls. "I wanted to go and touch her, but the lady kept backing away and backing away and backing away, withdrawing. That was my first indication that there was something wrong with me."

Ada didn't see her Caucasian relatives for ten more years. In the meantime, she began to excel in school, and in the summer after her high-school graduation Columbia Pictures selected her as one of the six most beautiful Indian girls in the country, in a contest that she had entered as a joke. With the selection came a movie contract and a role in *The Battle of Rogue River,* starring George Montgomery. According to the *Milwaukee Journal,* Ada had one line.

Ada to actor: "Did you meet the soldiers?"

Actor to Ada: "I do not speak to mere woman. I speak only to chief."

Ada quickly got fed up with Hollywood. She went back to Wisconsin, to the University at Madison, with the idea of becoming a doctor, but she soon realized that premed was not her strength; instead, she earned a degree in liberal arts. From Madison, she went to the New York School of Social Work at Columbia University, and worked at the Henry Street Settlement, organizing families floor by floor in the sixteen-floor buildings that made up La Guardia Homes, a subsidized low-income housing project on the Lower East Side. She would knock on the door of each apartment (there were eight per floor) to ascertain whether any of Henry Street's programs, ranging from dance to citizenship classes, were of interest to the resident. It was her first encounter with Hasidic Jews, Italian Americans, and Puerto Ricans. "I was all ears," she said later. "They were telling me things I never knew. For example, there were no gefilte fish in Wisconsin." (But there was plenty of other pike.) She also worked for two years for the New York Youth Board among, as she says, "kids with lots of energy and little to do" in Bedford-Stuyvesant, and then she returned to Columbia to obtain her degree. After she became an assistant secretary of interior, some of the girls she had sought to put on the straight-and-narrow many years earlier expressed their appreciation, on an occasion Ada refers to as part of her "circles and cycles," by taking her to tea in the Palm Court of the Plaza Hotel.

The Menominee (which means "people of rice") had lost their tribal status in the 1950s, when the federal government instituted its ill-conceived policy of termination of tribal designations. With the loss of federal recognition, the Menominee lost federal aid and benefits, and the reservation was impoverished overnight. By then, Ada had become a successful social worker—not unlike her mother, but with a college degree—and she had developed a fierce sense of pride in her tribe. She returned to Wisconsin and became a founding member of grassroots efforts to fight termination. "Ada came into a meeting with power," says Sylvia Wilbur, a coworker in the fight. "As you know, Indian people don't feel that that is the right way to be, especially if you are a woman. But Ada was able to do that." By 1973, Ada had succeeded in making the Menominee the first tribe to regain official recognition, and then she became the new tribal chairperson. Now she has jurisdiction over the bureau that her mother once worked for.

Like a figure out of a Louise Erdrich novel, Ada exudes moral authority. Her words come slowly and haltingly. But her sparing use of words originates in a place different than the disciplined silences of a Presbyterian minister. It is a natural flow, and it comes slowly because it comes from further down. In Congress, she would have offered a unique perspective. As the first Native American woman to get her party's nomination (on primary-election night she couldn't resist the opening "Me nominee"), she was a candidate almost too good to be true.

Her opponent in the 1992 race was Scott Klug, a liberal Republican finishing his first term after an upset victory over longtime Democratic Congressman Bob Kastenmeier. Kastenmeier's record of accomplishment in distant Washington had been no match for the polite presentation of a man who came into people's living rooms every night. Klug had been a local TV-news announcer, as several other Republican and Democratic challengers have been in recent elections. He began as a TV reporter in Wausau. From there he went to Washington, D.C., and then back to Wisconsin. He was everything Ada was not: glib, facile, quick with the right word and the right anecdote to the right audience, and full of statistics. Above all, he never offended. His attack centered on showing that Ada simply couldn't do the job—even to the satisfaction of the liberal constituency, which includes the University of Wisconsin. In a debate, Ada fumbled a detailed policy question, and he seized on that to clinch his case. Klug also knew how to cultivate and use the press. He was, after all, of the press, and locally famous at that. Almost everybody felt comfortable with him. Ada was something different.

The district's inability to see her inner strength mirrored the country's desire in 1992 to avoid confronting the reality of our lives and our history. Ada was battling racism and sexism, and she had known it would be an uphill fight. I felt that she was battling something deeper: the inability of people to see the real character of a politician. Too often it is the tongue and not the heart that moves people. Too often it is the focus-group phrase that carries the day, not faith or conviction or, least of all, the capacity to understand another person's suffering. The deep recognition of what it means to be human falls victim to the flow of staccato images and words. The facile, abbreviated analyses of TV shatter the structure of real thought. Entertainment masquerades as information.

James Billington, the librarian of Congress and an old friend, says that what America needs is "a pluralism of authentic convictions." Politics built on a shallow foundation cannot handle sincere convictions. How can a people that wages war on nature reflect God? How can a society with grating poverty amidst great wealth remain just? What is it that guides one through life? What is it that one yearns and strives for? Politics shrinks from even acknowledging these basic questions. It is easier to give a response based on a poll than one that flows from your heart. The practice of charge and countercharge rarely illuminates. The human experience is too elusive and changeable for campaign-style certainties. When a TV-anchor candidate (or any candidate) provides a sound bite as the answer to a complex problem, I say beware. When the Native American social worker who has spent a lifetime touching people struggles for words, I want to listen.

FEW IN American politics have desired to deal seriously with the burden of our Native American history. Most people know that we have wronged the original occupants of our continent, but they prefer to forget the destruction or to rationalize it. "They would have killed us if we hadn't killed them," some assert, as if the land had been taken in self-defense. Others recognize the carnage for what it was, but apparently believe that doing something about it could involve American society in a grotesque witch-hunt generations after the events. A few see that there is no simple way of summarizing all the interactions between Europeans and American Indians. The Scotch-Irish of Appalachia had a different experience with the Choctaws, Creeks, and Shawnees from that of the Baptists of Rhode Island with the Narragansets. The Yankees of northern Ohio related differently to the Kickapoos than the Dutch did to the Leni-Lenapes in New Jersey. The Spanish settlers who encountered the Pueblos were tolerated and sometimes welcomed when they rode their horses into the adobe villages of the Southwest. The Sioux and the Blackfeet, on the other hand, waged war on the Scandinavian settlers of the upper plains. Within several tribal frames of references, white settlers were a bolt from the sky, a gift from God. For others, decades of gradual contact through trade bred an unpleasant familiarity. For still others, such as the Crows or the Arapahos, the white man became a pawn in intertribal wars. The French and Indian War of 1754–63 had displaced eastern tribes farther west, thereby creating inter-Indian conflict where none had existed. For example, the Ojibwa, armed with French guns, pushed the nomadic Dakota Sioux west from what would become Minnesota and into conflict with the Mandans, Hidatsa, and Arikara.

No two tribes or groups of settlers were the same. Tribal history, the religion and the intent of the settlers, and the character of the land itself gave each encounter its own distinctive quality. The result, however, was the same: European Americans, by the end of the nineteenth century, owned America from coast to coast. Native Americans, conventionally estimated at a minimum of a million and a half strong when Columbus arrived, numbered two hundred and forty-eight thousand in 1890, and most of them lived on reservations. From the ruthless displacement of southeastern tribes to land across the Mississippi in the 1830s to the 1890 massacre at Wounded Knee, when the U.S. Army mowed down the ghost-dancing Sioux with Hotchkiss rifles, the American government systematically allowed, encouraged, or carried out the destruction of our country's aboriginal inhabitants.

I know that an American living now is not responsible for wrongs committed more than one hundred years ago, but the nation itself is responsible. When governments commit crimes, they must make amends to those who are the victims of crimes. If they fail to do so, they live with guilt. Confronting the dark pages of our history is essential to getting beyond them. Americans cannot naïvely espouse ideals that our own historic actions refute. Failure to come to terms with having broken treaties and destroyed hundreds of thousands of people undermines our moral authority. How liberating it would be to escape the hypocrisy and become a society that lives by its professed ideals! Making amends does not ensure future adherence to ideals or remove the knowledge of past wrongs—Americans will always live with that knowledge—but it would allow America to have a fresh start.

The history of U.S. policy toward Native Americans went through distinct phases, each of which was justified on humanitarian grounds even as more self-interested motives showed through. During the early years of the republic, there was no concerted Indian policy, only conflicts between Europeans and American Indians related to land—which, in the opinion of white settlers, Indians were not putting to its highest and best use. The Indians didn't understand the land's material value. They stood in the way of wealth creation. Progress for a free people who wanted to get rich required taking the land from the indigenes and using it for individual economic advancement. The first phase of federal "policy" came to an end when the whites who had destroyed the livelihoods of thousands of American Indians realized that they had to acknowledge what they had done and provide some recompense for the victims of white conquest.

The 1830s saw the first coherent strategy: removal. Today, the thought of uprooting a whole people against their will and sending them eight hundred miles overland to a vacant territory is almost beyond comprehension, but that is precisely what happened. The Creeks, Choctaws, Chickasaws, Seminoles, and Cherokees inhabited some of the best lands of Mississippi, Tennessee, Alabama, Georgia, Florida, and the Carolinas. Given the thirst of more and more settlers for "new land" and the size of the Indian territory (the Cherokees had fifteen million acres), there was no way for the federal government to enforce the prohibition in the Northwest Ordinance of 1787 against white encroachment on Indian land. All tribes east of the Mississippi were coerced into signing removal treaties, which, with few exceptions (the Black Hawk Wars in Illinois, the Seminoles in Florida, and some errant Cherokees in western North Carolina) were executed with token resistance. The removal in the 1830s of all the Indian tribes to land west of the Mississippi took the lives of thousands of Native Americans. Some eight thousand Cherokees alone succumbed to disease, inadequate food, and the trauma of moving through severe winter weather conditions on what has become known as "the Trail of Tears." As a policy, removal remains a blight on Andrew Jackson's historical record and one of the cruelest and most shameful official acts in American history.

Federal policy toward Indians changed in the 1880s, when a group of non-Indians, who named themselves Friends of the Indian, likened the circumstances of Native Americans to those of the emancipated slaves. Just as the abolition of slavery freed the black man to participate in white society, they argued, so the abolition of tribalism would bring about the social integration of the Indian. The Dawes General Allotment Act of 1887 aimed to eliminate tribal ownership of land and distribute it to individual Native Americans. Proponents of allotment held that the reservations (established during President Grant's administration) had kept out white influences and made Indians dependent on the federal government in ways that demeaned them and kept them indolent and lazy. The premise of allotment was to make the Indian into a property owner, a "modern economic man." Allotment would make up for the wrongs done to the Indian in the past by ending the horrors of the reservation system and allow the Indian to become a citizen in the fullest sense of the word. At the same time, government spending on rations to care for the destitute Indian could be reduced, and land would become available for sale to white Americans. And it worked out just that way. Allotment did not empower or liberate the Indian; instead, individual Indians and Indian tribes, in order to survive, sold their allotted land to whites. Under the Dawes Act, American Indians lost nearly two-thirds of their tribal lands, which decreased from one hundred thirty-eight million acres in 1887 to fifty-one million acres by 1934, when the program ended, with almost half the remaining land semiarid and virtually unusable.

In 1933, President Roosevelt appointed a reformer named John Collier as the new head of the Bureau of Indian Affairs. Collier considered Indian culture the antidote to the excesses of commercial society. He saw the attempts to transform Indians into property owners as destructive of their communal tradition. To Collier, reclaiming the Indians' tribal identity became central to offering white America a way out of the debilitating acquisitiveness of modern life. He persuaded Congress to end the sell-off of land under allotment, to make tribes self-governing units, and to give them economic assistance in the form of loans. But the annual appropriations were inadequate to fund the full program, and many tribal languages had no words to describe the law's concepts, such as budgets and economic development. More significantly, many of the Indians themselves resisted Collier's dream of a democratized reservation. The law improperly assumed that a referendum and a tribal constitution and council could eliminate the differences among clans and among villages, between pure and mixed blood, and between upholders of tradition and advocates of modernity within the Native American community.

The Indian New Deal ignored the Indian in his own context. It revived the idea of Indian sovereignty, respected many Indian traditions, and put democracy at the core of the experience envisioned for Indians by government bureaucrats. But it also was paternalistic, forcing the Indian to conform to the vision of a white man, who, determined to improve Indians' lot, failed to respect them on a deeper level. To Collier, Indian affairs was "an ethnic laboratory of universal meaning," as he wrote in his 1947 book, *Indians of the Americas: The Long Hope.* Most Indians would have preferred to be out of the laboratory phase.

The fourth federal policy toward Indians began when an aggressive government bureaucrat named Dillon Myer, who had administered the internment of Japanese Americans during the Second World War, became the new commissioner of Indian affairs in 1950. He saw similarities between reservations and the internment camps and became determined to make the Indians equal citizens under the law, integrated fully into the dominant white culture and free of the paternalistic grip of the bureau. In this he was joined by a group of conservative Western senators, who believed that government should get out of the business of supporting tribes anyway. These proponents of a new federal policy urged the termination of all trust arrangements and the elimination of tribal sovereignty. That meant placing the reservations under state jurisdictions and relocating the Indians to jobs in cities and elsewhere.

Even with fierce opponents, among them Indian-rights groups and Christian organizations, by the 1970s nearly one hundred tribes had been terminated, which included turning a stable, relatively prosperous Menominee reservation into a poverty area. The Menominee voted under Wisconsin law to convert the reservation into a separate county, and the land was transferred to a state-chartered corporation whose original shareholders were all tribal members. About twenty years later, after Ada Deer's successful effort got Congress to restore her tribe's designation, the Menominee agreed to divest the corporation of the land and return it to the tribe. In so doing, tribal members gave up something of personal economic value—their shares in the corporation—to regain the land-ownership form of their forebears.

The Menominee's action set an important precedent for other terminated tribes. It also signaled the beginning of an era of greater Indian activism. President Lyndon Johnson had proclaimed an end simultaneously to the policy of termination and to the temptation of paternalism. He called for a "partnership of self-help" with Native Americans. President Richard Nixon concurred and promised "a new era in which the Indian future is determined by Indian acts and Indian decisions." The American Indian, after two centuries, was finally at the center of federal policy about his future.

As Patricia Limerick writes in *The Legacy of Conquest:*

> One can ponder the history of federal Indian policy and still not feel wise enough to choose a course for the future. To this day, if one resolves to "help the Indians," it is not at all clear what one has resolved to do. "Helping the Indians" still puts the beneficiaries at risk of paternalistic interference, the imposition of the helper's standards of improvement. Cease meddling, and just let them alone? This suggests termination—the old impulse to cut the obligations and contracts of the past, reject the guilt for past injuries, and let the Indians look out for themselves. In a nation fond of simple solutions, loyal to an image of itself as innocent and benevolent, Indian history is a troubling burden. What balance of assimilation and tradition could restore morale to a demoralized people? . . . There is no bureau of Italian American Affairs, no bureau of Mexican American Affairs, no bureau of Black American Affairs. There is, and perhaps there will always be, a Bureau of Indian Affairs, an institutionalized statement that American Indians are not like any other minority. . . . A minority by conquest is not the same as a minority by immigration, and four centuries of history have not blurred the difference.

The irony, I believe, is that John Collier wasn't all wrong. In our current society, many of the values underlying the old native ways have a profound relevance. This is not to say that Native Americans were perfect. Read any of the accounts of scalping and torture in the intra-Indian wars. The fiercest and most violent battles were Indian against Indian: Ojibwa against Sioux, Crow against Blackfoot. Crow against Sioux. To dispel any notion that Indians often behaved against their enemies in wartime any differently from Bosnian Serbs toward Bosnian Muslims, just listen to Wooden Leg. He was a Cheyenne warrior moving among Custer's dead soldiers at Little Bighorn, as recorded by Thomas Marquis in his book *Wooden Leg: A Warrior Who Fought Custer:* " 'Here is a new kind of scalp,' I said to a companion. I skinned one side of the face and half of the chin, so as to keep the long beard yet on the part removed. I got an arrow shaft and tied the strange scalp to the end of it. This I carried in a hand as I went looking further."

Even the land, which tradition tells us Native Americans revered, was not protected from destruction. The Indians simply did not have the technology to obliterate an entire natural environment. The myth of an aboriginal paradise persists because there is no record of where Indian life diverged from the idealization embodied in it. Our literature and history have narrowed and simplified Native Americans. White America doesn't appreciate their diversity. There is no single Native American point of view—about anything, from the land to creation. Some tribes were patrilineal; others were matrilineal. The Plains Indians—the Indians of Hollywood movies and adventure novels—rode horseback on animals the Spaniards brought, hunted buffalo, and attacked wagon trains. They were as vastly different from the stable and rooted Pueblo villagers of the Southwest as the wealthy Lummi fishermen of the Northwest were different from the stealthy Mohegan hunters of the southeastern Connecticut woodlands. Native Americans were good and bad, generous and selfish, brave and cowardly, bloodthirsty and passive, respectful of nature and destructive of nature, anxious to change and resistant to change. The relentless advance of white settlers, farmers, miners, and ranchers forced different strategies of survival on different tribes at different times. In all cases, the range of choices open to Native Americans was narrowing as the Europeans advanced across the continent.

From the beginning, European settlers have viewed Native Americans as children or savages, and in both cases as inferior to Europeans. Now, in the 1990s, nearly a hundred years after the last Indian skirmish, we ought to begin to see them as equals who do not need idealizing, demonizing, or patronizing. After we clear away the human misery of the modern Indian predicament, the myths will call out across centuries, reminding us of a time when, in a relative sense, human life was in much greater harmony with nature than it is now.

Since the American and French revolutions, secular legitimacy ascends as tradition withers. To assume that ancient indigenous cultures still have relevance can be profoundly subversive, yet for me the old ways are not lost. I can imagine the continuity of life across generations, even centuries. I find old ideas powerful in the face of modernity. The very concept of what it means to be a "free" person was influenced by Native Americans. The European notion of the "free" Indian living at one with nature in the New World shaped the Enlightenment's sense of possibility. Even the institutions of our democracy can be traced in part to Native American thought. The Iroquois confederacy—with its impeachment of elected leaders (sachems selected by the respective sovereign nations of the Oneida, Cayuga, Seneca, Onondaga, Tuscarora, and Mohawk) and its establishment of a forum called a "caucus" to facilitate discussion and compromise—deeply impressed Tom Paine, Ben Franklin, and Charles Thomson, the secretary of the first Continental Congress. Though the American founders were more profoundly influenced by John Locke, the Scottish Enlightenment, and the democratic ideals of ancient Greece, for an example of living democracy in the New World they needed to go no further than the longhouse of the Iroquois.

What is particularly striking about the interaction of Americans with our indigenous peoples is how little we know about them. Our challenge is to see the Indians on their own terms and from the perspective of their own cultures, instead of simply looking for ways to fit them into the dominant white culture. But most ancient tribal politics have stayed a mystery. How the hybridization of tribes occurred remains unknown. The medical practices of the Hopi or the Ojibwa or the Yaqui of Mexico have barely been explored. The purpose of the Anasazi's five-hundred-room dwellings or their massive road system, which occupied vast areas of what is now New Mexico, can only be guessed at. The manifold creation myths and the ideas about man's relationship to nature have only been touched upon. Five hundred years after Columbus arrived, there is still much more for us to learn from our Native American heritage. But first we have to look for it.

IN THE mid-1970s, I began going to the Oglala Lakota Sioux reservation in Pine Ridge, South Dakota, to give basketball clinics with Phil Jackson. We would fly into Rapid City and drive an hour and a half to the reservation. The difference between giving a clinic in urban America and on a reservation was like the difference between the haunting chant of a Sioux medicine man and the angry staccato of a streetwise rapper. In urban America, the kids were wired with an energy that implied that they could make something of their lives. Their eyes darted from one place to another; they talked constantly and rarely listened. On the reservation, the kids were often nonverbal and unwilling to engage. They seemed far away as they sat impassively in front of me. Their eyes were dead.

To get the kids involved, I would challenge them to a foul-shooting contest. One day at Pine Ridge, I asked for volunteers. I expected that these kids would be hesitant, but three stepped forward. Two went out early. The third matched me four for five, four for five, five for five. I was impressed by his self-confidence and his concentration. Finally, I missed and he won.

My impulse was to keep the relationship with the young man going, to build on his ability to handle pressure. In a flash, I saw him as a leader. I probably also saw myself as doing good, affecting one life as the first step to affecting many. It was a romantic impulse, but I yielded to it. I asked his name. "Mike Sierra," he said. I inquired about him and discovered that he was an orphan. I decided I was going to give Mike a chance to escape the reservation, or to get the skills that he could use to change the reservation. I offered to send him to school in the East. He agreed. For a year, Mike went to a prep school in New Hampshire. It was not easy for him, because it conjured up memories of the Indian boarding school of his orphan youth. But his athletic ability gave him the self-esteem to persevere—until he broke his ankle in late spring.

In the summer, I put him in an Outward Bound program, thinking that the combination of physical challenge and the natural setting would build his confidence. Instead, he rebelled; his ankle had not healed yet, and his white partners were asking him to carry extra equipment. He argued with them, justifiably angry at these "white turkeys" who wouldn't carry their fair share of the burden. He felt the Outward Bounders were ungrateful when he paddled many miles to get help for an injured counselor. He finished the program but declined to do a second Outward Bound trip later in the summer. Because of this choice plus his unwillingness to meet several other requirements I had set (I had no experience in dealing with a rebellious seventeen-year-old), I refused to return him to prep school in the fall. He remained on the reservation and started to drift from place to place there and around the West, developing problems with drugs and alcohol along the way. Just as I would run around the country for a decade pleasing fund-raisers instead of facing up to the deeper problems of America and speaking with an authentic voice, so

Mike took a detour away from the development of his leadership potential. He became profoundly lost. Then he came under the influence of a medicine man named Sam Moves Camp, a Lakota Sioux from the Plains who had ministered to tribes across the country. Under Sam's guidance, Mike stopped running, faced himself, and began to grow. He ceased his substance abuse and determined to rebuild his life from the inside, committing himself to learning the Lakota tradition and seeking a life centered on the old ways.

I returned to the Pine Ridge reservation on occasion at the request of Phil Jackson's friend, Mike Her Many Horses, and eventually the tribe made me an honorary member, presented me with a peace pipe decorated with an eagle feather, and gave me a Lakota name that means Tall Elk. After I was elected senator, I did what I could to safeguard Native American interests, preserving the special tax treatment for treaty-guaranteed tribal fishing income, and protecting the Indians' most valuable asset, their water rights, through settlement of outstanding disputes on terms acceptable to them. Then, in 1983, several Lakota Sioux visited me with a request to redress an old wrong.

In 1868, the United States had signed the Fort Laramie Treaty with the Sioux, establishing the Great Sioux reservation and setting aside for the "absolute and undisturbed use by the Sioux" all of the land in South Dakota west of the Missouri River, including the Black Hills. The U.S. government agreed to keep all non-Indians off it. The treaty also gave the tribe hunting rights outside the reservation, in large parts of what would later become Nebraska, Montana, and Wyoming—the best buffalo-hunting area was there, along the Powder River.

Six years later, after decades of rumors, gold was discovered in the Black Hills by prospectors who had accompanied a military reconnaissance expedition led by General George A. Custer. Anticipating the tremendous explosion of interest, the Grant administration began to pressure the Sioux to sell the Black Hills to the government. A commission to establish a price failed to come up with one. The government offered six million dollars. The Sioux, having heard about the gold, wanted seventy million dollars. The negotiations became hostile and broke off. The Grant administration then asked Congress to stop the rations of food, medicine, and blankets that the U.S. government was providing pursuant to the Fort Laramie Treaty and an earlier one in 1851. Congress refused. Finally, to precipitate a crisis, the federal government removed the troops that had been patrolling the area to prevent non-Indians from entering the Black Hills, and prospectors and settlers poured in.

The administration then ordered all Plains Indians who were hunting in the outlying areas to return to their reservations by January 31, 1876, or they would be declared hostile and shot on sight. Communications were slow in those days, and because of this and the severity of the winter, many of the Indians could not return by the designated date. The secretary of the interior notified the secretary of war, and soldiers were dispatched to round up the errant Indians. The skirmishes of winter precipitated a wider conflict, and in the spring Crazy Horse and his Oglala band joined the Cheyenne to defeat an expedition of U.S. military personnel at Rosebud Creek, in what is now Montana. On June 25, 1876, General Custer came to his last stand by the Little Bighorn River. The Sioux and their Cheyenne allies killed all two hundred and sixty-six soldiers in Custer's contingent, and in so doing ignited the nation's enmity. Not since 1813, when the fierce Creek Red Sticks had massacred and scalped nearly two hundred and seventy soldiers and civilians at Fort Mims, Alabama, in an attempt to purge their nation of "evil" European influences, had a single event so mobilized the rage of white America.

When Congress, which was in the middle of its centennial celebration, heard of Custer's defeat, it passed a "sell-or-starve" amendment to the Indian-appropriations bill. Under the amendment, the federal government now set out to do what Congress heretofore had refused to allow it to do. The Sioux were denied all rations until they turned over the Black Hills and gave up all rights, including hunting rights, outside the Great Sioux reservation. In 1871, the Grant Administration had ended the recognition of American Indians as sovereign, and refused to make any more treaties with them. In 1876, on the brink of starvation, approximately one-third of the adult male Sioux (Sitting Bull, Crazy Horse, and Black Elk were still in the Powder River country or in Canada) signed an agreement (not a treaty) in which they gave up the Black Hills, the wider hunting rights, and all land to the Cheyenne River in exchange for government restoration of rations and nine hundred and seventeen thousand acres of worthless Cannonball River land in North Dakota. They literally gave up gold mines for welfare checks. To change the terms of the 1868 treaty would have required twice that number of signatures. In 1877, Congress passed legislation taking land in the western part of the Great Sioux reservation (7.3 million acres, including the Black Hills) and opening it up for settlers and gold miners. Congress used the insufficient signatures on the 1876 agreement as evidence of tribal support. After the murder of Crazy Horse, by Indian police, the Lakota Sioux were herded into the area of dirt buttes and badlands in southwestern South Dakota that became known in the early twentieth century as the Pine Ridge reservation.

Nearly fifty years later, aware that they had been blackmailed and starved into accepting the terms of the 1876 agreement and the 1877 "taking" legislation, the Sioux instituted a lawsuit against the government for illegally voiding the 1868 Fort Laramie Treaty. After years of litigation and appeals, the case reached the Supreme Court, which in 1980 finally affirmed the Sioux claim, taking note of an earlier judicial decision that "a more ripe and rank case of dishonorable dealing will never, in all probability, be found in our history." The justices ordered that the Sioux be compensated by the government—seventeen and a half million dollars for the value of the Black Hills in 1877, plus 5-percent simple (not compound) interest on that amount ever since, which came to slightly over one hundred and twenty-two million dollars, and which was placed in an account in the Treasury Department. The Sioux, however, refused to take the money. Money, they said, couldn't replace the loss of the land.

I had heard of the Fort Laramie Treaty and the massacre at Wounded Knee when I visited Pine Ridge in the 1970s. I had read accounts of the battles waged against the Sioux in *Son of the Morning Star*, by Evan Connell. I had known and spoken often with a lawyer whose firm had represented the tribe before the Supreme Court in its battle to get proper compensation. In 1983, when I met in my Senate office with Gerald Clifford and several other Sioux, I was given the chance to do something more than learn.

Gerald Clifford is of mixed blood, with finely chiseled features. His great-grandfather, Henry Clay Clifford, a white man, had been an interpreter who married into the Oglala tribe. His father was the basketball coach at Holy Rosary school on Pine Ridge. Gerald, who exudes a gentleness that belies his steely sense of purpose, was born and grew up on Pine Ridge. He left to attend college at South Dakota School of Mines in Rapid City and eventually became an aerospace engineer in California. He felt something missing in his life, so he gave up his job in the aerospace industry to go into a Catholic monastery for six years, only to realize that his real calling was back in South Dakota. In 1968, he returned to the reservation, where he learned the Lakota language and customs, including the importance of the pipe and the value of the sweat lodge and the fast. What he learned put him more in touch with himself and his natural surroundings. He came to believe that his future lay in studying and spreading the Lakota ways—not the dissolute and corrupt ways of many Lakota on the present reservation but the old ways of the ancestors, the wise ones.

Gerald's wife is Charlotte Black Elk, a descendant of the Lakota holy man who died in 1951 at the age of eighty-eight, and who became celebrated in the 1932 book by John Neihardt, *Black Elk Speaks*—a record of Lakota struggle and the visions that Black Elk had for his people. Charlotte is committed to keeping alive the Lakota language, religion, mythology, and culture. She grew up on the Pine Ridge reservation, in the village of Manderson, which is where the Crazy Horse faction of the Lakota settled in the early twentieth century. As a girl, she absorbed the stories of the elders and the rituals of the Lakota oral tradition, from the sweat lodge to the Sun Dance to the throwing of the ball. Today she speaks both English and Lakota, and spends the bulk of her time writing down the sacred texts she remembers hearing in her childhood, including the seven rites associated with the sacred pipe. Above all, she honors the message of Black Elk, who, in Jungian psychiatrist Joseph Henderson's words, "suggests that unless the life of the spirit is honored for itself alone without any need for acclaim or approval, it is not worth honoring."

In 1983, the Sioux Tribal Council organized a group called the Black Hills steering committee, consisting of representatives of all eight Sioux tribes. They drafted Gerald as coordinator and later elected Charlotte as secretary. Painstakingly, the group reached agreement that even though the gold mines had virtually been exhausted, what the Sioux should ask for was the land, the sacred Black Hills. (The Lakota Sioux had been in the Black Hills long before the Ojibwa pushed the Dakotas west.) The steering committee refused to take the one hundred and twenty-two million dollars sitting in the Treasury account, which would have been divided among eighty thousand Sioux. Instead, Gerald came to me, because of my basketball connection to Pine Ridge, and asked that I help them get back the place the Sioux call "the heart of everything that is."

The suggestion was a big-picture reform that remedied injustice. I had gotten into politics to do exactly that. After lengthy discussions and negotiations—between my staff and Gerald and the tribal representatives—I agreed to introduce a bill that would return to the Sioux 1.3 million acres of public land in western South Dakota, including some areas in the Black Hills now held by the U.S. Forest Service and the Bureau of Land Management. In addition, they would receive the money that the Supreme Court had allotted them, which by 1987 had grown to one hundred and ninety-one million dollars. It would be a sizable land settlement (the largest outside Alaska during the twentieth century), but the bill attempted to take into account the interests of non-Indians and also the South Dakota political environment. No private lands would be taken. Mt. Rushmore, Ellsworth Air Force Base, and other military installations, federal courthouses, and rights of way would be specifically excluded. Existing timber, mining, and grazing rights would be "grandfathered." No private landowner would be displaced. Rights of free passage through the 1.3 million acres to any private property would be guaranteed. A Sioux national park of small acreage and large purpose would house exhibits whose objective would be to help Americans to understand not only Sioux culture but Native American cultures generally—their history, their variety, and their message to modern America. This monument to indigenous peoples, if done properly, would complement the beauty of the Black Hills, deepen the message of Mt. Rushmore, and increase tourism for the whole state of South Dakota.

Introducing the Black Hills bill was like dropping a match onto a pile of oil-soaked rags. The entire South Dakota congressional delegation vociferously opposed the bill. They called me well-meaning but ill-informed. They also called me an Eastern intruder who was imposing a divisive solution, the consequences of which I didn't have to live with. South Dakota's Republican governor, the late George Mickelson, a forthright and admirable man, visited me and provided me with a lengthy memo. It held that the Sioux had no historical claim, because they had come to the area only in the 1800s, after having been driven out of Minnesota by the Chippewas. It challenged the constitutional basis for the action. It argued that the 1980 Supreme Court ruling was the final word. It claimed that the bill tried to establish a Sioux religion, thereby violating the constitutional prohibition of a state-sanctioned religion. It insisted that the bill's result, because of existing private claims, would be an unadministratable "checkerboard jurisdiction" that would create safe havens for criminals. It predicted that the Sioux couldn't manage the region's fish and wildlife. It asserted that the bill gave tribal courts jurisdiction over non-Indians in civil cases. It stated that the bill violated traditional Western water law. Finally, it claimed that the bill was not supported by all the Sioux.

A retired history professor from the University of Wisconsin examined the historical evidence and concluded that the Black Hills were not sacred to the Sioux. He said that the Sioux had "violated every treaty of the U.S. government on numerous occasions and by their acts nullified the [Fort Laramie] treaty [of 1868]." He further contended that "the government had bought and the Indians had sold the Black Hills, a bargain that subsequent generations appear to have confirmed by their continued acceptance of its benefits"—the infamous rations—and that "treaties with Indians are no different from any other public laws and are subject to contrary legislation by the Congress when it is felt to be in the interest of the country." No legislation had been passed overturning the 1877 Black Hills taking legislation, so he concluded that it was valid, notwithstanding the 1980 Supreme Court ruling.

I received several hundred letters, primarily from South Dakota, the bulk of which were against the bill. A sample:

> I believe you are the typical reformer who has all the answers but isn't quite sure what the questions are.

> I can foresee a rancher opening up a feed lot on his own land and within a fortnight find[ing] Indians worshipping there because they feel that Brave Brother Bill will put in claims for them for not only the feed lot but the entire ranch.

> The Indians are still Indians. The more you give them, the more you do for them, the more they want and the less they do for themselves. We have been supporting them for 100 years more than adequately. If you had to live with them or work with them or be around them, you will [sic] know what I'm talking about.

> Hey, Pal, watch what the hell you're doing. This idea to get the Black Hills is only a way for these people to get the government to support them some more.

> The bill is divisive and opens up the door to revolutionary activity.

> The whole proposal is preposterous and unjust, absolutely unthinkable unless you are to allow a few renegade fanatics to take over the coun-

try area by area. . . . Is it a crime . . . to be white, hardworking, honest, to try to make a living by the sweat of your brow, to raise and educate your children and provide a future generation of self-supporting individuals who will be able to pay taxes and "pay them our way" during their lifetimes, rather than be a drain on the already failing national economy? What would you expect of your children if you raised them to disrespect work, to feel the rest of society owed them a living and a free education that they really didn't have to use anyway and that some rare group of "taxpayers" would always be there to write their checks and take care of them? You certainly couldn't expect them to have any pride or ambition.

Some letters threatened physical violence if I ever set foot in South Dakota again. Gerald told me that he had expected this kind of response, and he attributed it to an overreaction on the part of people who did not see the reasonableness of the legislation. He began education sessions in South Dakota, to talk through the bill with whites and Native Americans, and he felt he was making progress with the few who attended. But the white community at large did not feel the need to compensate for past wrongs, regarded the Sioux as slothful and ignorant, and heard only "giving land to Indians."

Some whites said they'd like to help the Indians, aware that Pine Ridge was the poorest place in America, with a median annual income of thirty-five hundred dollars. Some railed against the "failed socialism" of the Bureau of Indian Affairs. But most often my correspondents complained about pouring taxpayer's money into a bureaucracy whose efforts had no impact on conditions inside the reservation. If the Sioux were given more land, many letter writers seemed to be saying, they would only "mess it up in the way that they have messed up their own lives." No white person I heard from appeared to believe that the work of Charlotte or Gerald to keep their heritage alive and accessible to all Americans had any value whatsoever.

I decided to go to South Dakota and get a firsthand sense of the controversy. In the spring of 1986, I flew to Rapid City, as I had many times before. Every time I get off a plane there, the sky seems bigger, the space wider. Between Rapid City and Pine Ridge, there is a stillness more overarching than the wind whispering through the pines or the prairie grass. There is a changelessness, a continuity, an assurance that nature can still be our guide. At the reservation, I gave a speech at the Oglala

Community College graduation and afterward watched the ceremonial dancers—some feathered and wearing trousers of animal skins, some in blue jeans—bobbing up and down, periodically freezing their body movements for a few seconds and then moving on, in a tribal-dance circle a hundred feet across. The constant drumbeat and the high-wailing chant took me back momentarily to an earlier time, when dance was a part of a living tradition, but I was under no illusion that what I witnessed was the original. Now the Indians danced as if they were trying to recapture what had been lost to time and the white man.

Most of the nondancers were overweight. They sat in aluminum folding chairs under a thatched sun-cover, eating potato chips, Fritos, and candy, and drinking soft drinks. Their storage of high amounts of body fat was no longer balanced by an active life of hunting buffalo. None of them shouted or applauded as the sweat rolled down the pockmarked faces of the dancers. They just sat and watched. One doesn't know how they felt, but it seemed to me that the Bureau of Indian Affairs and federal policy had turned these descendants of the original Americans into relics. It was as if America had created a Native American zoo, put the inhabitants in large open-air cages, fed them badly, ignored their health, and on occasion chided them for not using their "freedom" responsibly. Yet, even in the midst of this degradation, the dance of the few who were in good physical shape revealed a glimpse of what once had been a proud, confident, hearty people—a people always on the move, not above breaking their word to the white man, who had broken his to them so often, but unintimidated by the white man's achievements and desirous only of being left alone to express their relation to each other and the land in their own way and with their own symbols.

In my remarks at the graduation, I pointed out that Western thought since the eighteenth century had liberated us from superstition and at the same time denied us the moral certainty enjoyed in another age. And in so doing, it had assaulted the sense of harmony and balance that underlies traditional Native American cultures. The science that had improved the physical condition of our lives had also given us the power not just to rearrange nature but to destroy Mother Earth. The extroverted impulse of modernity that seeks to amass wealth, control nature, conquer lands, and use knowledge to order and shape a reality apart from self clashes with the promise of Native American mythologies, which celebrate the introverted aspect of life, whose path leads through self and family to God and to oneness with nature.

Millions of white Americans possessed an invigorating personal liberty. For those in a big city who were young, curious, and comfortable financially, there were almost no social barriers. But many other people in our cities and our suburbs, too, were longing for a new form of community, a sense of belonging, a deeper personal meaning that went beyond class or social position and allowed us to enter a communal tradition that nurtured the life of the spirit. I said that the Lakota nation had something to say to the rest of America; America needed to know why the Lakota call the Black Hills "the heart of everything that is." America needed to know why, for the Lakota (in a refutation of New Englander Robert Frost), good fences *don't* make good neighbors. Americans needed to understand the inclusivity of the Lakota belief that the children of the earth are two-legged, four-legged, winged—all things growing and moving, all with a right to live.

I returned again to South Dakota a year later. The Black Hills bill was beginning to move through the Senate Select Committee on Indian Affairs. I spent the night with a wheat farmer on his three-thousand-acre property, about a half-hour from Wall, South Dakota, home of the Wall Drugstore, where you can eat possibly the country's best cinnamon rolls. My host's father gave me some clippings chronicling JFK's campaign visits to South Dakota in 1960. He also gave me a massive folder full of papers that documented the argument that the Black Hills never belonged to the Sioux but to the Mandans, Hidatsa, and Arikara. Why, he suggested, didn't I try education and public jobs? Why did I want to inconvenience "legitimate" whites? Why couldn't I see that whites were still afraid of Indians and looked upon any land return as a threat?

I said that I was not suggesting that the federal government take any land away from private owners. The lands to be returned were all public lands, and the right of free passage through all 1.3 million acres to any private property was fully guaranteed.

Yes, he said, but even if you could keep your cabin on your own land in the Black Hills, and you could have the right to go through Indian land to get to it, the property value would drop. Who knew what the Indians might do? People would be afraid to drive through sections of the state under Indian control, he said—afraid for their lives, for if a white person were to be arrested on reservation land, that person would be tried in an Indian court. "I want to help them, you know," my host's father said. "I've been going down to the reservation for fifty years and I know how bad it is. The schools, the alcohol, the health care, the housing, and no jobs. It's terrible. But I just don't want to see land taken from farmers and ranchers who have worked so hard."

The only whites who expressed support for the bill were property owners in the northwestern part of the state, who, it was rumored, were going to be displaced by Honeywell Inc., which was planning to build a missile site and a test-firing range near land that would otherwise go to the Sioux. It appeared that only under the threat of missiles being fired next door did white South Dakotans prefer Indian neighbors. Only when the choice was between shrapnel or Indians did Indians prevail. The resistance to the bill was blind and still virtually total.

I had pushed to get a hearing on the bill in the Indian Affairs Committee. In the summer of 1986 we got the hearing. Pressure began to build. I was again accused of being an Easterner who didn't know anything about the West or the Indians. The two Republican senators from South Dakota—Larry Pressler and James Abdnor—were fervently opposed. Abdnor lost his race for re-election in November 1986, but Tom Daschle, the new Democratic senator, was equally opposed. Senator Malcolm Wallop of Wyoming sent me the draft of a bill he said he intended to introduce. It would give back a million acres in the New Jersey Pine Barrens (and the Statue of Liberty as well) to the Leni-Lenape.

Still, the Black Hills bill was a matter of principle. I wasn't going to give up. By March 1987, I had three senate cosponsors and thirteen house cosponsors, including six chairmen led by Morris Udall of Arizona and Jim Howard of New Jersey. The opposition in South Dakota planted letters to the editor in New Jersey newspapers and spread stories about the unfairness and futility of my efforts. Governor Mickelson visited my office again and argued that, if I were truly interested in the Native Americans, I should make efforts to ensure that the present reservation had adequate access to water, even if it took a new federal water project that benefited mostly local, predominantly non-Indian water districts. (Ultimately we passed such a project, with Gerald Clifford as its director and the Oglala Sioux in control of the central pipeline from the Missouri River.) The South Dakota attorney general, in a gross smear of Italian Americans, asked his state's congressional delegation to introduce a bill urging that New Jersey be given to Sicily. "I think most of us recognize that Sicilians run and own New Jersey anyway," he told them, "and I think it would be in everyone's interest that New Jersey become a Sicilian outpost here under their laws, speaking their language." Several New

Jerseyans asked me why I had introduced the bill. The wife of the state's most important newspaper editor said that I couldn't right all the wrongs, that some things were just "over."

Progress was slow and steady, passage a very long shot. My cosponsors and I were crossing a vast attitude desert an inch at a time. In the meantime, a totally unanticipated event had enlarged the desert.

Phillip J. Stevens, a millionaire businessman from Newport Beach, California, appeared in 1986 on the Oglala reservation in South Dakota. Stevens was fifty-nine years old, and he claimed to be part Sioux. A search of his ancestors, he said, had revealed that he was the great-grandson of Chief Standing Bear, one of the great Sioux chiefs. (There is some irony in the fact that Stevens owned Ultra Systems of Irvine, an aeronautical-engineering firm that, among other things, had designed part of the Minuteman missile, some of which were housed in underground silos beneath the wheat fields of South Dakota.) He further announced that he was in South Dakota to save his people. He urged that all the tribes appoint him as war chief and that the authority vested in the Black Hills steering committee, run by Charlotte Black Elk and Gerald Clifford, be delegated to him. If this was done, he said, he would personally finance a massive public-relations and lobbying campaign to convince the American people of the injustice of the 1876–77 agreement and legislation, and he would negotiate with the federal government to obtain not only a return of the Hills but more money.

Stevens sent agents to each of the eight Sioux tribes. They told the tribes that my bill was a sellout of Sioux interests. They argued that, in addition to the land, the tribes should get 3.1 billion dollars as compensation for damages caused by non-Indians' taking the gold, mineral, and timber resources of the Black Hills for over a hundred years. The hundred and ninety-one million dollars being held in escrow by the Treasury Department was a pittance unworthy of the tribes, they argued. After months of lobbying, the agents persuaded two of the eight tribes to withdraw their support from the bill.

Opponents could now use the division of the Sioux nation as a weapon to defeat the bill.

The possibility of the Sioux's ever receiving some three billion dollars in compensation was zero. How Stevens's agents got two tribal councils to vote for the withdrawal of support for the bill is a mystery. After Stevens's limited success, Gerald and Charlotte met with me in my office. It was a somber time, filled with long silences. We did not have a chance without the support of all the Sioux who made up the Sioux nation. The white man had once again divided Native Americans. In the nineteenth century, it had been a deliberate strategy of the U.S. government; now it was coincidence. Or was it? Why Stevens intervened, or who he really was, I'll never know, but the result was the same: no progress for Native Americans; no recognition of their uniqueness or relevance to the twentieth century; no respect for the culture and wisdom of Black Elk; no tangible expression of regret for what America had done and continues to do to its indigenous people.

At the meeting, I said that I would not introduce a bill in the next Congress unless there was tribal unity. I could hear the opponents already: "He doesn't even have Sioux backing." As I write these words in 1995, the two tribes remain officially opposed to the measure. Nothing has moved, except Chief Stevens, who has drifted out of the picture.

A few years later, a Brooklyn brewery introduced a brand of malt liquor called Crazy Horse. To name an alcoholic beverage after one of the Lakota heroes and sell it among his people, many of whom were struggling against alcoholism, strikes me as analogous to selling Malcolm X crack on the streets of Harlem. It is a deeply offensive act. Part of the white community loved it. Instead of campaigning for a national museum to explain Native American history and Lakota folklore with the monumental Crazy Horse sculpture, carved out of a mountain near Pine Ridge, as its symbol, Sioux activists had to campaign against the affront of naming a malt liquor Crazy Horse. The soaring potential of the Black Hills bill gave way to fighting against your garden-variety racist manifestation. Instead of people finding common ground, whites and Indians traded insults. How sad. How predictable!

The disastrous economic plight of Native Americans seems to breed get-rich-quick schemes. Because they were cheated out of land, denied equal access for grazing or mining, and denigrated at every turn by the white majority, it isn't surprising that faintly fanciful ideas have taken root among many of them. Some tribes have used the sovereignty of the reservation to bring in gambling halls, with visions of turning their reservations into another Reno, Las Vegas, or Atlantic City. In addition to gambling, a small group on the Pine Ridge reservation wants to start a bank to launder money from around the world; they see Pine Ridge as the onshore equivalent of the Cayman Islands or the Bahamas. One grandiose scheme has led to another, and each one has required more in the way of non-Indian expertise. These get-rich-quick white advisers have never watched the Sun Dance or sought to understand the promise of Native American mythology for twenty-first-century America. They see the reservations the same way a wealthy investor sees tax loopholes—as places to make a quick buck.

The expanding fantasies about capitalist success have run head-on into the simpler objectives of the young man who refused the second Outward Bound experience some twenty years ago. After his years of wandering, Mike Sierra found his voice as a leader. I could not have imagined a decade earlier that he would make it, but he has. Now he issues a clear call to conscience and to action. He says that the answer to the problems of Native Americans lies within the Native American community itself. He set out to master the traditional ways and live a nature-centered life, free of the stultifying grip of the Bureau of Indian Affairs, free of tribal politics, free of modernity's enticing but often deadly ways. No white man's welfare check could lure him back from his journey. In 1992, Mike proposed a plan of action whose purpose was to demonstrate that spiritual renewal must precede material advancement. His plan is to reconcile ancient Lakota customs with current sustainable-development techniques and to create a tradition-oriented presence on the Pine Ridge reservation which could be replicated on the land of other tribes. The Ti O'spaye, the Lakota term for special community, would establish a seed bank, grow all its own food, build its own structures, and sell the community's produce (corn, beans, squash, ten varieties each of melons and potatoes, and a hundred culinary herbs) to reservation stores and hospitals and to the farmers' market in Rapid City. Free-roaming turkeys, guinea hens, and chickens would provide meat for consumption and protect the gardens from grasshoppers. The plan, which has already gained support from the Kellogg Foundation, a German textile manufacturer, and the Administration for Native Americans, has the air of a nineteenth-century utopian community. Mike needs more resources to build structures, to buy equipment, to sustain a small workforce, and to properly establish a seed bank. He has written proposals, approached other foundations, asked wealthy people to help. So far, not enough people have come forward. Mike believes they will eventually. He is confident that his project will be a model for other impoverished communities across America. His serenity remains untouched.

Mike has offered something that many Americans think is naïve or foolish. One can never go back to an era before the computer, the combustion engine, and the railroad. But I wonder whether the key to understanding a more diverse world with different cultural inheritances isn't a journey deeper into who we are, not only as Presbyterians or Catholics or Jews, but as Americans. Along our path to a would-be comfortable modernity, we might find, if we look, that we have lost something that holds direct relevance to our future. The Iroquois believed that no decision should be made without considering its impact seven generations into the future. To live such an insight today, we must change our behavior—make amends for the past and make plans for a tomorrow that can be ecologically sound, fiscally responsible, racially and ethnically expansive, and personally healthful. When you drive around any Native American reservation today and see the joblessness and the violence, you realize that the first group that should learn the ancestral lesson is the Native Americans themselves. Many of them need the discipline of a warrior and the hard body of a brave. They need to escape the dependency of the bureau and the trap of whiskey and regain the shaman's sense of mystery rooted in nature. Most of them have forgotten the lessons of the elders and no longer can hear the whispers of the wind.

The balance of nature animated generations that lived on this American land before we came. By learning more about Native American peoples, we learn more about ourselves. To know the myths and life rituals of Native Americans who were inspired by centuries of living on the Great Plains, or in the woodlands of Wisconsin, or along the great rivers of the continent, or on the wild Northwestern coast, gives us a deeper understanding of those places and fills them with powerful memories. To remain ignorant of how the original Americans felt about these American places is like seeking to put a puzzle together with half the pieces missing. It can't be done. If we revere our land and seek to know the spirit of a place, we must know its past in a human as well as a geographical sense.

In the Black Hills, Mt. Rushmore rises, with the faces of Washington, Jefferson, Lincoln, and Teddy Roosevelt carved into its side. We know what these great presidents said. What we have yet to listen to carefully is what the mountain says.

15

The Creedal Society

LBEN BARKLEY, Harry Truman's vice-president, wrote in his memoir, *That Reminds Me,* about the constituent who came to him after each of his election victories and said, "I want you to know I voted for you. I fought for you, sweated for you, and almost bled for you. I don't want a thing in return—all I want is for you to be a good official." This went on through all Barkley's races: for prosecuting attorney, county judge, congressman, and senator. Finally, when he was elected vice-president, the man came back and said, "Mr. Vice President, now I have a request." A little apprehensive, Barkley asked what it was. His admirer replied, "I want you to help me take out my citizenship papers."

THE DRAMATIC INCREASE in immigration to America since 1980 has been part of a worldwide phenomenon that by 1992 saw a hundred million people living outside their native lands. This movement poses fundamental questions about national sovereignty, moral obligation, disparity of incomes, democratic processes, and national capacities for assimilation. For the people on the move, the need for adjustment is as painful as ever. The life of the new American immigrants, as for all those who came before, is a life caught between past and future, between the pull of remembered traditions and the push of new opportunities.

America claims to be a creedal society. Anyone who adheres to our American creed can become a citizen. The creed's touchstones are liberty, equality, individualism, democracy, and the rule of law. The tension among these values creates the dynamics of American politics. Virtually any person in the world can become American by raising his or her right hand and swearing sole allegiance to the flag and Constitution of the United States of America. America remains a living ideal.

Representing New Jersey for seventeen years, I have witnessed the power of the creed for thousands of my constituents. Citizens of my state are ethnically self-conscious, which means that they are aware of the boundaries charted by ethnicity even as they think of themselves first as Americans. Sections of New Jersey townships are dominated by ethnic groups who find the proximity with their fellow immigrants as reassuring in suburbia as it once was on the Lower East Side of Manhattan or other areas of New York. I have constituents who care deeply about British bigotry in Northern Ireland, Tamil grievances in Sri Lanka, and Armenian aspirations in Nagorno-Karabakh. I have constituents who remember Japanese cruelty in Korea, the jails of Salazar, the terror of the Red Guard, the rigidity of Iranian fundamentalists, the nights of fear in Argentina, the squalor of Palestinian refugee camps, the brutal repression of Soviet Jewry. The security of American life provides a sharp contrast to the past experience of millions of Americans.

People come to America for a multitude of reasons. They come seeking freedom from oppression: the oppression of totalitarian elites or—especially for women—the oppression of suffocating social mores and rigid family structure. Many immigrants come for the chance to make money; some arrive anxious to exercise their democratic political rights; some come for an American higher education and end up staying; a small number, opposed to the regimes of their former homelands, are fleeing for their lives. They come because they believe that merit will ultimately prevail, that if they work hard they can get ahead, that the country is big enough and fluid enough so that even the most unusual sect or group or individual can find a niche and be able to breathe free. Many do the lowliest work, in the belief that their children will have it better. They come with the recognition that it will be painful to lose the cultural moorings of their homeland. They will send money back to relatives in the old country. They will continue to observe old ethnic customs, but, with the passage of time and the birth of children, they will form American attachments. They will have no frame of reference in which to comprehend Boy Scouts, or Thanksgiving, or baseball. They will yearn for the warmth and closeness of the old country. They will feel hurt by the indifference and coldness of much of American society. They will struggle to understand the subtle class distinctions of their new world. Still, they come convinced, as surely as were the boatmen who headed down the Ohio toward the Mississippi or the settlers who crossed the plains, that their future will be more shining than their past.

If you ask people where most American families originally came from, the usual answer is England, the home of the white Anglo-Saxon Protestant. Until recently, this was the right answer, with the bulk of the British arriving in four waves of immigration during the eighteenth century. Now, in the last decade of the twentieth century, the most populous immigrant group is German. Fifty-eight million Americans in the 1990 census claimed German as "ancestry or ethnic origin," as compared with thirty-nine million claiming Irish and thirty-three million claiming English.

Whereas the Bradley side of my family was Scotch-Irish, the Crowe— or Kroh—side was German. My mother's great-great-great-great-grandfather, Gottfried Kroh, came from Germany to St. Charles County, Missouri, in 1796. That was about one hundred years after the first Germans—Rhinelanders fleeing high taxes, the threat of conscription, and excessive regulation of practically every aspect of life—found economic opportunity in Pennsylvania, having been drawn here by higher wages, cheap land, and a general atmosphere of freedom. By 1776, immigrants from the Rhineland numbered a hundred thousand, and Germantown rivaled Philadelphia. What precipitated the departure of my Krohs from Germany I do not know.

Gottfried's son, Michael, my great-great-great-grandfather, was killed in an accident hauling logs in 1818. Michael's father-in-law, James Green, had crossed into Kentucky from Virginia with Daniel Boone, and during the early Kentucky Indian troubles became his trusted companion. Michael's son, Martin, my great-great-grandfather, married Jane Jump, who was the daughter of one of St. Charles County's earliest settlers. Martin Kroh (now spelled Crowe) held public office as county clerk, assessor, and judge of the county court. The lives of these German ancestors were already far removed from Metternich, the Congress of Vienna, and the newly reconstituted German monarchies. As the tensions in Germany rose—because of periodic economic busts of an artisan and farm economy, and the Carlsbad Decrees, which increased censorship—Germans from Hanover, Bavaria, Saxony, Thuringia, and Westphalia left for America in growing numbers.

In the century after the end of the Napoleonic Wars, five and a half million Germans immigrated, as compared with the one and a half million who came here from just after the First World War through the fall of the Berlin Wall in 1989. From 1845 to 1854, three million immigrants arrived, of which Germans represented the largest group; the United States population at that time was twenty million, and this remains the greatest proportional wave of immigration in American history. When Germans settled in small numbers among Americans, they easily assimilated. When they established themselves as groups, they often clashed with their British American neighbors.

From 1815 until the mid-1850s, there were three separate efforts—in Missouri and southwestern Illinois, in Texas, and in Wisconsin—to create a "New Germany" in the United States. These enclaves were conceived as ethnically homogeneous communities that would be geographically isolated and economically independent of the rest of the country. The Germans of Missouri held to the German language and convinced the state legislature to print laws in German as well as in English. By the time of the Civil War, west Texas was a concentrated area of German language and life; before statehood in 1845, given its isolated location the area might well have become a new Germany. With their inherent rootedness, the closeness of their extended families, and their devotion to their traditional ethnic customs and social mores, Germans inevitably came into conflict with an aggressive Yankee Puritanism that sought to impose its own version of American culture. Since many of these newcomers had come to America in part to escape regulation and were enjoying freedom for the first time in their lives, resentment of Anglo regimentation grew. In Wisconsin, Germans called the Yankee attempt to prohibit alcohol a "temperance swindle" and an "outflow of Puritan bigotry."

Virtually no German immigrants of the nineteenth century supported the institution of slavery. They either disapproved of it or were indifferent to it. They forcefully opposed its extension to the territories. Their view was one of the reasons that Missouri, a slave state, did not secede from the Union. These progressive Germans believed in the Union. Although most Germans were Democrats, in some states—particularly Pennsylvania and Illinois—they helped to put Lincoln into office with their votes. They also helped to win the Civil War with their blood and bayonets. In the process, they seized the unique chance that war offers for a "different" group to integrate fully into American society.

My great-grandfather John Crowe entered the Union Army at age nineteen when Lincoln first called for volunteers. After a three-month term, he enlisted for three years. He fought with Grant at the Battle of Shiloh, participated in the siege of Vicksburg, and played a notable part in the Battle of Missionary Ridge. From there, he went on with the Union forces to Atlanta and "thence," as the Missouri Civil War history book says, "in all that followed with Sherman to the sea." He returned home to a farm outside Union, Missouri, in the winter of 1865, having been commissioned a captain. In the 1870s, John Crowe was elected sheriff of Franklin County and later served as probate judge, before retiring to the farm. A document put together for a Crowe family reunion in 1923 notes that "the Judge, though a Republican, never endorsed any of the extreme measures of his party either in or out of the army and though he fought the armies of the South, he never made war on private citizens. His sympathies were, in part, with the Southern people, aside from their attempts to break up the unity of the Nation."

Indeed, the Crowe family split in the Civil War. John's first wife was Minerva Breckinridge, the daughter of Asa, a descendant of the historic Breckinridge family of Kentucky. When she died, he married Sarah Hendrick, whose relatives fought for the Confederacy. After the Civil War, my Unionist great-grandfather lived in the same house in Union, Missouri, with one of his wife's Confederate relatives. No matter how much my great-grandfather supposedly sympathized with Southern people, for twenty-one years these two men never spoke, and each time the "rebel" walked into the room, my great-grandfather spat into a nearby cuspidor. The Crowes held grudges and were known for being stubborn. My father used to refer to people by saying they were "as hardheaded as a German" or, in one of his classic mixed metaphors, "as bullheaded as a Crowe."

Historically, the hardest German American heads were not liberals such as Carl Schurz or Gustav Koerner, who urged their countrymen to speak English and went into public life (Schurz became a U.S. senator) to make their new society more tolerant of pluralism. The stubborn Germans were those who, in the face of the xenophobia, of the Know-Nothings, asserted their Germanness by resisting assimilation. They started German social clubs, insisted on speaking their native tongue in churches, rarely married outside the group, and refrained from partisan political activity. They sought to have German spoken in the public schools, and when, in 1854, Wisconsin prohibited this, German Lutherans and German Catholics established parochial schools in which German was the language of instruction. As late as 1900, six hundred thousand children of German immigrants were being taught in the German language. Until the First World War, most Americans of German descent tended to refer to themselves as German-Americans (with a hyphen).

Many German Americans naturally opposed the United States' entry into the war. When President Wilson made the decision to fight the Kaiser, they experienced what one of them said was "perhaps the greatest trial that any foreign element in a country ever had to face." German American pastors felt paralyzed. The war had put them between the land of their spirit and the land of their citizenship. Once the United States was at war, nativism was ascendant again. The only way a German American could retain his American identity under these circumstances was to eradicate his affinity for things German. Many changed their names. In his autobiographical work *Palm Sunday,* Kurt Vonnegut put it this way: "The anti-Germanism in this country during the First World War so shamed and dismayed my parents that they resolved to raise me without acquainting me with the language or the literature or the music or the oral family histories which my ancestors had loved. They volunteered to make me ignorant and rootless as proof of their patriotism." The German language was banned in many states, and the German vote as a bloc vote disappeared after the First World War.

The Second World War further weakened the attachment that most Americans of German descent felt to the fatherland. Two bloody wars between the United States and Germany within thirty years drove German group identity in America underground, and the Holocaust all but eliminated it completely. To generations of native Germans born during or after the war, the Holocaust was inexplicable—a vast silence in their lives. To the older generation, it was a source of shame; nothing could ever redeem them for having allowed it to happen. In both Germany and

Austria, Jews had brought extraordinary effort and creativity and brainpower and given birth to much of what is best about modernity. Then the irrational underpinnings of German society had opened up and swallowed six million people. It was an unimaginable horror. Admit you're German, and you carry the burden of all three twentieth-century catastrophes.

But there is still a Steuben Day parade in New York. Carl Ratches still serves good sauerbraten in Milwaukee. Hermann, Missouri, still celebrates the Mayfest rites of spring. The Octoberfest revelers still fill the beer garden of the German American Club in Clark, New Jersey. The descendants of Germans who fled Bismarck's anti-Catholic *Kulturkampf* are still devout, and they lead the Right to Life movement in Bismarck, North Dakota. A few German singing societies still offer fellowship and group expression in the hill country of Texas. But the promotion of German high culture as "German" is declining. Bach and Beethoven and Kant and Goethe belong to the world. German Americans no longer think that raising American culture to German standards is the way to say thank you to America for their freedom.

German politics, even today, is inherently suspect, regarded as harboring authoritarian tendencies. American high schools tend to teach Spanish or French as a second language, not German. The German American Bund is dead. There are no more rallies in Madison Square Garden. It is as if a ghostly swastika hovered over such enterprises. Nevertheless, individuals of German background are conscious of their heritage.

During my years in Crystal City, I never thought of myself as German, any more than I considered myself Scotch-Irish. I was just American. Although my stepgrandfather had emigrated from Germany at age twelve, and cooked spareribs and sauerkraut every Wednesday, and drank his beer each afternoon at four o'clock, I didn't recognize these things as ethnicity. They seemed to be only individual habits. Even his stories about being lifted off the ground by disciplinarian schoolteachers pulling his ears were offered, and received, as stories of the perils of childhood in general rather than of a childhood spent in Germany. The German Americans of my youth were the women in South St. Louis who scrubbed the front steps of their homes every Saturday morning, occasioning my father to comment, "You can eat a meal off those Germans' steps, they're so clean." Germans were the people who ate the big hot dogs and brewed Busch Bavarian Beer. What did I have in common with them—or with my Kroh ancestors, for that matter? I didn't embrace or explore the German side of my family. My understanding of things German, as well as of the immigrant experience in America generally, came only after I was married.

My wife, Ernestine, is a German-born naturalized citizen. She is constantly caught between two worlds, living in a society much different from the one she grew up in. She was four years old when the Second World War began, and her early childhood memories of the Bavarian city of Passau are of a railroad station full of soldiers in transit and a city without men. They were off to war. The place was eerily empty, populated only by the elderly and women. She was free to roam, to sneak into movies, to feel bold beyond her years.

Her father, Sepp Misslbeck, served in the German Air Force in a support role almost exclusively on the Western front in France. Her mother, Erna, an outspoken individualist with fierce family loyalty, nearly ended up in the Passau jail as a political prisoner for a public outburst against Hitler's war. In the spring of 1944, Erna had spoken out during a movie newsreel showing German defeats in the East. Her remarks were reported to the Nazi authorities, who construed them, correctly, as antiregime. A few days passed, and then a local official warned her one evening that the Nazis would be coming to get her at eight o'clock the next morning. Only one thing could save her: Hitler gave pregnant women special status, and Ernestine's mother was pregnant with her second child. But she needed an official proof immediately, because if they took her she would never be able to see a doctor. She woke up her own doctor at 1 a.m. to obtain a certificate of pregnancy. When the Nazis came the next morning, she coolly pulled out the certificate, and they left. Apparently, the Führer needed all the babies he could get.

My wife, above all, was a child of the defeat. She recalls watching the faces of wounded German soldiers streaming through Passau in retreat. She remembers that in the last few months of the war her mother took her and her baby brother to live with a farmer, so that they would have food. Everyone was panicked, wondering whether the Russians, who were known as rapers and pillagers, would arrive before the Americans. After the surrender, her father moved the family to his hometown of Ingolstadt. There, she remembers the victorious Americans' dispensing chocolate, cigarettes, and C-rations. But her family's pride and rigidity prevented them from close associations with Americans, who were both admired and resented. Her mother tells stories about American officers in the first wave of occupation, before her husband had returned, who brought her chocolate, which she accepted, judging their interests as genuinely humane because she was again obviously pregnant. Ernestine will never forget the brutally cold winters of 1946 and 1947. In Frankfurt, there were nine hundred overcoats for four hundred thousand people. The mayor of Stuttgart reported seventy-one overcoats for a population of three hundred and thirty thousand. In Frankfurt, only a quarter of the prewar houses were still standing, and everywhere people were hungry. As if it were not hard enough for the occupying forces to care for the surviving German nationals, eight million refugees, at a rate of five thousand to ten thousand per day, arrived in Germany from Soviet-occupied Germany and Austria, as well as from Poland and other nations in the East.

Ernestine's father was briefly a POW, but he was released once the Allies had determined that he was free of any Nazi connections. He began a new life selling wooden tableware to American GIs and bartering the American "currency"—cigarettes—for milk and meat for his young family. Shortly after arriving in Ingolstadt, Ernestine's mother took ill with phlebitis, pleurisy, and the complications from nursing without adequate nutrition. For eight years she was bedridden, leaving Ernestine to raise, with the arrival of her sister, both younger siblings. Ernestine attended a Catholic girls' school, where some of the teachers were returning war veterans, extremely well-educated and well-traveled, but traumatized, ill-tempered, and starving. Her only social activities outside the school were 5 a.m. tennis matches with her male admirers.

Sepp Misslbeck, thin and energetic, was urged by Allied authorities to enter local government. The field was open, since anyone who had been associated with the Nazis was barred. Ernestine's father did not like the newly returned communists or the socialists, but neither did he want to join the emerging Christian Democrats. He started his own party—the Independent Voters—which was neither ideological or religious but dedicated only to improving the nuts and bolts of local government in Ingolstadt. In the meantime, Ernestine was chafing under her premature maternal responsibilities and the claustrophobia of a small town. Eventually she left home and her university studies for America. Her father became a councilman in Ingolstadt; later, in the 1960s, he would rise to mayor, and would bring a major natural-gas pipeline to this mid-sized Bavarian industrial town.

Ernestine married in America, had a child, divorced, earned a Ph.D. in comparative literature from Emory University in Atlanta, and became a college professor. In 1974, she married me. Our daughter, Theresa Anne, was born in 1976. Ernestine stood beside me and campaigned superbly in my three races for the U.S. Senate. It was not uncommon, given her strength, directness, and likability, for people specifically to request her appearance at campaign and fund-raising events.

Ernestine saw America less as the economic and political promised land than as a place in which she could breathe freely, far from the stifling atmosphere of a small German city. She did not come seeking riches or political freedom. Like thousands of others, she came for personal reasons, having to do with family interaction, social mores, and the role of women in the Old World. After each trip she took back to Germany, she would remark, "I could never again live there." But she would say, too, "I'm reminded every day in countless ways that my impulses aren't American. It's so exhausting to constantly have to make an effort to understand." The family and community rituals that gave her childhood meaning with all their order and predictability were the moments whose stultifying impact prompted her inner conflict and from which she most wanted to flee. She sensed there was more to life than dinner at six with father as king. But, at the same time that she prized her American independence, she missed the intensity and the communality that flowed from those moments. As with most first-generation immigrants, her head tells her how wonderful America is, but her unreflected assumptions still rest in her natal place. Her academic specialty, German literature, keeps her involvement with Germany constant. The rhythms and rituals of American life do not come naturally to her. She has had to learn them. Some, such as baseball, she has never mastered.

Living with her every day gives me a deeper impression of how incomplete the immigrant's experience is. It makes me aware of the tremendous courage it takes to leave a native land for a new one filled with the unknown. It makes me appreciate the experiential richness of living in two cultures simultaneously, with the world as a setting. It chastens me to see how much I have taken for granted about the "right" way to do things. The "right" way is nothing more than the way in which I was brought up, the way that others around me automatically accepted.

There are other ways to see things and do things. The challenge and the joy is remaining open to learn from them.

The American creed, with its volitional power and dedication to abstract ideals, remains expansive and generous at its best moments. Unfortunately, it is often marred in its realization by persistent prejudice against nonwhites, or other "out groups" of the historical moment, such as Germans, Irish Catholics, Italians, Greeks, Jews, or Poles. Attributing hostile or socially unacceptable characteristics to an "out group" absolves the host society of any responsibility to relieve the group's privation or suffering: the group's shortcomings, not the society's, are the problem. World history is replete with examples of this phenomenon, and the potential for such thinking resides in each of us. Its effect in America has been to diminish the power and sweep of the American creed, "that all men are created equal; that they are endowed by their Creator with certain unalienable Rights; that among these are Life, Liberty, and the pursuit of Happiness." Resistance to Asian Americans is a part of this sad aspect of our history.

The Chinese started coming to America in sizable numbers in the 1850s and 1860s. They came to trade and to export goods back to China. They worked as laborers in the gold mines of California. They helped to build the first transcontinental railroad. Leland Stanford, the president of the Central Pacific, made special efforts to recruit them. By the 1870s, factory owners had started hiring Chinese labor in California.

The inhospitality of white Americans toward the Chinese came to a head in 1871. The *Almanac of American History* carries the following entry for October 24, 1871: "Race riots erupt in Los Angeles, California, against the Chinese. Fifteen laborers are lynched in the ongoing violence which has begun to characterize opposition to Oriental immigration. Aside from vicious racial antipathy, there is also the fact that the Chinese work harder, better and longer for less money than anyone else. They are also sober and clean." In other words, the Chinese created problems because, even though they looked different from whites, they seemed fervently to practice the Protestant work ethic.

The Chinese of San Francisco shaped a different and more popular impression. Twenty-five thousand of them crowded into a small area of brothels and gambling halls called, plainly, Chinatown. The opium dens, the gambling parlors, and the scarcity of families—only 5 percent of the hundred and sixteen thousand Chinese in California in 1876 were women—caused religious crusaders to join with the union leaders angry at the competition from Chinese laborers. The political backlash was fierce: by a vote of 150,000 to 900, California in 1879 voted in a state referendum to exclude all Chinese from the United States.

California—and Oregon too—had refused to ratify the Fifteenth Amendment to the Constitution, on the ground that, if the vote was given to blacks, it would have to be extended to Chinese as well. The new California Constitution specifically denied Chinese the right to vote or to work for a corporation. The U.S. Circuit Court threw out both of these provisions within a year, ruling them a violation of the Fourteenth Amendment, but the court could do nothing about the popular mood, which continued to build against the Chinese.

In 1882, led by the California congressional delegation and supported by many labor and business interests, Congress passed the Chinese Exclusion Act. The act allowed continued immigration of Chinese merchants and students, but Chinese laborers were prohibited. Courageously, President Chester Arthur vetoed it, but Congress overrode the veto, and for the first time since slavery, people from a particular country and of a particular race were denied the chance to profess the creed and thereby become Americans.

As if to fill a void, residents of another Asian country—Japan—began to immigrate in large numbers to the United States at the end of the nineteenth century. Unlike the Chinese, they immediately sought to Americanize themselves. Progressive and adaptable, they relinquished the ways of their old world. But with the emergence of Japan as a world power after the Russo-Japanese War of 1904–5, they, too, became suspect.

"Unwilling to remain wage earners," Patricia Limerick reports, "many Japanese immigrants set themselves to acquiring property, becoming farmers instead of farm workers. . . . Far from refusing to participate in American life, many of the Japanese were acculturating too successfully, in the judgment of their white competitors." The more the Japanese sought to fit in, the more the white establishment feared they were attempting to colonize the West Coast.

Around the turn of the century, the mayor of San Francisco, James Duval Phelan, thundered that the Japanese were "not the stuff of which American citizens can be made." In 1906, the San Francisco Board of Education ordered the segregation of all "Oriental" students in the public schools. President Theodore Roosevelt, who was involved in delicate negotiations with the Japanese on armaments and the future of Asian spheres of influence, labeled the board's action a "wicked absurdity." He convinced San Francisco officials to repeal the order in exchange for his promise to reduce Japanese immigration. After a congenial negotiation, the United States and Japan entered into the 1908 Gentlemen's Agreement, which kept Japanese laborers out of the U.S. In the same year, the Asiatic Exclusion League of North America raised the prospect of Japanese Americans as a fifth column. It asserted that Japanese Americans were ready when the time came to respond to the call of the emperor and rise up against the United States.

Urged on by the Native Sons of the Golden West, a chauvinist agriculture group, and alarmed that the 2 percent of the population that was Japanese was producing 90 percent of some crops, California in 1913 passed the Alien Land Law, which had the effect of prohibiting Japanese immigrants from buying or bequeathing land. Even leasing land for more than three years became illegal. Finally, in 1924, Congress banned Japanese immigration in a way similar to the 1882 Chinese Exclusion Act. Moreover, Japanese already in the United States were to be considered ineligible for naturalization. In the 1930s, when Japan invaded Manchuria, people in America of Japanese descent began to worry. By 1938, sensing the growing public antipathy toward Japan, they feared the worst for themselves if war should break out between Japan and the United States.

When I was a senior in college, one of my roommates was a nisei, a second-generation Japanese American. Dan Okimoto had been born in the relocation center at the Santa Anita racetrack. His parents were on their way from their home in San Diego to a detention camp in Poston, Arizona. Pursuant to an executive order signed on February 19, 1942, by President Roosevelt and a policy carried out by California Attorney General Earl Warren and the first director of the War Relocation Authority, Milton Eisenhower, all people of Japanese ancestry on the West Coast were detained as security risks and transported to internment camps far from the Pacific Ocean. "A Jap's a Jap," Western Defense Commander John L. DeWitt told the press. "It makes no difference whether he is an American citizen or not. . . . They are a dangerous element, whether loyal or not."

After Pearl Harbor, in order to mobilize America for war, the U.S. government—with the aid of academics like anthropologist Ruth Benedict and moviemakers like Frank Capra—sought to portray the Japanese enemy in government-produced movies and books as alien to all things Western and fanatically devoted to the emperor. The propaganda rubbed off on Japanese Americans, who were not regarded as individuals capable of breaking free from tradition and embracing the American creed. Instead, they were lumped with Japanese militarists and labeled a threat to U.S. security.

To understand the Japanese internment, one must comprehend the shock created by the Pearl Harbor bombings. FDR vividly etched it in the public mind by declaring December 7, 1941, "a date which will live in infamy." For the first time since 1812, a foreign power had attacked American soil. The sense of security that oceans had provided Americans was shattered. Fear ran rampant. There was a genuine panic about Japan's striking California next, and that panic spread quickly as it fell in rich fields of xenophobia.

There was no evidence of blind loyalty to the Japanese emperor among residents of Japanese descent, but even that was held against them. Earl Warren demonstrated this logic at work. Some people, he said in 1942, "are of the opinion that because we have had no sabotage and no fifth column activities [in California] that means that none have been planned for us. But I take the view that this is the most ominous sign in our whole situation. . . . I believe that we are just being lulled into a false sense of security and that the only reason we haven't had disaster in California is because it has been timed for a different date."

The Japanese American Citizens League tried to counter the suspicions with a statement of loyalty rooted in the American creed. "I am proud that I am an American citizen of Japanese ancestry," it began, "for my very background makes me appreciate more fully the wonderful advantages of this nation. I believe in her institutions, ideals, and traditions; I glory in her heritage; I boast of her history; I trust in her future." Notwithstanding the declaration, a hundred and seventeen thousand residents of Japanese descent, two-thirds of them American citizens, were sent to camps in the interior. Many of them sold their property for fear it would be destroyed or confiscated while they were interned. According to the Federal Reserve Bank of San Francisco, such sales resulted in total property-value losses of four hundred million dollars.

Dan Okimoto's parents were Christian missionaries. His father had rejected the military tradition of his family in Japan, and his mother had rejected strong family opposition to her conversion to a "foreign" religion.

Both of them, at the behest of the Christian missionary community in Japan, had immigrated to the United States in 1937, in order to minister to the large Japanese immigrant community in California. Five years later, the Okimotos found themselves in an internment-camp barracks, with living quarters measuring twenty-five feet by twenty-five feet for their family of six. The man who had left Japan because of its rising militarism found himself and his family detained because of the fear of that militarism.

Most of the Japanese sent to internment camps stayed, as Dan's family did, for the duration of the war. At the same time, Japanese American males were asked if they were willing to sign up for combat duty. Many said yes. Among them was Daniel Inouye, whose segregated Japanese American unit performed heroically in Italy. Inouye lost an arm in proving his loyalty, while his fellow Japanese Americans lived behind barbed wire. Later, he became one of the most respected U.S. senators of the last fifty years, representing Hawaii with distinction from the first days of its statehood.

In addition to the combat request, all Japanese Americans were asked to renounce any allegiance to the Japanese emperor. The irony of asking American citizens, detained because of their ancestry, to profess loyalty to the country that denied them the full rights of citizenship was not lost on residents of those camps. The journalist Gene Oishi said that the requirement "was comparable to asking Joe DiMaggio, the son of Italian immigrants, to forswear allegiance to Mussolini."

In the summer of 1945, my roommate's family left the camp in Poston and returned to San Diego to resume caring for the souls in that city's small Japanese community. The church in San Diego paid Mr. Okimoto a hundred and forty dollars a month to support his wife, three sons, and a daughter. Often, parishioners would leave food on the Okimotos' doorstep, not wanting to embarrass the family by an open acknowledgment of their poverty. Dan's parents preached hard work as well as religious conviction. They pushed their children toward attainment of a principled excellence. All four were models of performance in school and on the athletic field. In addition, they grew up with the tribulations that came from being Japanese American.

In a 1971 autobiography, Dan wrote:

When others called me "Little Nip" or "Slant Eyes," I usually purged the pain away by laughing. When I was a child and my toys from Japan

broke, I was told that the Japanese were no more than a race of imita-
tors who could produce only cheap, second-rate goods. In movies
showing scenes from World War II, I learned that the sinister "Japs"
taking such sadistic pleasure in killing and torturing almost uniformly
brave American soldiers were representative of a whole nation, and I,
although of Japanese descent, was expected to share this popular view.
It is not perhaps surprising that I tried as best I could to disassociate
myself from "bad" Japanese in as many ways as possible, for I wanted
to be above all an "American," whatever meaning that may have had.
But this attempt was doomed to failure, for I was not after all representative of the central figure of middle-class American mythology,
the WASP in all his white-skinned, blue-eyed glory. In spite of that, I
was American and hardly knew whether to love or hate that which I
was and wanted to be.

When Dan came to Princeton, he knew virtually nothing about Japan
beyond family stories. Although his parents had spoken Japanese occasionally, they had not taught him the language, and his twelve years of
California education had focused exclusively on American and European
history. Not one course in his high school had introduced Asia or any
other non-Western region of the world. Baseball, basketball, and football, yes. Proms and sock hops, yes. American politics and literature,
yes. Johnny Mathis and Elvis, yes. Japan, no. At the urging of his Princeton adviser, he enrolled in Japanese language and East Asian history
courses. He read Japanese writers and poets. He studied the intricacies
of Japanese politics. He spent his junior year in Japan for intensive language training and exposure to the society. Princeton was opening a new
world for my roommate, so that he might understand his heritage. At the
same time, it offered painful reminders about white American ethnocen-
trism. As one of only a few nisei at Princeton, Dan was once asked by the
assistant dean of the college to speak before the board of trustees.
    "What's the subject?" my roommate asked.
    "Princeton, as Asians see it," the dean replied.
    "Sir, I'm afraid I don't qualify for the assignment."
    "What do you mean?" the dean replied, puzzled.
    "You see, sir, I'm not really an Asian."
    Then what was he? the dean wanted to know.
    "Just an American—in disguise."
    The exchange provided the title for his autobiography, and in the

summer of 1971 he made a brief publicity tour to promote the book. One of his stops was St. Louis. I happened to be visiting my parents at the time, so I accompanied him to the studios of KETC-TV on a hot June night. The format of the show included an interview by the host and telephone calls from the television audience. In the interview, Dan talked candidly about his family's experience at Poston and the stain on American history represented by the Japanese internment, and his resultant identification with the civil-rights movement and the aspirations of African Americans. He talked about the promise of America and about how lucky he felt to be American. He described his California childhood—his football-star brother, his years at Princeton, his father's Christian commitment.

As I sat in the studio, I began to glow with admiration for his candor and convictions. I had not known all the things he said about Poston, and I felt ashamed. How could this Poston have happened in America? I thought. In college I had studied the effect of American xenophobia on immigrants during the Palmer Raids and the Red Scare of 1919. I had written a college paper about anti-Catholic xenophobia in England during the Popish Plot of 1678 and another one on Bismarck's *Kulturkampf*. I had seen the dogs and fire hoses of Birmingham police chief Bull Connor attack black civil-rights advocates. I had heard my cousin making anti-Japanese remarks as she watched TV documentaries of the Second World War in the vain hope of spotting her husband, who had been lost at Midway. I had read about the anti-"Hun" propaganda in the First World War. I had heard anti-Semitic and anti-Italian slurs in my youth. I knew all of this, but I wasn't quite ready for the telephone calls that came when the host opened the lines.

Caller #1: "If Mr. Moto doesn't like America, tell him to go back to Japan."

Caller #2: "I don't know why you're complaining; you've done well in America."

Caller #3: "I lost my husband at Pearl Harbor. You can't trust these Japanese. How do we know what you say about these camps is true? I don't trust you."

Caller #4: "Tell the Japs they're lucky that we didn't drop another atomic bomb on them."

Caller after caller spewed out an irrational hatred toward Japanese. Much of it flowed from the painful memory of war with its great loss of

American lives and incredible brutalities visited upon American prisoners of war by the Japanese, but none of the callers apparently registered
the fact that my roommate was American, not Japanese. The diatribe,
beyond being a failure to acknowledge what he said and a shocking
demonstration of the closed-mindedness of prejudice, evinced a selec-
tive memory of the historical record. While it is true that the Japanese
were themselves chauvinistic, even racist, toward Koreans, Chinese,
and Caucasians, and while no one should forget what they did in
Nanking, Burma, or the Philippines, at the same time, America had
overreacted and diminished our finest traditions by creating the camps.
Anyone who introduced facts that ran counter to American history portrayed as one uninterrupted extension of freedom, faith, and wealth
risked outraging the popular mind. If the truth teller didn't look "American"—that is, Caucasian—it seemed he simply was not believed. This
would not be the last time I would observe such reactions, and it would
always be painful.

In my first three years with the New York Knicks, the doctor at
Madison Square Garden was a Japanese American named Kazuo Yaniga-
sawa—or "Yana," as we called him. During Knick games or New York
Ranger hockey games, you could usually find Yana with a half-chewed
cigar in the corner of his mouth, playing poker in his office under the
stands with some of the Garden's security employees. He was a powerfully built man with a gruff exterior, and he liked to crush even the
biggest player's hand in a prodigious handshake. He treated our torn lig-
aments and battered cartilage with care but with little coddling. In my
third week as a Knick, I was hit by a speeding sportscar—an MG—in
midtown Manhattan. It was nighttime, and raining, and I saw the car's
headlights out of the corner of my eye. Luckily, by reflex, I jumped up
and to my left, rolled over the MG's hood, and fell into the street. The
young woman who drove the car was trembling as we exchanged addresses and called her parents. I then dragged myself to St. Clare's Hospital, on West 52nd Street, where Yana was on staff, and where, after a
quick exam, he told me to quit complaining—there was nothing seriously injured. After I had sat out the next two games, he told me to get
back on the court.

In the summer, when I would be in New York running in Riverside
Park and shooting in vacant gyms to get back into shape for the coming
season, Yana and I would often eat dinner together at Delsomma's, on

47th Street. It was while I ate those meals of salad, sirloin steak, and cantaloupe that I heard about Yana and the camp director.

During the Second World War, Yana was a medical student at Columbia, but his family, like Dan Okimoto's, had been sent to an internment camp, this one in Utah. He was determined to get them out. Through the medical school, he asked Herbert Lehman, the director of the Office of Relief and Rehabilitation and later a U.S. senator from New York, to intervene in behalf of his family. Lehman made the inquiries, and the answer came back that if Yana could bring his family to New York—about as far from the Pacific as you could get—they would be released. But he had to go out to the camp to get them and personally escort them to New York.

When Yana arrived, the camp director, a Japanese American, welcomed him and asked if he would like something to eat. Yana, young and unsure, said yes. The camp director took him back to his luxurious living quarters, opened a refrigerator stuffed with food, and removed two big steaks, which he broiled—one for himself and the other for Yana. Then he took Yana to his family, who were living in a crowded barracks room and ate beans and rice for nearly every meal. They told Yana that they hadn't eaten meat in months. Because of the desert climate, their room was often cold at night, and during the summer the daytime temperatures reached a hundred and twenty degrees. The camp director, they said, insisted that the detainees treat him with the deference due a commanding officer in the military. He never socialized with his fellow Japanese Americans who were confined. When Yana left with his mother and sister, he vowed never to forget the camp director.

One night about twenty years later, Yana was on call in St. Clare's emergency room when an ambulance arrived with the victim of an auto accident on the West Side Highway. The patient appeared to have several broken bones. Yana examined the injuries; they were serious but not life-threatening. He was about to give the patient a shot of painkiller when he looked at the man's face. It was the camp director. There were no luxurious quarters now; no refrigerator full of steaks; no insistence on deference to power. There was only a body screaming in pain. After all those years, Yana paid a particular homage to the memory of his mother and sister. He paused, just for a moment, and in doing so gave the camp director the equivalent of a bone-crushing handshake.

America eventually confronted the Japanese American internment.

In 1988, Congress passed the Civil Liberties Act, which contained an apology to Japanese Americans for the internment and gave monetary compensation to the survivors. A Japanese American congressman from California named Norm Mineta, who had lived in an internment camp in Wyoming, was a major force in its passage, and he drew support from such unlikely sources as Senator Al Simpson, who, as a member of a Boy Scout troop from a nearby Wyoming town, had visited the camp where Mineta was interned. The Civil Liberties Act is a monument to the persistence of its principal Senate advocate, Senator Spark Matsunaga of Hawaii, who pursued his objective relentlessly and respectfully, putting himself on the line with colleague after colleague. It passed the Senate, 67–27. By March 1994, 79,342 Japanese Americans had received an apology and more than one and a half billion dollars. The Civil Liberties Act of 1988 stands as testimony to the power of memory and a model for how a democratic society can try to overcome the dark chapters in its past.

LATINOS ARE a new American ethnicity. Because they are truly multiracial, they pose a challenge to the usual American concept of race that demands a person to be either black or white. Whether they are Cuban, Puerto Rican, or Mexican, their first language is Spanish and their first religion usually Roman Catholic. Yet Mexico is a nation of mestizos, criollos, and indigenes. Cubans and Puerto Ricans trace ethnic strains back to Spain as well as to the Yoruba of West Africa. In Puerto Rico there is a saying, *"Si no es Dingo, es Mandingo,"* which, loosely translated, means that if your ancestors are not from one tribe, they're from another. In Mexico City, in the education ministry, there is a mural depicting a myriad of racial combinations that make up the Mexican nationality. By the time of the Revolution of 1910, after centuries of intermarriage between Spanish immigrants and the native peoples, fewer than one and a half million out of fifteen million Mexicans were criollos—pure European stock. Children in one family often have different shades of skin, which is taken only as one of their individual attributes. Puerto Ricans and Cubans also have a mixed Spanish and African ancestry.

I represent the second-largest Cuban American population in America—after Miami, where Cuban Americans make up 42 percent of the population. Many of the Cubans fled when Fidel Castro seized power.

They arrived in America penniless. Often whole families lived off what one person alone would have found meager sustenance. These refugees were the professionals and small-business owners of the old Cuba, the former clerical employees of American corporations operating in Cuba, Cubans who doubted Castro's messianic promises. In his book *Latinos,* Earl Shorris points out that nearly one-third of the Cubans who came to the United States in 1959–62 were professionals, with technical and managerial skills. Another third had worked in sales or clerical jobs. Thirty-six percent had graduated from high school or had attended college for a time, compared with 4 percent of the whole Cuban population. They brought their entrepreneurial skills, and their energy and drive were awesome. In Miami, they established their own financial institutions, which made loans primarily to the Cuban community. This *socioismo* was no more complicated or heinous than the old-boy network that operates in places such as Wall Street. Cubans poured their lives into reclaiming their middle-class status, and the amount of money they made was the easiest way for them to measure their progress. As a Cuban woman with a Cuban Ph.D. who went from welfare to wealth in twenty years told Shorris, "For a Cuban, the problem is not to have money, but to be able to make money."

In New Jersey, the Cubans settled in Hudson County, an older urban community that had begun to deteriorate as upwardly mobile Italian Americans and Irish Americans left for the suburbs. They followed the familiar path of those who live in two cultures simultaneously. Like immigrant children of other nationalities, young Cuban American girls, who had more quickly assimilated American language and customs, accompanied their mothers on shopping trips, acting as translator and negotiator and assuming responsibility far beyond their years. Above all, in the face of rejections that came because of their differentness, Cuban Americans didn't become discouraged. Constant work paid off for them in New Jersey. The one-room apartments gave way to three-room apartments. Slowly, the neighborhoods changed and the cities—Union City, North Bergen, and West New York—revived. Churches reopened. Small businesses thrived. Law offices were established. Cuban restaurants attracted customers from miles around. Suburban Spanish classes took field trips to these booming Cuban neighborhoods to practice the roll of the language.

Hudson County was once the home of political boss Frank ("I am the law") Hague, the longtime mayor of Jersey City. In one mayoral race, when he was faced with an opponent named something like John L. Smith, who threatened to reduce his margin of victory from the usual 85 percent to 80 percent, Hague convinced three loyal partisans to change their names to John E., John A., and John C. Smith respectively and file as candidates so that they would split the Smith vote. Hague could then argue that any decline in his performance came from running against four John Smiths, not one. Hague died in 1956, but his Democratic machine lived on under John Kenny; it opposed Medicaid/Medicare in the 1960s, because Medicaid/Medicare would impede the dispensing of free health care at the Frank Hague Hospital as a perk for being a loyal party-precinct worker.

In the 1970s Union City was run by Mayor/State Senator Billy Musto, a cagey and knowledgeable Hudson County politician who knew how to balance political claimants. He once told a nice but unqualified local pol, whom the machine had tapped for a congressional race, that if he wanted to win the general election he should follow "the Winnebago strategy." When the untutored candidate asked Musto what that meant, the reply came. "Nick, you get in the Winnebago and don't come out until after the election." Going to a Democratic dance in the seventies at Schutzen Park—a cluster of buildings housing ballrooms and dining rooms, on a property where blacktop had replaced grass and the largest structure was an old-age home—was like visiting another era. You expected young Frankie Sinatra of neighboring Hoboken to walk in at any moment. The tables were covered with platters of rice, chicken, and sausage and plates of pasta. Men stood at a bar behind a partition at one end of the room sipping rum, vermouth, or Chivas on the rocks. On the stage at the other end was the dance orchestra, its members identically clad. Well-dressed Cuban Americans and Italian Americans in dark suits and long gowns fox-trotted around the floor. The center of the scene was a table just in front of the orchestra, where Musto sat barking orders in a raspy voice over the din of music and the babble of various petitioners. A seemingly endless stream of constituents shook his hand and kissed his cheek. He reciprocated by smiling and cupping the back of the person's head. Democratic majorities were 70 percent in Hudson County; in Union City, they were 80 percent.

The Hudson County political machine nurtured the Cubans, teaching them the ways of American politics. And the Cubans in turn extended the machine's life, giving it their loyalty—up to a point. Ultimately,

Cuban Americans did not want to be "controlled," nor did they want their "vote delivered." They challenged the machine in the early eighties, and in 1984 Musto went to jail for bribery and Cuban Americans took political power. In 1992, the Cuban Americans of Hudson County elected New Jersey's first Latino congressman, a young, talented Cuban American Democrat named Robert Menendez, whose considerable talents could someday make him America's first Cuban American senator or governor.

Cuban Americans are well known for their virulent anticommunism and for their constant call to overthrow Fidel Castro. They are Republican more often than Democrat (except in Hudson County), because JFK aborted the Bay of Pigs invasion in 1961. To Cuban Americans, that betrayal, however pragmatic, condemned their countrymen to more than thirty years of living under a dictator who tolerated no dissent. Armando Valladares's book *Against All Hope* lays out the horror of Castro's jails, where torture was the norm for anyone who threatened the regime, even with words. I'll never forget a town meeting in West New York where a man who was a well-known political prisoner showed up. He had just been freed from prison in Cuba. I asked him how long he had been incarcerated, and he replied, "Twenty-two years, ten months, two weeks, three days, one hour, and fifteen minutes." Every week, thousands of Cubanos mail money home to help family members still trapped on Fidel's island.

Cuban Americans loved Ronald Reagan not only because they saw him as a fervent anticommunist but also because he (unlike Kennedy) tried to overthrow a communist government—this time in Nicaragua. In 1986, when I voted to support a hundred million dollars of military aid to the contras, just about the only group of my constituents who voiced approval of the vote were Cuban Americans. Some of them came to me with tears in their eyes, overwhelmed because finally a Democrat, a representative of the party that had welcomed them to New Jersey and nurtured them to political maturity, had understood how dangerous communism was in their view, and how only force could stop communist revolutionaries from consolidating power.

Just as in old Cuba, where white Cubans had their clubs and black Cubans had theirs, and where—up until the very eve of the revolution—thousands of white foreigners came every year to have sex with mulatto prostitutes, the issue of race remains unresolved within the Cuban American community. Cubans have always lived at a trade crossroads, in a world that was part black, part white. This mixture of African and Spanish shaped the island's music, its gene pool, and even its religion. The white revolutionary José Martí and the black general Antonio Maceo fought together for Cuban independence and for much more. In his nineteenth-century essay "My Race," Martí wrote, "With what justice can the white racist, who believes his race to be superior, complain of the Negro racist who considers his race specially privileged? . . . How can the Negro racist, who insists on the special character of his race, complain of the white racist?"

In the early months of the Clinton administration, Mario Baeza, a black Cuban American lawyer from New Jersey, was proposed for assistant secretary of state for Inter-American Affairs. He met with virulent opposition from the organized Cuban groups (both Democrat and Republican) based in Miami. If you're not from Miami, you're suspect. Ask any Cuban American researcher from the North who is interested in how Miami works. Miami Cubans said that it was ideology, not race, that generated their opposition: Baeza was viewed as insufficiently anti-Castro, because he had once served as the lawyer for a group of companies who went to Cuba on a trade mission. The real reason was much simpler. No one knew Baeza. He had not paid his dues to the Cuban American community.

Blacks in Miami say they missed their "day in the sun" during the civil-rights movement, because just at that moment the Cubans arrived, carrying the privileged status of ideological refugees along with the additional government benefits that went to anticommunist freedom fighters. Everything from government construction jobs to highway development has served the Cuban community more than the black community. When you visit Overtown or Liberty City, it is possible to understand why there have been more explosions of black violence in Miami than in any other American city in the last twenty years. José Martí's vision of racial harmony remains unfulfilled.

Ultimately, Cubans are different from other Latinos because they are exiles. As Shorris has written, "The nature of the immigrant is to flee the past; the exile seeks only the return of his former glory; he wants only the opportunity to act upon his nostalgia." For more than thirty years, they have lived with split families, dreams of return, and unremitting hard work. On Castro's island, it is hard work for no objective and little benefit, since the ideal of the socialist society is dead. On the mainland, it is hard work to earn money and to divert attention from the pain of exile—the pain of living without what sustained you in your youth and gave you a sense of continuity. With the passage of time, it seems fewer and fewer Cuban Americans want to return to the island on that inevitable day when Castro is no longer there. Younger Cuban Americans have settled into American society. They are not yearning to go home— this is their home. When Fidel exits and the dream is no longer deferred, it will be ironic if Cuban Americans pass it up. Then there are days when I think that Cuba by 2020 will be the fifty-first state.

IN 1982, from my discussions with American bankers about Mexico's international debt, and in particular from the stories of the Mexican oil boom of the 1970s and the profligate spending that resulted from it, I knew that there were aspects of the financial tale which I couldn't understand until I knew Mexico better. Beyond a basketball players' union meeting in Acapulco in 1970 and a visit to a few Tijuana bars while I was staying in the home of another college roommate from California, I knew virtually nothing about our neighbor to the south. I began by reading Octavio Paz and Carlos Fuentes. I studied the history of Mexico from before the arrival of the Conquistadors in the sixteenth century to the present. I read the eyewitness account in the journal of Cortés's lieutenant Bernal Díaz del Castillo, William Prescott's prodigious history of Spanish exploration, James Cockcroft's account of the intellectual origins of the Mexican Revolution, 1900–1913, and Alejandro Morales's *The Brick People,* a novel about nineteenth-century Spanish California. Slowly, Mexico began to come into focus. The vast amounts of money and corruption involved in politics, the turbulent colonial and political history, the bitter conflict between the Catholic Church and the revolutionary one-party state, even the romance of the place—its haunting and stark art, its preoccupation with the symbols of death, and its respect for the magical— all intrigued me. I began to visit Mexico several times a year to get a sense of how it felt and functioned today in relation to its history.

On one of these early visits, my wife and I spent two days in the National Museum of Anthropology in Mexico City. It is built in the grand public style of Mexico, with giant stone slabs for walls and vast open spaces surrounding the buildings so they can breathe. Inside lies Mexico's national story. The various halls describe the native civilizations of Mexico: the Olmecs, the Mayans, the Zapotecs, the Toltecs, and the Aztecs. Each had a complex culture long before Europeans arrived in America. When you are standing before the model of Tenochtitlán, with its canals and lakes protecting the Mexico City of the Aztecs, it is easy to imagine the awe that Cortés and his army of Spaniards must have felt upon seeing it. And in the Aztec tradition, after they arrived and conquered, they bred with the native women, snuffing out most vestiges of the old civilization.

Spain's fascination with Mexico, in the words of Bernal Díaz, was "for God and for gold," but neither objective completely caught the motivation or the breadth of the story. Cortés, de Soto, Ponce de León, Coronado, and Cabrillo joined Columbus, Pizarro, and Magellan to create the most remarkable worldwide exploration in history. As Samuel Eliot Morrison has written, "In one generation the Spaniards acquired more new territory than Rome conquered in five centuries." These great Spanish adventurers had explored and staked out the American Southwest and Southeast nearly seventy years before the British landed at Jamestown. Two hundred years before the first Scotch-Irish would cross the Cumberland Gap, the land from Salina, Kansas, to the shores of California (an area larger than Europe from the Elbe to the Atlantic) had been claimed and explored by Francisco Vásquez de Coronado and his men. At a time when the imaginations of European rulers were confined within narrow geographical boundaries, Coronado's accomplishments, financed by the Spanish crown, seem almost unimaginable in scope: the discoveries of California, the Grand Canyon, the ancient Hopi civilization, and the Great Plains covered to the horizon with buffalo.

Mexico gained its independence from Spain in 1821 and became a federal republic in 1824, but administrative control of the great empty land, ruled from faraway Mexico City, was no easier than it had been under the Spanish crown. It could not be protected from wandering Americans looking for land. Encouraged by Mexico, thirty thousand American settlers were living in Texas by the mid-1830s, bringing with them black slaves in defiance of Mexican law. Mexico had prohibited further immigration from the United States in 1830, but settlers continued to arrive, and the Mexican government eventually dispatched its military to take control of the area. Texans resisted. Sam Houston defeated the Mexican general Antonio López de Santa Anna in 1836 at San Jacinto, and the Republic of Texas was born. The United States offered to buy the area south of the Nueces River—today's central Texas—but Mexico refused.

In 1846, with Texas now in the union, Mexico and the United States went to war over the land north of the Rio Grande. President James K. Polk had promised in his election campaign to settle the disputes over our borders with Mexico and Canada. He precipitated the war with Mexico, and while Generals Zachary Taylor and Winfield Scott were fighting the Mexicans—along the Rio Grande and in the corridor from Veracruz to Mexico City, respectively—Polk sent General Stephen Kearny and seventeen hundred men out from Fort Leavenworth, Kansas, to lay claim to the land all the way to California. The war completed America's territorial aggrandizement, adding to the United States California, Texas, Nevada, and Utah, and parts of Arizona, New Mexico, Colorado, Kansas, Oklahoma, and Wyoming—all of which had been Mexican or Spanish territory for over three hundred years. To the Whig congressman Abraham Lincoln, the war was an abomination, and he voted against it. To the proponents of Manifest Destiny, such as Senator Thomas Hart Benton of Missouri, the peace settlement should have included all of Mexico.

To anyone living today, it is just so much ancient history—until you visit the Museo Nacional de las Intervenciones, in Mexico City. The museum is located in a residential neighborhood, far from the bustle of downtown Mexico City and the usual tourist track. Not many foreigners visit the museum, part of the Iglesia de Los Angeles de Churubusco. As you enter the gates of the courtyard, there is a plaque honoring the Irish Catholic mercenaries who deserted from General Zachary Taylor's army (appalled by its wanton murdering of women and children and its destruction of Catholic churches) and fled south to defend the church when it was attacked on August 20, 1847, by Scott's forces, who had marched inland from Veracruz. To the right of a wide stone walk leading to the museum entrance is a garden, where cedars and eucalyptus trees tower above fan-leafed palmettos. Bougainvillea, hibiscus, and flowering vines take up every inch of space, all but obscuring the building's barred windows. The vibrancy of the natural setting contrasts poignantly with the cracked and ancient stones of the aging structure. Inside, in meticulous detail, the entire history of the relationship between Mexico and the United States is documented. Each American affront is there, including

Sam Houston's war for Texas, Polk's war for Manifest Destiny and the 1848 Treaty of Guadaloupe Hidalgo (which gave the United States more than half the territory of Mexico for fifteen million dollars and American assumption of monetary claims held by Americans against Mexico), Woodrow Wilson's invasion of Veracruz in 1914, and the pursuit of Pancho Villa in the Sonoran desert (over the objections of both the dictator Huerta and his opponent, the constitutionalist Carranza). The exhibit is blatantly intended as an indictment, but the fact of the indignities cannot be denied. Nor can one go through these halls without understanding the ambivalence that many Mexicans feel toward the United States.

Just as American settlers poured across the border into Texas in the 1820s and 1830s in a virtual occupation, so now Mexicans push north across the border in search of livelihoods for their families. In 1990, there were twenty-one million people of Mexican descent living in this country; fourteen million of them were natural-born American citizens, and three million were illegals. In the previous decade, 28 percent of the legal immigration and 50 percent of the illegal immigration to the United States came from Mexico. Once, in an El Paso tenement that had eight tiny apartments and one communal toilet and shower, I asked a woman who was living in two rooms with six other Mexican immigrants why she had come to America. She said that she and her husband had left their land and a house in the Mexican state of Sonora because there were no jobs. It had come down to feeding the horses and cows or feeding her children, she said. Without the horses and cows, however, there could be no livelihood. They sold the livestock and headed north. She and her husband, who worked day jobs around El Paso, came across the border because the alternative was starvation.

In Los Angeles County, there are 3.3 million people of Mexican heritage. There are lawyers, doctors, editors, and successful entrepreneurs, but most of them are laborers. They work as bricklayers, plumbers, auto repairmen, shoemakers, leather workers, tile setters, sheetmetal workers, gardeners, food processors, housecleaners, waiters, florists, bellmen, and construction workers. Every day four hundred and thirty thousand of them board buses for the two-hour trip from East Los Angeles to the Westside, where they work. More Latinos—the overwhelming majority of whom are Mexican—live in poverty in Los Angeles than do blacks, Asians, and Anglos combined, and 75 percent of all male workers earning less than ten thousand dollars per year are Latino. Given the low wages, housing often consists of one-story stucco homes in East or South Central Los Angeles, with as many as twenty-seven people sleeping in three shifts in one house. For over one million of these people, who suffer disproportionately from tuberculosis and other diseases not rooted in behavior, there is no health insurance. Latinos are hard workers, with strong families that stay together. Their children are filling the public and parochial schools of Los Angeles. Between 1980 and 1990, Los Angeles County public schools, which are now 64 percent Latino, lost one hundred and seventy-seven thousand Anglos and thirty-three thousand blacks and gained ninety-two thousand Asian children and two hundred and forty-six thousand Latinos.

The immigration explosion of the 1980s could occur because of well-established immigration patterns built up over many years. Early in the twentieth century, the Santa Fe and Southern Pacific Railroads built their lines into Mexico. As Roberto Suro points out in his book *Remembering the American Dream: Hispanic Immigration and National Policy,* these transportation routes offered thousands of Mexicans a means to move to factory work during the industrialization of the American West. When the violent Mexican Revolution of 1910 created national turmoil, taking more than one million lives in a nation of fifteen million, the first wave of Mexican immigration occurred, with nearly a million and a half Mexicans fleeing across the border. Mexican workers were not excluded from coming to the United States by the 1924 immigration law that effectively barred most foreigners. They were a labor supply that could contract or expand, depending on the American need for labor.

To deal with labor shortages during the Second World War, the government created the *braceros* program, in which Mexicans worked officially as temporary contract laborers in the United States for up to six months. After the war, this pattern became a way of life in the Southwest, particularly in Texas and California, with as many as four and a half million Mexican workers coming north as part of the program. When recessions occurred, the *braceros* were unceremoniously deported—sometimes at gunpoint. In 1964, when the program was eliminated, the immigrants kept coming, illegally. By the 1970s, the migratory routes had become an accepted part of life on the Texas and California borders. The support networks were already in place. Ninety percent of the immigrants joined relatives already in the country. When the Mexican economy went into a tailspin in the early 1980s, the California economy was booming, and the flow of people north turned into a gusher.

In the summer of 1993, our daughter, Theresa, worked in rural Guanajuato, the site of one of Mexico's old colonial capitals, set in a beautiful valley and surrounded by small towns and gigantic chili fields. She told us that she did not meet one man who had not worked at some time in the United States. They would tell her about the hardships of heading north; the perils most frequently mentioned were starvation, rattlesnakes, and the treacherous currents of the Rio Grande. The U.S. border patrols seemed to be of no particular concern. Wayne Cornelius, of the Center for U.S.-Mexican Studies at the University of California, San Diego, reports in a study cited by Suro that in the 1980s "40 percent of all residents in traditional Mexican communities, including children and infants, had migrated at least once (some legally and some illegally). Most adults had made several trips." If people flow north, money is what flows south. In 1990 Mexicans remitted $3.2 billion to relatives and friends living in Mexico.

In 1986, Congress passed a landmark piece of legislation sponsored by Senator Alan Simpson and Congressman Romano Mazzoli aimed primarily at dealing with illegal immigration. It allowed migrants who could demonstrate continuous residence since January 1, 1982, to become legal simply by declaring themselves within eighteen months of the law's passage. Almost three million people—roughly two-thirds of the nation's total illegal population—availed themselves of the amnesty and stayed. No longer would they have to work without benefits and for a salary below the minimum wage, afraid to protest the exploitation for fear of exposure to the authorities.

Under the new law, anyone who entered the country illegally after 1982 was to be deported, but enforcement of the new law rested on employer sanctions: companies that hired illegal aliens would now be subject to fines of up to ten thousand dollars per worker and the owner would get six months in jail if he engaged in a pattern of violation. By targeting the jobs themselves, the law was an attempt to eliminate the principal incentive for illegal immigration into the United States. The attempt did not succeed, in large part because the enforcement of these sanctions was inadequately funded. Mexican workers continued to stream across our borders.

Americans in the midst of wage stagnation and corporate downsizing increasingly saw these immigrants as unwanted. The distinction between legal and illegal immigrants blurred. Even politicians far from the border perceived them as a threat: in 1985, Ed Koch, the mayor of New York, called for the U.S. Army to police the two-thousand-mile border between the United States and Mexico. Chicago politicians called for constant helicopter fly-overs. Along the border near San Diego, the United States erected a ten-foot-high steel wall that stretched for fourteen miles. In Nogales the wall consisted of old slabs of airport runways. Farther east, across from Ciudad Juárez, on the El Paso border, the U.S. immigration police stood round-the-clock watches in Dodge vans at half-mile intervals for the purpose of deterring and apprehending illegal immigrants. The Mexican American Republican mayor of Pomona, California, Eddie Cortez, was stopped and treated roughly by border agents who aggressively demanded documents that would prove he was a legal U.S. resident. Cortez, who had been elected on a tough law-and-order platform, pulled out his mayor's ID and the agents apologized. "If they can treat a mayor like this," he said, in words many Latinos felt, "who knows how they treat a normal Hispanic person just going about his business. The whole immigrant population is at risk."

Pete Wilson, the Republican governor of California, played the anti-immigration card in his 1994 re-election campaign. He knew that, though Latinos were 25 percent of California's population, they were only 11 percent of the registered voters. He offered them up to pacify middle-class Californians' frustration and fear about tough economic times in the state. In one of his TV commercials, he showed illegal immigrants jumping out of boats onto a beach like an invading army; another one showed them running across the border at night, headed north. Reminiscent of the anti-Asian crusades of the nineteenth century, opponents of immigration argued that immigrants—and in particular Laotians, Cambodians, and Mexicans—were burdening the social-service systems, paying little in taxes, bringing in new kinds of diseases, and taking jobs from Americans. Wilson won easily, and ballot proposition 187, which, among other things, forbade the children of illegal immigrants to attend California public schools, passed overwhelmingly—notwithstanding a 1982 Supreme Court decision that declared it unconstitutional for a state to bar the child of an illegal immigrant from getting a public-school education.

Having failed to persuade the federal government either to enforce

employer sanctions as the law required (some of Wilson's own businessmen supporters who employ illegals in their fields and factories didn't
want the sanction law enforced) or to provide financial help to cope with
the dramatic illegal inflow, Californians voted to turn school principals
into policemen and to stigmatize all Mexican American first graders. In
the city of San Diego, 37 percent of the first graders speak Spanish at
home. Proposition 187 in its most benign interpretation conveyed a
strong plea to Washington for help, and at its most virulent served up an
election-year brew of demagoguery and xenophobia. (In 1995, Wilson
tried to ride the antiforeigner wave to the White House but failed.) A
study by the Urban Institute in Washington, D.C., which revealed that
immigrants nationwide paid twenty-five billion dollars more in taxes
(even illegals pay sales taxes) than they received in benefits and services
each year, seemed to have no influence on the debate. But to deny a
teenager an education because a parent is illegal doesn't end the public
cost. It simply puts the young person on the street, where ultimately police costs associated with crime will exceed saved costs associated with
education.

The best way to stop the mounting flow of illegal immigrants—in addition to tougher enforcement of employer sanctions and the creation of
a computerized databank for all entrants on visitors' visas (52 percent of
illegals are tourists, overwhelmingly non-Mexican, who overstay their
visitors' visas)—is to make it unnecessary by creating jobs in Mexico.
That was one of the ideas behind the North American Free Trade Agreement. In the long run, NAFTA will create jobs in Mexico, which will reduce illegal immigration as well as guarantee more purchasers for
American goods.

On one of my early visits to Mexico, I met Carlos Salinas de Gortari,
who was then the budget director in the administration of President
Miguel de la Madrid. Although he was a key player in de la Madrid's economic reforms, many people considered him too much of a technocrat
to become the next president. He was small, thin, bald, and mustached,
and he looked more like an accountant than a leader of ninety million
people who, on the whole, still respected machismo. In the course of our
conversations, I raised the possibility of free trade between the United
States and Mexico. Salinas rejected the idea, saying that the differences
between the two countries and the history of United States intervention
argued against such a union.

Salinas took office as president in 1988 and embarked on the next phase of Mexico's bold economic and political reforms. He continued to cut the budget deficit. He lowered tariffs unilaterally, privatized vast segments of the public economy, and moved aggressively against tax evaders and corrupt labor-union leaders. These economic reforms required foreign investment to generate new jobs in place of the jobs lost in economic restructuring. In 1990, Salinas went to Europe to seek closer economic ties with France and Germany. To his surprise, they weren't interested. The French were worried about GATT and the European agricultural policy. The Germans were preoccupied with unification and had little capital for investment in Mexico. Even Spain was more interested in investing in Europe than in the New World. Salinas returned to Mexico emptyhanded and discouraged.

Salinas then went to Japan. Indeed, he was a bit of a Japanophile (he sent his children to the Japanese school in Mexico City). He dreamed of making Mexico a Pacific power, and Japan was the crucial relation. It had amassed billions in investment capital in the 1980s, and Mexico's economic reform should by now have made it attractive to investors. After Mexico took advantage of the debt rescheduling under the Brady Plan, some American capital began to flow south, but not enough. Unfortunately, when Salinas arrived, Japan was in the midst of a real-estate crash, which resulted in plummeting wealth, and his overtures to Japanese businessmen were virtually ignored.

Only after his rejection by Europe and Japan did President Salinas contemplate the unthinkable. The United States remained the only alternative. In 1990, aware of the history of conflict between the two nations and the anti-American sentiments of Mexico's intellectual elite, Salinas nevertheless proposed that Mexico, the United States, and Canada be made a free-trade area. It was a startling step, based on the assumption that such a free-trade area would convey enough stability to financial markets so that foreign investment would skyrocket.

President George Bush, himself a veteran of Mexico's oil business, saw the opportunity and negotiated an agreement. When the Clinton administration came to power, it was decided, after much internal debate, to support NAFTA, adding side agreements on environment and labor safeguards to the original text of the agreement. NAFTA, it seemed to me, could be comparable to the Louisiana Purchase in its long-term influence on the character of America and its strategic implications for our future. It was an opportunity that might never come again.

The congressional debate focused almost entirely on the economic aspects of the agreement, and in particular on the number of jobs it would generate or lose. The labor unions asserted that NAFTA would lead American factories to head south of the border, where wages were lower. The supporters of NAFTA argued that the agreement would create a larger market for American goods, since Mexicans purchased 70 percent of their imports from the United States. Furthermore, it was argued, the United States, Canada, and Mexico as an economic unit would be stronger in relation to competitors such as Japan and Germany than any one of us could be alone. The result would be job creation in the United States. The figure both sides in the debate settled on was two hundred thousand jobs: supporters said that it would create two hundred thousand jobs, and opponents said that it would cost that number. In an economy where the creation of two million new jobs per year is not unusual and a hundred and thirty million jobs exist overall, it was a minuscule number. Although any job loss is painful to the person losing the job, and every politician has to be sensitive to his constituents' legitimate troubles, the job issue ought not to have been the paramount aspect of the agreement. Issues of political structure and social integration were equally important.

When the peso crisis hit at the end of 1994, it was clear that Mexico, with its paltry savings and dangerous dependence on foreign capital, was not nearly as resilient as half a dozen Asian countries. The new Mexican President Ernesto Zedillo Ponce de León recognized that regaining economic balance required more than the international guarantee of fifty billion dollars, which had stemmed the panic. The broad support that comes only with true democracy was now his only hope, even if it risked ending the one-party rule of the Institutional Revolutionary Party (PRI). Zedillo dissolved the Supreme Court, proposed a judicial-reform law, offered amnesty to the Chiapas rebels, assured a fair gubernatorial election in the state of Jalisco, and appointed a lawyer from one of the opposition parties to the sensitive post of attorney general.

Whether all these changes will be enough to ensure stability cannot be foretold. The economic deterioration has certainly stunted NAFTA. An economy in free fall is not a good customer. The difficult reduction in the number of agricultural workers that NAFTA would anyway entail becomes harder in a country that is generating few new jobs in the nonagricultural sector. Even with a U.S.-led infusion of capital to shore up the value of the peso, the outcome of the crisis remains uncertain, but the direction toward greater integration with the U.S. holds steady. Besides, Mexican stability has always been underestimated. Zedillo is counting on its continuance as he seeks to rekindle economic growth with strong free-market policies. There are too many human bonds across too much American territory for thoughts of severing ties to be relevant. Mexico's refusal to lurch back to a protectionist, state-dominated economic approach is in part due to the interdependence that NAFTA has created. The realization grows that Mexico's future is part of our future (and vice versa), for better or worse, so Americans need to take the long view.

Carlos Fuentes has said that the difference between the United States and Mexico is the difference between eighteenth-century England and sixteenth-century Spain. NAFTA in the long run offers a chance to bridge that social and cultural gap. Free trade would regularize and normalize contact between Mexicans and Americans. It would transform many border cities. Mexican culture—its art, its architecture, its literature—would begin to shape how Americans think about themselves. Slowly, mestizo history would become as accessible as Taco Bell. American influence on Mexico, meanwhile, would contribute to Mexico's post-NAFTA political evolution (as it already has) by relentlessly pushing democracy and greater governmental accountability to all Mexicans. The agreement itself would amount to a sign of American respect and acceptance after two centuries of neglect. Mexicans and Americans—like Canadians and Americans—would increasingly come to think of each other as brothers, not "others."

Americans would also discover new aspects of their own past. Woodrow Wilson's five-volume history of the American people does not have one sentence about the sixteenth-century Spanish period in the Southwest. Charles Beard's 1927 sixteen-hundred-page history of America devotes only a few pages to the accomplishments and impact of the Spanish. But Samuel Eliot Morison gave due respect to Spanish exploration. By integrating Mexico through NAFTA, we would be absorbing a historical tradition as well as a market. We would be integrating Spanish history into our own history, thereby escaping the denial and distortion that have prevented us from learning from our Spanish ancestors. We would finally be acknowledging in a new way the triumph of Ponce de León, de Soto, Cortés, Coronado, and the other Conquistadors.

Mexicans in turn would come to see the country in which twenty-one million of their relatives live not as an arrogant and dangerous foreign country, but as a nation whose people wanted to chart a new life together with them. As the diverse but still Anglo influence of the United States mixed with the diverse but still Spanish-Indian influence of Mexico, the people of both countries would be enriched, and out of that interaction would evolve a distinctly North American (or—as some Europeans still refer to us—"New Worlder") society.

THE RECOGNITION of difference among peoples of the world and citizens of America need not be divisive if it springs from curiosity and is tempered by tolerance and goodwill. These democratic virtues provide a bond that can hold together a disparate and increasingly fractured world. The insistence that all Germans are suspect because of the Holocaust is little different from the anti-Semitic mindset that characterizes all Jews as Shylocks. The same mindset that sees only similarities among Chinese, Japanese, and Koreans sees no differences between Cubans and Mexicans. The various ethnic perspectives brought here by the immigrants are as indispensable to our understanding of this free land as are the ancient beliefs of the Native Americans. Asian American immigrants in the 1980s added much-needed economic dynamics to every community they made their home. The arrogance of majority status, whether in religion or culture or everyday impulse, is rooted in ignorance. America is at its best when it is flexible instead of rigid, and respectful of individual citizens, instead of enamored of an unimpeachable elite.

Knowing how difficult a meshing of worldviews is even at the family level, I can appreciate how challenging such a course would be at the level of statecraft. But anything less is superficial and in the long run doomed. Respecting and paying attention to another's values and assumptions about life are important. JFK's visit to Mexico is still remembered there, in part because he visited the basilica of the Virgin of Guadaloupe. Ronald Reagan's visit to Danilov Monastery in Moscow sent the right message of respect for the faith of millions of Russian Orthodox believers. Yet even more important than such symbolic visits is building the connections of insight, understanding, and commonality among all societies—an imperative undertaking if the world is to become more peaceful and more prosperous.

Accentuating difference tends to make us forget our common humanity, yet it is this individuality that shapes a person's identity. Such is the guiding paradox of America. Taking American diversity as an opportunity to understand another point of view reveals it as a real American strength. The inability of many whites to get beyond the stereotypes of Chinese or Japanese or Mexicans or Cubans simply denies the potential for our own enrichment. Conversely, the refusal of some minority people to give whites any benefit of the doubt—much less to trust them—further isolates us from one another.

Herman Melville wrote, "We are the heirs of all time, and with all nations we divide our inheritance." In that sense, America has been generous with its bounty and its spirit. In the process, America has become with each succeeding wave of immigrants a more significant society. That is the way it will always be, if our actions follow our creed. America for the first time in history could be a world society, organized on liberal-democratic principles. Like the blacks, Indians, Portuguese, Manxmen, Nantucketers, and Polynesians on Melville's *Pequod,* but with a different fate, we can help each other when the task is clear and our determination is strong. New Americans add energy, dynamism, and hope. New Americans add freshness and new insights. New Americans in tune with the cultural rhythms of India, China, or Brazil can propel American exports throughout the world. New Americans possess the ability to hold multiple perspectives simultaneously, and in their contact with the rest of us enrich our future. In the invocation to his great poem "John Brown's Body," Stephen Vincent Benét wrote about American diversity:

> All these you are, and each is partly you,
> And none is false, and none is wholly true.

16

Across the Great Divide

I HAVE STRUGGLED with the issue of race for most of my adult life. On its face, racism is stupid. Common sense tells us that no one person is exactly like any other person. Each is unique. Race as a category in a multiracial society should ideally have very little meaning.

America is not yet such a society. Cursed by two hundred and forty years of slavery and more than one hundred years of systematic and degrading discrimination against blacks, and buffeted by generations of black survival techniques, white guilt and denial, and racist assumptions and actions, America is a nation obsessed with the interplay between African Americans and white Americans.

Like most Americans, I grew up with black and white difference and distance all around. No racist incidents took place in Crystal City, and many blacks had factory jobs, earning the same money as whites. Nevertheless, there was a clear division in town, revealed most obviously in the housing arrangement: all the town's blacks lived together, in "Old Town," a small neighborhood a few blocks from my home. From an early age, I knew that the way some of my white friends regarded black people was wrong. Wanting to be accepted by my schoolmates for who I was and not because of who my father was made me sensitive to others who were also looking for acceptance. When kids derisively called me "the banker's son," I didn't like it. I didn't like being attacked for something I couldn't change, and I knew that what people called each other reflected their feelings. Friends could say things to each other in jest that if said to a stranger might offend, but I was sensitive even to that kind of gentle name-calling. When I was an NBA rookie, the Knicks' captain, Willis Reed, started calling me "Bradley" rather than "Bill." It annoyed me, and finally, at an airport one day, I said, "Willis, you call every other player on the team by his first name. Would you please do the same for me?" He smiled and said, "OK . . . Bradley."

When I was fourteen, Central High School in Little Rock, Arkansas, was forcibly integrated by order of President Dwight Eisenhower. On television, I saw the federalized National Guard troops, helmeted and uniformed, escort black students into the high school through taunting white mobs. It all seemed so foreign from Crystal City, where I had been playing Little League baseball with black friends since I was nine, where an African American was vice-president of his newly integrated high-school class, and where every afternoon, for three hours alone in the high-school gym, I practiced my basketball moves, pretending I was Elgin Baylor.

But, as I reflected later, I didn't have one black female friend at the time. I had never danced with a black partner. No one in the town had declared interracial dating an issue; such associations were simply taboo. I had been as brainwashed as anyone when it came to the question of who was beautiful and who was not, and in Crystal City the issue was buried so deeply that it never surfaced.

The fundamental issues of race have to do with identity in a society that proclaims equality but until the late sixties had antimiscegenation laws on the books. In America, a person who has one documented black ancestor is considered black by the U.S. census, however far removed that ancestor is. This "one-drop" principle originated at a time when slaveowners wanted to claim as many slaves as possible, even those with "one drop" of African blood. The categories of our discourse don't allow for multiracialism. Gone even are the days when the census would classify people as mulattoes, quadroons, and octoroons. The current census categories force a person to be either white or black. These narrow categories deny the reality we see with our eyes. Americans of color are not all black or all white. They are a mixture of hues that should define their individuality, not their sameness. In a society where racial consciousness does not dominate, racial variety can be an individual attribute, not a category so broad that it blocks us from seeing personal uniqueness. To label someone as multiracial who needs the comfort and support of black identity is wrong. To deny someone the option of asserting mixed parentage and a multiracial identity is also wrong. The key, it seems to me, is to allow people to define themselves.

When I went to Princeton, I developed a broader understanding of the history of race in America. A course on the Civil War introduced me for the first time to the Reconstruction as a time of black achievement. My basketball success pitted me against better and better players, who were often African Americans, and in all-star competitions my roommates on the road were often black. Gradually, the impulses of my high-school days became the convictions of my college years. Racial discrimination became the ultimate evil for me.

The civil-rights movement of the sixties broke the racist grip on America. It was as if the country had been awakened from a bad dream, with an invitation to a better future. What made the movement striking was its summoning up of an American conscience, rooted in American ideals and based on a powerful message of redemption. The movement's oratory extended the Christian metaphors that Abraham Lincoln had used during emancipation and war, and breathed new life into their meaning. What drove the movement—in addition to its talented leaders, such as Dr. King, who shared his "dream" and told us about the view from the "mountaintop"—were the thousands of people of all races and religious faiths who boarded the freedom caravans, sat at lunch counters, refused to go to the back of the bus, and marched in orderly protests. For me, a photograph in *Life* of white Catholic nuns from St. Louis marching in Selma said it all. Their civil disobedience anticipated arrest, and they welcomed arrest as a part of their moral act. The movement, though mostly black and clearly with social and political equality for blacks as its goal, achieved a universality that superseded race. It challenged all Americans in a very personal way, asking each of us to displace exploitation of others with respect, and alienation with love. The moment was full of hope for those who lived through it. Sadly, the moment passed.

I remember one hot July evening in 1967, walking into the common room of our barracks at Air Force Officer Training School in San Antonio. The news was on TV, and there were shots of tanks in the streets and soldiers with guns and helmets.

"Where is this?" I asked, wondering if we were at war somewhere other than in Vietnam.

"It's Detroit," someone said.

I stood in a state of shock. Detroit? I had read about and seen pictures of the Watts riot in Los Angeles two years earlier, and also of disturbances in Harlem, Jersey City, Birmingham, Jacksonville, Chicago, Cleveland, and Milwaukee, but now American tanks were patrolling the streets of Detroit and the National Guard was occupying Newark. The march toward greater equality seemed stalled, or maybe even derailed. The war in Vietnam had sucked up the country's resources, and now, with urban riots in which people broke the law not as a moral act of civil disobedience to bring about a greater good but simply in defiance of the state, I feared the disappearance of political consensus for reform.

The disturbances of the late sixties—unlike the race riots in Wilmington in 1898, Atlanta in 1906, and Chicago in 1919, which had been started by whites—presented an inexplicable phenomenon. Why would African Americans, approaching a peak of political influence, seek to lash out blindly at white America? I have never heard a good explanation. Some suggested that the rioting flowed from the civil-rights movement itself, which had lowered barriers so that black anger could burst into the open. Some said that television news, by bringing the power of protest into living rooms, had encouraged other groups of African Americans to imitate the techniques of protest but without the moral and substantive underpinnings of the civil-rights movement. Others blamed leftist political radicals for naïvely attempting to turn the dismantling of Jim Crow and the widening of black opportunity into a class movement aimed at overthrowing the "power structure." Apologists for the rioters said that the violence kept the focus on unaddressed social and economic conditions and simply evidenced black insistence that they be dealt with. A less charitable view was that the criminal element within the African American population had decided that they could break the law without consequences and did so without regard for the inevitable white backlash. Still others pointed out that automation was creating rising desperation and high levels of black unemployment, displacing unskilled African American factory workers in Northern cities just as the mechanized cotton picker had displaced them two decades earlier in the South. Whatever the reason, the violence precipitated a polarization between blacks who regarded themselves as victims and whites who resented black claims. Many whites felt betrayed by the violence and perplexed about how it could possibly promote the agenda of love and justice that lay at the core of the civil-rights movement. Biracial cooperation suffered.

The re-emergence of Richard Nixon and the splintering of the Democratic Party, as well as the spread of urban disturbances, provided the backdrop for my actions and aspirations. Vietnam dominated the concerns of people I knew. I had friends who were writing speeches and organizing for Eugene McCarthy and friends who were working for Bobby Kennedy. For them, change would be found in direct political action. I wasn't ready for politics yet.

Then, one evening in April 1968, a black teammate called me. I could tell he was crying. "Someone has shot Dr. King! Dr. King's been shot! What's going to happen next?" I hung up and turned on the television. Robert Kennedy, campaigning before a black audience in Indianapolis, said:

> Martin Luther King dedicated his life to love and to justice for his fellow human beings, and he died because of that effort. . . . Those of you who are black . . . can be filled with bitterness, with hatred, with a desire for revenge. . . . Or we can make an effort, as Martin Luther King did . . . to understand . . . with compassion and love. . . . For those of you . . . filled with . . . distrust at the injustice of such an act . . . I can say that I feel in my own heart the same kind of feeling. . . . I had a member of my family killed. . . . But we have to make an effort in the United States, we have to make an effort to understand. . . . What we need . . . is not division . . . not hatred . . . not violence or lawlessness; but love and wisdom, and compassion toward one another and a feeling of justice toward those who still suffer within our country whether they be white or . . . black.

His conviction seemed to comfort the crowd, and his message of calm had a credibility unlike anyone else's in America. I thought, A few more weeks in the season, then Oxford. Then I've got to do something in support of better race relations.

A year earlier, in 1967, I had decided not to take my exams at Oxford but to join the Air Force, play pro ball, and then return to complete my degree in politics, philosophy, and economics. Now I had to make up for the two Rhodes Scholar years I had spent reading biographies and novels, traveling, and doing a modicum of course work. I returned and took up residence at a motel on the outskirts of town. After surveying the two years of work on which I would be tested, I laid out a study plan for the remaining forty-five days and started in. Just as in my freshman year at Princeton University, when I saved myself from academic embarrassment by an intense period of twelve hours of study a day, I thought I could do a large part of two years' work in six weeks. About three weeks in, I knew it would be impossible, but I kept going. I ate all three daily meals at the motel restaurant, visited none of the pubs, and called none of the friends with whom I had whiled away my time from 1965 to 1967. My only diversion was the television set in my room.

That was the spring of the student revolt in Paris. The English-speaking French commentator on the BBC, who looked like Yves Montand, and Tariq Ali, the Oxford Pakistani radical who was the BBC's expert on the student left, predicted widening revolt. Danny the Red—Daniel Cohn-Bendit, the leader of the French students on the barricades—and his cohorts provided me with a gripping break from moral philosophy, economic theory, international relations, and comparative political institutions. Then, on June 5, one week before exams, I turned on the BBC and there was the kitchen of the Ambassador Hotel in Los Angeles.

Robert Kennedy had been shot on the night he won the California primary. For the next five days I dropped much of my exam preparation and just watched television. It had been Robert Kennedy—in the summer of 1964, before he became a U.S. senator from New York—who spoke to Washington interns in the big ballroom at the Sheraton Woodley Hotel. He said that public service was a noble profession and politics a crucial skill. He urged us to accept less comfort ourselves in order to give more Americans a better chance. He asked us to excel at being human. He made a profound impression on me, and I was not alone. In 1966, the Oxford basketball team, which was composed almost entirely of Americans, had voted to forfeit its quarter-final game in the English championships in order to hear him speak at the Oxford Union. I also remembered his visit, earlier in the spring of 1968, to the Medical Center at Indiana University, where he told the young medical students that they had it too easy and that they ought to care for the poor. I remembered his rapport with Chicano leader Cesar Chavez, and his visit to Pine Ridge, South Dakota, to call attention to the poverty on Indian reservations. I remembered the respect he accorded to party politicians and union members, and the respect and loyalty they showed in return. I remembered the metaphorical torch he carried—the torch signaling the approach of a better world.

Whether he stood on car tops in South Africa or Poland or Watts or Toledo, people literally reached out to touch him. He embodied the promise of his brother's abbreviated presidency, but he extended it with his own separate style. His contradictions were obvious: he was ruthless and gentle, idealistic and operational, decisive and hesitant, optimistic and fatalistic. He attracted and repelled at the same time. His speaking style was halting, full of a staccato depiction of American reality, not a soaring evocation of America's past greatness. He often seemed to cut against the grain. He might not have made it to the nomination. He seemed different—more truth teller than politician, and truth tellers rarely win the political prize. On the night he was shot, he had only five hundred and twenty-five delegates—less than half what he needed for the nomination. But if he had won the presidency, I believe America would have been noticeably different. The America of Richard Nixon or even of Jack Kennedy would not have been the America Robert Kennedy would have helped to shape.

Robert Kennedy seemed to have a deeper level of conviction, a fuller capacity for love, a keener perception of evil, a more complete understanding of the fragility of life than most political candidates. He came to the presidential spotlight after his brother had been assassinated and the nation had gone through the convulsions of sorrow and lost possibilities, followed by the escalation of war and then the explosion of race violence in cities. Like Lincoln, who allowed one of his in-laws, the widow of a Confederate officer, to live as a family member in the White House during the Civil War—or like FDR, whose valiant and uncomplaining struggle against polio gave heart and hope to a nation flat on its back economically—Robert Kennedy confronted the ironies of his times every day, within his immediate and intimate life experience. America's trauma was his personal trauma to a surprising degree.

As I sat in the Oxford motel watching the funeral at St. Patrick's Cathedral in New York, I heard Senator Ted Kennedy say that his brother was "a good and decent man, who saw wrong and tried to right it, saw suffering and tried to heal it, saw war and tried to stop it." I saw the shots of people saying farewell along the route of the funeral train as it headed south from Penn Station to Washington, where he would be buried near Jack at Arlington National Cemetery. Now, almost thirty years later, when I take the train from New Jersey to Washington, I can conjure up the faces of the people on television back in 1968 who lined the railroad tracks—the Irish of Harrison, the Italians of Newark, the blacks of Elizabeth, the Poles of Linden, the Hungarians of New Brunswick, the Princeton students, the Trenton steelworkers, the office workers of Burlington, the Quakers of Philadelphia, the Presbyterians of Wilmington, the Catholics of Baltimore, the housewives, the veterans, the trainmen—all who stood silently and watched. Occasionally, they lifted their hands to wave goodbye. At times, they saluted. Some were crying. "The good, they die young," as the song goes.

Ten days later, I finished my exams with a sigh of relief, earned my degree by the slightest of margins, and went on to Harlem, where I had agreed to spend the summer in the Urban League's Street Academy Reading Program. I worked in a storefront office at the intersection of Lenox and 116th Street. The summer was full of memorable characters. Harv and George were two young white Christians who had transferred their lay ministry to the streets. Harv was a barrel-chested man from Paterson, New Jersey. George, bespectacled and curious about people, had come to Harlem by way of suburban Chicago and Princeton. They had a black partner named Herb, a former gang member gone straight. Every day, these three negotiated the terrain of poverty programs and private philanthropy, of emerging black nationalism and Black Muslim consciousness. One of the Muslims they met was Hammas, a teacher of Islam, who captivated George, as he would later sway Lew Alcindor to become Kareem Abdul-Jabbar. Every meeting of the Street Academy team had an intensity I'd rarely known, and yet, at the same time, each day was filled with the monotony that makes up many poor people's lives. On weekday mornings, I took the A train up Eighth Avenue from 50th Street to 116th Street and walked two blocks east to the storefront, where I arrived to hear stories of the previous night's confrontations. I wrote a fund-raising brochure, so that potential corporate sponsors would understand how a street school worked, and I analyzed different strategies for building black capitalism in urban America. Twice a week, I conducted a reading class for about eight young male students. We read books about the African empire in Timbuktu and about the history of African Americans in this country. I was reading many of these books for the first time.

A white friend of mine who worked in the program was stabbed in the back one morning in broad daylight as he walked through Morningside Park. He left the city and went back home to Florida. People advised me not to stay in Harlem after dark, but for me that was when the street life became interesting. People sat on the stoops or hung out the windows, while their radios blared. Groups of men played dominoes or cards, shot dice, just talked. It was a new world for me, so different from Crystal City or Princeton or Oxford.

Two days a week, I left work a little early and took a train to Philadelphia, where I played in a summer basketball program called the Baker League. During my rookie year in professional basketball, I had failed to make it as a guard. Too slow to handle quick players, I had played expecting to make a mistake, and I usually did. I had become hesitant and frustrated. Much ridicule had been heaped upon me. Angry patrons at Madison Square Garden threw coins at me and spat at me from the exit overhang when I went to the dressing room. People accosted me on the street and called me a bum. Cabdrivers berated my ability.

There was only one way to proceed. I needed to sharpen my basketball skills for my second year with the Knicks. "If you're not practicing," Ed Macauley, one of my basketball mentors, once said, "remember, someone somewhere is practicing, and, given roughly equal ability, if you two ever meet, he will win." I was determined that during my second year I was not going to fail because I hadn't made the effort.

Ninety percent of the players in the Baker League games that summer were black. Nearly all of the games took place in the small gym of the Bright Hope Baptist Church, whose pastor was the father of the future congressman William Gray. Our team, Jimmy Bates's B-Bar, was coached by a slight, milk-chocolate-hued African American named Sonny Hill. He was a sweet-talking, energetic Teamsters' union representative with encyclopedic basketball knowledge. He encouraged me with observations and pointers, and, more important, he gave me playing time, so that I got back some playing rhythm. He was just the right person for me that summer. In the final game, Jimmy Bates played Gaddis Real Estate, whose best player was the great Earl "the Pearl" Monroe. I scored fifty-two points; Earl scored sixty-three. Gaddis won in double overtime—but I was back.

As time passed in pro ball, more African Americans became distinct individuals to me. Yet I often saw other people reacting to my teammates because of their skin color and not the quality of their personalities, and then I became deeply offended. I never made commercial endorsements, in part because I felt they were offered to me because I was a "white hope" as much as because I was a good player. Racial harmony on the team and in society became a compelling imperative for me.

For ten years, from September to May, I traveled across America with the Knicks. Basketball was our work—something we did every day, together. During those years, my best-known teammates were Willis Reed, from Bernice, Louisiana, and Grambling College; Dick Barnett, from Gary, Indiana, and Tennessee State; Walt Frazier, from Atlanta and Southern Illinois University; Dave DeBusschere, from Detroit and the University of Detroit; and Earl Monroe, from Philadelphia and Winston-Salem State University. We created one of the first basketball teams to capture the imagination of a national TV audience, and we won the hearts of basketball fans in New Jersey, Connecticut, and New York. It was an extraordinary group of human beings.

I wish I had a hundred dollars for every time in the last twenty years that someone—usually a white person—has asked, "What was it like to play on the Knicks and travel with your teammates?"

"What was it like? What do you mean?"

"Well, you know, guys who came from such . . . different backgrounds and had such different interests from yours."

"You mean that most of them were black? That I was living in a kind of black world?"

"Well, yes," they'd say. "What was that like?"

"Listen," I'd say, "traveling with my teammates on the road in America was one of the most enlightening experiences of my life."

And it was. I saw that if you're black in America, you never know when the next moment might bring a slight, a slur, or a slug. One night, after a game, Earl Monroe was standing in the rain outside the Garden and hailing a cab for his girlfriend. Four white guys on the curb started shouting, "Hey, boy! Hey, look at the boy in the rain." Earl ignored them at first, but then one thing led to another until a fight ensued, leaving Earl the morning after with a swollen eye and a seething anger.

Besides enjoying the warmth of my black teammates' friendship and the inspiration of their personal histories, besides seeing the powerful role of family in their lives and the strength of each one's individuality, I began to understand distrust and suspicion. I came to know the meaning of certain looks and certain codes. I found myself in racial situations for which I, as a person of a different race, had no frame of reference. I sensed the tension created by always being on-guard, by never totally relaxing. I felt the pain of racial arrogance directed my way. I knew the loneliness of being white in a black world. And I realized how much I will never know about what it is to be black in America.

I worried about all of that for a while, but then I forgot it, because I'd known for a long time that no one is just black or just white. We are all just human, which means we are neither as virtuous as we may hope nor as flawed as we may think. The essence of humanity is treating one another with respect. Some people do it with words but not with deeds. Some of us aren't able to do it even with words, because we're prisoners of the words themselves. My Uncle Cecil worked forty years in the lead factory next to African Americans who made the same wage and took the same risks, but when my beloved Aunt Bub spoke, she didn't talk about African Americans with respect. She'd say, "I'm just from another age, I guess, but . . ." and then she'd go off on a tirade that would appall me. She didn't hate, but her language was racially abusive. I often wondered how I could love someone who was so flagrantly wrong on the fundamental moral issue our nation confronted. At first, I would get angry and argue with her, and she would be reduced to tears. "But you're still my baby, aren't you?" she would ask. Or I would leave the room. Or I would plead that, no matter what she felt, it hurt me to hear her say it, so would she please stop.

After I left Crystal City for college, I saw Aunt Bub less and less. I'd talk with her on the phone occasionally. "Don't forget you're my baby," she'd say, "no matter how big you get." Or she'd pop up at a Knicks game somewhere, often ready with a postgame comment about my black teammates which would distress me anew. Yet I couldn't forget that she had been my second mother when I was growing up; I wouldn't have dreamed of withholding my love. The conflict was never resolved.

One of the last times I saw Bub, she weighed under a hundred pounds. We sat in the living room of her two-room apartment in Crystal City and she told me about the chemotherapy and the doctors and how Medicare paid her bills and how she was able to live on her Social Security check. She said life had been good to her. She showed me a picture of her newborn grandson and recalled the good old days. ("Remember, whatever happens, you're still my baby.")

Then, right out of the blue, she said, "I'm glad you didn't run for president."

"Why?" I asked.

"Because you would have chosen Jesse Jackson as your vice-president, and then the blacks"—she used another word—"would have killed you." Silence.

She died in 1988, and the most moving tribute at the funeral was a song sung by a black friend of hers—the wife of a local doctor—whom my aunt had obviously loved and who, it was also obvious, had loved my aunt. Had I been wrong about my aunt all these years? Race relations, I thought, were never simple.

In the 1960s, there was a tacit assumption that once the legal barriers fell and more people of both races interacted on an equal basis, as part of a spiritually transformed national community, they would see the foolishness of racial discrimination and abandon it. What happened instead was that discrimination went underground. As law professor Derrick Bell has written in *Faces at the Bottom of the Well,* "Today, because bias is masked in unofficial practices and 'neutral' standards, we [African Americans] must wrestle with the question whether race or some individual failing has cost us the job, denied us the promotion, or prompted our being rejected as tenants for an apartment. Either conclusion breeds frustration and alienation—and a rage we dare not show to others or admit to ourselves."

There is no good answer to this dilemma, particularly on America's number-one equity issue—equal opportunity for employment. Quotas requiring businesses to reflect the area's black population in their workforce regardless of qualifications reduce the process of living together to a numbers game, raise white suspicion and anger, and increase black self-doubt. Doing nothing, however, conveys to those who want to discriminate that they can do so with impunity. Just as school districts in the South resisted integration after *Brown* v. *Board of Education* by assigning pupils to schools on bases other than race—such as supposed availability of classrooms, or the psychological state or mental aptitude of the students—so businesses or landlords intent on discrimination frequently find obscure disqualifications for black applicants. It is in the area between quotas and doing nothing that there is the deepest misunderstanding, the most frequent misrepresentation, and the greatest opportunity. To many whites, affirmative action means ignoring merit and giving blacks special treatment. To many blacks, it means countering racist presumptions and attitudes so that decisions can indeed be based on merit. Both groups have overstated their case.

I oppose quotas, and I believe that affirmative action must have a context to be successful. The more affirmative action is rooted in the search for what Peter Gabel, the president of New College of California, calls a "spiritually transformed civil society," the easier it will be for all people to understand what is being affirmed. Racial justice is more than a numbers game.

I often ask constituents at town meetings if any of them believe that discrimination based on race has any justification. None raise their hands. But what does one do when discrimination occurs? What course of action is available? Most people don't have enough money to hire a lawyer to sue under the civil-rights laws. More important, how does one prevent discrimination? Or, if it occurs, how does one stop it? Or, if it persists, how does one create a remedy for the person discriminated against?

During the debate on the 1964 Civil Rights Act, Senator Everett Dirksen (R.-Ill.) told President Lyndon Johnson that Republicans would join Southern Democrats to filibuster the bill if LBJ insisted on putting in an administrative enforcement mechanism against employment discrimination similar to that used by the National Labor Relations Board in labor disputes. LBJ agreed to remove the teeth from the bill, and now the only way to seek a remedy for discrimination is by filing a lawsuit before one of hundreds of federal judges. Not only does the cost of such a remedy exclude most people who are discriminated against, but federal funds for legal services for the poor are frequently cut from the budget. When people persist for years with expensive litigation until a verdict, judges will offer their own interpretations and issue their own remedies, which will be shaped in part by the racial lens through which they view life. When the separate decisions are compiled into a collective body of work, what emerges is a minefield of muddled thinking.

The Equal Employment Opportunity Commission (EEOC), with ninety-seven thousand unresolved cases of claimed job discrimination based on race or gender, has made a mockery of attempts to counter racial discrimination. Administrative delays go on for years, as lawyers speak of pain in legalese. Lawyers make millions defending corporations against frivolous as well as serious complaints of discrimination. The EEOC can only urge the parties to agree. It can neither force them to do so nor issue a verdict itself. At some point, those who feel discriminated against usually give up on an administrative resolution, and if they can afford it they take their case to federal court, where it can drag on for many additional years. Employment discrimination cases clog federal courts unnecessarily and burden managers in the workplace, who are called upon to supervise complainants while awaiting a decision. But above all, individuals who are discriminated against rarely get relief.

The only way to cut through the delay is to guarantee and shorten the time for an administrative review. Then individuals and employers can have some hope of getting a resolution—yes or no—on a charge of job discrimination. A way to accomplish that objective would be to give the EEOC the same cease-and-desist authority the National Labor Relations Board has. Panels of experts would develop a familiarity with the circumstances of discrimination, and a body of precedent would be created. With such a process adequately funded, there would be less posturing and more decisions in a timely manner—much to the relief of both corporations and of individuals.

The concept of merit-based affirmative action offers much hope. For example, at Harvard, out of ten thousand applicants three thousand are qualified, from which the admissions office selects one thousand. If you're the child of an alumnus, you're given special consideration. If you are an athlete or a fine musician, you are given weighted consideration. If you are from Montana, not Massachusetts, the need for geographical diversity in the freshman class helps your chances. In such a process, once an individual makes the qualified pool of applicants, being black is just another positive attribute for admission to a university preparing people to live in a pluralistic society.

Whites need to be assured that blacks with lesser skills don't get preferences. Blacks need to be assured that if they have shown their ability, they won't be shut out because of subjective racial judgments. That is, of course, what an affirmative-action plan is—an effort to find qualified members of a minority who have been overlooked and who, in a nation insufficiently integrated, don't normally come to employers' attention. As Clifford Alexander, the first black chairman of the EEOC, wrote in 1991:

> If you are starting an affirmative action program at your company or institution, you develop your plan in a systematic and businesslike

way. You assess your present utilization of minority workers in each
job category. Then you determine the percentage of black people with
skills, knowledge and ability to do the job where you recruit your
workforce. When there is a significantly smaller percentage present in
any job category than those who are available with requisite job skills,
you set up a plan of action to close the gap. That plan, as with all other
aspects of management by objective, sets a specific goal and a timetable
for reaching that goal. . . . Nowhere in the presidential executive orders, or in federal regulations requiring the development of affirmative action plans by government contractors, does anything require a
preference for black people. . . . Nowhere in an affirmative action plan
is there any discussion of giving something extra to black people or any
provision for hiring black people who do not have qualifications to do
a specific job.

To hire blacks of lesser talent so that your company's image is politically correct violates the law and endangers all of affirmative action's
gains. Some benefits and programs that posture as affirmative action are
nothing of the kind. For example, it is indefensible to grant giant tax de-
ferrals to companies in the name of affirmative action because they sell
radio and TV stations to firms owned in part by well-to-do minorities.
Looking beyond the easy hiring of black superstars, however, takes leadership. Former Texas Governor Ann Richards once said that she simply
had to tell her staff that a position would remain unfilled until they found
a talented black. With a little more effort, they found a talented black.
But how we determine talent—test scores, performance reports, academic record, trajectory of personal growth—remains subjective.

IN 1991 AND 1992, I gave a series of speeches on relations between blacks
and whites in America. The first speech came about by chance. In the
summer of 1991, President George Bush, still basking in the glow of the
Persian Gulf War, had favorability ratings of 80 percent. Few Democrats
dared criticize him. One evening I was walking through the Senate
Democratic cloakroom and a TV set was blasting the evening news. Bush
was saying that a civil-rights bill, which had been pushed tirelessly by
Republican Senator Jack Danforth, was "quota legislation," and that, if
the quotas were not removed, he would veto it. I stopped to watch the
rest of the segment, and my anger started to rise. I saw his remarks as a

harbinger of the 1992 political campaign and a signal that he would once again play the race card.

Several times in my Senate career, I had encountered blatant racism. In the early 1980s, the issue of Bob Jones University emerged. Bob Jones University, in Greenville, South Carolina, did not allow interracial marriages or interracial dating among its students, and said that the religion of its ruling body prohibited it from doing so. The IRS revoked its tax exemption, and the university contested this decision. The Reagan administration sided with Bob Jones. The Bob Jones case became an issue because the Reagan administration had proposed a bill to grant tax credits to parents of children in private or parochial schools, and since a May 1983 Supreme Court ruling did not clearly outlaw all varieties of favorable tax treatment for a university that discriminated based on race, all subsequent legislation had to be explicit about prohibiting racially discriminatory practices in any recipient of a federal-tax benefit. During the summer of 1983, the bill was making its way through the Finance Committee. I had committed to support tuition tax credits during my first campaign in 1978, and now I wanted to make good on my pledge. I had initially backed the idea of tax credits (long before my active tax-reformer days) because of the large Catholic-school population in New Jersey and, in particular, because of the role that parochial schools played in urban settings. Often more than 30 percent of the students in these schools were non-Catholic, and 50 percent were black or Hispanic. Under financial pressure, the Newark Archdiocese had begun closing its schools during the late seventies. Tax credits, while benefiting individual taxpayers, would have the effect of making tuition cheaper and more accessible to people. It might also provide some room for tuition increases, which would help the schools' finances. In depressed American cities, the choice was not between public schools and private schools but— given the dysfunction of many urban public schools—between private schools and chaos. At the same time (and it was a fine line), I didn't want to subsidize segregationist academies in the South or the North. So when the administration's bill reached the Finance Committee in the summer of 1983, I insisted on language that clearly stated that parents could take the tax credit only if their child went to a school that did not discriminate on the basis of race.

Late one July afternoon, Reagan's assistant attorney general for civil rights and several other Justice Department lawyers came to my office.

They were reluctant to support the antidiscrimination provision I was proposing. I was incensed; I told them that if they wanted my support for the credit, it had to have the nondiscrimination provision. The proponents of the nondiscrimination language won on a vote in the Finance Committee, with no help from the assistant attorney general. In November 1983, the amended bill failed on the floor, with the Reagan administration making only a token effort to support it.

The next time I experienced racism in government policy making was that October, when Jesse Helms opposed making the birthday of Dr. Martin Luther King, Jr., a national holiday. When he alluded to what he called Dr. King's "action-oriented Marxism," I hurriedly wrote and delivered a scathing speech that charged him with playing the old Jim Crow politics. He wasn't at all fazed. He seemed to be saying, "This is just how I get re-elected in North Carolina."

In 1988, the race card was played more subtly. The Bush presidential campaign skillfully linked the Democratic candidate, Michael Dukakis, with a black man named Willie Horton, who had raped a woman and stabbed a man while on furlough from a Massachusetts prison, where he had been serving time for murder. Oddly, the first politician to mention Horton (but without racializing it) was not Bush but Senator Al Gore. In the New York Democratic primary that spring, he attacked Dukakis for his prison-furlough program. The Republicans, though, emphasized Horton's blackness. They didn't discourage an independent committee from running a TV ad with Horton's picture in it, and simultaneously Bush referred to Horton on the stump. Republicans denied exploiting the race issue, claiming that the ad was about crime, not race. Few people believed them. Dukakis's postconvention lead vanished in part because of this shrewd linkage of black violence to his record as governor of Massachusetts.

So, in 1992, when Bush labeled Danforth's bill a quota bill, something in me snapped. I knew Bush was not a racist. (Ultimately, he signed a version of the bill.) He was a decent and honorable man who had an admirable sense of public service. He had always been a moderate Republican who was considerate of staff and believed in playing by the rules. Yet he was obviously doing this for political reasons. For me, it was a sad flaw in his character. I decided that if he intended to use race to get votes again, he would not do so with impunity. I wrote a speech that detailed Bush's record on race issues. I asked him to explain why, as an unsuccessful candidate for the U.S. Senate from Texas in 1964, he had opposed the Civil Rights Act of that year. In making the speech on the Senate floor, I laid out the economic losses that black Americans had sustained during the Reagan years. I quoted Bush as saying one thing to a black audience and then doing something quite different. I questioned his ability to lead on the issue of race and his interest in doing so. I talked about his go-along attitude during the Reagan era, when twenty years of progress on race relations almost came to a halt. I asked Bush to tell the American people how he encountered race as an issue in his own life. I challenged his convictions and said that as a political leader on race relations he had failed to further the country's long-term best interests.

Two weeks later, in a second speech, this one at the National Press Club, I tried to do what I'd asked President Bush to do. I described my own racial awakening during childhood; I talked about the meaning of my years with the Knicks, and I recounted what I had learned during my travels as a senator, listening to the voices of black people.

The best political minds had counseled me to talk about race only before a targeted (meaning black) audience. Advocating aid for urban America, which was a part of the speech, was generally interpreted as taking from whites to give to blacks, who by implication lacked personal responsibility. To call America to a higher moral ground or to highlight black self-destruction risked alienating both races. For a white person to push black Americans to broaden their own self-perception was thought by the experts to be as likely to succeed as the prospect of finding, in Derrick Bell's words, "a white Michael Jordan." The political battlefield was littered with the corpses of good intention and high ideals. But as I thought about their comments, I became more centered than I had been for years. I knew I could no longer listen to the voices of perpetual caution. I knew I had to find a way to say and do what I felt most deeply.

Since 1968, the winning side in American politics had been the side that played on white fears by using black stereotypes to pit white against black. Lyndon Johnson had sensed such an outcome when he said after passage of the 1964 Civil Rights Act that he thought it was good for America but bad for Democrats. When the civil-rights movement was displaced by radical politics and the protest marches became urban riots, Richard Nixon knew he had the law-and-order issue. Bobby Kennedy had never tolerated violence as a means to achieve a political objective. As attorney general, he had been the nation's top cop. But Bobby was gone. Now Nixon put Democrats on the defensive. For the next twenty years, virtually every Republican presidential candidate used the tactics that Nixon had pioneered. They worked. The racist actions of these Republican candidates were subtle. They targeted their listeners by direct mail or telephone or they used code words. They didn't advertise their views. They just made sure that enough of the "right" people knew them.

I told the reporters that in 1992 things would be different. Because of Bush's record of opposition to the 1964 Civil Rights Act, there was an opening for counterattack. His position would be indefensible once it was known. Most independent voters and liberal Republicans did not consider themselves racist; many were progressive on race. They would be appalled to learn that Bush had opposed the desegregation of lunch counters and hotels.

Not one reporter who asked about the speeches suggested that I had been motivated by moral reasons; other than African American reporters, only a few remarked that I had shown courage or raised issues of national importance. To many journalists, a politician's actions boiled down to politics; in this case, the questions were about what the speeches did for my supposed presidential aspirations. Earlier in my life, I had fought against the public's impulse to regard athletes only as dumb jocks. An athlete has a brain, and a politician has a heart. The denial of intelligence in one and moral sensibility in the other is stereotypical thinking.

Racial consciousness often prevents white people from seeing their own interests clearly. This is particularly true among Americans of modest means. Today's white workers, under strain from downsizing, global competition, and the application of information technologies, see affirmative action as a fundamental threat to their economic well-being, notwithstanding that many more whites lost their jobs in the 1982 recession alone than black workers have been helped by court-ordered affirmative action since the program began. The point is that the bond between working people is economic. It is against the common enemy of poverty and declining opportunity that blacks and whites and others should be able to find common ground.

Thirty-seven million Americans live in poverty. Ten million are black. Nearly fifty-four million Americans earn under thirty-five thousand dollars a year. Slightly more than eight million of them are black. Almost six million of the country's ninety-seven million households earn over a hundred thousand dollars a year. Of these households, 170,028 are black.

When it comes to distribution of wealth, the disparity is even greater. The median net worth for white households in 1991 was $44,408. For black households, it was $4,604.

The problem of the poor is inadequate economic growth unfairly shared. When growth soars, the wealthy benefit disproportionately, which partly explains why the wealthiest 0.5 percent of Americans own 37 percent of the financial assets and 56 percent of all private business assets. When economic growth plummets, the wealthy lose, but they have more flexibility and options to protect themselves than do the poor, who stand defenseless, watching their jobs go and their savings dwindle. For politicians in tough economic times to take the frustration of white workers and channel it toward black workers bespeaks a callous meanspiritedness. It will do nothing to improve the standard of living of either poor whites or poor blacks. Affirmative action didn't cause poverty, and if there were no affirmative action poverty would remain. The African American that a poor white has to make room for because of affirmative action seems insignificant as a job threat in comparison with government mismanagement of the economy or companies that fire workers for short-term boosts to the bottom line. If whites of modest means could see their class interest as clearly as they see what they think is their racial interest, they would stand a chance of advancement—perhaps even through interracial political solidarity.

But even well-off whites need to see how racism hurts their long-term self-interest. In this global economy, America can't compete with the burden of an increasingly larger population in poverty or just above the poverty line. A society 40 percent of whose citizens have high skills, 40 percent low skills, and 20 percent no skills cannot be a prosperous society. If America can't offer all its citizens the hope of a higher living standard through work, then the American dream will become a nightmare and we will all be at each other's throats. Only by reducing poverty sharply and providing increased job opportunities will America be able to maintain its optimism.

Racial thinking obstructs America from seeing how to reduce poverty, because many in the white majority view many blacks as undeserving and unwilling to work. But to refuse more resources to fight poverty because you don't want to help blacks actually hurts more whites than blacks, because poor white people outnumber poor black people by thirteen million. Only by reducing poverty, the bulk of which is white, can Americans achieve economic security. Only by ending racial thinking can America sharply reduce poverty. White America has to see its own self-interest clearly.

Nowhere is the issue of race more urgent or less candidly faced than in urban America. Race and the American city are inextricably bound together in fact and in the public perception. The people who live in America's cities are poorer, sicker, and less educated, and their circumstances are more violent than at any point in my lifetime. The physical problems are obvious: old housing stock, deteriorated schools, aging sewers and bridges, a diminished manufacturing base, a doctor-starved health-care system that fails to immunize against measles, much less educate about AIDS. The jobs have disappeared. The neighborhoods have been gutted. The tax base has withered. A genuine depression has hit cities, with unemployment in some areas at the levels of the 1930s. Rather than devising ways to cut poverty, too many politicians talk only about affirmative action or welfare.

What is less obvious in urban America is the crisis of meaning. Without meaning, there can be no hope; without hope, there can be no struggle; without struggle, there can be no personal betterment. Absence of meaning, derived from overt and subtle attacks from racist quarters over many years and furthered by an increasing pessimism about the possibility of justice, offers a context for chaos and irresponsibility.

Development of meaning starts at the very beginning of life. Increasingly, large numbers of children are not getting the attention or the resources they need. Too many grow up without fathers. More than 40 percent of all births in the twenty largest cities of America are to women living alone. Among black women, more than 65 percent of births occur out of wedlock. In 1961, when I left Missouri for Princeton, 13 percent of the children born in St. Louis were born to single mothers. In 1994, that number had jumped to 68 percent. Among African American women in St. Louis, it was 86 percent. The children of these mothers are in general poorer and less attended to than they would be in a two-parent household. The uncertainty of life for the single mother produces frequent uprooting and relocating, which further disorients the child. Though many single mothers raise their kids successfully, there are millions of others who are too young, too poor, and too unloved. Many of their children are thrown out on the street early, without any frame of reference except survival. These children have no historical awareness of the civil-rights movement, much less of the power of American democracy. They become ticking time bombs, ready to explode in their own and our nation's future.

To expect kids who have no connection to religion, no family outside a gang, no sense of place outside "the 'hood," no imagination beyond the cadence of rap or the violence of TV, to find meaning in their lives is like expecting them to find water in a desert. If you don't believe me, just ask a group of young black males how many of them are fathers. Only a few hands go up. Then ask them how many have made babies. Most of them raise their hands; sex to them has little to do with love and nothing to do with fatherhood or responsibility. Nor can they be expected to believe that government is on their side. Their contact with government has not empowered them, it has diminished them. They see government at best as incompetent (look at the schools, the streets, the welfare department) and at worst as corrupt (the cops and building inspectors on the take, the white-collar criminal who gets a suspended sentence, the local politician who molests children). And replacing a corrupt white mayor with a corrupt black mayor won't make the difference.

They find their role models elsewhere. The prevalence of crack and cocaine makes a bad situation into a disaster. A Los Angeles police officer told me that a search of a fourteen-year-old's bedroom revealed more than twenty-one thousand dollars in cash stuffed in the mattress— the booty of the drug trade. For every kid with twenty-one thousand dollars in his mattress, there are hundreds dodging the police and making forty dollars a night selling cocaine vials on the streets. They dream of becoming a drug kingpin, not a mayor, or a principal, or a minister. In such a world, calls to "just say no" to drugs or to study hard for sixteen years so that you can get an eighteen-thousand-dollar-a-year job are heeded by only a few. The culture of crack undermines our most cherished virtues. Instead of desires rooted in the values of commitment and service to community, as expressed in black churches and mosques, desires become rooted in the immediate gratification of the moment. Our mass media feed this lust with messages of conspicuous consumption, and these kids become trapped in the quicksand of American materialism. Television sells provocative images of sex, violence, and drugs, regardless of their corrosive effects on the work ethic and sense of community that informed an older generation. And with no awareness of how to change their world through political action and no reservoirs of self-knowledge, these children are buffeted by violence and swamped by narcissism.

Every day, the newspaper tells of another murder in the inner city. Both the number of murders and the number of other violent crimes has doubled in the twenty largest cities since 1968. Ninety percent of all violence is committed by males, and they are also its predominant victims; indeed, murder is the highest cause of death for young black males. Fear covers the streets like a sheet of ice. Visit public-housing projects where mothers send their kids to school dodging bullets; talk with young girls whose rapes go uninvestigated; listen to elderly residents express their constant fear of violation.

What is new is white fear of random violence. Suburban subdivisions used to advertise by promoting the pleasures of outdoor life or the prestige of the community. Now they advertise personal safety, with guards and gates. To a white person, no place in a city seems safe. Walking the streets is often likened to Russian roulette. At core, this fear is a fear of young black men. Never mind that in a stereotypically racist society, all black men have to answer for the violence of a few black men. Never mind that Asian Americans fear both black and white Americans, or that in Miami and Los Angeles some of the most feared gangs are Latino or Chinese. Never mind that the ultimate racism is whites ignoring violence when it isn't in their neighborhoods, or that black Americans have always felt afraid in certain white neighborhoods. Never mind all that.

There are two phenomena today. There is white fear, and there is the appearance of black emboldenment. Today, many whites, responding to a more violent reality heightened by sensational news stories, see young black men traveling in groups, cruising the city, looking for trouble, and they are frightened. Many white Americans, whether fairly or unfairly, seem to be saying of some young black males, "You litter the street and deface the subway, and no one, black or white, says stop. You cut school, threaten a teacher, 'dis' a social worker, and no one, white or black, says stop. You snatch a purse, you crash a concert, break a telephone box, and no one, white or black, says stop. You rob a store, rape a jogger, shoot a tourist, and when they catch you, if they catch you, you cry racism. And nobody, white or black, says stop."

It makes no difference whether this white rap is the exact and total reality of our cities: it is what millions of white Americans believe. In a kind of ironic flip of fate, the fear of brutal white repression felt for decades in the black community, and the seething anger it generated, now appear to be mirrored in the fear whites have of random attacks from blacks. White scorn grows when a cowed white politician convenes a commission to investigate a black lawyer's charges of racism, and the anger swells when black spokespersons fill the evening news with threats and bombast. White disgust hardens when black citizens fail to criticize a black official who is corrupt, incompetent, or hateful.

Most politicians avoid confronting the reality that causes the fear. They don't want to put themselves at risk by speaking candidly to both blacks and whites about violence and saying the same things to both groups. In effect, they appear indifferent to black self-destruction. And black violence only hardens this indifference—not just to the perpetrators but to all African Americans.

But when politicians refuse to talk about the reality that everyone knows exists, they cannot lead us out of our current crisis. I will never forget a visit in Newark with a nine-year-old girl who had AIDS, contracted at birth from a heroin-addicted mother. She lay in the hospital bed playing with a coloring book. She had a big sore under her nose that wouldn't heal. The doctor took a toy rabbit from his pocket and gave it to her. She smiled and cuddled it to her face. "We're just trying to make her comfortable," the doctor said quietly. "She'll soon die at home. Ten percent of Newark will die of AIDS by 2000 and many of them will be children." (By 1995, more than ten thousand people had died of AIDS in Newark. The doctor's prediction seems on target.)

I have often felt that the future of urban America will take one of three paths: abandonment, encirclement, or transformation.

Abandonment means recognizing that, with the growth of suburbia (thanks to subsidized single-home ownership and highway systems), corporate parks, and the malling of America—and with communications technology advancing so fast that the economic advantages of urban proximity are being replaced by the computer screen—the city may have outlived its usefulness. Like the one-company small town whose industry leaves, the city, some say, will wither and disappear.

Encirclement means that people in a city will live in separate enclaves. The racial and ethnic walls will go higher. The class barricades will be manned by ever-larger security forces, and communal life will disappear. City politics will amount to splitting up a shrinking economic pie into ever-smaller ethnic, racial, and religious slices; it will be a kind of *Clockwork Orange* society, in which the rich will pay for their security; the middle class of all races will continue to flee, and the poor will either be preyed upon or join the army of violent predators. What will be lost for everyone will be freedom, civility, and the chance to build a common future.

Transformation means winning over all segments of urban life to a new politics of common effort. Answers won't come only from the elite who determine what the new society will look like. Instead, the future will be shaped in large part by the people from inside the turmoil of urban America. Transformation requires listening to the disaffected and the powerful alike. Transformation is as different from the politics of dependency as it is from the politics of greed. Its optimism relates to the belief that every person can realize his or her potential in an atmosphere of nurturing liberty. Its morality is grounded in the conviction that each of us has an obligation to another human being simply because that person is a human being.

William Watley is the pastor of St. James African Methodist Episcopal Church, which sits on Martin Luther King, Jr., Boulevard halfway up the Court Street hill, overlooking downtown Newark. Reverend Watley grew up in St. Louis with his father, mother, two grandmothers, and a great-grandmother. He was raised in the crucible of the black church (with its unique role as the center of black spiritual, social, political, and economic life), where his father, after years as a common laborer, felt the call and became a preacher. He made sixty-five dollars a week, and the family lived in a modest parsonage next to the church in Kinloch, an all-black community in St. Louis County. They often visited relatives in Festus, where Watley's father had a good friend who was also an AME pastor. Watley remembers the Saturday mornings of playing badminton and horseshoes in the yard and evenings of listening to the assembled pastors preaching their sermons to each other and sharing the techniques that stirred their congregations. He recalls that Ed Collins, a high-school basketball star for Kinloch and a member of Watley's father's church, was asked one Sunday around Christmas why he had a long face and replied, "I ran into Bill Bradley." (Crystal City had beaten Kinloch in the Normandy Christmas Tournament.)

Reverend Watley's first awareness of race came when the integration of Little Rock's Central High School dominated the news. He was seven years old. His mother used his questions about the Little Rock Nine to explain the racial past of America, to convey that there were still white Americans who didn't affirm the rights of black people, and to emphasize that, whatever the swirling racial currents in white America, he should know that he was just as good as anyone else. When he was eleven, the family moved to Carondelet, in German South St. Louis, where he attended his first integrated schools. Slowly his racial consciousness began to take shape. In the sixth grade, he wrote an essay on the injustice that blacks had encountered in America. "I couldn't go to the movie theater that my white classmates went to," he recalls. Watley went to Beaumont High School in St. Louis, where he did well enough in academics and school activities to be named in 1963 for Boys' State, an assemblage of outstanding high-school students. Six blacks, out of seven hundred and twenty delegates, attended the statewide convention that summer. But Watley, familiar with the politics of the church, was like a fish in water. He ran for state treasurer of Boys' State and won. The audience at the convention gave him a standing ovation for his speech. More important than the victory was his encounter with a black female counselor, who encouraged his college ambitions. She opened the door for him at St. Louis University, telling the college recruiter that, while his academic record was just above average, he would not disappoint them if the university would just give him a chance. He was awarded a scholarship that covered tuition, but he continued to live at home, which he believes kept him rooted in the black community. To supplement his scholarship, he held numerous jobs—working in the library, selling *Collier's* and Fuller brushes door to door, and selling ladies' shoes at a local department store and furniture at a place that, as he puts it, offered terms of "one dollar down and one dollar a month for the rest of your life."

After St. Louis University, he entered a seminary in Atlanta. For his fieldwork, he was invited by a friend of his father's in the AME church to minister to nine hundred black migrant farm workers in southern Pennsylvania. It was in this ministry that Reverend Watley first encountered blacks exploiting blacks. A worker would be paid fourteen cents for a bushel of tomatoes, but the black crew leader took two cents for Social Security and two cents for the "bonus plan." (If the workers stayed until the end of the picking season, then the two-cent deductions were returned to them as bonuses.) The crew chief also charged the workers for food and transportation, so that by the time they got to the fields they were deeply in debt. When the workers got sick, the crew leader would lend them money for the doctor or dentist but charge fifty cents on the dollar as interest. When people in the barrackslike housing weren't feeling well, the crew leader sent in the German shepherds. On occasion, when manpower was low, a crew leader would go to Baltimore, find drifters, get them drunk, throw them in the back of the truck, and drive back to the farm, having made them an offer they couldn't refuse.

After his educational summer in Pennsylvania, Watley returned to the seminary in Atlanta more determined than ever to fight for justice. Along with his heavy academic load, he pastored a church of two hundred and fifty people, about a hundred miles north of Atlanta, where he carried a pistol during services because of death threats from neighboring white landowners. He graduated from the seminary first in his class.

From Atlanta, Watley went to New York, entering a joint Ph.D. program at Columbia University and Union Theological Seminary, and began pastoring at various churches in the area, eventually leaving the East to become the president of Paul Quinn College in Waco, Texas. There Watley says he discovered that he was no Texan, and in 1981, after a disagreement with the chairperson of the school's governing board, he was relieved of his duties. Deeply hurt and in doubt that he would ever pastor again, he and his family moved back with his parents. For eight months he drew unemployment and began to sort out his life. He experienced the proverbial "dark night of the soul." In 1983, he took a position with the Consultation on Church Unions, headquartered in Princeton, New Jersey. Less than a year later, he was offered the post at St. James and, after much prayer and reflection, took it.

His goal was to make St. James central to the lives of the Newark community. He instituted Thanksgiving Day and Christmas Eve candle-light services and, in a real innovation, added a Wednesday service at lunch hour. The community responded, flocking to listen to his message of hope, which was delivered in powerful style. Membership grew to more than three thousand. Attendance swelled from an average Sunday turnout of one hundred people to three hundred for the 7:30 a.m. service, six hundred for the 10:45 service, and seven hundred for the Wednesday noon service. Equally important, he reached out to the white community, appearing at Chamber of Commerce events to offer invocations and seeking to be the pastor for all Newark. The first time he spoke at the Newark Council of Higher Education, several of the representatives from the New Jersey Institute of Technology, Rutgers Newark, Essex County College, and the New Jersey College of Medicine and Dentistry did not even know where St. James was located. The office of the editor of the state's major newspaper, the *Star Ledger,* sits two blocks from St. James, overlooking the vacant lot that is the site of Reverend Watley's dream, St. James Preparatory School.

"When you tell people that a black church wants to build a high school in Newark," Watley says, "people look at you as if to say, 'You must be kidding.' " But St. James, which numbers three hundred teachers among its members, established a long-range planning committee, and that committee has recommended that St. James build its own preparatory school, starting with two hundred and fifty students and increasing to five hundred. Watley sees the school emphasizing education in a global context that is at once technical and ethical. Businesses tell him that they can train someone to operate a computer but they can't make people ethical. By emphasizing the cross-cultural, Watley acts on his belief that the fiercest competition for the next generation will come from Asia. He recounts a story of a visit to China, where out in the countryside a small boy walked up to him proudly and said, in crystal-clear English, "Good morning, sir." Impressed, Watley decided to see that those young people who attend St. James Prep would have the same multilingual capacity. In addition to providing a basic education, he wants foreign languages, international studies, and technology as required disciplines at St. James Prep. "Ain't gonna be no more white guilt to scare up," he says. "Unless inner-city kids learn to function in a global context, they're not going to make it."

The spirit behind the effort is very much out of his experience at Paul Quinn College, and similar to the rationale of the United Negro College Fund. "Part of our job is to take kids with sixth-grade educations and prepare them to go to MIT," he says. He wants to touch kids as he was touched by the counselor at Boys' State. He wants to take not only A students, but also C students without much interest in academics, and turn them on to education. "That's why it has to be in Newark," he says. "If you can make it in Newark, you can make it anywhere."

Watley is trying to raise ten million dollars for the school, which, as the architects have conceived it, will be a five-story structure with a state-of-the-art library, media center, and gymnasium. In addition to classrooms and administrative offices, there will be a credit union, a family-development center which will provide primary health care, and a bookstore to serve the needs of the wider community. From his members he has raised one million dollars in contributions, which sits in a bank account, and from other sources he has received another $1.5 million. If he can raise an additional two million dollars, he can get a bank-able loan for the rest, and the professional consultants hired by the long-range planning committee have shown that, with tuitions of fifty-five hundred dollars annually, he can cover the cost of operating the school and paying the debt service on a $6.5 million loan. Reverend Watley says that there is still extreme skepticism in Newark's white commu-nity, even though he has received some corporate support along the way. In a city where only 25 percent of the eleventh graders passed reading, writing, and math proficiency tests in 1992 (statewide it was 74 percent), Watley's dream seems ambitious. Yet, given per-pupil expenditures in the Newark public schools of $10,700 in 1992, his tuition seems reasonable and his openly moral vision offers even more.

Reverend Watley's efforts illustrate that beyond the state and the market lies the civil society. That's where citizens such as Watley demonstrate leadership. They are working in their neighborhoods, with or without government funds. They are there because of a commitment to their neighbors. With the erosion of manufacturing jobs and the flight of middle-class blacks to the suburbs, their presence is often the only thing that stops a neighborhood from drifting into chaos. A creative gov-ernment policy would entail not establishing another giant centralized bureaucracy but providing resources to institutions and people, who are already doing the jobs in the neighborhoods while struggling against the odds. What prevents us from adopting a fresh approach are the old bat-tles between Democrats and Republicans, liberals and conservatives, about the relative roles in our society of government and the private sector.

I believe that through self-reliance, discipline, and determination a person can overcome virtually any obstacle, achieve any goal. But I can also imagine forces beyond your control—ill health, violent disaster, economic trauma—that overwhelm your prospects. While conservatives preach the sufficiency of self-help, urban schools become warehouses rather than places to learn, black infant-mortality rates and black unem-ployment rates skyrocket, and a generation is lost to guns in the streets. Self-help is important, and initiative deserves reward. But the struggle for equal opportunity in economic, educational, and political matters, as well as real progress against poverty and crime, do require the help of government. Transformation means both a deep renewal from within urban America led by authentic local voices and help from the outside that recognizes the insufficiency of local resources.

THE ISSUE of race in the context of contemporary American views of what is liberal and what is conservative came alive with great force when, in 1991, President Bush nominated Clarence Thomas, an African American conservative, to fill the seat on the Supreme Court being vacated by Thurgood Marshall. The drama began when the president held a press conference and quickly denied that race was a factor in his decision. He mounted no campaign, made no major speech, and rallied no group of Americans; instead, he said that "Judge Thomas's life is a model for all Americans, and he's earned the right to sit on this nation's highest court."

Many subtle and not-so-subtle messages were contained in Bush's nomination of Judge Thomas. The messages were that Thomas had not needed government help, so why should help be extended to others; that white America had no responsibility for the failure of blacks; that racism hadn't held Judge Thomas back, so why were other blacks always whining about its effect on their lives; and that an administration that nominated a black for the Supreme Court had answered the critics of its racial policies.

I struggled with the president's assertion that Clarence Thomas was "the best person for this position"—thinking about the seven hundred and fifty thousand lawyers in America, the ten thousand judges, the five thousand law professors. I thought about the eight hundred and seventy-five black judges and the two hundred black law professors. I thought about the American Bar Association's "average" rating of Thomas. I had to disagree with the president.

Although Judge Thomas said in his confirmation hearings that he would be impartial on questions of law, the skill of a judge is not some mechanical, computerlike balancing act. Since the Supreme Court dispenses justice, what goes into one's conception of a just society will have an influence on decisions, as would one's reading of American history, with its tensions between liberty and obligation, freedom and order, exclusion and participation, the dominant culture and the countless subcultures, the individual and the community. Where a justice placed himself in our historical narrative depended on how thoroughly he had learned our past, how insightfully he had read his times, how well he knew himself, how clearly he thought about his values.

Clarence Thomas presented himself to the Judiciary Committee for confirmation just as President Bush had introduced him to the public—by highlighting the personal. He chose to emphasize not his reading of the law or his political philosophy, not his public record, but, rather, his politically attractive personal journey. When questioned, he constantly referred back to the personal, as if he were a candidate repeating a sound bite.

"I don't think there was a dry eye in the house," said the president of Thomas's opening story about growing up in Pin Point, Georgia, in a poor family at a time of blatant racial discrimination.

The great African American novelist Richard Wright, in writing about his book *Native Son,* gave another view of such tears: "I found that I had written a book which even bankers' daughters could read and weep over and feel good about. I swore to myself that if I ever wrote another book, no one would weep over it; that it would be so hard and deep that they would have to face it without the consolation of tears." Fifty years after Wright penned those words, America couldn't afford to sentimentalize black life. Significant parts of the African American community were being devastated and were self-destructing daily. We should have been taking Wright's "hard and deep" look.

To see Clarence Thomas's story as one of solely individual achievement was a dangerous mistake. I didn't diminish his personal accomplishment or discipline. I admired them. But even on this personal level, what he chose to share of his story was missing a lot. It was a story of overcoming odds, of hard work, of tremendous dedication and self-reliance. But it was also a more complex story, involving an authoritarian grandfather, women who had sacrificed themselves for the man of the family, a dedicated group of nuns who had given guidance and inspiration, luck (as he said, "someone always came along"), historical change (the civil-rights movement), and affirmative action by Holy Cross and Yale. Clarence Thomas's philosophy of the 1980s implied that only self-help was necessary, but his own life experience refuted that view. Self-help was necessary, but far from sufficient.

Thomas's self-help story didn't ring true for those not lucky enough to have gotten even the small breaks. But the conservatives loved it. Who needed the state at any time in life, if all of us could make it on our own?

Who needed Social Security or college assistance or health care for the poor, if all of us could make it on our own?

As I watched the confirmation process, I became profoundly saddened by its limitations and by what it did to Thomas. People who had known him since his college days agreed on one thing about him. Not Pin Point, Georgia; there were Pin Point, Georgia, stories in the lives of millions of Americans, both black and white, who had struggled against the odds. The thing that had separated Clarence Thomas from other people and had marked his individuality was his point of view: he was an outspoken conservative. He had worn conservatism like a badge, until his confirmation process. In doing what he perceived to be necessary (or what he had been told was necessary) to attain one of the most important positions our country offers, he had allowed himself to be manipulated into the ultimate indignity—being stripped of his point of view. In his Pin Point beginning, racism had denied him his individuality. During the confirmation hearings, he denied his own individuality through his refusal to assert those views that had given his genuine identity, as opposed to his racial identity, its boldest definition in the first place.

Thomas might have been a good friend with a great sense of humor and a high moral character. One could have been all that and still not have been a person we would want building the legal framework for our children's future. I found his record troubling, his performance before the Judiciary Committee puzzling, and his life experience potentially an important influence on the present court. His nomination posed a fundamental question for me: Did one make the judgment about him on the basis of his individuality or his race? Did one vote against him because of his record, or for him because, as Maya Angelou had said in an op-ed column about Clarence Thomas, "he has been poor, has been nearly suffocated by the acrid odor of racial discrimination, is intelligent, well trained, black, and young enough to be won over again"?

Given the heightened and proper sensitivity to blackness in the last twenty-five years in America, one asked whether there was something latent in Thomas that would blossom if he had lifetime tenure. Would his rigidity, his reactionary views, his intolerance be replaced by a more flexible, balanced perspective?

Some people argued that Thomas was unpredictable and might just bite the hand of those who had advanced and promoted him for his conservatism. Blackness, they said, will prevail over individuality. By blackness, they presumed a set of experiences that led to views that were not necessarily liberal, but were different from Thomas's stated positions. But what was the essence of blackness? A common sharing of the experience of oppression? A common network of support to nurture the spirit, mind, and body under assault? A common determination to add to the mosaic of America that which was uniquely African American? A common aspiration that all black Americans could live with dignity, free from racist attacks, overt discrimination, and sly innuendo—and without deep, lingering distrust of white Americans? Yes, all of these commonalities, and probably many others I had never even thought of, went into blackness, but would they offset Clarence Thomas's political philosophy and his public record, both of which ran against the common currents of black life? To assume such a sea change was irrational. It denied him the individuality that was God's gift to every human being. Qualities of mind and character attach to a person, not to a race.

Thomas's paradox was real. The individuality that had allowed him to survive in a world of hostile, dangerous racism was the individuality that seemed to have made him numb to the meaning of shared experience. Those who called Clarence Thomas the "hope candidate" did not mean hope in the transcendent sense of "Keep hope alive." Instead, they hoped that those qualities which had characterized his individuality up to that point could be transformed. I doubted that it was possible. I doubted that he could be "won over again." Therefore, it was on the basis of his individuality, as I had been allowed to know it from his public record, his professional work, and his confirmation process, that I cast my vote against Judge Thomas. I made that decision and said so before Anita Hill ever arrived on the scene.

FRIDAY MORNING before Election Day in 1992, I was in Detroit, at the hotel inside the airport terminal. It was 7 a.m., and I was doing sit-ups in front of the TV. The *Today* show was broadcasting a fragment of an interview with President Bush taped the night before on his campaign plane. Sensing defeat, Bush looked exhausted. "What is your strategy for turning things around?" the interviewer asked, and "What about Iran-contra?" Then Bush was asked a question I had publicly asked him in the Senate speech in 1991, and that I had urged countless reporters to ask him for more than a year: "Why did you oppose the 1964 Civil Rights Act?"

Bush said something about states' rights, that he was wrong to have done it, and that when he was wrong he admitted it, unlike Governor Clinton. I felt a small moment of triumph. At least he had had to answer the question, even if it was four days before the election, in only one of many interviews. He had had to face his record on race relations.

My last stop in Detroit that day—I would fly home to New Jersey that afternoon—was Pershing High School. The student body was 85 percent African American and 15 percent Kaldean (Iraqi)—the latter being part of the 1980s immigration wave. The event was to be a joint appearance with Senator Don Riegle of Michigan. I got there early. Kids were standing in front of the school and I went up to them and started talking. I asked them questions, but I didn't identify myself as a U.S. senator. They were suspicious at first; then they loosened up. "Where are all the TV cameras?" one kid asked. "They're over at Bloomfield Hills," said another, referring to one of Detroit's wealthy suburbs. "They only come here when there's bad news."

It was October 30, and that night would be Devil's Night, which in Detroit had become a night of violence and fire setting. The previous year there were sixty-two fires, but things were looking up; in 1984, the number had been four hundred, and one of them had burned down a whole apartment building. In 1994, more than three hundred teenagers would be arrested for violating the Devil's Night curfew.

"What are you guys going to do tonight?" I asked.

"Stay home," they said.

"We're not going out."

"Too much danger on the streets tonight."

"I don't want no trouble; I'm staying home, even if the fellas come to get me."

Riegle arrived, and as we walked into the high school, I noticed a middle-aged black man talking with the vice-principal. He had tears in his eyes. I asked him what was the matter. He said that several nights ago his son was walking home and some Kaldeans had pulled up next to him in a car and made a derogatory remark. His son had said something back to them. They had taken out a gun and shot him in the neck. Now he was in the hospital. "He's a good kid, and I just wanted to tell the principal and the counselor why he's missing class," the father said, as he headed out the door.

In the board room off the principal's office, Riegle asked the vice-principal, "Can I do anything for you?" The vice-principal shook his head and took a deep breath. "There's too much, Senator. This is the first year of open enrollment in Detroit, which means that any kid can go to any high school. We were prepared for eighteen hundred, but because we're regarded as a good school, twenty-four hundred arrived. We've had to get extra teachers, because classes are not allowed to be larger than twenty-four. We're still a little overwhelmed."

Schools in urban America are beset by multiple problems: students in poor health, streets filled with danger, buildings in disrepair, families without enough parental time and less take-home pay, teachers who are overworked and called upon to ensure safety as well as teach mathematics and history, administrators who become detached from the crisis and make holding on to a paycheck more important than improving the school, state legislators who mandate higher test scores without providing the needed resources and thereby force pragmatic principals to sacrifice genuine education and teach for the test, and parents who hate sending their children into a cauldron of drugs and blood but don't have any good alternatives.

How can you expect a school such as Pershing to succeed (even though it sometimes does) when it has to deal with so many of the non-educational needs of its students? And Pershing is one of Detroit's better schools. How can we expect urban schools—which, on average, are funded at levels 36 percent lower per pupil than suburban schools—to produce the same results? Or how do we enforce accountability and inspire performance in urban schools such as Newark's, which get per-pupil funding similar to wealthier districts but have facilities that are falling apart after one hundred years of use? Increasingly, as the schools become unable to provide education, students become less interested in learning. There are too many schools in which the 10 percent of the students who don't want to learn and are often disruptive make learning impossible for the 90 percent who do want to learn.

Urban schools offer fewer subjects, fewer labs, smaller libraries, older textbooks, and fewer extracurricular activities, such as sports and music. They cannot compete with suburban schools in any of these areas. Often the money goes for administration and not to the kids. Many urban students feel like the senior at a Camden, New Jersey, high school who told the sociologist Jonathan Kozol, "So long as there are no white children in our school, we're going to be cheated. That's America. That's how it is."

Inside the Pershing High School auditorium, twenty-four hundred kids filed in for the assembly in an orderly way. A fifty-piece marching band that had an overrepresentation of drums played ten times louder than it should have. "Why are there so many drums?" I wondered. The kids continued to file in, and the band played on. When the kids were all seated, the band played on. My temples reverberated from the sound waves. Finally, the assistant principal signaled the band teacher, who signaled the band, but the band played on. The assistant principal motioned vigorously to cut it, and finally, mercifully, the band stopped. I thought, I'm the one who's been gapped generationally. Was this the way my father had felt when my bedroom radio was blasting Buddy Holly, Elvis, and Chuck Berry?

Riegle gave a version of his Clinton stump speech, touting the virtues of the Arkansas governor. I spoke about pluralism, democracy, and the economy, and I said that to really succeed you have to work ("If you're not practicing, remember, someone somewhere is practicing, and, given roughly equal ability, if you two ever meet, he will win"). I said to love your neighbor ("Ask yourself what you owe another human being simply because he or she is a human being"). Quoting a camp-meeting speaker from my high-school days as a member of the Fellowship of Christian Athletes, I said that "those who love you are watching you, and they're expecting the greatest from you." I felt connected with the audience, which seemed to be listening.

I saw these kids as doctors, engineers, philosophers, lawyers, scientists, businesspeople. Yet if they were similar to thousands of other high-school students in urban America, their chances were declining each day. Black children in urban America had to overcome so much merely to start on an equal footing with kids growing up in small towns or suburbia.

I remember a fifteen-year-old African American male from Baltimore who testified in 1991 at a hearing of the Commission on the Future of the African American Male, an ambitious but poorly organized effort to identify the particular problems of young black men. There were three of us on the panel that day—Mayor Kurt Schmoke of Baltimore, a black computer executive, and me.

We asked the young man what he wanted to be, what his hopes were, and what he feared. He said he wanted to be an NBA player, but if he couldn't make it—because he knew that only very few had the ability to make the NBA—then he'd like to work for the CIA or the FBI.

He said that his fears were four. First, he feared that he'd get killed. Seven young men had been killed in his neighborhood in the past year. Second, he feared that his parents would be killed and that he would then lose the world they had created for him, with its opportunity and emphasis on education, and he would have to live with relatives or foster parents who wouldn't care as much about his education. Third, he feared AIDS. "I don't mess around," he said, "but look at the great Magic Johnson. It only takes once." Finally, he said that he knew that if he had the ability to make the NBA he could, but he wasn't sure that, even if he had the ability, he could get into the CIA or the FBI. He feared lingering discrimination.

After we heard his testimony, we looked at each other and shook our heads. This web of omnipresent violence, discrimination, and sexual turmoil has come to define reality for many—too many—urban kids. Here was a young man who wanted to play by the rules, whose values are the values we all espouse, yet he was clearly endangered in a way most other kids are not.

How different life in Detroit is from life in Bloomfield Hills, I thought, just as Newark is different from Short Hills, South Central Los Angeles from Brentwood, Philadelphia from Villanova. The urban kid who wants to do well has to cope with so much. Nobody—not even U.S. senators—wants to face up to the moral bankruptcy that permits these lives to be lost. We are allowing a violent Third World country to emerge in our midst, and we are doing little to avert it.

No one levels about these realities. Most white people look at integration as if it were a one-way street, ignoring how much they have to learn about those who don't look like them. Too many black people, particularly in groups of blacks and whites, look for an excuse, or claim victimization, when confronted with black pathology. White racism lives, but so does black denial. The stakes are too high for either to be tolerated.

We must aim at the behavioral problems—racism among whites and self-destructive behavior among African Americans—or accept the status of a second-rate nation that wallows in hypocrisy, sudden death, and a slowdown of our economic growth. No longer can we keep running away from making decisions. Denial will not remedy our society. Either institute a death penalty that can be administered often enough to test its deterrent value or stop playing politics by masking the revenge impulse as a criminal-justice policy. Either force juvenile delinquents to go to school in prison, and to get drug treatment if they're addicted, or don't be surprised if they commit another crime when they get out. Either get rid of the welfare system and replace it with something else that puts a floor under a family in economic free fall, or stop trotting out a tired old version of the Welfare Queen for racial reasons at election time. Either convict violent offenders and keep them locked up, or don't be surprised if vigilante groups proliferate. Either make control of handguns more common sense than constitutional crisis, or stop decrying murders caused overwhelmingly by handguns. Either talk openly about domestic violence and mobilize community resources against it, or pay the price of repressed emotions and continued abuse of women and children. Either recognize that a job is the best antidote to crime, or be prepared to accept further social disintegration.

The Federal Crime Bill of 1994 was a fine piece of work that included more financing for prison construction, more money for police in local jurisdictions, and more innovations such as special drug courts that will give an overburdened judiciary some relief. Still, it dealt directly with only those 5 percent of the crimes committed in this country that violate federal laws. Only 13 percent of all crime-fighting resources are controlled by the federal authorities. The answer to crime will be found closer to home than to Washington, D.C. What Washington can do is call for a rebellion against violence and measure its progress, so that we aren't all panicked by the latest horror story on the six o'clock news. Joining together as citizens to stop violence requires us to see beyond color to self-interest furthered by civic action.

By the year 2000, 57 percent of the people entering the workforce will be native-born whites. This means that the economic future of the children of white Americans will depend increasingly on the skills and talents of nonwhite Americans. If we allow nonwhite Americans to fail because of our current penny-pinching or our timidity about straight talk, America will become a second-rate power. If they succeed, America and all Americans will be enriched. You cannot separate their futures from our chances. This isn't ideology; it's demographics. All of us will advance together, or each of us will be diminished.

In 1994, according to the National Assessment of Educational Progress taken by the federal Department of Education, only 4 percent of the twelfth graders in the country achieved an "advanced" rating and 30 percent scored "below basic"—that is, they were nonfunctional readers. Among African Americans 54 percent were "below basic." Failure to improve current educational performance will produce a human and national disaster.

If we can't revive the Pershing High Schools of this country—and I doubt that we can do so without radically altering the Detroits—then maybe we need to create boarding-school communities that instill values in the students while educating them. Good teams usually have good coaches. Good platoons have good sergeants. Good schools most often have good principals. In many urban environments, you need institutions that are part platoon, part school, part team, but dedicated to lifting kids to another level of self-perception.

Some will say that I am advocating the removal of the child from the family. I'm saying that even with a good family, a child's chance of success, given rotten schools, dangerous streets, and poverty, is, again, like a game of Russian roulette. In such an environment, the option of a boarding school becomes more a lifeline than a noose. At a minimum, we ought to find ways to support leaders such as Reverend Watley and schools such as St. James Prep. Every year we delay dealing with the larger urban problems, they become more intractable; ultimately, they will be unsolvable. America will rise or fall based on how well we guide, educate, and strengthen those kids in the auditorium at Pershing High School.

So we have come full circle. From a society that practiced two hundred and forty years of slavery and another century of legalized discrimination, we Americans emerged in the 1960s to look at ourselves in the mirror and rededicate ourselves to making the founders' ideals a reality for all Americans. Now, thirty years after that optimism and the moral uplift of the civil-rights movement, we find ourselves facing each other across the great divide—a chasm of racial thinking. The division is based also on education and class, with only the most educated of the black and white races able to keep hope alive. At the same time, there is a growing and threatening emergence of a class of young African Americans detached from all connection to the deeper currents of our national ideals, and a growing number of poorly educated whites perversely ready to blame blacks for their deteriorating economic predicament.

No longer can we indulge ourselves by assuming that we can live apart from the turmoil. Things have gotten too bad. Now it's a matter of survival. Unless we can save the poorest, most disconnected among us, we will not save ourselves.

The more we can see beyond color to the uniqueness of each person, the clearer we can see the reflection of our national potential. The more we can see African Americans as individuals whose hues enliven a multiracial society, the closer we will be to shedding the racism of our history. Only then can we say that America truly works. Isn't that our challenge, to reach out to fellow Americans and mobilize the good people of all races for action, and provide the moral leadership worthy of our ideals? Having shed the peculiar institution of slavery and blown away the insidious aroma of Jim Crow, we stand on the threshold of a new century, hoping not only to contain our negative impulses but to fulfill our best impulses—and the promises of our founders. That can be our particular destiny, to let America be America again.

17

Promises to Keep

URING MY YEARS in the Senate, the middle class has been very much on my mind. Crystal City was middle-class; my family considered itself middle-class. The vast majority of households in New Jersey and America are middle-class, earning between twenty thousand and a hundred thousand dollars a year. Depending on family size, many people who earn more than a hundred thousand dollars a year identify with the middle class. Being middle-class means you have a job and make enough money to live in a house, buy a car, and enjoy a few amenities. You aspire to send your children to college; you want health coverage for your family; you expect to have a pension in your retirement; and for two weeks a year you go on a vacation. You also worry about money, because, as you earn more, you always end up spending more. Above all, you have always assumed that your children's standard of living will be higher than your own, as yours is higher than the standard of living once enjoyed by your parents.

In many ways, the middle class has given America a stability that other nations lack. It serves as the ballast in our ship of state. It is a force for moderation, and it peoples the institutions of our civil society—our churches, synagogues, community organizations, school boards, and civic clubs. The PTA, the Red Cross, and the Elks are quintessential middle-class organizations. Mothers Against Drunk Driving and the Sierra Club are equally middle-class. Over time, middle-class families have changed. Fewer resemble Ozzie and Harriet. Divorce has become commonplace. The need for two parents to work has left less time for the kids and for community involvement. Still, the children of middle-class families are the majority of the young, and they seek to achieve, knowing that most of America is in the same economic boat as they are.

When I worked for tax reform in 1986, I was thinking of the middle class. Because of loopholes in the tax code, too many people with the same income paid different amounts of tax. I believed that many hard-working Americans would be better off if loophopes were fewer and rates were lower; that way, they could keep more of each additional dollar they earned, and equal incomes would pay about equal taxes. In 1991–92, when I sought a new way for individuals to finance their college education (by allowing people to repay government loans as a pre-arranged percentage of their future income), I was thinking of the middle class—not just eighteen-year-olds who, thanks to a college education, could expect at least to double their income over a lifetime, but also mothers who had raised their children and now wanted to go back to school to learn more so they could earn more, and fathers who had lost their jobs and needed retraining to obtain new work. On beach walks in the mid-eighties, when hypodermic needles were washing up on the Jersey Shore, I saw the outrage of middle-class families whose two-week vacations had been blighted, and it hammered home the need for action to stop the pollution. On all these issues, I tried to keep my word to those who work hard and play by the rules. But as America moved into the nineties, middle-class voters became angry and frustrated. Their economic circumstances stagnated, their kids worried about whether they would do as well as their parents, and, as I learned in the election of 1990, politicians paid the price. Yet I believed that what was happening to the middle class was more than a temporary squall. At times, it seemed like a full-scale economic hurricane.

KEVIN DOLAN IS a New Jerseyan who played by the rules. He grew up in a stable Irish immigrant family in the Bronx, where he went to high school. He graduated from Manhattan College in 1968 and shortly thereafter he joined the Marine Reserves. His first job was with Consolidated Edison. During his five years with the big utility, he met his future wife, who was working as a secretary for the FBI. Con Ed sent him to night school to get his M.B.A., but because Con Ed needed engineers and not managers, Kevin left and went to work for Citibank in the mid-1970s.

John Reed, who is now Citibank's CEO, had just taken over the operating group on Wall Street, where Citibank processed all its checks, and Kevin joined his team. They worked from 7 a.m. until late at night, with daily morning and evening briefings. Their objective was to cut costs. Kevin proudly says that he felt he was back in the Marines. Of the dozen recruits who started, only three completed the project. Kevin says that the Ivy League guys felt the work was too hard and dropped out. Reed and his team, by replacing people with computer workstations, eventually reduced the organization's personnel from eight thousand to three thousand.

Kevin's success on the Reed team led to bigger things. He went from the back office to run Citibank's personnel operations in Ohio for a year, and then he was sent to Puerto Rico for three years. He and his wife had three children, and life was good. He was promoted quickly, becoming the head of international personnel. In that post, he developed great expertise in handling pay and tax issues for forty-nine different nationalities, at branch offices in ninety countries. He called the job his "Ph.D." But then, almost a decade after the first layoffs, John Reed, by now the president, brought in the consulting firm of McKinsey & Company to do another analysis, with the goal of cutting corporate staff groups from twenty-four hundred people to a thousand. Kevin sensed that Reed was after a further flattening of the corporation, notwithstanding its human cost. As every person in the organization had to lay out in detail his or her daily activities to the consultants, the anxiety and tension began to grow. With thirty people reporting to him in the international-personnel office, Kevin knew his group was a target. He saw what was coming and left before the ax fell.

From Citibank he went to Shearson Lehman, which, in going global, had a real need for Kevin's international expertise. When he arrived as the head of international personnel, he found only an empty box on the organizational chart. There was no office. He had to set it up and staff it. He traveled 70 percent of the time, establishing offices in Hong Kong, Japan, London, and elsewhere around the world. He was doing well financially—until the crash of 1987, which hurt Shearson's revenues, and the absorption of E. F. Hutton in 1988, which doubled Shearson's over-head. Kevin helped execute the layoffs in Shearson's surplus offices abroad; and then, since his policies and pay programs had been comput-erized and the company was retrenching, his whole management level was eliminated, and he was out of work in his mid-forties. Once again, the computer and the need to improve the bottom line had cost him his job.

After being unemployed for six months, Kevin got a job at J. Walter Thompson, through a Manhattan College networking connection. He spent four years there, modernizing the agency's international-payroll system, bringing his Citibank Ph.D. to yet another company. In late 1987, the agency had been absorbed by WPP, a large British advertising and public-relations company that was looking for diverse, well-priced acquisitions. Things went well for a while but then they turned sour. Nineteen ninety-one was a bad year for advertising, and WPP started cutting the U.S. subsidiaries. Once again, Kevin's job was eliminated. This time he was unemployed for more than a year. He had never felt so powerless.

"I remember walking down the street, looking up at the buildings, and wondering if I would ever work again," he says. "You make tons of calls, and very few people call you back. When they do, they have noth-ing for you. You send out all these letters, and you're constantly getting rejected. It really starts to eat at your ego. Unemployment compensa-tion, when I was out, was three hundred dollars per week, which is twelve hundred dollars a month. COBRA medical [continuing medical coverage] for a family of five, like mine, was seven hundred dollars per month. You're getting twelve hundred, but seven hundred of it goes for medical. So you've got five hundred dollars to live on, for a family of five. We got to a point, when I was out over six months, where there was no more severance and my unemployment was up. I started using a food pantry at one of the Catholic churches. My wife was embarrassed about it. I went up there and started volunteering, and they gave me food. So here I am, a hundred-and-fifty-thousand-dollar-a-year senior vice-presi-dent—board member for a college, and everything else—in a food pantry. You know, bringing food home for my family."

WITHOUT A VIBRANT, innovative private sector, all of us suf-fer. Those who achieve should get their reward. Those who provide the capital and take the risks can move us all to higher ground. But justice has another facet, which requires us to recognize and meet the needs of those American people and places in distress. Without achievement, there can be no prosperity; without justice, there can be no stability. The plight of those who are wounded on the periphery of our society commands our compassion and requires us, morally, to take action, but when those who are caught in the storm are in the majority, it is a different order of problem.

Kevin Dolan eventually got a job with an out-placement firm, for 40 percent less in salary, but he was thankful. Now his career is to help other fired employees weather the storm of job loss. "For me it was a little bit easier than for others," he says, "because I was savvy in the market. I'd learned to work in four different cultures—utilities, banking, Wall Street, and advertising. I was president of my alumni association. I was good at networking. But you give a guy twenty-five years at IBM, fifty-two years old. . . . Financially, he's got kids in college. Absolutely brutal! IBM has a lot of suicides. You put in years at a company, really work hard. They shouldn't be able to just throw you out and say, 'Here's six months' severance,' and it's over! I think our system today is much too severe. Golden parachutes protect the top guys, so there is no empathy. You have safety nets for the poor. But you don't have them for the middle class. I see lots of people losing their car, house, everything they've worked for for twenty-five years. I see lots of marriages breaking up. I see the fabric of our society, middle-class America, being torn apart by this greed for profit. The employees have no voice, no advocacy, and it's wrong."

THE TWO GUIDING ASSUMPTIONS of the Democratic Party for the last forty years have been, first, that the middle class is in good economic shape, so that it does not have to be the object of government's concern, and, second, that the middle class would tolerate and even support a policy that put the problems of the poor at the top of our government's agenda. Today both of those assumptions are false.

To begin with, middle-class wages have been deteriorating for a long time. The journalist Simon Head, in an article in *The New York Review of Books,* points out that production and other nonsupervisory workers, who account for 80 percent of the American labor force, earned an average of three hundred and fifteen dollars per week in 1973. By 1994, that weekly wage had dropped to two hundred and fifty-six dollars, a 19-

percent decrease. Over the same period, output per capita in the nonagricultural private sector increased by 22 percent. Far from receiving the annual 2.5-to-3-percent real wage increases plus benefits that workers got from about 1950 to 1975, workers today are not benefiting from increased productivity. They're losing ground. From 1991 to 1993, median family income dropped by more than a thousand dollars a year. By 1985, one-third of all workers toiled under new labor contracts that included wage freezes or reductions. The economist Frank Levy points out that in the early 1970s the average wage for a worker with a high-school diploma was twenty-four thousand "in today's dollars." Now it is around eighteen thousand. In 1973, it took 25 percent of a family's income to pay for health care, utilities, and housing. In 1993, it took 31 percent. On top of that, in the 1980s the percentage of the workforce with pension plans decreased from 50 percent to 43 percent. But beyond stagnant or declining wages, the middle class faces a bigger problem: the increasing prospect that what they had assumed would never change—their means of livelihood—is now endangered.

America is in the midst of an epochal economic transition, recently described by Peter Drucker in a remarkable essay in *The Atlantic Monthly* entitled "The Age of Social Transformation." We are moving to an information-based economy, in which neither capital, labor, nor raw materials will be as important as knowledge—its use and application. The brain surgeon needs an operating room, but his knowledge is what he makes available to patients. Understanding how to get information about a changing reality will be the essence of knowledge, and, as is the case with capital, those who have learned to acquire it will likely acquire more. The zest for lifetime learning will be the entrepreneurial energy of a knowledge-based society.

As more offices and workplaces use information better, productivity will skyrocket. Teams of individuals with specialized skills will look outward to customers rather than inward to the boss. The computer, telecommunications, and entertainment industries will converge. Home shopping will be common. The successful entrepreneurs will be those talented individuals who harness the Internet or develop a means by which different computer networks can communicate with each other, sharing software and databases. The premium will be on adaptability and creativity. American innovation in the area of information technology (particularly software) is the best in the world, by far. We have leaped ahead of other nations. This decisive advantage will expand our exports, spur economic growth, and generate enormous national wealth. But the flip side of burgeoning productivity is significant job disruption.

As in the earlier transition from agriculture to manufacturing, severe dislocations will coexist with enormous opportunity. The nature of work itself has already begun to change. In what is fast becoming the old days, the industrial sector was epitomized by the automobile assembly line making the same car, and the service sector by insurance-company clerks lined up in rows of identical desks processing the same form; the historical task of a worker was to repeat a process over and over. That was the job. Out of about a hundred and thirty million jobs in America, roughly ninety million still amount to repetitive tasks. With the advent of information technology and automation, each of these jobs is endangered by a machine. In 1994 there were a hundred million computers in the world. By 2000 there will be a billion.

Like millions of Americans, I am not a child of the information revolution. (Since you've read this far, I'll admit to you that I wrote this book with No. 2 pencils.) I've asked countless experts to describe the shore toward which the information wave carries us. As I have come to understand the direction we're heading in, I am in awe of its potential to change life for the better. Still, I worry how many boats will sink before we hit land.

During the 1980s, 1.8 million workers in the manufacturing sector lost their jobs. By 1990, manufacturing employees had dropped from nearly 30 percent of the workforce to 16 percent. The number of steelworkers dropped from seven hundred and twenty-one thousand in 1979 to three hundred and seventy-four thousand in 1992, but the same amount of steel was produced, as the country exported more and imported less. From 1989 to 1993, the job loss in manufacturing surged: nearly another 1.8 million workers lost their jobs, and only six hundred thousand of them got new jobs in the service sector. Drucker estimates that by 2010 the manufacturing sector will employ only 12 percent of all workers.

Joe Biden recently told me that at the Hercules Corporation's research center outside Wilmington, the downsizing has accelerated and become brutal. When employees arrive at their office building on Monday morning, they know they have been fired when they see a Pinkerton Security man standing outside their office door. Usually he tells them that he's sorry and he knows they've worked hard for twenty-two years, but could they please have their desk cleaned out by noon—and if they don't mind, he'll stand at the door, because the company doesn't want to take the chance that the computer system will be sabotaged. On Mondays at the Hercules center, no one carpools, because it's impossible to predict who will be going home at noon.

From the 1960s on, organized labor gave its consent to automation, the major vehicle of downsizing and a precursor to the information age. Instead of insisting on a shorter workweek, so that more people could stay employed, organized labor opted for retraining, so that those who lost their jobs would get the education they needed to fill the jobs that technological change would supposedly generate. In his provocative book *The End of Work,* Jeremy Rifkin notes that from 1960 to 1967 the number of collective-bargaining agreements that included retraining provisions rose from 12 percent to 40 percent.

Having given up on attempting to control the production and work process with a shorter workweek, labor explained the continued job loss and wage stagnation in manufacturing by stigmatizing international competition. At almost every town meeting I hold, foreign competition is cited as the cause of middle-class distress, along with high taxes to support government programs. The claim is that the United States is losing good high-wage manufacturing jobs to cheap labor in Third World countries. The facts don't sustain this view. Using robots and computer-aided design to customize products and deliver them immediately to the consumer is the wave of the future, not uniform assembly-line production. In such a world, having the factory near the market and organized to receive parts just in time for customization will be essential. In an article in the April 1994 *Scientific American,* the economists Paul Krugman and Robert Lawrence note, "The concern widely voiced during the 1950s and 1960s that industrial workers would lose their jobs because of automation is closer to the truth than the current preoccupation with a presumed loss of manufacturing jobs because of foreign competition." We spend only 2 percent of our national income on manufactured imports from low-wage countries. Our competition comes from high-wage countries, and technology is the force that shakes up the job market. Krugman strengthens the case in a working paper published by the National Bureau of Economic Research:

> In 1990 the trade deficit in manufacturing was $73 billion, corresponding to approximately 700,000 manufacturing jobs. In that year,

the average manufacturing worker earned about $5000 more than the average non-manufacturing worker. Thus the loss of "good jobs" in manufacturing due to international competition could be said to have corresponded to a loss of $3.5 billion in wages that year. That may sound like a large number, but U.S. national income in the same year was $5.5 trillion. That is, the wage loss from de-industrialization in the face of foreign competition, was less than 1/15 of one percent of national income.

During the 1980s, the amount of investment made in information hardware led to a veritable upheaval in employment and productivity. One trillion dollars was invested in such hardware during that decade, with more than $860 billion going to the service sector, so that by 1992 every white-collar worker had ten thousand dollars of capital equipment behind him. Deregulation meant greater competition among bloated corporate bureaucracies in banking, telecommunications, air travel, cable TV, insurance, trucking, and financial services. Globally, deregulation brought large foreign investments to the United States, in pursuit of a share of the world's largest market. But these foreign investors also viewed reducing American employees as a quick way to improve the efficiency and financial performance of their multinational companies. (Witness Kevin Dolan and WPP.)

By the early nineties, the gains in productivity suddenly accelerated in the service sector, and from 1990 to 1994 they rose to three times what they were in the 1980s. As the service industries began to discover the potential of their expensive hardware, and software became more user-friendly, they realized how many thousands of workers were unnecessary. As with steel, you could produce more with fewer workers. Eighty-three thousand employees lost their jobs with AT&T between 1991 and 1995. Over the same period, IBM cut eighty-five thousand employees, NYNEX twenty-two thousand, Boeing thirty thousand, Union Carbide fourteen thousand, GTE seventeen thousand, Bank of America twelve thousand, GM seventy-four thousand, Sears fifty thousand, Pacific Telesis ten thousand. One and a half million middle managers alone became victims of the information revolution. With labor costs making up 70 percent of total business-production expenses (80 percent in services) and ninety million workers performing repetitive tasks in the American economy, further reductions in personnel are likely.

The strategies to save labor costs are numerous and reflect the new power of information technologies. "Re-engineering" is a concept that targets any job that requires an individual to do the same thing every day. At IBM Credit, re-engineering collapsed five departments into one, and productivity increased an incredible 1,000 percent. At Bell Atlantic, one department saw its payroll drop from $86 million to $6 million. At Ford, three hundred and seventy-five jobs were eliminated in the accounts-payable department, in an attempt to emulate Mazda, where five people did all the work. The management consultant Michael Hammer, one of the leading proponents of re-engineering, claims that three-fourths of middle management will eventually disappear. "Lean production" is another new management technique that produces more with less, encouraging collaboration between worker and manager, who together, bypassing middle management, constantly tinker with the production process to streamline it. "Out-sourcing" sheds costly workers who have expensive fringe benefits. Chrysler now has outside companies producing 70 percent of its cars, and some economists predict that the out-sourcing market for services in the information sector will increase from $12.2 billion in 1992 to $30 billion by 1997. Finally, temporary workers are increasingly brought in on a project-by-project basis. Manpower, Inc., with its seven hundred and fifty thousand available temporary workers, is one of the biggest employers in America. The Department of Labor in 1987 reported that a full-time worker's average wage per hour was $7.43, whereas the part-timer's was $4.42, and three times as many full-timers got health-and-pension coverage as did temps. The Clinton administration announced that in the first six months of 1993 the economy had created one million two hundred and thirty thousand jobs, but it neglected to say that seven hundred and twenty-eight thousand of them were part-time. When a laid-off TWA mechanic was told about this robust job creation, he said ruefully, "Yeah, my wife and I have four of them."

From the early twentieth century, there has been concern over the question of whether technology creates more jobs than it destroys. In the last epochal economic transition, from farm to factory, there were enough new jobs in industry to offset the decline in jobs on the farm and in homes (Peter Drucker points out that domestic servants were the second-largest part of the workforce in 1900). These new blue-collar workers enjoyed the most dramatic increase in standard of living of any one group in American history. The capacity for job creation also held firm in the early days of automation, as the service sector boomed to pick up the slack in manufacturing. New technology has always generated more jobs at better pay, but now advances in the use and application of information rapidly shrink the manufacturing and service sectors both, creating job loss and drastically lowering purchasing power. At a time when the whole thrust of business is to downsize and the pool of workers performing repetitive tasks is ninety million, the critical question is whether new companies that create new products and services will be able to generate enough jobs at reasonable pay to offset the continued shrinkage. For example, Jeremy Rifkin reports that roughly ninety-seven thousand jobs have been generated in the biotech industry in the last ten years, an industry universally regarded as the wave of the future. Yet, for the national unemployment rate to drop by 1 percent, the information society must create the equivalent of eleven biotech industries. If you stand in the way of technological progress (if that's possible) you risk being labeled a Luddite and you are in effect advocating a lower standard of living in the long run. But to allow the dramatic rearrangement of our work lives with the bottom line as the only guide— though it may immediately yield maximum corporate profits—risks dragging down the standard of living in the short run, and maybe for much longer, for millions of middle-class employees.

Over the last twenty years, American families, who increasingly live with greater uncertainty, less pay, and fewer benefits, have sent mothers to the workplace to make ends meet. By 1990, 45 percent of all married couples worked. Today 40 percent of the children in America live in families where both parents work. If you add the 27 percent of kids who live in single-parent homes, then fully two-thirds of American children have a "time deficit" and often a "resource deficit" with their parents. Lower pay has led to fewer hours of real parenting. Unable to pay for adequate child care, and living apart from relatives, many middle-class families have left their children alone with TV, which has become the storyteller and a persuasive shaper of values. Very quickly, economic stress leads to child neglect—which, in turn, often leads to passivity, poor school performance, even to drug use for many kids, and to marital stress for the parents.

IN SUCH CIRCUMSTANCES, who can the middle class turn to? Churches can't offer sufficient material help. Universities are peripheral.

Unions represent only 11 percent of all private-sector workers. Executives are under their own pressure to produce a better bottom line. Investors don't care about corporations' keeping their word in ways that consider the humanity of each worker. Only government can moderate or prevent the insecurity that the transformation of the American economy has brought to middle-class lives. Only government can balance the clout of private power.

But hostility toward government has been cultivated in many circles for many years. After the hope of the New Deal and the idealism of the Great Society, government popularity went into a long decline. Lately, Speaker Newt Gingrich and the Republicans have successfully stigmatized government by claiming that it is not on the average guy's side but, rather, is the cause of the average guy's problems. The result is that the middle class looks at government and thinks "taxes," not "power." Government has been so devalued that even those who today would benefit most from it have been blinded to its potential.

What can governmental power do to help Kevin, the unemployed Hercules technician, or the TWA employee and his wife working four jobs, or others of the middle class caught in the midst of these swirling changes? First, policy makers must cultivate a certain frame of mind. In her new book, *No Ordinary Time,* Doris Kearns Goodwin points out that when the United States entered the Second World War, FDR sought a partnership between government and business, in order to produce the greatest quantity of war goods in the shortest time. Business, as part of these negotiations, tried to get FDR to back away from the workers' safeguards of the New Deal, such as the minimum wage and the forty-hour week. Even in the midst of war, with the private sector threatening a slower mobilization if these laws were not repealed, FDR refused, seeing the social gains for workers and the elderly as nonnegotiable. FDR was aware that if he showed a willingness to retreat on these hard-won victories, the private interests would push to have even more provisions repealed. By resisting the private-interest pressure, he sent a message about being a strong leader and about what he believed was in the long-term economic interest of America. "While our Navy and our Air Force and our guns may be our first lines of defense," FDR said, "it is still clear that way down at the bottom, underlying them all, giving them strength, sustenance and power, are the spirit and morale of a free people."

Today government must make it clear that reneging on our commitments to the poor is not a prerequisite for helping the middle class. The middle class and the poor alike share a need for a farsighted yet tightfisted government that reorients power relationships—more like the progressives than the New Dealers. The private interests that destroy the lives of workers are not thinking about tomorrow. If we get higher productivity but we sacrifice the middle class (arguably the finest achievement of American society in the last hundred years), then we will have a hollow and short-lived prosperity. I'm all for rewarding risk taking and innovation. I want no government control of profits or stigmatizing of success. But I want us to think about the long run, in human as well as economic terms, and act accordingly. In order to ride the crest of the information wave, we need not shove America's loyal and most stable segment of citizens off the edge.

Political leaders need to redefine our circumstances. For Mark Hanna, politics was a matter of weighing the economic interests of business, labor, and farmers and giving business the advantage. For FDR, who still accepted economic interests as the integrating force of politics, government had to collect and redistribute the fruits of land, labor, and capital, so that workers would have the means to support their families and the combined purchasing power to keep the economy afloat. Today knowledge—the economic wherewithal—is not susceptible to the same control by government. It cannot be taxed or regulated. Drucker points out that knowledge is not economic. It cannot be quantified. So, when its use disrupts an economy, the course to take becomes uncertain.

Because we travel in uncharted waters, we need new thinking. The very flexibility, mobility, and adaptability of Americans is our biggest advantage. Government must be examined not in the context of the old dichotomies of liberal/conservative or private/public but in the context of a common effort to grapple with new problems posed by a new era.

In addition to balancing the budget, providing the lowest possible tax rates on income, and shifting part of the tax burden to unnecessary consumption, we need to facilitate the transition to the new economy by cushioning its disruptive impact on individual human beings. The government should require a former employer in firms above one hundred workers to pay a laid-off employee's medical expenses for no less than a year. Someone who dedicated ten years of life to a company deserves at least that. Before homes of employees who lost their jobs through no fault of their own are foreclosed, government should encourage banks to work with people, help them manage, carry them for a while—just as my father did. The age at which you can sell your house without having to pay taxes on the proceeds should be lowered from fifty-five to forty. Pensions should be portable, so that sequential careers don't leave employees emptyhanded at retirement.

Beyond restoring fiscal common sense and providing the cushion, the basic issue is greater power in the workplace. Employees need enhanced clout. Perhaps an answer is to make it easier for unions to organize if they can show that they are democratically run. Worker councils, or even company unions, would allow employees to shape their world. Mandatory profit-sharing would spread the gains of rising productivity. Expanding employee stock-ownership plans (ESOPs) would conceivably help. As corporations find that managing a workplace of temps, consultants, part-timers, and contract workers is harder than they imagined, a loyal workforce, not one always looking over its shoulder to the next job, will seem a more attractive alternative. To encourage the broadest possible hiring instead of the longest overtime, government should consider making overtime a minimum of twice regular wages. Flexible work hours would give parents a chance to structure work so that they could spend more time with their young children.

But I think there are deeper questions embedded in our current circumstance. The people guiding the economic transition are highly skilled technocrats striving to increase their corporations' efficiency and productivity. But they are also managers, concerned with personal bonuses, the bottom line, and quarterly performance reports. To improve profitability at the expense of laying off middle-class employees seems a worthwhile exchange to some managers, even if the employees who remain are overburdened and overworked. In such cases, the middle class becomes the victim not only of technological change but of the quest for profits and bonuses. According to the Congressional Budget Office, from 1977 to 1989 personal income in this country grew by $740 billion. The wealthiest 1 percent, six hundred and sixty thousand families, got two-thirds of this increase and saw their average annual income go from $315,000 to $560,000. While this group was getting a 77-percent increase in income, the middle class as a whole received a paltry 4-percent increase.

Why this harsh treatment of the middle class? The answer is simple— because they are weak and the boss is strong. When Kevin Dolan lost four jobs, he had no one to turn to. When the TWA machinist lost earning power, he had no leverage. When the loyal employees of the Hercules Corporation got thrown out with three hours' notice, they simply had to cope. Not only are employees vulnerable to solely corporate decision making but too often they remain excluded from contributing their view of how best to conduct the process of change, as if all wisdom rested with consultants and upper management. The form has yet to emerge, but the need to involve employees in dealing with the future—even a frightening future—should be obvious.

Beyond power disparities between the employee and the management, there is a need for corporations to be more accountable for their broader impact on us all. The only current measure of corporate performance is the financial balance sheet. If profits are up, share price usually follows and management is declared a success. But what about the workers whose lives have been diminished, even destroyed, by downsizing, and what about the environment that has been decimated by corporate decisions to extract more, dump more, cut more? Ultimately, corporations have a public purpose. For example, Penn Central's corporate charter requires it to transport passengers on its railroad. Because the public has granted limited liability to the individuals who run corporations, the public can insist on a more thorough disclosure of corporate performance. If corporations, treated as individuals under the law, can evade all individual responsibility for their actions, then the public is not being served by the corporate form. A more complete corporate balance sheet is in order, so that the world will know how corporate decisions affect our lives.

The true costs of corporate actions should be made public. Corporations that pass all costs of environmental cleanup on to the taxpayer get a free ride. Corporations that pull out of communities reduce the property tax base and take with them the communities' hope for better schools. A corporation's record on human rights or severance packages for its dismissed workers should be as accessible to the public as the size of its sinking fund. Why shouldn't the actions of the best corporate citizen become the required norm? Any good executive knows that treating fired workers shabbily endangers the loyalty of those who remain. The illusion that we can price goods without accounting for environmental cleanup is the ultimate in short-term thinking. With a fuller accounting, talented young people can refuse to work for a company that is a bad corporate citizen, and the public at large will have a way to determine whether the charter it has granted is serving the larger general interest.

In many ways, the sense of powerlessness felt by the middle class parallels what has happened to other groups in America at different times in our history, when private interests focused only on short-term results and avoided thinking about the future. I've always admired the progressives, such as Teddy Roosevelt and Woodrow Wilson, who enabled the private sector to flourish but in a way more responsive to national purpose. In my service in the Senate, I have sought a balance between the public and the private interests: between the rights of property owners and the needs of society, between the big corporate players and the forgotten players—the urban poor, Native Americans, unskilled workers, small farmers, even fish and wildlife. I've seen many private interests attack government when it limits them and petition government for aid when it can help them: the big farmers in California's Central Valley, financiers like the people who took over and sold the steel plant at Martins Ferry, countless corporate interests who with every tax bill seek to lower their own taxes in a way that leaves the rest of us paying more. Efforts on the Central Valley Improvement Act, the Pyramid Lake Settlement Act, and the Tax Reform Act of 1986 all showed that it is possible, with perseverance and goodwill, to reconcile diverse interests, and to make a market fairer and more efficient at the same time. But finding the balance between public and private interests is not always a cool, detached process. It can deteriorate into a bitter fight. That was the lesson of South Dakota and the Black Hills, and of the 1994 mining-law reform bill.

Seeing child laborers in sweatshops in the early twentieth century awakened compassion in even the coldest hearts and mobilized citizens to activate government to stop the exploitation. Seeing Bull Connor turn his dogs on blacks in Alabama in the 1960s moved good people to action on civil rights. Likewise, really listening to the stories of dashed dreams, broken marriages, and crushed self-esteem from middle-class Americans, who above all played by the rules, compels us to action. Our values drive us to use government to ameliorate the suffering and moderate the disorientation of a middle class displaced by economic change. That, in the long run, benefits all of us. More is at stake than anyone realizes. I'm reminded of that every Fourth of July, when I walk in parades along streets lined with middle-class families sitting in lawn chairs, wearing baseball caps, waving small American flags. They are proud of their country. They raised their kids and taught them to believe in its promise. They fought in its wars and supported its schools with their taxes. Life for most was work, home, and community, and when work goes, it affects all the rest. Too many of these Americans are embarrassed and in pain. To do nothing for them in their moment of need would be a betrayal.

But beyond compassion lies self-interest. A corporation that has released twenty thousand workers is a corporation that should be worried about the workers who remain. How will they feel about a company that has just "re-engineered" a department out of existence? Will downsizing, in its many forms, downsize the whole economy in the long run? Will insecurity lead to a deadening of creativity, risk taking, and innovation? Are we headed, as a friend of mine said, for a Hollywood economy, where no one has a job but everybody is "working on a few projects"? What happens to people's trust, loyalty, sense of belonging, and sense of pride in creating something that lasts and sustains?

Kevin Dolan again: "In the old days, back in the Marines, it was dawn to dark. Because you knew how you got promoted, and there was a quid-pro-quo. You were going to make it happen, and it was going to work. People aren't doing that anymore. They're saying, 'Why should I bust my chops? I'm not going to be here that long. They could cut us tomorrow.' Trust makes marriages work, and helps corporations work, too.

"A corporation can always keep going, just tightening, tightening. The problem they're going to have is the morale of the people who are left. Among the survivors, morale is very, very low. There's no trust level anymore. You've got employees who feel alienated. So, even if they are information workers and they ought to be happy, they're not. They're scared. Many of them are looking for the next position. In the old days, it was a psychological contract. You went to the company, you worked, you did a good job. Like my father and maybe your father, a lot of people worked for thirty-seven years or so, retired, got a pin, and they were happy. That does not exist anymore.

"I think, if you take all these millions of people who have been laid off and, as in my case, are probably earning twenty to forty percent less than they were making before—they have to work a second job. Things are really tight, and they don't see a future, because everything has contracted, contracted. People start to lose faith in their government, their country, and so forth. Then you start seeing some of the things that Bill Bennett is saying. [William Bennett, former secretary of education, established in 1992 a leading index of social indicators, patterned after the index of economic indicators.] Seeing the rise in teen pregnancy, suicide, and the breakup of families. And while you can say it's a failure of morality, it's economically driven."

E V E R Y   M A J O R societal transformation forces men and women to ask basic questions. One of my favorite stories, Leo Tolstoy's *The Death of Ivan Ilyich,* makes the point well. Ivan Ilyich is a midlevel bureaucrat in Czarist Russia. He is lying on his deathbed, recalling his life, his friends, his passions, his failures, his understanding of life. As he ruminates, he becomes bitter. Finally, he wonders whether his whole life has been led in vain and all the things that all the highest-placed people admired have been false—whether his "scarcely noticeable impulses," those which he "immediately suppressed," have been true and all else false. Facing death or living in a time of transformation encourages us to raise such questions.

The very speed at which the transformation is taking place not only displaces workers without regard for length of service or loyalty to the company but puts heavy demands on those with the greatest talent. The very complexity of large organizations means that fewer people are able to run them well. The relentless pressure forces increasingly larger numbers of highly educated professionals to stop and ask themselves what their lives are all about. These are the employees who are working sixty hours a week to make their companies go forward. They are headed toward success, but they can never get away from work. Faxes, conference calls, Federal Express, e-mail follow them practically everywhere. While the information revolution is improving productivity in some places, it has exacted a price in family time and in the relaxation time from which much of creativity springs. Many of those who by outside assessments would be viewed as winners think of themselves, in personal terms, as anything but. My father knew something important as he sat with his thoughts in his white folding chair under the blue cabana in Palm Beach, deciding that he wanted no calls from the bank when he was on vacation. FDR, while he was president of the United States, often disappeared from sight for two-week cruises to recharge his creative energies. The young information worker, tied to his beeper, fax, and modem, is not a free person. Quality of life is more than work, even if work, as Joseph Conrad said, is "the sustaining illusion of an independent existence." The information revolution and automation were supposed to lead to a life of greater leisure for many and greater creativity for the few.

Instead, they have led to unemployment for too many and a rat race for the few.

I remember one luncheon at an investment-banking firm where the talk turned to productivity and its impact on lives. One person recalled that twenty years ago an employee of the firm would make a three-day train trip to Chicago to get another firm's business, whereas today clients log in by computer in an instant. A second person expressed surprising hostility toward one of the investment bank's biggest clients, a major U.S. corporation, because the firm—following the competitive bidding policy of a cost-cutting, re-engineered corporate financial department—no longer gives the bank its exclusive business. "I used to worry about that company day and night," he said. "Now I forget their existence as soon as I walk out the office door." As they spoke, I sensed that if we as a nation don't handle the effects of the information revolution with sensitivity toward those disoriented by its impact, something could be irretrievably lost—the goodwill of our people toward each other and their country.

Ultimately, work life is embedded in one's community and private life. American civilization is like a three-legged stool, with government and the private sector being two legs and the third being civil society, the place where we live our lives, educate our kids, worship our God, and associate with our neighbors. The governing ethos of the private sector is to get as much as you can for yourself; for government, it is to pass laws telling other people what is right for them. But the ethos of civil society is giving something to another person without the expectation of a return. As de Tocqueville pointed out, American civil society mediates between the government and the private sector and creates the context for political action and the forums in which individuals can do great things for their communities and families.

The failure to appreciate the importance of civil society lies at the core of our policy dilemma. Because we do not look for ways to strengthen and encourage the combination of community institutions, families, and religious institutions, we are left in a sterile debate about government versus the private sector, as if they were mutually exclusive areas of American life. Liberals have a government program for every problem—a program preferably controlled by a central bureaucracy in Washington. They hold that spending money on a problem is inherently worthwhile, regardless of maximum efficiency. They don't see that wasting government money endangers the legitimacy of government itself. Too often, many liberals have refused to emphasize the role that hard work, self-reliance, and individual responsibility have to play in devising a solution to poverty or pathology. Conservatives, on the other hand, fail to acknowledge that government can be used to promote the common good. Their answer is to preach self-help and leave the safety net up to private charities. But noble individual actions, both in terms of available resources and in the coordination of their impact, are clearly inadequate to deal with the struggle for survival by the poor or the increasingly bewildered panic of the middle class. What is missing in the conservative approach, in addition to resources, is an appreciation that without a vibrant civil society there are only individual acts of goodwill, which, if not rooted in a context of institutions, add little to the experience all of us share. There is a third way, which emphasizes governance, not government. Governance is something we do for ourselves, by participating in our community and taking charge of our lives, not in a context without government but with a government that supports our efforts.

In the years ahead, the private sector will produce all the goods we want with millions of fewer workers. Because of our gigantic national debt, government cannot be the employer of last resort, the role it played in the Depression. If neither government nor the private sector will employ enough people, that leaves only the institutions of civil society. In *The End of Work,* Jeremy Rifkin argues that our policy challenge is how to take the strength of the private sector, with its burgeoning productivity, and the wherewithal of government, with its power to tax and to channel new resources, into a third sector to create jobs in the civil society—jobs that will deal with social problems. Current volunteerism is insufficient, both in terms of the number of volunteers and the effect on the larger economy. If the worry—in a world of rising productivity and declining employment—is inadequate purchasing power, more volunteers cannot be the single answer. Using the resources controlled by government (cutting corporate subsidies to pay for employee subsidies) and the private sector (encouraging social entrepreneurship) to create paid jobs in civil society answers the worry about where the purchasing power will come from. In addition, the civil society, with adequate resources, can make progress in dealing with the social issues of our time—the poverty, violence, and family disintegration of the underclass; the damaged self-esteem and diminished income stemming from middle-class job loss; and the general problems of addiction and absence of meaning that affect Americans of all classes—because civil society is rooted in people's lives and doesn't shy away from values as the basis of action. Now that large bureaucracies have shown little ability to run social-service programs, and business enterprises readily admit their inability to solve our social problems, the importance of civil society bursts upon our attention. Within civil society lies the zest to deal with what ails us as a nation.

The third sector cannot be shrunk by computers or destroyed by information technology. Mentors, teachers, nurses, day-care providers, pastors, surrogate parents and grandparents, athletic coaches, music directors, and others who give to others, reach out as individuals to those in need. No computer can evoke the smile of a child. It is common sense to connect senior citizens who want to help with children in need of adult influence, and to link displaced middle managers with institutions dedicated to community. The institutions of civil society are moved by idealism and a sense of service, and even if you're receiving a small wage, your commitment is fundamentally different from the pursuit of profit or power which underlies the private and public sectors. Whether they are large institutions, such as giant churches, research universities, and modern hospitals, or small ones, such as community-development corporations, private foundations, and local churches, they know their purpose and can focus energy to achieve their mission. If each of them succeeds, the society benefits.

In what Peter Drucker calls a society of organizations, the government is not irrelevant. It must be the force that sets the standards, establishes the policies, and helps with resources and with defining the common good. The organizations execute policy, following government's lead. The third way emphasizes governance—a governance in which the institutions of the third sector assume a larger responsibility. Whether it is in confronting the poverty and pathology of urban America or in reclaiming the lost dreams of displaced workers, government has a central, but new, role.

In Bertolt Brecht's *The Life of Galileo,* a character says, "Unhappy is the land that breeds no hero." To which Galileo responds, "Unhappy is the land that needs a hero." Brecht was referring to a national hero, but it is in our local communities that the real heroes live. They are individuals like Dorothy Bradley, Deborah Floyd, Ada Deer, and Reverend Watley, whose humanity calls out to us. They are the parents who raise their children, the citizens who engage one another in pursuit of a communal objective, and the individuals living out their spiritual values every day. The microchip cannot determine what is right or wrong. A new drug cannot end hatred. No government and no private sector can ever make those facts different. It is only each of us, alone with our consciences, who will shape the American future. Even rising income inequality derives in part from the absence of a morality that tells today's economic superstars how much is enough. Achieving personal excellence and extending a helping hand to others are what will get us through. If a new man or new woman can be created out of the ashes of the twentieth century, with all its wars, hatred, and tragedy, it will be here in America. We made those promises to ourselves long ago. Optimism is one of our great virtues. No circumstance is beyond improvement. No predicament is hopeless. In an age where change is the rule, our nation, which was born out of change and remains dedicated to its healthy cultivation, will not only survive but prosper. As Robert Frost wrote, we have promises to keep, and miles to go before we sleep.

18

A River That Still Runs

HERE ARE MOMENTS along the road of American politics that stay with you forever. They emerge not only from memorable stories or election verdicts but from introspection, triggered by some event that comes unexpectedly and releases a chain of thought that leaves you in a different state of mind.

I experienced such a moment one night in Montana in 1987, on the occasion of my first visit to that state, when Max Baucus and I spoke at the state party rally in Bozeman. After the rally, a young man drove me to a guest house, where I would spend the night—an old Victorian home that had been converted into a bed and breakfast. My room had a four-poster bed and a radiator that was popping overtime. In six hours, I would be picked up for an early-morning flight to Denver, where I would change planes to get back to New Jersey. A drive, a flight, a performance, a hotel, a sleep, and a drive, a flight, a return.

I sat down on the edge of the enormous bed and looked through the book the Democratic Party had given me to show their appreciation for my visit to Montana—*A River Runs Through It*, by Norman Maclean. There it was on the first page, second paragraph—right out of the Westminster Shorter Catechism. "Man's chief end is to glorify Almighty God and to enjoy Him forever." I remembered memorizing the whole catechism for confirmation in the Presbyterian church, when I was thirteen years old. Suddenly, I was swept up in a rush of memories about the religious faith of my youth.

There were perceived vital differences between the branches of Protestantism in the Missouri of my childhood. Like siblings, Protestants battled over the smallest of things, and these battles took the pettiest of forms. But most Protestants of whatever denomination would acknowledge their shared origins as rebels. Presbyterians, Methodists, Lutherans, and their American cousins, the Southern Baptists, did not disagree on basics—as they did with Jews or Catholics, who were different. History taught that the Jews had helped the Romans kill Christ and the Catholics had sold salvation for money. In some people, the sense of these differences ran deep. Intermarriage was discouraged; after all, in what faith would you bring up the children? I could never generate much sectarian energy, however. Disparaging people for eating fish on Friday seemed outlandish to me. And if Jews were so bad, why were my parents always going out to dinner with the Goldmans? Beyond Catholics, Jews, and mainline Protestants, I knew very little. Mormons, Jehovah's Witnesses, the Church of Christ, and the like were never even mentioned around our house—there weren't any in the neighborhood. In the religious environs of my childhood, they might as well have been Muslims, Buddhists, or Hindus.

My mother was raised Methodist. As she tells it, her father, my Grandpa Crowe, was a strong-willed man. He insisted that Sunday dinner at Riverside take place at 3 p.m. and that the whole family be in their places at the table. After the table was cleared, the family would go into the music room, where he would play the guitar, banjo, or violin, and everyone else would sing. At 7 p.m., he left the house for another week of flogging Old Judge coffee on the road. The Missouri Pacific Railroad had agreed to allow a train to stop at Riverside—the property bordered on the tracks, which ran along the Mississippi and then swung west—on Sunday nights to pick him up, after he had demonstrated to its management how much business he brought them in coffee cargo. Samuel Howard Crowe wore a big black Stetson hat and went from town to town selling coffee, staying in different hotels five nights a week, and writing his wife every night he was away, for twenty years. He took his religion seriously. Once, he made a small investment in a bank in Arkansas. When the 1929 crash precipitated a national banking crisis and the little bank failed, Samuel Crowe promised—even though he wasn't required to by law—that he would make each depositor whole. For five years, he took a big part of his earnings and repaid depositors. He believed that he had a moral obligation. Partly as a consequence of his repayments, my mother went to the Central Methodist College in Fayette, Missouri, with little more than a pillow, a Sunday dress, and two dollars and fifty cents a month for spending money. Formal worship, Bible reading, and church activities were a part of her life from the beginning. The family was required to attend services every Sunday. The services generally lasted two hours, and when you went with the Crowes, you knelt when you prayed. Never mind that only Catholics, Episcopalians, and Lutherans knelt; when Samuel Howard Crowe knelt in the Herculaneum Methodist Church, you knelt.

Though my mother had been terrified of her father, she also inherited his energy and his fervent religious faith. My father came from a less intense religious background. He was raised a Presbyterian, but he revealed his religion more in his style than in expressed conviction: he was reserved, undemonstrative, gentle, and kind, but never explicitly religious. His daily experience shaped his religious perspective. He had no interest in abstract ideas. The condition of his body, the work at the bank, and the comfort of his home determined the level of his satisfaction. Philosophy and literature were as mysterious to him as physics and calculus. His idea of good painting was a realistic rendering of breaking waves or moving trains. The walls of his bank office were filled with pictures of trains. The walls of his home were adorned with breaking waves. Still, when it seemed suitable for the family to go to church, my father insisted that it be Grace Presbyterian, which just happened to be across the street from our house. My mother went along with this. Every Sunday, we were to be found in the last pew. I was never sure whether it was John Calvin's theology or the church's convenient location that determined my father's choice.

Most religion reeked of hypocrisy, as far as my father was concerned. "The last person I trust," he said on more than one Sunday afternoon after a particularly monotonous sermon, "is the preacher. Preachers use religion to cover up a bad credit record. In some cases, they steal, ask forgiveness of their parishioners, and leave town." For my father, nothing was more emblematic of virtue than a good credit rating, keeping your word, saving your money, and never, ever getting close to the "unethical"—a word defined by him in terms of money or sex. Once he was asked by an absentee owner to appraise for sale a five-thousand-acre tract of land along the Mississippi. No one else in the area knew that a sale was contemplated. When I asked my father why he didn't bid for it—or, better yet, buy it—he said, "Because it would have been an abuse of my position. I know people who do worse, but I couldn't. The bank's reputation is too important. I want to sleep at night with a clear conscience and a good name."

At any rate, I grew up a Presbyterian. My mother transferred all the devotion and fervor she had learned among the Methodists to the Presbyterians. She taught Sunday school, directed the youth choir, taught in summer Bible school. By the time I was ten, I was in full rebellion against religious authority. My Sunday-school teacher became so concerned about the state of my immortal soul that he told my parents about my constant contrarian views. My mother disregarded the warning, knowing that my well-developed sense of guilt would bring me around. "So go ahead and stay in bed, miss Sunday school," she would say. "It's OK with me if you're irresponsible." Needless to say, I never was. For me, religion was a course of study, and very similar to history. The Westminster Catechism deconstructed the mysteries of grace, faith, and predestination. John Calvin, John Knox, and John Wycliffe were historical figures for me, like Napoleon, George Washington, and Franklin Roosevelt. In this I resembled my father, whose approval of a sermon depended on how much history or current events the minister wove into it. To him, religion ought not to be emotional in any overt way. He hated sermons that were "full of shouting."

My mother, perhaps prompted by her Methodist upbringing, occasionally took me to a camp meeting. We sat under a big tent, on wooden folding chairs, and sang "The Old Rugged Cross" and "In the Garden." In later years, when I read about the Great Awakening in the eighteenth century, the Cane Ridge revivals in 1801, the burned-over district of upstate New York, and the zeal of various fundamentalist sects, I would think back to those revival evenings of song and salvation. But by the time I reached high school, the ascetic side of my personality, with its Westminster Catechism foundation and its sports discipline, had hardened into a steely conviction that only with hard work, complete self-control, and careful study would I even have a chance of coming closer to the distant God that ruled the universe.

Consequently, I was not prepared for the flow of emotion that hit me as a junior in high school when at my mother's suggestion I attended a Fellowship of Christian Athletes conference in Wisconsin. At the conference, sports greats Don Moomaw, Paul Dietzel, and Fran Tarkenton spoke of Jesus Christ as if they were describing a friend. Religion, for a Presbyterian, was a matter of creed. Presbyterians were not as ritualistic as Lutherans or, certainly, Roman Catholics. Jesus was a historical figure, whose teachings lived through the interpretations of the founders of Presbyterianism. The evangelicals, however, referred to Jesus as if He were a living person, and much was made of "conversion," as a watershed event in the life of a believer. The faith of the evangelical was intimate. One was not simply born into the faith; one was "called," one had "an encounter" with Jesus, and decided to become a Christian as an act of will. The evangelicals' version of Christianity was of an individually tailored experience of inner freedom and peace and rock-solid certainty: "Once you believe, you are saved." When you "accepted" Christ, your life changed. He became your personal savior.

The Christian-athlete role models at the FCA conference told emotional stories about sick people healed, obstacles overcome, games won, success achieved. They gave "testimonies" about how they had been changed once they let Christ into their lives. I was powerfully moved, especially by the speech of a former Baylor football player, who reminded us that "those who love you are watching you and are expecting the greatest from you" (a line I've used often since then). The timid rebellion and firm self-discipline of my childhood gave way to a rush of tears. I felt my breath grow short as the speeches reached their emotional conclusions. I knew I was yielding to the moment in a way that I never had before. I felt that I would never be the same.

I returned to Crystal City to proselytize my school and my team. I convinced the high-school coach, who did not attend church, to allow me to play some of the summer's speeches, which I had tape-recorded, for the high-school basketball team. I spoke at Grace Presbyterian Church. I gave my first sermon, the most evangelical ever given from that pulpit. "Bill's so idealistic," my mother's friends said. My father didn't say anything.

I had a turbulent first year at Princeton, nearly flunking French, always doubtful that a small-town boy could make it there. After bungling an oral French exam in March, I returned to my room in Henry Hall, threw myself down onto my bed, and burst into tears. Everything seemed to be falling away. I didn't know what to do. In a desperate search for comfort, I played a record of speeches from the FCA conference. One of my childhood idols, basketball star Bob Pettit, said, "We're not playing for the state championship or the world championship, but for the victory of Christ in the hearts of men." I heard the strains of "How Great Thou Art." ("I see the stars, I hear the rolling thunder. . . . Then sings my soul, my Savior God to Thee, how great Thou art, how great Thou art.") I made agreements with God about what I would do if He let me just get through this first year. I waited for God to appear. I felt the reassurance of faith. I took comfort in religion. Shortly thereafter, I formulated a story about this episode, similar to those I'd heard two years earlier at the conference. The act of telling audiences of high-school kids the story about the French exam and Bob Pettit gave me peace. I had convinced myself that this was my "personal experience" with Jesus. I had "converted" to Christianity.

My growing celebrity as a basketball player began to attract attention from fellow believers. I was invited to speak at churches around New Jersey, to offer my testimony about why and when I became a Christian. I started teaching Sunday school at the First Presbyterian Church in Princeton. I attended an occasional Bible class with a fundamentalist teacher. I felt the sting of Episcopalian chaplains, who made snide comments about my Christian fundamentalism. Such stigmatization from fellow Christians appalled me. The differentness I felt as a freshman from a small-town high school was compounded, as I became further differentiated because of how I chose to worship God.

Two summers later, I went back to FCA camp. It was 1964. I had spent most of that summer in Washington, D.C., where the soaring promise embodied in the 1964 Civil Rights Act had brought out my political aspirations. I arrived at the camp strongly anti-Goldwater and pro–civil rights. To my surprise, many of the college players with whom I shared a cabin did not support the Civil Rights Act. I noticed, for the first time, that there were no black athletes in attendance; I began to find my fellow athletes insensitive and ignorant of our nation's history. I could not fathom how those who professed such faith in Jesus Christ could so adamantly refuse to see that prejudice and discrimination against black people were affronts to Christian values.

In my senior year, the requests from churches became insistent. How could I say no to a speaking request—wasn't I a Christian? Why couldn't

I fly to Vancouver in three days for a revival? I should think of the Lord and my work for Him, not my senior thesis.

Slowly, I began to see that fundamentalism had a downside. It did not tolerate debate, nor did it seek balance. It appeared to be less a God-centered existence than a man-ordered set of demands. It was less a kinship within a Christian community that tolerated difference than it was an intrusion by people single-mindedly focused on their own organizational objectives. Religious commitment without thought became nothing more than emotions that one day soothed and the next day assaulted me. I retreated into myself.

While at Oxford, I participated in a Billy Graham crusade, even though I was still struggling with my conscience. As I stood on the platform at Earl's Court in London before an audience of several thousand, I did not respect myself. I was speaking as if religious fervor continued to dominate my life. I was denying how strongly and how negatively I had reacted to the narrowness of view and uncharitable attitude of many who professed the same faith to which I was testifying. I felt dishonest for pulling the emotional strings once again. Then, one Sunday, in the church I attended at Oxford, the minister preached a sermon that blatantly defended white Rhodesian power. I walked out, never to return.

The years passed. My life experiences broadened, deepened. I saw more, felt more, questioned more, experienced more. Life became fuller. Religion seemed less urgent. Still, something ached in me when I heard friends, people I respected and loved, denigrate religious faith.

THE CERTAINTY and smugness of self-proclaimed atheists mirrors the absolutism of fundamentalists. It allows for none of the inner freedom essential in the search for a meaning to life that is deeper than that offered by the material world. It seems to me that seeking to formulate your own spiritual values does not deserve ridicule. Such derision appears as the ultimate act of arrogance. Because religious faith doesn't work for one person doesn't mean that someone else can't legitimately live by it. People everywhere in the world seem more than ever to yearn for an inner peace, a oneness with themselves and their world. Christianity offers one way to achieve it; Buddhism, Judaism, Islam, Confucianism, Hinduism offer others. Men and women who live palpably as people of God come from many different religions. Increasingly, I resist the exclusivity of "true believers." Isn't it better to remain open, so that you may learn from another's truth? Only one thing is unarguable: without a body of convictions, life becomes a series of events in futile pursuit of utopia on earth, or of endless material possessions, or of sybaritic comfort, or of self-satisfied mastery of a narrow series of intellectual disciplines. Secular absolutists suggest that the ultimate in life is pleasure, or knowledge, or money, or political power, or detachment, or success, or freedom. I don't accept those goals as ultimate. Slowly, I have come back to an appreciation and understanding of that first faith, in all its nonverbal, stern, mysterious, unrelenting power. Like the Scotch-Irish who met in open fields so as to be unadorned and unencumbered by religious structures, I seek my own individual faith.

Man's purpose, I believe, is to glorify God not in an overly pious way, or in a socially self-conscious way, or in a naïve and rigid way, but in a way that returns to the old faith. The old faith for me can be found in the Westminster Catechism, but I sense it also in the interaction with others who were brought up differently. I admire the erudition, the depth of conviction, and the openness to debate of some Roman Catholic priests. The gospel singing in the African Methodist Episcopal Church or a black Baptist congregation brings tears to my eyes and fills me with a yearning to share the suffering all of us experience. I remain open to the idea, as the professor of comparative religion Diana Eck has written, that "God really encounters us in the lives of people of other faiths." Just think of Gandhi's example of a love that puts one's own life on the line for justice because one sees that both justice and love are inseparable, one being the social manifestation of the other.

The old faith constitutes a partnership of judgment and love. It is in the dynamic between the two that you encounter the terrifying excitement of choice. If you choose faith, then you move beyond ritual to a search for your own individual path. You become engaged in a process of remaking yourself—by what you do, what values you adopt, what you teach your children, how closely you listen to a neighbor, how good a steward you are for future generations, how sincerely you try to understand another person's suffering and joy, and how loving you are, not only to those who love you but also to strangers.

Politics rarely touches these subjects, and too much of American society avoids them. Too many people are trapped in a hedonism exacerbated by wealth; and even the poorest, most desperate parts of our society are in the grip of the pleasure/money syndrome. Sectarian politics increasingly shape our post-cold-war world. Yet people shy away from appreciating the heterogeneity of worldviews embodied in the world's religions, and even fewer see in them any relevance to their own lives. Many of us can't abide a catechism that glorifies God, because we want to be in control; we want to be the center ourselves. The spiritual is too often devalued. So what to do?

Are possibilities for renewal and wonder gone? Are we left with just our minds and our bodies in a duel for dominance over our personalities? Or can we see beyond ourselves? Can we give thanks for those who commit their lives to make things better for urban poor, coal miners' wives, Native American children? Can we truly identify with the panic of hardworking family men who have lost their jobs because technological change has made obsolete the skills that once made them useful? Can we comprehend the true joy of giving to others? Can we share without regret? Can we see the strength it takes to be humble? Can we go beyond respect to see the connection among all faiths that help people understand their times and live their lives? Can we let go of the anxiety and fear that prevent us from truly engaging another human being? Can we get beyond skin color or eye shape to see the commonality among all people? Can we respect the deep time of canyon walls or the timelessness of rivers like the Mississippi? Can we appreciate the rituals of the Sioux or imagine the awe of the Spanish Conquistadors and the plainsmen who first encountered the vastness and beauty of our land? Can we sense the fullness of life, even as we feel our own lives rushing by? Can we see our lives as one link in a long chain—a part of a larger story that continues after we are gone?

These are the questions I have asked myself on moonless nights with a sky full of stars, and I still do. I know I am anchored in nature, in God's grace, and in humanity's potential to grow. All of these combine, even in the darkest hour, to make life's mystery full of excitement and possibility.

Afterword

I N 1976, when I finished writing *Life on the Run,* I knew I had said what I wanted to say about the life of a professional basketball player on the road in America. Having put that experience into perspective, I was ready to move on to something else. The book was integral to the decision. The act of writing has always been a method of clarification for me, a way of getting down to how I really feel about an issue, a decision, a place, a person. Although putting things down on paper never came easily to me (*Life on the Run* went through twelve drafts, and most of this book even more), I knew the importance of the writing process to the way I thought. It was natural, then, that by the early 1990s I had the desire to take stock again.

When I started writing this book, I had no idea how I would feel at the end. As usual, the beginning phase was the hardest, but once the basic structural issues were resolved, I took pleasure in elaborating and sharpening the main themes. During this two-and-a-half-year period, whenever I experienced something—a meeting, a vote, an insight, a story—I found myself slotting it into the book and evaluating whether it added clarity or deepened a feeling. Increasingly, I felt at ease with what I was saying about the levels of my experience as a public person. I didn't know what the future would hold for me or for America, but I felt that whatever it might be, I would have had my say.

As I completed the manuscript, a different emotion emerged. Living life intensely has a momentum and exhilaration of its own. Thinking about events you have experienced, and developing perspective about them, in some way completes them, and finding the words to express that perspective brings about a sense of closure. So on August 16, 1995, I announced that I would not run for re-election to a fourth Senate term. I love the life of a senator, even on its bad days. It's the greatest elective job in the world. Yet the Senate is not the only place to serve. I am leaving the Senate, but I am not leaving public life. When I started the book in January 1993, I did not know it would lead to this decision, but it has. My life as a U.S. senator is almost over, but then again, I've always preferred moving to sitting still.

Montclair, N.J.
October 1995

Acknowledgments

IN WRITING this book I have owed much to others.

I thank my editors: Jonathan Segal, who was my editor for *Life on the Run* and now, with this book, nearly twenty years later, showed an even steadier and wiser hand with the editor's pencil; Sam Vaughn, who picked apart a line of thought almost as well as he dissected a paragraph; and Sara Lippincott, whose sensitive attention to the entire text raised its quality several levels, and whose unrelenting attention to detail was as challenging as it was reassuring.

I thank friends who read all or part of the manuscript and offered candid and helpful comments: Marcia Aronoff, Bob Bauer, Doug Berman, John DesPres, Anita Dunn, Betty Sue Flowers, Mark Foulon, Ann Gearen, John Gearen, Simon Head, Rita Jacobs, Tom Jensen, Patricia Limerick, Carolyn Lukensmeyer, John McPhee, Jim McPherson, Tom Ochs, Dan Okimoto, Gene Peters, Sydney Pollack, Richard Rorty, Don Roth, Tom Singer, Marta Tellado, Robb Westbrook, John Wideman, and Charles Wilkinson.

Over the period of nearly three years, four people—Leslie Hatamiya, Chris Eidschun, Fritz Eidschun, and Meg Hawthorne—deciphered my handwriting and presented me with clean, typewritten pages in the margins of which I could scribble again, and I am most grateful to them.

I thank my agents: Paul Gitlin, who kept getting deals too generous for me to accept, and Art Klebanoff, who knew why I wouldn't accept them.

I thank the people of New Jersey, who in giving me their votes and their trust gave me the chance to serve.

Finally, and above all, I thank my first reader and first editor, my wife, Ernestine, who encouraged me to do this book and understood how important writing it was to me, and who made the personal sacrifices and gave the constant support that made it possible.

Index

ABC News, 199
abortion, 38–9, 45, 61, 191, 206, 208, 242, 264
Abscam scandal, 73
Adams, Brock, 186, 188
adoption, foreign infant, 43
affirmative action, 208, 365–73, 384
Afghanistan, 128; Soviet aggression in, 130–3
Africa, 336
African Americans, 24, 26, 51, 54, 73–4, 297, 328, 340, 342, 344, 354–93; affirmative action, 365–73; in basketball, 361–64; charges of racism by, 376–7, 384–7, 390; discrimination against, 24, 328, 340, 354, 357, 363–93; education issues, 365, 367, 378–83, 386–92; employment issues, 354, 357, 365–77, 379, 384; exploited by African Americans, 379–80; in politics, 154–7, 208–9, 383–6; race riots, 357–8, 371; single mothers, 374–5; violence, 375–7, 390–1; white stereotypes about, 371–4, 376–7
agriculture, 84, 102, 217, 285, 400, 403, 407; immigrant, 328, 329, 350–1; and Western natural-resource interests, 102–16, 217–25, 227–35
AIDS, xiii, 33, 176, 374, 377, 390
Air Force, U.S., 31, 68, 127, 129, 356, 358
Akaka, Dan, 227

Alabama, 86, 296, 409
Alaska, 85, 86, 215, 226, 227, 307
alcohol, xiii, 150, 176, 245, 291, 302, 314, 317, 320
Alexander, Clifford, 367–8
Alien Land Law (1913), 329
American Revolution, 283, 286, 287
Ames, Aldrich, 133
Angola, 130–1
anti-Semitism, 333, 351
apartheid, 128, 141
Appalachia, xii, 32, 267–89, 290; federal assistance in, 270–1; Scotch-Irish settlers of, 283–9, 294
Argentina, 96, 99, 130, 318
Arizona, 109, 115, 146, 226, 230, 342, 343
Arkansas, 35, 71, 88, 287, 355, 378
Aronoff, Marcia, 70
Arthur, Chester, 328
AT&T, 402
Atlanta, 21, 22, 357, 379, 380
Atlantic Monthly, The, 399
auto industry, 251, 265, 400, 403
automation, 401–2, 404, 411

B-1 bomber, 68
B-2 stealth bomber, 68
Babbitt, Bruce, 204, 226

Baker, Howard, 73, 76, 86, 204
Baker, Jim, 97–8, 196–7
Baker League, 361
Balanced Budget Amendment, 81
Baltimore, 389
bankruptcy, 258–60
banks, 402, 417–19; home mortgages, 406; of
    1930s, 91; 1980s weakening of, 46, 96–8; of
    1990s, 47, 406; savings-and-loan crisis, 47,
    97, 145–7; small-town, 3–5; Third World
    debt, 95–101
Barkley, Alben, 64, 65, 317
Barnett, Dick, 363
baseball, 9, 10
basketball, xi, 6, 9, 12, 17, 20–30, 40, 60, 92,
    94, 118–21, 127–8, 149, 172–3, 189, 197,
    200–2, 212, 237–8, 251, 301, 334, 355,
    356, 362–3, 371, 421
Baucus, Max, 236, 237, 239, 416
Bayh, Birch, 189, 206–7, 211–13
Bayh, Evan, 211–13
Bayh, Marvella, 207, 211
Begala, Paul, 200
Bell, Derrick, 365, 371
Bell, Jeffrey, 31, 148
Bennett, William, 410
Bentsen, Lloyd, 83, 85
Berlin, 141
Biden, Joe, 62, 87–8, 138, 189–90, 198, 204,
    400–1
Billington, James, 294
Blackfeet, 295, 299
Black Hills, S. D., 295, 303–16, 409
Boren, David, 131, 134
Bosnia, war in, 45, 299
Boston Globe, 199
Boxer, Barbara, 116, 177, 189
Bradley, Bill (William Warren): in Air Force
    Reserve, 31, 127–8; as basketball player, xi,
    6, 12, 17, 20–30, 40, 60, 92, 94, 118–21,
    127–8, 149, 172–3, 189, 197–8, 200–1,
    237–8, 251, 301, 334, 355, 356, 362–3, 371,
    421; campaign style and trips, xi–xii, xiv–xv,
    30–2, 35, 39–43, 142–3, 172–93, 201, 210,
    236, 267–80; childhood of, 3–8, 12, 16,
    117–18, 149, 253, 354–5, 417–20; on civil
    society, 382–3, 412–15; at Clinton–Bush–
    Perot debate, 195–200; on Clinton-Gore bus
    tour, 36; decision to leave Senate, 427; early
    political experiences, 6–10, 29–30, 59–61,
    71; education of, 7–9, 14, 16, 18, 59–60,
    117–27, 129, 358–61, 420–2; on Energy and
    Natural Resources Committee, 61, 101, 107,
    111, 214–16, 224, 225–9, 236, 279; ethics

of, 182–4, 409, 422–4; *The Fair Tax,* 93;
    family of, 201–2, 205–6, 210, 324–7; on
    Finance Committee, 61–3, 92–4, 369–70;
    first Senate speech, 61; on foreign-policy
    issues, 124–44, 201; fund-raising efforts,
    172–84; German background of, 319–21,
    323–4; on immigration issues, 317–53; on
    Intelligence Committee, 73, 99, 128–38;
    international travels of, 118–38, 144, 236; on
    labor relations, 250–66; *Life on the Run,* xi, 30,
    426; media on, 24–6, 60–1, 122–3, 183,
    236, 280; on media scrutiny of politicians,
    145–61; on middle-class issues, 394–415; on
    Native American issues, 290–316; 1978
    Senate race, 18, 30–2, 35, 40, 92, 147–9,
    172–4, 178; 1984 Senate race, 40, 41, 46,
    107, 178, 180; 1988 national convention
    speech, 21, 22, 27; 1990 Senate race, 39–43,
    46, 177, 178–86, 202; 1992 national
    convention speech, 17–28; presidential
    ambitions, 179, 183–4, 200–5; privacy of,
    147–50, 201–2; on racial issues, 354–93,
    421–2; on religion, 416–24; as Rhodes
    Scholar, 119, 122–7, 129, 236, 358–61, 422;
    Scotch-Irish background of, 267, 280–89,
    319; Senate career, xii, 30–2, 38–43, 48,
    60–1, 90, 101, 112, 128–38, 147, 178–86,
    202, 267, 409, 427; as speaker and television
    performer, 18–28, 61, 189–93, 239–41, 371;
    staff of, 42, 70, 179, 184; on tax reform,
    92–5, 395, 409; television commercials of,
    40, 178, 182, 184; on Third World debt,
    95–101; on Clarence Thomas nomination,
    383–6; in Tokyo Olympics (1964), 59, 120;
    in town meetings, 37–9, 191, 366, 401; on
    water reform, 101–16, 232–4; women
    candidates supported by, 154–7, 186–93,
    239–49
Bradley, Dorothy, 239–49
Bradley, Ernestine, 177–8, 200–2, 205–6,
    324–7
Bradley, Hugh, 281
Bradley, Susie, 3–16, 91, 117–18, 200, 319,
    417–19
Bradley, Theresa Anne, 326–346
Bradley, Warren, 3–16, 29–30, 91, 117–18,
    149, 200, 281, 321, 323, 354, 411, 417–19
Brady, Nicholas, 98–9
Brady Plan, 98–9, 349
Brandeis, Louis, 150, 204
breast cancer, 205–7, 241
British Americans, 319, 320
Brokaw, Tom, 25
Brown, Jerry, 20, 21, 204

Brown, Ron, 20
Brown v. *Board of Education,* 9, 365
Bryan, William Jennings, 164
Buckley v. *Valeo,* 171, 173–4
Bumpers, Dale, 227
Bureau of Indian Affairs, 297, 309, 310, 315
Bureau of Land Management, 84, 221, 223, 234, 307
Bureau of Reclamation, 84, 101, 107–8, 224
Bush, George, 22, 47, 54, 98, 142, 143, 151, 171, 178, 212, 349, 368–71; 1992 presidential campaign, 113–15, 194–200, 201, 278, 369–72, 386–7; on racial issues, 368–72, 383–4, 386–7; Clarence Thomas nomination, 383, 384
bus tours, political, 35–7
Byrd, Harry F., Sr., 63
Byrd, Robert C., 48, 62, 73, 75–82, 129, 189
Byrne, Brendan, 148, 173

California, 53, 171, 173, 174, 181, 211, 215, 216, 220, 225, 233, 287, 314, 342, 343, 359; immigrants in, 327–31, 344–8; water reform in, 101–16
campaign debt, 145–6
campaign finance, 162–93, 210; *Buckley* v. *Valeo* loophole, 171, 173–4; direct-mail solicitation, 177; ethics, 175–6, 182–6; history of, 162–72; PACs, 176–7, 181, 184–5; reform, 45, 171, 183, 184–6, 193; telemarketing solicitation, 177; and Western natural-resource interests, 225
campaign tactics, dirty, xiv, 32, 147–9, 207–9, 370
Canada, 262, 349, 350
cancer, xv, 364; breast, 205–7, 241; cervical, 272; lung, 272
capitalism, 7, 260, 315
Carey, Ron, 263
Carter, Jimmy, 46, 47, 49, 67, 68, 75–6, 116, 139, 179, 204
Carville, James, 201
Case, Clifford, 31, 172–3
Casey, William, 99–100
Castro, Fidel, 131, 336–41
cattle grazing, 84, 217, 219–21, 225–6, 307, 314
Caudill, Harry, *Night Comes to the Cumberlands,* 271
census, 356
Central Intelligence Agency (CIA), 99, 129–39; covert operations, 130–6; post–cold war, 138–9
Central Valley Project (CVP), 101–16, 214, 409
cervical cancer, 272

Chafee, John, 69, 70, 86
Chandler, Rod, 188
chauvinism, 54, 188, 294, 334
Chemical Bank, 97
Cheyenne, 299–300, 304
Chicago, 154–5, 170, 181, 250, 257, 347, 357
child care, 264, 265, 404
children, 265, 391, 407; discipline lacking in, xiii, 375–6; immigrant, 337, 345, 347–8; in labor force, 261–2, 409; middle-class, 394, 395, 404, 409, 414; single parents of, xiii, 374–5, 404; urban poor, 374–7, 386–92
China, 54, 121, 127, 128, 130, 137, 139, 140, 218, 220, 260, 327, 381
Chinese Exclusion Act (1882), 328, 329
Chinese immigrants, 327–8, 351
Choctaws, 294, 297
Church, Frank, 86, 189, 206
cigarette smoking, xiii, 160, 276
Citibank, 396
cities, *see* urban America
Civil Liberties Act (1988), 336
civil rights, 59–60, 76–7, 262, 340, 556–61, 366–71, 374, 409, 421
Civil Rights Act (1964), 59, 60, 71, 366, 371, 372, 386–7, 421
civil society, 366, 382, 394; importance of, 382–3, 412–15; jobs in, 413–14
Civil War, xii, 53, 60, 220, 245, 281, 320, 321, 356, 360
Clean Air Act, 89
Clean Water Act, 89
Cleveland, 162–3
Clinton, Bill, xiv, xv, 35, 178, 188, 203, 211, 246, 251, 340, 389, 403; debate style, 195–201; NAFTA negotiations, 349–50; 1992 presidential campaign, xiv–xvi, 21, 27–8, 35–7, 113–15, 142–3, 151, 182, 194–200, 203–4, 245, 260, 266, 278
Clinton, Hillary Rodham, 35, 188, 197
Clinton-Gore bus tours, 35–7
coal, 250, 252, 268–71, 278–9
Coelho, Tony, 107
Cohen, Bill, 86
cold war, 68, 124, 126, 130, 133; end of, 44, 45, 133, 138–44
Collier, John, 297–9
Colorado, 109, 214, 215, 221, 226, 230, 343
comeback, political, 211
Commission on the Future of the African American Male, 389
Commission on Presidential Debates, 195
communism, 124–7, 140–1, 170, 208, 339; collapse of, 44, 45, 133, 138–44, 239

computer industry, growth of, 44, 263, 264, 377, 396–7, 399–403, 412

Congress, U.S., 59, 129, 162, 221; immigration policy, 328, 329, 336, 346, 350; Indian policy, 296–9, 303–5, 308–14; 1984 elections, 51–2; reintroduced bills in, 113; *see also* House of Representatives, U.S.; Senate, U.S.

Congressional Record, 81

Connecticut, 94–5, 363

Constitution, U.S., 81, 185, 328

coordinated campaign, 185

corporate executives, xiii, 115, 265

corporate PACs, 176, 184

corporate responsibility, 408

corruption, political, 170, 175–6, 185

Cranston, Alan, 146, 147, 189

Crazy Horse, 304, 305, 314

Crédit Mobilier, 175–6

Creeks, 294, 296, 304

crime, 47, 100, 150, 159, 348, 375–6, 382, 390–1; New Jersey, 33

Crowe, John, 321

Crowe, Samuel Howard, 5, 417–18

Crowe, William, 196, 198

Crowe-Carraco, Carol, *The Big Sandy,* 278–9

Crystal City, Mo., 3–16, 35, 117–18, 197, 198, 252–3, 323, 354–5, 364, 417–20

C-Span, 21, 90, 142

Cuba, 130, 140, 336–7, 340–1

Cuban Americans, 336–41

Culver, John, 85, 206

Cuomo, Mario, 198–9

Cushing, Cardinal Richard, 8

Custer, George A., 299, 303, 304

Cutler, Lynn, 188–9, 192

Czechoslovakia, 128, 237–9

Daley, Richard, 198

D'Amato, Alfonse, 113, 209

dams, 105–16, 167, 221, 224, 231–4

Danforth, Jack, 74, 87, 368–91

Daschle, Tom, 312

Dawes General Allotment Act (1887), 297

death penalty, 390

debates, presidential, 31, 194–200, 201; Clinton–Bush–Perot, 194–200; Dukakis–Bush, 194–6, 199; format and location, 195; Lincoln–Douglas, 195; Nixon–Kennedy, 8, 194, 195

debt, 95; campaign, 145–6; national, xiii, 44–5, 46, 57–8, 191, 413; personal, xiii, 45; Third World, 95–101, 341, 349

DeBusschere, Dave, 21, 251, 363

DeConcini, Dennis, 146, 147

Deer, Ada, 290–4, 298

defense, 49, 50, 54–5, 70, 74, 88, 129; 1990s downsizing of, 44, 45, 47, 142; nuclear weapons strategy, 68, 70, 130, 133, 142; post–cold war, 138–44; Reagan program, 68

Defense Intelligence Agency (DIA), 129, 136

Delaware, 61, 62, 400

Delaware River, 32, 33, 112, 252

democracy, xiv, 37, 48, 153, 162, 175, 286, 298, 318, 351; pluralistic, 144

Democratic Congressional Campaign Committee, 168, 169

Democratic National Committee, 49–50, 64, 188

Democratic National Convention, 198; of 1984, 199, 205; of 1988, 21, 22, 27, 198; of 1992, 17, 20–8, 35, 205

Democratic Party, 7, 8, 9, 60, 63, 64, 142, 146, 198, 226, 321, 338, 339, 358; and economic troubles, 46–58; identity crisis of 1980s–90s, 49–58; and labor issues, 264–6; and middle-class issues, 398–9; 1994 election losses, 51–2; social programs and values, 49–58, 398; "yellow-dog," 269–70; *see also* politics; presidential elections; *specific politicians*

Denver, 230

Depression, 4, 5, 7, 12, 15, 46, 53, 65, 91, 108, 143, 154, 225

deregulation, 402

Detroit, 251, 357, 386–92

Dewey, Thomas, 7

discipline, 382–3; lacking in children, xiii, 375–6

divorce, 398

Dixon, Alan, 154–5

Dolan, Kevin, 410–11

Dole, Bob, 67, 69, 77–8, 82, 113, 170, 204

Domenici, Pete, 74

domestic violence, 391

Douglas, Paul, 209

downsizing: defense, 44, 45, 47, 142; job, 372, 396–411

drought, 105, 109, 111

drug use, 159, 300, 327, 375–6, 388, 391, 404; by politicians, 148–51

Duberman, Martin, 60

Dukakis, Michael, 145, 194–5, 199, 211, 370

Duke University, 118–19

Durenberger, David, 134

Durkin, John, 206

economy, xiii, 24, 40–51, 139, 189, 286; Appalachian, 268–72, 278, 284–7; and foreign-policy issues, 137–9, 143–5; immigrant, 328, 337, 345–51, 352;

information-based, 399–404, 411–12, 414; international, 44, 45, 47, 54–5, 262, 373; job downsizing, 372, 396–411; manufacturing, 250–66; middle-class burden, 31, 44–50, 57, 191, 395–415; and NAFTA, 348–52; Native American, 314–15; New Jersey, 32, 33, 40–2, 45–6, 215, 260; of 1930s, 77; of 1940s, 405; of 1970s, 46, 54, 67; of 1980s, 46–51, 143, 257–64, 345–7, 369–70, 372, 396–7; of 1990s, 44–7, 143, 200, 251, 259–60, 265–8, 347–8, 395, 397–414; and politics, 46–58, 143, 406; and racial issues, 372–4, 382, 390–2; and Third World debt, 95–101; and wealth distribution, 372–4, 391–2, 407; and Western natural-resource interests, 101–16, 217–35
education, xii, 45, 89, 112, 246–7, 263, 291–3, 318; college loans, 42, 89, 112, 278, 395; community colleges, 270, 276–8; federal aid to, 89, 276–8, 395; of immigrants, 328–9, 337, 347–8; New Jersey, 34, 78, 140–1, 369, 380–2, 388; and racial issues, 328, 365, 367, 369–70, 378–83, 386–92; segregated, 24, 328–9, 355, 365, 369, 378–9; tax credits, 369–70; urban schools, 374, 378–83, 386–92
Eisenhower, Dwight D., 7–8, 60, 355
elderly, xiii, 46, 57, 254–5; health care, 270; Social Security, 53
Eller, Ronald, *Miners, Millhands, and Mountaineers*, 268
employee stock-ownership plans, 66, 407
employment, xii, xiii, xiv, 6, 45, 191, 260, 337, 350; in civil society, 413–14; information age, 399–404, 411–12, 414; middle-class, 395–415; power in, 407–11; quotas and affirmative action, 208–9, 365–73, 384; racial issues in, 365–77, 379, 384; *see also* industry; labor; unemployment
endangered species, 106, 231–4
entertainment industry, 51, 399
environment, 48, 54, 84, 269, 300, 349, 409; endangered species, 106, 229–34; legislation, 89, 220–7, 233–5, 279; New Jersey, 32, 33, 225; pollution, 32, 33, 54, 108–9, 139, 182, 225, 227–35, 252–3, 278–9, 395; soil erosion, 15, 278–9; water reform, 101–16; Western natural resource and land issues, 101–16, 214–35; workplace toxins, 278–9
Equal Employment Opportunity Commission (EEOC), 366–7
ethnicity, 9–10, 24, 34, 139–40, 250–1, 267–89, 317–53; diversity, 144, 318, 322, 352–3; Chinese, 327–8, 352; German, 319–27; Japanese, 328–36, 352; Latino,

336–53; Scotch-Irish, 267, 280–9, 319; *see also* immigrants; race and race relations
European exploration and settlement, 13–14, 105, 220, 295, 296, 300, 301, 341–4, 351

Fahrenkopf, Frank, 142
Fair Tax, The (Bradley), 93
family, 49, 269; deterioration of, xiii, 57, 375, 404, 413; immigrant, 319, 345; middle-class, 394–7, 404–5, 410–11; parental leave, 265; of politicians, 201–2, 205–7, 209–13; Scotch-Irish, 284; single-parent, xiii, 374–5, 404
Farley, Jim, 64, 65
federal budget, 41; balancing, 50; deficit, xiii, 44–5, 46, 50, 57–8, 93, 100, 137, 412
Federal Bureau of Investigation (FBI), 73, 129, 147
Federal Crime Bill (1994), 391
Federal Home Loan Bank Board, 146
Federal Reserve, 46, 47, 67, 97
Feinstein, Dianne, 116, 189
Fischer, David Hackett, *Albion's Seed,* 283, 285
fish, 108–10, 229–34, 303
flag burning, 61
floods, 14–16, 103, 106, 278
Florida, 181, 296, 336
Florio, Jim, 39–41
Floyd, Deborah, 272–80
food stamps, 407
Ford, Gerald, 31, 172, 195
Ford, Wendell, 85
foreign policy, 45, 54–5, 124–44, 201, 339; Afghanistan war, 130–2; intelligence operations, 124–39, 142; Iran-contra, 135–6; post–cold war, 138–44; Vietnam War, 124–7, 132–3
Fort Laramie Treaty (1868), 303, 305, 308
France, 14, 324, 349, 359
Frank, Barney, xiv
Franklin, Benjamin, 301
Frazier, Walt, 17, 363
French and Indian War, 295
Frost, Robert, 8, 415
fundamentalism, 419–22
fund-raising, *see* campaign finance

gambling, 34, 327; Indian, 314–15; sports betting, 112
gang culture, xii, 375, 376
Gantt, Harvey, 209–10
Garn, Jake, 113, 115
Garner, John Nance, 167, 168
gender equity, 262, 265, 294
General Mining Act (1872), 223–5

Gentlemen's Agreement (1908), 329
George, Walter, 63
Georgia, 63, 79, 296, 385
Gephardt, Richard, 10–11, 179, 198, 199
Gergen, David, 25
German immigrants, 319–27
Germany, 12, 117, 118, 123, 124, 126, 137, 141, 201–2, 319–25, 349, 350, 352; World War II, 322–5
Gingrich, Newt, 403
Glenn, John, 146–7, 189
gold, 220, 303–5, 313, 327, 342
Goldwater, Barry, 59–60, 204
Gorbachev, Mikhail, 87, 131, 132, 138, 142
Gore, Albert, Jr., xiv, 35, 370
Gore, Albert, Sr., 66
Gore, Tipper, 35
government, federal, 51–2, 107, 136, 162, 375, 412–13; aid to Appalachia, 270–1, 278; cynicism about, xiv, 37, 50–1, 375, 405; and economy, 46–58; Indian policy, 293, 294–316; and middle class, 398–9, 405–6, 412–15; and money, 163–94; racist policymaking, 368–71, 377, 383–6; Republican cuts in, 48–52; town meetings, 37–9, 192, 204, 366, 401; Western land management, 215–35; *see also* politics
Grady, Bob, 115
Graham, Billy, 422
Gramm, Phil, 86, 196, 197, 200
Grant, Ulysses S., 176, 303, 304
grazing, 84, 217, 219–21, 225–6, 307, 314
Great Britain, 117, 118–19, 122, 124, 281–3, 318, 319, 359
Great Society, 53, 270, 272, 405
Green, David, 52
Gumbel, Bryant, 24–5
gun control, 185, 391

Hamill, Pete, 24
Hamilton, Alexander, 52, 53
Hanna, Marcus Alonzo, 162–6, 170, 193, 406
Harkin, Tom, 182, 189, 204
Hart, Gary, 179, 189, 204, 205
Harvard University, 367
Hatch, Orrin, 131, 132
Hawaii, 80, 331
health care, xiii, xv, 83, 191, 205, 262, 265, 266, 276–8, 338, 394; for elderly, 270; 1990s debate and legislation, 77–8, 89–90; for the poor, 374
health insurance, xiii, 44, 46, 256, 260, 263, 345, 397, 403, 406
heart disease, 272

Hecht, Chic, 73, 131
Heflin, Howell, 73–4, 86
Heinz, John, 85
Helms, Jesse, 57, 76, 78, 86, 177, 208–9, 370
Hill (Anita)–Thomas (Clarence) hearings (1991), 87, 155, 187, 188, 386
Hitler, Adolf, 324
Hoffa, Jimmy, 255
Hollings, Fritz, 185
Holmes, Oliver Wendell, Jr., 92, 204
Holocaust, 140, 322–3, 352
Holzman, Red, 21
Homestead Act (1862), 219, 220, 230
homosexuals, 197, 208
honoraria, 68–9
Hoover, Herbert, 7
Horton, Willie, 370
House Intelligence Committee, 129, 134–5
House of Representatives, U.S., 10–11, 30, 61, 113, 129; 1940 elections, 167–70; 1994 elections, 51–2; *see also* Congress, U.S.
House Ways and Means Committee, 93
housing, low-income, 270, 376
Houston, Sam, 342, 344
Howard, Jim, 312
Huffington, Michael, 174
Hughes, Langston, 22, 24
Humphrey, Hubert, 62
Hungary, 121–2, 123
Hunt, Jim, 208

IBM, 398, 402, 403
Ickes, Harold, 106
Idaho, 86, 214, 215, 226, 227
Illinois, 13, 35, 154–6, 209, 267, 296, 320, 321
illiteracy, 391
immigrants, xii, xiv, 34, 140, 144, 218, 250–1, 265, 294–5, 317–53, 387; Chinese, 327–8, 352; economy, 328, 337, 345–51, 352; German, 319–27; illegal, 344–7; increase of, 317, 320, 345; Japanese, 328–36, 352; Latino, 336–53; legislation, 328, 329, 336, 346–8, 350; and politics, 338–9; racism against, 327–36; Scotch-Irish, xii, 267, 268, 280–9, 294, 319
independents, 208–9
Indiana, 207, 211
individual responsibility, xiii–xiv, 318, 375, 413
industry, 6, 36, 52–3, 84; auto, 251, 265, 400, 403; automation, 401–2, 404; biotech, 404; California, 108–9; computer, 44, 263, 264, 377, 396–7, 399–403, 412; export, 96, 97; foreign competition, 401–2; New Jersey, 32, 33; 1990s decline, 252, 262, 264, 396, 407;

steel, 250–66, 400; Western natural-resource interests, 217–35
inflation, 46, 54, 99
information-based economy, 399–404, 411–12, 413
infrastructure, 15–16, 167, 224, 231–3, 272; California, 101–16; New Jersey, 33
Inouye, Daniel, 80, 331
intelligence operations, 124–39; post–cold war, 138–9, 142
interest rates, 46, 48; of 1970s, 67; of 1980s, 96, 257, 258; of 1990s, 45, 47
International Monetary Fund (IMF), 96–8
international trade, 44, 45, 47, 54, 262, 348–52, 401–12
interpreters, 137–8
Iowa, 35, 85, 131, 189
Iran, 130, 133, 135
Iran-contra scandal, 135–6, 178
Ireland, 281, 318
Irish Americans, 319
iron, 250, 252
Iroquois, 301, 316
irrigation, 102–16, 219, 224, 229, 233
Islam, 138–9
Israel, 123, 124, 130, 141, 172
Italy, 123, 331

Jackson, Andrew, 207, 285–6, 296
Jackson, Henry "Scoop," 48, 62, 67–70, 83, 188
Jackson, Jesse, 27, 57, 204, 365
Jackson, Phil, 21, 236, 243, 301
Japan, 88, 89, 98, 120, 126, 137, 138, 139, 259, 298, 318, 332, 349, 350; World War II, 329–36
Japanese Americans, 24, 328–36, 352; interned during World War II, 329–36
Javits, Jacob, 209
Jefferson, Thomas, 52, 53, 207, 216, 218, 285, 286, 316
Jews, 172–3, 318, 323, 327, 333, 352, 417
jobs, *see* employment; industry; labor; unemployment
Johnson, Lyndon B., 53, 65, 79, 89, 121, 125, 126, 127, 154, 167–9, 178, 193, 270, 299, 366, 371
Johnston, Bennett, 74, 80, 111, 226–7
Jones (Bob) University, 369
Jordan, 123, 124, 141
Jordan, Barbara, 17

Kansas, 286, 342, 343
Kassebaum, Nancy, 86
Kaye, Michael, 18
Kean, Tom, 40
Keating, Charles, 146–7
Keating Five, 146–7

Kemp, Jack, 202
Kennan, George, 124, 125
Kennedy, John F., 8, 27, 35, 93, 127, 170, 250, 311, 339, 352, 360
Kennedy, Robert, 59–60, 92, 358–61, 371–2; assassination of, 359–61
Kennedy, Ted, 48, 49, 79, 82, 92, 171, 177, 207, 208, 360
Kentucky, 65, 85, 267–89, 319–20; politics, 269–71, 277; Scotch-Irish settlers in, 283–9
Kerrey, Bob, 138, 182, 189, 204
Keynes, John Maynard, 126–7
King, Martin Luther, Jr., 24, 356, 358, 370
King, Rodney, 160, 191
Klug, Scott, 293
Kohl, Herb, 174
Koppel, Ted, 87
Kosygin, Aleksei, 137–8
Kroh, Martin, 319–20
Krugman, Paul, 401

labor, 6, 51, 53, 165–6, 250–66, 268, 349; child, 261–2, 409; in civil society, 413–14; corrupt leadership, 257–64; downsizing, 372, 396–411; foreign competition, 401–2; gender equity, 261, 265; immigrant, 327–8, 337, 344–51; information age, 399–404, 411–12, 414; legislation, 261, 262; middle-class, 395–415; and NAFTA, 349–51; of 1970s, 257; of 1980s, 257–64, 386–7; of 1990s, 252, 262–6, 395–403; pension benefits, 256, 258–66; power of, 407–11; racial issues, 365–77, 379, 384; re-engineering, 403, 410; reform, 262, 264–6, 407–11; retraining, 395, 401; small business, 47, 51, 337; strikes, 6, 257, 258, 261; temps, 403, 407; unions, 6, 143, 242, 250, 255–66, 268, 350, 400–2, 407; wage increases, 398–9, 407; *see also* employment; industry; unemployment
LaBow, Ronald, 259
La Follette, Robert M., Jr., 76–7
Lakota Sioux, 401–16
Latin America, 208; debt, 95, 96, 98–9
Latinos, 24, 51, 53, 54, 199, 336–53, 369, 376
Lautenberg, Frank, 174
Lexalt, Paul, 233
Leach, Jim, 138
lead, 252–4
leadership, xiii–xiv, 24, 202; moral, xiii–xiv, 24, 46–58, 91, 183; presidential, 202–5
lean production, 403
Lehrer, Jim, 199
Leone, Dick, 148, 173

Leopold, Aldo, 220
Lewis, Ham, 90
Lewis, Michael, 25–6
Lewis and Clark, 218, 237
Life on the Run (Bradley), xi, 30, 426
Limerick, Patricia, *The Legacy of Conquest,* 218, 219, 244, 299, 328
Lincoln, Abraham, 58, 195, 207, 267, 285, 316, 321, 343, 356, 360
Lindsay, John, 20
Lithuania, 138
Little League baseball, 9
Long, Huey, 64–6, 67, 77
Long, Russell, 48, 49, 62–7, 75–6, 78, 83, 84, 92, 93–4
Los Angeles, 101, 160, 181, 191, 196, 327, 344–5, 359, 375, 376
loss, political, 210–11, 246, 249
Louisiana, 62–6, 75, 80, 218, 281
low-income housing, 270, 376
Lubensky, Lloyd, 259
Lugar, Dick, 86
lung cancer, 272

MacNeil/Lehrer NewsHour, 199
Magnuson, Warren, 206
Maine, 74, 76
Mansfield, Mike, 76, 80, 88–9
Mao Tse-tung, 121
Marquis, Thomas, *Wooden Leg: A Warrior Who Fought Custer,* 299–300
Marshall, Thurgood, 383
Mashek, John, 199
Massachusetts, 370
Matsunaga, Spark, 336
McCain, John, 115, 146, 147
McCarthy, Eugene, 358
McCarthy, Joseph R., 72
McClellan, John, 87–8
McClure, Jim, 75, 86, 228
McCurdy, Dave, 198, 199
McGovern, George, 49, 189, 195, 204, 206, 210
McKeller, Kenneth, 65
McKinley, William, 162–6, 170
media, xiv, 16, 18–19, 21, 24, 35, 65, 69, 77, 84, 89, 90, 114–15, 137, 145–61, 164, 293–4; on Bradley, 24–6, 60–1, 122–3, 183, 237, 280; on 1992 presidential election, 35; partisan, 159, 207; political TV ads, xiv, 32, 36, 40, 147, 184, 185, 208–9, 370; politicians scrutinized by, 145–61, 194–200, 201; on racial issues, 372, 376–7; sensationalism, 157–60, 209, 376; strategy, 159–60; *see also* newspapers; radio; television

Medicaid, 62, 66, 89, 156, 270
Medicare, 62, 89, 270, 338
Melcher, John, 236
Melville, Herman, 353
Mendendez, Robert, 339
Menominee, 290–4, 298–9
mergers and acquisitions, 51
Metzenbaum, Howard, 86, 189
Mexican Americans, 336, 341–53
Mexico, 137, 301, 336, 341, 346, 351; debt, 96, 98–9, 341, 349–51; history, 341–4; and NAFTA, 348–52
Miami, 336, 337, 340, 376
Michigan, 214, 267, 357, 386–7
Mickelson, George, 307, 312
middle class, xii, 337, 394–415; economic burden, 31, 44–50, 57, 191, 395–415; employment issues, 395–415; fears, 44–6, 57, 395–7, 399, 401; future of, 405–15; New Jersey, 33, 45–6; and politics, 398–9, 405–6; power of, 407–11
middle management, downsizing of, 402–3
Miller, George, 111–16
Miller-Bradley bill, 111–16
Mineta, Norm, 336
mining, 84, 214, 220–9, 303–4, 307, 314, 327; coal, 268–71, 278–9; fraud and reform, 222–9, 279, 409; strip-, 279
Mining Law Reform Bill (1994), 227
Mississippi, 70, 296
Mississippi River, 12–16, 101, 214, 252, 285, 288, 295, 417; floods, 14–16
Mississippi Valley Committee, 15
Misslbeck, Erna, 324–6
Misslbeck, Sepp, 324–6
Missouri, 3–16, 18, 30, 36, 101, 117–18, 142, 169–70, 190, 197–8, 252–5, 281, 287, 319–21, 323, 354–5, 417–19
Missouri River, 14, 101, 237, 303, 312
Mitchell, George, 76, 78, 80, 89–90, 113, 129, 138, 189
Mondale, Walter, 93, 179, 203, 204, 205, 211
money, political, *see* campaign finance
Monroe, Earl, 21, 363
Montana, 76, 215, 216, 220, 226, 229, 236–49, 303, 416; politics, 239–49
moral leadership, xiii–xiv, 24, 91; and politics, 46–58, 183
Moral Majority, 206–7
Morgan, Bob, 206
Moseley-Braun, Carol, 73–4, 154–7
Moynihan, Pat, 62–3, 74, 174, 190
Muir, John, 220
Mulford, David, 98

Murray, Patty, 186–93
Muskie, Ed, 74
Musto, Billy, 338–9
Myer, Dillon, 298

National Basketball Association, xi, 172, 389;
    1970 championship, 26–7, 29; 1973
    championship, 30
National Congressional Club, 177, 208–9
national debt, xiii, 44–5, 46, 57–8, 191, 413
National Labor Relations Board, 261, 262, 264,
    366, 367
National Press Club, 371
National Reconnaissance Office (NRO), 129–30
National Recovery Act, 77
National Rifle Association, 185
National Security Agency (NSA), 129, 136
Native Americans, xii, 12, 13, 24, 53, 56, 105,
    189, 215, 216, 217, 219, 224, 231–4, 243,
    246, 283, 286, 290–316; culture, 307, 310,
    314–16; economy, 314–15; federal policy
    on, 293, 294–316; legislation, 296, 298–9,
    303–14; and politics, 293–6, 298–301, 306;
    reform, 295–6, 299–314; reservations, 291,
    293, 295, 297–8, 301–16, 359
NATO, 124
natural resources, Western, 103–16, 214–35,
    317
Nazism, 324–5
NBC radio network, 65
Nebraska, 286, 303
Nelson, Gaylord, 207
Nevada, 109, 214–16, 220, 222–4, 226, 230,
    244, 343; Pyramid Lake Settlement, 231–5
New Deal, 53, 63, 405–6
New Hampshire, 179
New Jersey, xi, 9, 12, 18, 32–5, 61, 78,
    139–40, 295, 361, 363, 369, 378–82, 394;
    agriculture, 108; crime, 33; economy, 32,
    33, 40–2, 45–6, 215, 260; education, 34, 78,
    139–40, 369, 380–2, 388; environment, 32,
    33, 225; ethnic diversity, 144, 318, 323,
    336–40; geography and population, 32–4;
    politics, 18–19, 30–5, 37–9, 149, 166,
    172–4, 178–81, 203, 337–9; taxes, 39–41,
    46, 94–5; town meetings, 37–9
New Mexico, xii, 74, 109, 199, 214, 215, 220,
    224, 230, 301, 343
New Republic, The, 25
newspapers, xiv, 18, 24, 114, 115, 152, 164,
    196, 200, 293, 376; partisan, 157, 207;
    politicians scrutinized by, 152–60;
    sensationalism in, 157–60; *see also specific
    publications*

New York, 34, 291, 318, 334–5, 347, 361–2;
    1992 Democratic national convention, 17,
    20–8, 35, 205
New York Daily News, 24
New York Knicks, 12, 17, 20–8, 29–30, 40,
    94, 127, 128, 149, 172–3, 201, 238, 251,
    334, 355, 362–4, 371
New York Review of Books, The, 398
New York State, 62, 181, 214, 363, 419
New York Times, The, 24, 196
Nicaragua, 54, 130, 135–6, 338
Nightline, 87
Nixon, Richard, 7, 8, 126, 138, 170–1, 178,
    194, 211, 299, 358, 360, 371–2
Norris–La Guardia Act, 261
North, Oliver, 136, 177
North American Free Trade Agreement
    (NAFTA), 262, 348–52
North Carolina, xii, 56–7, 177, 195, 208–9,
    214, 240, 267, 296, 370
North Dakota, 217, 323
North-South issues, 54
Northwest Ordinance of 1787, 296
Nunn, Sam, 68, 74

obesity, xiii, 276
Occupational Safety and Health Administration
    (OSHA), 252, 264
Oglala Lakota Sioux, 301–16
Ohio, 36, 146–7, 164–7, 250–2, 256–7, 267,
    280, 295, 396
oil, 46, 48, 54, 60, 66, 75, 83, 94, 102, 139,
    214, 215, 219, 221; independent, 167–9;
    1970s shortages, 215, 270; and Third World
    debt, 95–6
Okimoto, Dan, 329–34
Oklahoma, 56, 216, 286, 287, 343
Omnibus Water bill, 111–16
Operation Desert Storm, 127
Oregon, 215, 328
out-sourcing, 403
overpopulation, 54
Oxford, Bradley at, 113, 118–19, 122–7, 129,
    237, 358–9, 422

Packwood, Bob, 93, 94
Paine, Thomas, 301
Pakistan, 131, 132
parental leave, 265
Paris, 359
parks, national, 84, 220, 221, 225, 307
partisan politics, 7, 22, 86–7, 113–15, 207–8;
    and economy, 46–58; and end of cold war,
    142–3; in savings-and-loan scandal, 146–7;
    see also Democratic Party; Republican Party

Paulson, Allen, 258

Pearl Harbor bombings, 329, 330, 333

Pelosi, Nancy, 199

Pennsylvania, 35, 36, 59, 61, 174, 181, 283, 286, 319, 321, 379

Penny, Don, 19–20

Pension Benefit Guaranty Corporation (PBGC), 256, 258, 259

pension benefits, xiii, 256, 258–66, 394, 399, 403, 406–7

Pentagon, 127

Perle, Richard, 68

Perot, Ross, 195–200, 245

Pershing II missiles, 132

Persian Gulf War, 127, 368

personal debt, xiii, 45

Philadelphia, 34, 283, 290, 319, 362

Phoenix, 230

Pinchot, Gifford, 220, 221

Pittsburgh, 250, 286

Pittsburgh Plate Glass Factory, Crystal City, Mo., 6, 9, 13

pluralism, 139–40, 144, 322, 352–3, 367

Poland, 134, 325

political-action committees (PACs), 176–7, 181, 184–5; corporate, 176, 184; independent, 185

politics, xiv, 45, 318; bus tours, 35–7; corruption, 170, 175–6, 185; cynicism about, xiv, 37, 375, 405; and economy, 46–8, 143, 406; end of cold war, 142–4; fund-raising, 162–93; and immigrants, 338–9; Kentucky, 269–71, 277; loss in, 210–11, 246, 249; media scrutiny of, 145–61, 194–200, 201; middle-class issues, 398–9, 405–6; moral leadership, 46–58, 183; Native American interests, 293–6, 298–91, 306; New Jersey, 18–19, 30–5, 37–9, 149, 166, 172–4, 178–81, 203, 337–9; partisan, 7, 22, 47–8, 86–7, 113–15, 142–3, 146–7, 207–8; personal life of politicians, 201–13; of power, 60; and principle, 46–58; privacy issues, 147–61, 201–2; racial issues, 368–72, 377, 381, 383–6; reform, 103–4, 185–7; Scotch-Irish tradition, 285–9; small-town, 8; television ads, xiv, 32, 36, 40, 147, 178, 179, 184, 185, 208–9, 370; Western natural-resource interests, 103–16, 214, 224–35; *see also* campaign finance; Congress, U.S.; debates, presidential; Democratic Party; government, federal; House of Representatives, U.S.; presidential elections; Republican Party; Senate, U.S.; *specific politicians*

Polk, James K., 343, 344

polls, 32, 35, 93, 103, 124, 137, 179, 196

pollution, 32, 33, 54, 108–9, 139, 182, 225, 229–35, 252–3, 278–9, 395

Ponce de León, Ernesto Zedillo, 350–1

postal service, xiii

poverty, xii, 49, 53, 55, 197, 262, 294, 331, 344–5, 359, 372–5, 405–6, 413, 414; Appalachian, 268–72, 278; immigrant, 344–5; New Jersey, 33; and racial issues, 372–7, 382

Powell, John Wesley, 219, 224

prayer, school, 264

presidential elections, 7, 201; dirty campaign tactics, xiv, 32, 147–9, 207–8, 370; of 1896, 162–5; of 1932, 64; of 1940, 167–70; of 1948, 7; of 1952, 7–8; of 1956, 7–8; of 1960, 8, 170–1, 194, 195; of 1968, 126, 171; of 1972, 126, 195; of 1980, 49–50, 206; of 1984, 46, 93, 145–6, 179, 205; of 1988, 46–7, 170, 179, 194, 195–6, 370; of 1992, xiv–xvi, 17, 20–8, 35–7, 42, 47, 113–15, 142–3, 151, 179, 182, 194–200, 203–4, 245, 260, 266, 267, 278, 369–72, 386–7; of 1996, 199

presidential leadership, 202–5

press, *see* media

press conferences, 38

Pressler, Larry, 312

Princeton University, 9, 14, 16, 26, 31, 33, 59, 60, 118–22, 124–5, 166, 172, 332, 356, 359, 420–1

principle, political, 46–58

prisons, 390, 391

privacy of politicians, 147–51, 201–2

prostitution, 244–5, 327, 339

Proxmire, William, 86

Pryor, David, 70–2

public lands, Western, 214–35; Indian interests, 303–16

Public Works Administration, 15

Puerto Rico, 336, 396

Pyramid Lake Water Settlement Act (1990), 233–5, 409

Quakers, 282–3, 290

Quayle, Dan, 206–7

Quayle, Marilyn, 207

race and race relations, 9–10, 21, 24, 42, 191, 354–93, 421–2; black/white stereotypes and fears, 371–7, 392–3; civil rights legislation, 59, 60, 71, 357, 366–72, 386–7; discrimination, 9–10, 24, 156, 158, 294, 314, 327–8, 333, 340, 354, 356, 363–93;

economic issues, 372–4, 382, 390–2;
education issues, 328, 365, 367, 369–70,
378–83, 386–92; employment issues, 354,
357, 365–77, 379, 384; in government
policymaking, 368–72, 377, 383–6; media
on, 372, 376–7; of 1980s, 369–70, 371;
"one-drop" principle, 355–6; Oriental
immigrants, 327–36; quotas and affirmative
action, 208–9, 365–73, 384; riots, 357–8,
371; single mothers, 374–5; in the South, 48;
Clarence Thomas hearings, 383–6; urban
American, 357–8, 371–83, 386–92; wealth
distribution, 372–4; *see also* ethnicity; *specific
races*
radio, 65, 117–18, 159, 160, 169, 196, 368;
talk-show hosts, 158
railroads, 15, 86, 164, 175, 176, 217, 222, 229,
327, 345, 408, 417
Rather, Dan, 25
Rayburn, Sam, 168–9
Reagan, Ronald, 31, 46, 54, 68, 178, 205, 206,
211, 233, 264, 339, 352; defense program,
68; economic program, 46, 48–51, 143,
257–64, 369; Iran-contra, 136; labor
relations, 257–64; racial issues, 369–70, 371;
tax reform, 48–51, 93–5, 369
recession, xiv, 96; of 1990s, 44
Reed, Willis, 17, 26, 355, 363
re-election, 89, 112–13, 147
re-engineering, 402, 409
reform, 91–116, 191; campaign-finance, 45,
171, 183, 184–6, 193; labor, 262, 264–6,
407–11; mining, 222–9; Native American,
295–6, 299–314; tax, 92–5, 258, 395, 409;
water, 101–16, 233–5
Regan, Don, 97
regulation, federal, 49, 52, 53, 402
religion, 4, 14, 282, 284, 287, 288, 307, 328,
330–1, 336, 352, 369, 375, 380, 416–24
Republican National Committee, 165
Republican National Convention (1992), 196–7
Republican Party, 7–8, 9, 60, 86, 163–4,
227–8, 286, 339; and economic troubles,
46–52; end of cold war, 142–3; fund-raising,
162–71; middle-class issues, 405; 1994
election gains, 51–2, 405; racial issues,
368–72; Regan program, 48–51; *see also*
politics; presidential elections; *specific
politicians*
reputation of politicians, 148–62
responsibility: corporate, 408; individual,
xiii–xiv, 318, 375, 413
retirement, 260
Rhode Island, 69

Richards, Ann, 198–9, 368
Richardson, Bill, 198, 199
Riddick, Floyd, 75
Riegle, Don, 146
Robb, Chuck, 136, 189
Robertson, Oscar, 29
Rockefeller, Jay, 82, 174, 198, 199, 270
Rockefeller, John D., 165, 174
Rockefeller, Nelson, 170
Rodino, Peter, 29
Roe v. *Wade,* 242
Roosevelt, Franklin D., 7, 15, 22, 53, 60, 63–6,
77, 91, 95, 168–70, 297–8, 329, 330, 360,
405, 406, 411
Roosevelt, Theodore, 53, 164–6, 167, 220–1,
316, 328–9, 409
Rostenkowski, Dan, 93
Russell, Richard, 79
Russia, 48, 68, 87, 107, 112–14, 121–4, 126,
130–5, 137, 137–8, 237, 318, 324, 352;
aggression in Afghanistan, 130, 131–2;
economy, 132; end of cold war, 138–42;
nuclear weapons, 130, 139, 142

St. Louis, 197–8, 217, 255, 323, 333, 374,
378–9
Salinas de Gortari, Carlos, 348–9
Salomon Brothers, 48
Sandinistas, 140
Sanford, Terry, 209
San Francisco, 102, 205, 327, 327–30
Sapoch, Betty, 181
savings-and-loan scandal, 47, 97, 145–7, 178
Schurz, Carl, 321–2
Schweiker, Richard, 59
Scientific American, 401
Scotch-Irish immigrants, xii, 267, 268, 280–9,
294
Scotland, 281–2
Scranton, William, 59
Seattle, 186–93, 203, 216, 230
Securities and Exchange Commission, 53, 152,
171
segregation, 24, 328–9, 355, 365, 369, 378–9
Senate, U.S., xii, xiv, 7, 29, 30, 59–90, 273;
Bradley's career in, xii, 30–2, 38–43, 48,
60–1, 90, 101, 112, 128–38, 147, 178–86,
202, 267, 409, 427; Bradley's 1978 race for,
18, 30–2, 35, 40, 92, 172–4, 178; Bradley's
1990 race for, 39–43, 46, 177, 178–86, 202;
campaign fund-raising, 172–84, 188–9;
committee chairmanships, 70, 83–4, 88–9;
dirty campaign tactics, xiv, 32, 147, 207–9,
370; filibusters, 76–8, 81, 89, 112–13, 227;

Senate, U.S. (*cont.*)
  foreign-policy issues, 124–38; honoraria,
    68–9; 1940 elections, 169–70, 190; 1984
    elections, 208; 1994 elections, 51–2, 136;
    offices, 84–5, 86; procedure and style,
    59–90; re-election to, 89, 112–13; reform
    bills in, 91–116; staffers, 69–70, 84, 85;
    votes and obligations, 61–2, 69, 74, 77–8,
    86, 89, 90; Western natural-resource
    interests, 214, 224–33; *see also* Congress,
    U.S.
Senate Appropriations Committee, 80
Senate Armed Services Committee, 70
Senate Energy and Natural Resources
  Committee, 61, 67–8, 70, 83, 84, 86, 101,
    107, 111, 116, 214–16, 224, 225–9, 236, 279
Senate Ethics Committee, 146–7
Senate Finance Committee, 48, 61, 62–3, 66–7,
    83, 84, 92–4, 369–70
Senate Indian Affairs Committee, 311, 312
Senate Intelligence Committee, 73, 85, 99,
    128–39
Senate Judiciary Committee, 29, 383–6
Senate Rules Committee, 85
Senate Subcommittee on Water and Power,
    101–2
sensationalism, media, 157–60, 209, 376
sex, xiii, 151, 158, 159, 160, 294, 375;
  abstinence, xiii; *see also* gender equity
Seymour, John, 111–13
Shearson Lehman, 396–7
Shelby, Richard, 86
Simpson, Alan, 87, 198, 336, 347
single parents, xiii, 374–5, 404
Sioux, 295, 299, 301–16
skilled workers, shortage of, 260
slavery, 297, 320–1, 328, 342, 354, 355, 392,
    393
small business, 51, 337; of 1990s, 47
small-town America, 3–16, 35; banks, 3–5;
  Clinton-Gore bus tour in, 35–7; politics, 8
social programs, 36, 44, 50, 53–4; Democratic
  Party, 52–6; Reagan cuts in, 50, 51; *see also*
  specific programs
Social Security, xiv, 53, 62, 65, 95, 255
soil erosion, 15, 278–9
South, 78; race relations in, 48
South Africa, 128, 130, 141
South Carolina, 296, 369
South Dakota, 190, 216, 217, 290, 294, 359,
    409; Sioux land interests, 301–16
Spain, 342, 349, 351
special-interest groups, 41, 50, 52
spies, 130, 133–4

sports betting, 112
standard of living, 1990s, 45
Stark, Lloyd, 169–70, 197
State Department, U.S., 129
steel industry, 250–66; decline of, 250–2,
    257–9, 400, 402
Stegner, Wallace, 222, 225–6
Stennis, John, 70–1
Stevens, Phillip J., 313–14
Stevens, Ted, 82, 85–6, 114
Stevenson, Adlai, 7
Stewart, William, 222
stock market, 48, 53, 396
suburbs, 51, 387; growth of, 377
Supreme Court, U.S., 27, 171, 173, 204, 305,
    307, 308, 347, 369; Clarence Thomas
    nomination, 383–6

Taft, Robert, 7
Taft-Hartley Act (1947), 261
Talmadge, Herman, 79
tax, 31, 40, 62, 76, 83, 88, 92, 100, 176, 191,
    348; and campaign-finance reform, 185–6;
    credits, for children in private or parochial
    schools, 369–70; earned-income credit, 66;
    federal cuts, 31, 48–52, 66, 92–5, 148;
    federal increases, 65; inheritance, 65;
    loopholes, 92–5, 258–9, 395; middle-class
    burden, 31, 49, 50, 405, 408, 409; New
    Jersey, 39–41, 46, 94–5; of 1930s, 65; of
    politicians, 150, 152; property, 46, 408; and
    racial issues, 368, 369–70, 374; Reagan
    program, 48–51, 93–5, 369; real-estate,
    263; reform, 92–5, 258, 395, 409; school,
    46; state increases, 39–41, 243; urban, 374;
    windfall-profits, 75–6
Tax Reform bill (1986), 93–5, 258, 395, 409
Taylor, Zachary, 343
Taylor Grazing Act (1934), 219–20, 225
Teamsters Union, 255, 263
technology, 44; information, 399–404, 411–12,
    414; 1990s growth of, 44, 45, 47, 252, 264,
    265, 269, 372, 377, 396–404, 407, 411–12,
    414
teen pregnancy, 410
television, xiv, 18–19, 21, 24–8, 87, 89, 117,
    137, 142, 147, 152, 293–4, 333, 357, 359,
    363, 368, 375, 404; New Jersey, 34; political
    ads, xiv, 32, 36, 40, 147, 178, 179, 184,
    185, 208–9, 370; politicians scrutinized by,
    152–61, 194–200, 201; presidential debates,
    8, 194–200; "simulated" news, 160; violence
    on, xiv, 160, 191, 375; *see also* specific
    programs

temporary workers, 403, 407

Tennessee, 65, 267, 284, 287, 296

terrorism, 139

Texas, 83, 97–8, 167–9, 181, 215, 272–75, 287, 320, 323, 342–45, 347, 371, 380

Third World countries, 141; debt, 95–101, 341, 349; labor, 401, 402

Thomas, Clarence, 87, 155, 187, 383–5

Thomases, Susan, 35

Thompson, J. Walter, 397

Thurmond, Strom, 76–7

timber, 84, 214, 217, 219, 225, 229, 307, 313

Today show, 24, 196, 386

Tokyo Olympics (1964), 59, 120

totalitarianism, 140–51

tourism, 34, 233, 307, 348

Tower, John, 68, 74, 85, 272–5

town meetings, 37–9, 192, 204, 366, 401

toxic-waste dumps, 33, 225

trade, 83, 88, 262; international, 44, 45, 47, 54, 262, 348–52, 401–12; and NAFTA, 262, 348–52; subsidies, 62

trade unions, 255–66

transportation, 88, 345, 408

Treasury, U.S., 95, 97, 98, 176, 304

Treaty of Guadaloupe Hidalgo (1848), 344

Truman, Harry S, 7, 57, 59, 90, 125, 169–70, 190, 193, 197, 261

Tsongas, Paul, 182, 204

Turner, Frederick Jackson, 216–17

Twain, Mark, 15, 16, 217, 221

Udall, Morris, 312

Ukraine, 140, 260

unemployment, xii, xiv, 36, 44, 228, 263, 316, 350, 357, 372, 406; downsizing as cause of, 396–411; easing, 406–7; middle-class, 396–8, 404–14; of 1930s, 65; of 1990s, 45, 47, 259–60, 397–8, 404–14; and racial issues, 372–7, 382; urban, 374, 382; *see also* labor

United Nations, 128

urban America, xii, 12, 33, 414; crisis of meaning in, 374–5; future of, 377–83; racial issues, 357–8, 371–83, 386–93; schools, 374, 378–83, 386–92; violence, 33, 375–6, 382, 390–1; Western growth, 228; *see also specific cities*

Utah, 109, 113, 215, 221, 226, 244, 334, 342

values, American, 4, 5, 49; loss of, xiii, 57, 375, 404

Vandenberg, Arthur, 64

Vietnam War, 54, 59, 124–7, 132–3, 153, 196, 199, 358

violence, xii, 24, 57, 316, 370, 375, 413; black, 357–8, 375–7, 390–1; domestic, 391; and drugs, 375–6; race riots, 357–8, 371; random, 376–7; on television, xiv, 160, 191, 375; urban, 33, 375–6, 382, 390–1

Virginia, 63, 141, 163, 275, 280, 281

Volcker, Paul, 67, 98

volunteerism, xiii, 53, 270, 413

Vonnegut, Kurt, *Palm Sunday*, 322

voter registration, 45

voting rights, 328

Wagner Act, 53, 260

Wallop, Malcolm, 115, 312

Warren, Earl, 329, 330

Washington, D.C., 71–2, 160, 273–5

Washington Post, 60

Washington State, 62, 67, 68, 158, 186–7, 193, 215, 216, 230

water, 214, 215, 217, 219, 224–8, 229–35; Indian rights, 303, 312; industrial pollution, 252–3; reform, 101–16, 233–5

Watergate scandal, 7, 30, 129, 153, 171, 178

Watley, William, 378–82

Weicker, Lowell, 85

welfare, 36, 44, 50, 53, 62, 66, 74, 197, 264, 270, 315

West, 214–49, 341–4; frontier myth, 215–24, 230; Indian land interests, 303–16; natural-resource interests, 101–16, 214–35, 307; water reform, 101–16, 233–5; women in, 239–49

West Virginia, 62, 79, 81, 82, 170, 174, 250, 267, 270

Wheeling-Pittsburgh Steel, 250–2, 256–66

White, Byron, 27

Whitman, Christine Todd, 40, 41, 182

Wilder, Lilyan, 19

Wilkinson, Charles, *Crossing the Next Meridian*, 223, 234–5

Willets, Harry T., 126

Williams, Harrison, 73

Wilson, H. H., 60

Wilson, Pete, 111–12, 115, 347–8

Wilson, Woodrow, 53, 60, 167–8, 183, 190, 193, 344, 351, 409

Wisconsin, 175, 290–4, 298, 320, 322

women, 51, 192–3, 197, 265, 276; candidates supported by Bradley, 155–8, 187–94, 239–49; Native American, 290–4; Republican attitudes toward, 198; Western, 239–49; working mothers, 265, 404, 407

Works Progress Administration, 53
World Bank, 98
World War I, 322, 333
World War II, 53, 83, 117–18, 137, 143, 291, 298, 322–5, 345, 405; Japanese-American internment during, 329–36
Wounded Knee massacre, 295, 305
Wright, Jim, 146

Wright, Richard, 384
Wyoming, 109, 115, 120, 214, 215, 221, 226, 227, 303, 336, 343

xenophobia, American, 288–9, 322, 329–34

young professionals, xiii

A NOTE ABOUT THE AUTHOR

Bill Bradley was a three-time basketball All-American at Princeton, winner of the Sullivan Award as the country's outstanding amateur athlete, a gold-medal recipient at the Tokyo Olympics, and a professional player for ten years with the New York Knicks, during which time the team won two championships. He served in the Air Force Reserve from 1967 to 1973. Elected to the Senate from New Jersey in 1978, 1984, and 1990, he has authored extensive legislation, including the Tax Reform Act of 1986. He serves at present on the Senate Finance Committee, the Energy and Natural Resources Committee, and the Special Committee on Aging. Mr. Bradley is the author of *Life on the Run* and *The Fair Tax,* and has written for *The Wall Street Journal, The New York Times,* and other major publications. He is married and has one daughter.

A NOTE ON THE TYPE

The text of this book was set in a typeface named Perpetua, designed by the British artist Eric Gill (1882–1940) and cut by the Monotype Corporation of London in 1928–30. Perpetua is a contemporary letter of original design, without any direct historical antecedents. The shapes of the roman letters basically derive from stone-cutting, a form of lettering in which Gill was eminent. The italic is essentially an inclined roman. The general effect of the typeface in reading sizes is one of lightness and grace. The larger display sizes of the type are extremely elegant and form what is probably the most distinguished series of inscriptional letters cut in the present century.

Composed by the Haddon Craftsmen,
a division of R. R. Donnelley & Sons,
Scranton, Pennsylvania

Printed and bound by R. R. Donnelley & Sons,
Harrisonburg, Virginia

Designed by Cassandra J. Pappas